THE POLITICS OF PASSION:
NORMAN BETHUNE'S WRITING AND ART

Edited and introduced by Larry Hannant

The Politics of Passion: Norman Bethune's Writing and Art

UNIVERSITY OF TORONTO PRESS
Toronto Buffalo London

© University of Toronto Press Incorporated 1998
Toronto Buffalo London

Printed in Canada

ISBN 0-8020-0907-7

Printed on acid-free paper

Canadian Cataloguing in Publication Data

Bethune, Norman, 1890–1939
The politics of passion : Norman Bethune's writing and art

Includes bibliographical references and index.
ISBN 0-8020-0907-7

1. Bethune, Norman, 1890–1939.   2. Surgeons – Canada – Biography.
3. Surgeons – China – Biography.   I. Hannant, Larry, 1950–   .   II. Title.

R464.B4A3 1998   617 .092   C97-932481-5

University of Toronto Press acknowledges the financial assistance to its
publishing program of the Canada Council for the Arts and the
Ontario Arts Council.

To Bill Livant,
mentor and friend

Contents

viii   Contents

Maps appear on pages 120, 121, and 196.

Illustrations

Acknowledgments

When I began this book, I had no thought that it would introduce me to people of such immense generosity and dedication to knowledge. But serendipity has its ways. I'm delighted to be able to say that Norman Bethune has brought me into contact with three admirable scholars – Roderick Stewart, Myron Momryk, and Bill Livant.

I called Roderick Stewart unannounced one day with a problem concerning Bethune. I wasn't sure what reaction to expect from him. My experience with others who have striven to make Norman Bethune their personal property led me to be wary. But on that occasion and on many others over the course of months, Rod freely gave of his time as well as his knowledge of Bethune without thought of anything but deepening my own understanding. Myron Momryk, too, showed genuine enthusiasm for the project and expended effort beyond all call of duty to put pertinent information into my hands. Although Bill Livant and I have been acquaintances for some time, when I mentioned my work on Bethune to him, he also went out of his way to give me the benefit of his own thoughts and writing on the subject. Not only is this a far better book because of him, but in the course of our discussions we have also deepened our kinship. In each of these men, I have been gratified to find scholars with a profound respect for historical inquiry. None of them will necessarily agree with the interpretations he sees before him, but I trust that their high regard for the process will be undiminished by possible disagreements with the conclusions.

Ted Allan's involvement with Norman Bethune's image and his relationship with me have been chequered. Throughout his life, Allan attempted to control Bethune's memory, for his own financial advantage. (See 'A Note on Sources.') Much as I deplore that, I want to acknowledge directly Allan's role in this book. In co-writing *The Scalpel, The Sword*, the first primarily non-fiction book on Norman Bethune, Allan did much to acquaint people worldwide with a truly impressive man. I was one of those millions moved by the book. Although I recognized it as flawed, I began to use it in a class on popular history that I taught at the University of Victoria. One day I observed to my students that it was regrettable that all of Bethune's powerful writing and art had not been collected into a single volume and published. With that germ of an idea, I contacted Allan to propose such a book.

We talked by telephone and corresponded several times after that, but we didn't have the opportunity to meet until just weeks before his death in Toronto. Although seriously ill, he was able to give me some details about Bethune's life in Spain. When I left Allan, I hoped to see him fully recover to collaborate with me on this project. Unfortunately, that was not to be. And as much as I deplore his restrictive hold on Norman Bethune's work, I recognize that this book would have been better if Allan were alive today to supplement my own knowledge.

Aside from those mentioned above, many people deserve credit for helping me in various ways on this project. John Lutz, as always, gave me ongoing encouragement and thoughtful comments on parts I asked him to read. Readers' comments to University of Toronto Press on the unpublished manuscript gave me both useful criticism and insight into the extent to which Bethune's name can still spark political reaction. I received diligent research assistance from Jamie Disbrow, Lise Murray, Edward Lentz, and Andy Parnaby. Jamie Disbrow, Carol White, and Lisa Woodsworth enlivened my stay in Ottawa, and Neil Docherty and Salah Bachir did the same in Toronto. Tom and Gina Cody and their daughters generously opened their home to me in Toronto.

Karen McIvor, Peter Dale Scott, Emil Bjarnason, Jay Stewart, Peter McNair, Keith Ralston, Kay Macpherson, Patrick Lawson, Greg Kealey, Reg Whitaker, Victor Howard, Min-sun Chen, Bob Howell, Roseline Ross, Patricia Roy, Ruth McDonald, Wendell MacLeod, and Yola Sise, among others, have given me leads, encouragement, and ideas.

Archivists and librarians too numerous to mention offered courteous and efficient assistance at the National Archives of Canada (NAC), the Parks Canada Bethune Memorial House at Gravenhurst, Ontario, the Archives of Ontario, the Baldwin Room of the Metropolitan Toronto Library, the Osler Library at McGill University, and the University of Victoria Interlibrary Loans Office. They include Carole Séguin, Guy Tessier, Marina Royo, Wayne Lebel, and Maryellen Corcelli. I particularly wish to thank Anne Goddard, Carol White, and Teresa McIntosh at NAC, June Schachter at the Osler Library, and Bernard Lutz at the National Film Board.

Eugene Link persisted in a quest to rediscover slides of Bethune's mural *The T.B.'s Progress*. Irene Kon tracked down the painting *Night Operating Theatre*, and pursued people in Montreal who knew Bethune.

Rob Ferguson at University of Toronto Press was a patient and friendly editorial sounding-board. Copy-editor Ken Lewis caught many of my errors and made deft rewriting suggestions.

I had able translation assistance from Rosa Stewart, Bryan Nethery, and Marc Hunter, and Stuart Daniel provided excellent map-making skills. June Bull, Derry Perkin, and the helpful souls at ByteMarks Electronic Publishing turned huge volumes of oft-times barely legible typescript into computerized copy ready for editing.

Jim Hamm, as always, gave me good advice, even though I didn't necessarily follow it. I wish also to thank Maggie Thompson for her assistance, support, and encouragement. In Calgary, my family – including Elenora and Ted Barber, Wayne Barber, Sandra and Glen Heming, and Diane Field – have been sources of reassurance and help.

For all the assistance they've given, I hold none of these people in any way responsible for any errors of fact or interpretation in this book; these are exclusively mine.

My daughter, Caila Thompson-Hannant, has, I think, learned lessons in both history and justice through this book. She remains, as ever, a loving foundation of help and inspiration to me.

THE POLITICS OF PASSION

1

Introduction

Norman Bethune is not well known in the country of his birth, but internationally he might be the most famous Canadian. His fame is well justified. Born in 1890, in the 1920s his successful career as a doctor was shattered when he contracted tuberculosis. It was then a lethal disease, and he prepared himself to die from it. But in 1927, he insisted on a radical medical procedure which spared him. Attacking life with new zeal, he quickly made his name known as a crusader against tuberculosis. He gained both favourable attention and notoriety in medical circles as an iconoclastic thoracic surgeon seeking to eradicate the 'white plague.' He would become still more prominent in the 1930s for his political involvement on the side of progressive causes in Canada, Spain, and China. As a communist, during 1936–7 he initiated a pioneering blood transfusion system to assist the democratic forces fighting fascism in the Spanish Civil War. During the next two years, he gave magnificent assistance to the Chinese communists in their struggle against Japanese aggression, advancing the use of mobile operating units virtually at the battle front. When he died in 1939, succumbing to blood poisoning contracted while he operated on a wounded soldier, he became a revolutionary hero to millions in China and beyond. (Readers unfamiliar with the outline of his life may wish to consult the chronology in Appendix 2.)

His renown arises in part from two significant English-language biographies. They differ greatly in approach and, sometimes, in facts. Ted Allan and Sydney Gordon's *The Scalpel, The Sword* was the first treatment of Bethune, published originally in 1952. Allan was acquainted with Bethune on and off for about eighteen months in 1936 and 1937. Although he was alternately fascinated and frustrated by Bethune, Allan considered him 'the most exciting man I had ever met.'[1] *The Scal-*

pel, The Sword reflects that veneration. Indeed, hero-worship is one of its flaws. Frequently it damns not by faint but by excessive praise, substituting idolization for accuracy. In preparing this volume, I have come upon an important reason for Allan and Gordon's reverent approach – the source of a substantial part of their book is a Chinese work of fiction. In writing *The Scalpel, The Sword*, Allan and Gordon had a significant problem. The last two years of Bethune's life were spent in China, where he performed perhaps his most impressive work. Appropriately, almost half of their biography dwells on his sojourn in China. Yet neither author travelled to China to conduct research. Instead, Allan and Gordon drew extensively from a Chinese novel, *Doctor Norman Bethune*, written by Zhou Erfu and first published in 1948.[2] Zhou was no ordinary novelist. By 1938 he was an insider of the Communist Party of China, and in 1978 he became the vice-minister of culture in the People's Republic of China. With fiction as its foundation, *The Scalpel, The Sword* presents an unrealistically heroic Bethune, and that, coupled with a loose regard for exactness, causes many readers to question the portrait.

Allan and Gordon were members of the Communist Party of Canada when they wrote the book, and the project was written with the official assistance and cooperation of the Communist Party of Canada.[3] This connection accounts for both weaknesses and strengths. The flaws are glaring. For example, Bethune's membership in the Communist Party of Canada, beginning in 1935, is hushed up; his conflict with Spanish officials which got him recalled from the blood transfusion unit in Madrid is whitewashed. Nonetheless, Allan and Gordon's communist affiliation gives *The Scalpel, The Sword* an orientation that remains true to Bethune's essence. Their success lies in their ability to convey something evanescent but nonetheless critical – Bethune's indomitable spirit.

Just over two decades later, in 1973, historian Roderick Stewart wrote a very different biography, *Bethune*.[4] In contrast to *The Scalpel, The Sword*, Stewart's work is a thorough and factually accurate portrait of a complex man. I am indebted to Stewart's biography for piecing together the details of Bethune's life. But it, too, shows signs of imbalance. It emphasizes Bethune's self-destructive traits over his positive energy. It sets him on an apparently undeviating road of frustration and ruin but neglects his capacity to change and grow, to teach and to learn. The concluding sentence says much about Stewart's approach: 'He died as he lived, lonely and in combat.' Indeed, neither biography satisfactorily deals with the question of transformation in Bethune's practice and outlook. Allan and Gordon present an unvarying saint, Stewart a sinner.

Yet if Bethune was anything, he was dynamic, not static. Students who have studied both books have observed that *The Scalpel, The Sword* seems to be 'inside' its subject, *Bethune* 'outside.'[5] The result is a sometimes dichotomous portrait. *The Politics of Passion* is an attempt both to allow Bethune's own words and art to show his 'inside,' and to provide some of the 'outside' context in which that writing and art were produced. Stewart's 1977 book, *The Mind of Norman Bethune*, was a similar work, although considerably less comprehensive than this volume.[6]

The Politics of Passion is not intended to be a new biography of Bethune. Yet in important ways it rewrites the Bethune legend and shines a revealing light on the man, the artist, the revolutionary. It uncovers previously unknown historical documents relating to such conundrums as Bethune's dismissal from Spain and such controversies as his romantic and political attachments. For example, a remarkable report recently obtained from the Communist International archives in Russia and deposited in the National Archives of Canada demands a rethinking of our speculative knowledge of why Bethune was sent home in disgrace from Spain in 1937. The document refers to a mysterious Swedish woman, Kajsa von Rothman, Bethune's lover, who Spanish authorities believed was politically tainted and even a fascist spy (see chapter 5).

In order to re-examine Bethune's significance, we must reread Bethune. *The Politics of Passion* is intended to reintroduce us to the man himself. So I have made every effort to go to the original source, Bethune's own words, in his handwriting or from his indestructible typewriter. This has allowed me to make some small corrections to the historical record. For example, Bethune's account of one of his marathon journeys in China has been reprinted in varied forms, including a pamphlet published in 1938 by the Canadian League for Peace and Democracy, *From Hankow to Sian*. Returning to Bethune's original letter on which the pamphlet was based has allowed me to replace several passages cut from the original which offended the political tastes of the pamphlet's publishers. They thought, for instance, that North American audiences should not be told that American fighter pilots serving the Chinese nationalists in 1938 were disliked because they drew several times the pay and benefits of their Chinese counterparts. Having Bethune's typescripts, however, has also allowed me to conclude that such editorial rewriting by the Communist Party was extremely rare. Indeed that is virtually the sole significant instance of tampering with Bethune's work.[7]

This volume also reproduces most of Bethune's artistic works. This includes the mural *The T.B.'s Progress*, which depicts the fears and trials faced by him and other tuberculosis sufferers. Bethune drew the mural on brown wrapping paper pinned to the walls of his residential cottage at the Trudeau Sanatorium at Saranac Lake, New York. Created in 1927, it was originally some twenty metres long and incorporated eleven large panels with accompanying poetry. *The T.B.'s Progress* was lost for many years, and the original appears to have disappeared entirely at the American military base of Fort Bragg, North Carolina. But by great fortune, Professor Eugene P. Link of the State University of New York discovered antique-style slides of the mural images and donated copies of them to the Osler Library at McGill University, which has granted me the right to reproduce them.[8] In addition, this book reproduces all of Bethune's oil paintings, several sketches, and a photograph he took of Mao Zedong.

I have arranged Bethune's writing and art to correspond with the chronological order in which it was produced and have organized it into blocks that correspond to the major divisions of his life. In order to improve clarity, I have occasionally made silent, minor changes in spelling, punctuation, hyphenation, and the like. I needed to do this only rarely, since Bethune's writing was usually correct – an impressive feat, because for months in China he was entirely cut off from English speakers and printed communication. All significant alterations (again, intended to improve clarity) are contained within square brackets.

A small number of Bethune's letters to his wife, Frances, were retyped by Ted Allan from the handwritten originals. Occasionally, Allan has inserted ellipses where he could not make out Bethune's script. Lacking the originals, I have been forced to work from Allan's copies, and have reproduced them intact, with Allan's ellipses.

This volume is comprehensive – it includes almost everything of Bethune's writing which has survived. For reasons of space, I have been forced to leave out eleven of his more esoteric articles published in medical journals, all of them listed in the Bibliography. Everything else that I have been able to discover by Bethune has been included. Readers interested in learning the tangled tale of how I have located these materials will wish to consult 'A Note on Sources' at the end of the volume.

One point of style in this volume is that where I quote from Bethune's writings in the chapter introductions and brief notes before each selection I have not used footnotes, reasoning that the reader can refer to the text of the document itself immediately following. With regard to the names of Chinese people and places, of which Bethune included scores in recording his treks over half of China, I have preserved Bethune's spelling. In a very few cases, however, I judged that modern readers familiar with Pinyin Chinese transliterations might be confused by Bethune's Wade-Giles versions. In those few instances, including familiar names such as Mao Zedong and well-known places such as Beijing, I have made the change to Pinyin usage.

We think of Norman Bethune as the complete political activist. But if we look more closely, we see that politics was a preoccupation only for the last four years of his forty-nine–year life. Before he came to politics, Bethune's life was marked by passion. He possessed a passionate soul, a great rage for life, a consuming curiosity about the world, a profound desire to serve his patients, and an unyielding hatred of the injustice and disparities of wealth that nurtured disease. Acting on this passion led him to politics and made him a communist. His life was a journey from apolitical exuberance to political intensity.

Bethune was a writhing mass of contradictions – at once a troubled, discomforting, disturbing person to be with, but also an attractive personality whose energy and enthusiasm could enliven as mundane a chore as shopping.[9] Bethune radiated passion and bestowed it on those around him, regardless of whether or not they wished to be so blessed or afflicted.

Equally important, Bethune's life was dominated by a deep need to express himself, and he did so with characteristic zeal and abundant talent. In surgery, love, politics, painting, sketches, poetry, letters, short stories, photography, radio broadcasts and plays, public speaking, even medical articles and instruments, Bethune's intense desire to communicate his passions found outlets. In all these endeavours, Bethune's creativity and inventiveness shone through, helping him to produce highly original and often arresting written and visual images. Inez Fisher, the wife of Bethune's long-time friend Lincoln Fisher, probably best summed up Bethune's talent after she saw him dash off a plea for decisive tuberculosis treatment which ridiculed conventional medical care. It wasn't great literature, she wrote, but 'his mode of expression was nothing short of a gift from the gods.'[10]

The Politics of Passion is an attempt to reopen that gift from the gods, to lay it out for a contemporary audience, to revive Bethune through his creative works. It presents Bethune from his fiery heart – unvarnished, invariably blunt, exerting all the power of his pen, his spoken words, his paintbrush. Bethune is long dead; we cannot directly know his physical energy, his emotional volatility, his tirades against the complacency that perpetuated lethal diseases such as tuberculosis. But through his work, we can behold the product of some of his intensity.

In this volume, I also hope to reacquaint people with the wide-ranging gifts of a man who, as Lee Briscoe Thompson has observed, rejected compartments in life, who was at once doctor, poet, painter, revolutionary, designer, photographer, and propagandist.[11] In his own life and in society, Bethune emphasized connections between apparently discrete phenomena. In this regard, he had a fundamentally ecological vision. He believed that each cell is integral to the whole. So he was convinced that in fighting Japanese aggression in China he was also striking a blow against fascism in Europe and the wretchedness of capitalism in 1930s Canada. From China, he advised Canadian comrades: 'You keep on your fight, we will do the same here. It is all the same battle. We are bound to win.' Similarly, in the simple virtues of the Chinese Eighth Route Army peasant-soldier, Bethune detected the best of the democratic characteristics of the Spanish, Canadian, and other peoples. In ostensible enemies – the injured Chinese partisan fighter and his wounded Japanese counterpart – he saw brothers conscripted into a 'community of pain.'

Bethune's own experience with and knowledge of tuberculosis also reinforced his belief in links between what seemed to be separate aspects of society. He came to understand that illness was closely related to economics and politics. Bethune did not originate the saying, but he frequently repeated it: 'There is a rich man's tuberculosis and a poor man's tuberculosis. The rich man recovers and the poor man dies.'[12] Hence it was useless to try to cope with the disease in isolation. Economic and political injustice also needed to be cured. In the course of a lifetime of struggle against disease, he moved from believing that the curative process was individual and technological (symbolized by his own triumph over tuberculosis) to seeing it as economic, social, and political. Indeed, today's resurgence of tuberculosis among the poor and homeless throughout the world indicates that we need to return to Dr Bethune's prescription if we hope to come to grips with the disease.[13]

In reading Bethune's writing, what kind of man do we see? What kind of thinker? What kind of communist? Bethune's words show him to be highly emotional, by turns angry, impatient, and demanding. No less apparent is a deep compassion for people. Bethune loved humanity, but he was equally fascinated by the individual and the adventure of personal life. Even at the time when he was most deeply immersed in communism, for instance, he could write a short story like 'The Dud,' which celebrated a modest triumph in the life of an old Chinese peasant.

Bethune was also an acute observer. His lengthy reports from China were packed with detail about the complexities of building a new society immediately adjacent to the front lines in the battle with Japan. But this keen vision did not always progress to profound thought. Bethune was a doer, not a philosopher. For example, just before being recalled from the war in Spain, he wrote a long letter back to Canada on the nature of art. 'An Apology for Not Writing Letters,' however, was mostly an unsatisfying jumble – reflecting his mental anguish at being sent home from Spain – and not a deep inquiry. Only his summary, in which he described the role of the artist, was eloquent and striking: 'He makes uneasy the static, the set and the still. In a world terrified of change, he preaches revolution – the principle of life. He is an agitator, a disturber of the peace.'[14] It could have been Bethune's own epitaph.

As for his communism, Bethune was clearly an activist, not a theoretician. He insisted on the need for revolutionary change, led by a vigorous political party with deep roots among the people. In 1939 he remarked on how much he admired the Chinese Communist Party, whose strength was based on its 'enormous advantage of 20 years' actual experience.' The Chinese party put its efforts into 'teaching the masses local self government' and emphasized order and honesty in government, he reported. His language is instructive. Even in this period, Bethune's writing is virtually bereft of either the trappings or the structural foundations of Marxist philosophy. What we see is a humanist in a red cape. Ultimately, Bethune was most concerned about people; their health and happiness was the paramount issue. For Bethune, communism was a means for people to liberate themselves from fear, poverty, exploitation, and premature death. Fascism, by contrast, imposed exploitation by violence. Which side was he on? Bethune unhesitatingly chose communism, but it was a choice based on life's exigencies, not deep theoretical study.

Libbie Park, a medical colleague of Bethune's in Montreal, recalled that he once said, 'I wish I could write in a loud voice like Paul de Kruif.'[15] De Kruif was a bacteriologist who wrote many popular books promoting modern science as a 'conqueror' of disease in the nineteenth and twentieth centuries. Bethune's aspiration to be such a bold writer is a clue to his ambition as an artist. Bethune did not match de Kruif's literary output or success, yet this should not be taken to mean that Bethune did not write in a loud voice. His writing was not always outstanding, but, like his political consciousness, it grew and matured as he became more committed to principled causes. The very best of his writing, composed in Spain and China towards the end of his life, does far more than just evoke the intense action there, it conjures up the very soul of the anti-fascist struggle. Passing beyond mere left-wing reportage, it is at once commanding and analytical, empathetic for the victims of fascist violence and burning with hatred for the perpetrators of it.

These elements are present in his crowning written achievement, 'Wounds.' A polemical essay he wrote in China in 1938, Bethune properly called it 'one of the best things I have written.'[16] 'Wounds' is worth dwelling on momentarily, for it illustrates not just the majesty of Bethune's writing but also its contemporary relevance. It recalls a long night of operating on Chinese soldiers brought to him after a battle with the Japanese army in north China. After striving to remedy the horrific injuries they have sustained, Bethune asks: 'Any more? Four Japanese prisoners. Bring them in. In this community of pain there are no enemies. Cut away that bloodstained uniform. Stop that haemorrhage. Lay them beside the others. Why they're alike as brothers!' And these wounded brothers, he wrote, had counterparts on the other side of the social and political ledger, the 'brothers in blood' who finance, instigate, and perpetrate wars for their own profit. 'These men make the wounds,' he concluded.[17]

'Wounds' is important not just because Bethune regarded it as his finest writing. It also represents the most concentrated expression of the unity of passion and politics in him. The essay connects the 'inside' and the 'outside' – the subjective and the objective – of both Bethune and China. It portrays the dialectical unity of Bethune the doctor and Bethune the activist. Equally, it integrates the pain of a maimed Chinese boy-soldier and the agony of a China apparently supine before the Japanese Imperial Army. It bridges Bethune's personal compassion for the boy who will never run again and his intellectual grasp of the wider significance of that torment: 'Don't pity him! Pity would diminish his sacrifice. He did this for the defence of China.' 'Wounds' is Bethune's passion and politics knit together into a memorable whole.

Bethune wrote 'Wounds' in December 1938. Less than a year later – ironically, tragically – he would succumb to a wound himself. After his death, much changed in the turbulent twentieth century. Aside from his vibrancy as a historical character, does he have anything relevant to say on the eve of the twenty-first century? Reading 'Wounds,' the answer must be yes. His intense experience with disease and war taught

Bethune that common folk on both sides suffer most from it. To end their suffering, they needed to identify and unite against those who ignore disease and foment war. More than half a century after Bethune's death, half a century of unprecedented slaughter worldwide, we can still draw inspiration from 'Wounds.' It commands us to identify the root cause of conflict and to break its power.

2

Adventurer:
Youth to December 1927

Norman Bethune was born on 3 March 1890. Or was it 4 March 1890? Ontario birth registration records give the former date, but Bethune himself celebrated his birth on the latter.[1] The dispute over the precise date is probably less significant than the fact that Bethune had a *chosen* birthday, not a chance one. And how appropriate that the one chosen is the only date on the calendar which issues a command. 'March forth' was exactly what Norman Bethune did.

As a second child, Bethune was born to rebel. He was nothing if not restless, indeed driven. His life ranged over three continents – North America, Europe, and Asia – and he was seldom settled for long. He may have acquired this wanderlust from his youth, when his Presbyterian minister father shifted his family from town to town across Ontario. By the age of thirty, he had laboured and taught in Northern Ontario bush camps, completed his medical degree at the University of Toronto, and served two tours of duty in the First World War, one as a stretcher bearer, the second as a medical officer in the Royal Navy.[2]

In 1920, then a resident medical officer at the West London Hospital, Bethune met Frances Campbell Penney. Nurtured by her conventional upper-middle-class Scottish family, Frances had much that Bethune found attractive – beauty, culture, and intelligence. Although he was an extremely eligible young bachelor, he had only a small income, and what little money he had was consumed by his taste for clothes, art, and high living. Lack of money may have delayed their wedding. In August 1923, after Frances received a legacy from her uncle, the couple married at the London Registry Office. They immediately set off for an extravagant honeymoon in Europe – six months of visiting art galleries, skiing, and touring, during which they dispensed with much of Frances's inheritance.

The couple then moved to North America, where Bethune hoped to settle into practice as a physician. Unable to find a suitable opening in Canada, Bethune and Frances took up residence in Detroit. There they embraced the good life that America in the booming 1920s promised – a comfortable apartment, clothes, books, fine art, and dining. And to pay for it, a busy life for Bethune in private practice and teaching. But even in the midst of this getting and spending, preoccupied with enjoying life's adventures to the fullest, Bethune noticed those on the bottom end of the social ladder whose work made possible the luxury of those on the upper rungs. His practice in Detroit included poor immigrant and working-class clients who frequently had no means to pay for his services, and he was known for the generosity he extended to them.

The whirlwind of apparent success and happiness began to fly apart in 1925, when Frances left him. They were very closely bonded emotionally, and people who knew him much later believed he remained dependent upon her.[3] But she grew to resent his domineering manner with her. On the day of their marriage, he had declared, 'Now I can make your life a misery, but I'll never bore you – it's a promise.'[4] She began to fear that the misery was vanquishing the adventure he promised. Seeking an escape from the frequent arguments arising from money, sex, and their different personalities, she left him in the fall of 1925 to visit a friend in Nova Scotia, then crossed the continent to spend Christmas with her brother in California. She returned to him in 1926, but the reconciliation was only partially successful. In June 1927, she initiated divorce proceedings, and the Michigan court granted the application in October. Flamboyant in the face of adversity, Bethune received the telegram announcement and immediately wired Frances back with his congratulations and a proposal of marriage.[5]

The shock of his separation from Frances was compounded by another blow: in the fall of 1926, Bethune was diagnosed as having tuberculosis. This was a fatal disease for many, and the threat dramatically transformed both his life and his need for written and artistic self-expression. It ended his fast, high-rolling pursuit of pleasure and wealth and forced him to rest. He was confined to sanatoria – first the Calydor Sanatorium at his birthplace of Gravenhurst, then the Trudeau Sanatorium at Saranac Lake, New York. Here he was given time, indeed was compelled, to examine his life, his goals, and his uncertain future. This helped to generate the first trickle of a huge volume of writing and art. His most important artistic work during this time was a multi-panelled mural which he called *The T.B.'s Progress*. Drawn in colour on brown wrapping paper encircling the walls of his residential cottage at the Trudeau Sanatorium, the mural vividly conveyed the dimming of Bethune's hopes under the pall of tuberculosis. Bethune himself later regarded the drawings as relatively unimportant and dismissed the captions as 'bits of poetry (so-called!).'[6] But we see in them the first elements of an impressive artistic output produced over the years that followed.

Tuberculosis also triggered a radical shift in his attitudes towards medical practice. It began with his own treatment. Impatient with the prescribed cure of bed rest, Bethune studied diligently and chanced upon an article about an experimental treatment, artificial pneumothorax. This involved injecting air into the pleural cavity surrounding the affected lung, giving the lung a chance to heal. But the doctors at Trudeau rejected the procedure, and Bethune had to vigorously insist on being given it. Reminded of the risk, he is reputed to have threatened to perform the pneumothorax on himself if they refused.[7] It's uncertain whether his actual argument was quite so dire, but in any case he won the round. The pneumothorax was done, and it had remarkably rapid and positive results. In December 1927, just six weeks later, Bethune was healed. Freed from the fear of death and the constraining comfort of what he called 'Trudeau Sanctuary,' Bethune rose to greet the challenges of a new life.

In the winter of 1911–12, Bethune took a break from medical studies at the University of Toronto to indulge the adventurer and the latent missionary in his soul. Under the auspices of Frontier College, then called the Camp Reading Association, he became a labourer-instructor in a logging camp in Northern Ontario. His letters to the Frontier College office in Toronto presented a young man both practical and playful.

Martin's Camp
Nov. 12, 1911

Dear Miss McMeekin –
Please pardon, if you can, my slowness in reporting, and attribute it not to forgetfulness, but as a combination of work, lack of time and sore hands – the latter possibly being the greatest. I am very happy to report that everything is, to use a trite medical term, progressing favourably. I formally took possession on the 19th day of October and declared the building open that night. The next seven days were spent in laying in a

supply of wood, plastering and arranging the comforts of an effete civilization in conformity with the strict mission style furnishings of my bungalow.

I have commenced work on the road and must confess, find it a little hard, with the resultant effects – blisters and fully-developed symptoms of a kink in my vertebral column. However, I enjoy it, and am sure I shall like it immensely later on.

Would you be so kind as to send me the following?

a small English dictionary
a couple of pads of this paper
some copies of *Illustrated London News, Black & White*, etc.
envelopes
a few Bibles and a couple of quarterlies
a dozen paper-covered, Alexander's Hymn book, used by the revivalist committee – 'Where is my wandering boy tonight' and all those kind of songs, you know – see note.
Note – this is *not* a joke.
Two of each – those little books, paper bound, for beginnings in English form

German
French   They are simple sentences & common words
Pollack   translated. I noticed some in the other camps
Hungarian

I have at home some old school books which would be useful & mother will send them down to you. Will you please enclose them with the above?

I wonder if you could send the *Saturday Evening Post* every week? It is read with a great deal of interest. If you find it impossible, will you subscribe to it, in my name for I will gladly pay the subscription to have it in the camp.

I am sending you a list of my records, on a separate sheet. Would be very grateful if a couple of dozen more records could be sent. Some of the records here are practically useless from rough usage, resulting in crackling, etc. providing a combination of shrills and shrieks not included in the original definition of harmony by the great Wagner.

I assure you I appreciate your kindness more than I can say in sending the [University of Toronto] *Varsity*. It was extremely thoughtful of you.

But where, oh where, did you collect that exhibition of old masters? They make a truly wondrous & stirring effect on walls of the drawing room. I wake up every morning with a start, to find the gloomy menacing eye of that immense bull fixed intently on my helpless form. It's as good, believe me, as an alarm clock.

Forgive my unseemly levity. The boys appreciate them immensely & they brighten the place up in a surprising fashion.

Can I hope to have a letter from you shortly?

I remain, yours truly,
H.N. Bethune

December 31, 1911
A. Fitzpatrick, Esq. [the Frontier College administrator]
Toronto

Dear Sir,
Your card of the 19th received, also instructions. I have been notified that the books, etc. have arrived at Whitefish and will come in by the first team.

I am glad to be able to report that the work is proceeding very well and the men, especially the English-Scotch, appreciate the Reading Camp a great deal. At Christmas, the usual jumping took place, reducing to a great extent the classes.

Please send instruction books in Polish & French as soon as possible. There are about a dozen men in the camp who cannot speak English. It is extremely desirable that they know something at least about the language when they leave in the spring. These books are small & plain-lettered, with simple sentences. On one side is a sentence in Polish, on the opposite page is the corresponding English. I noticed some of these books in Fraser's camp. Until they come, very little can be done along this line.

We had the misfortune to break a small part of the gramophone, so could not use the new records. You may be able to get it in Toronto. It is a thin piece of flexible steel – one of the rods of the governor. [A sketch of one part was included here.] It – with its mate, regulates the speed. Fastened to the centre of each is a small spheroid of lead, so that in position the whole is like this [another sketch]. All attempts at makeshifts were found to be useless.

I am leaving this afternoon with a Pollack who had his leg broken yesterday – a simple fracture of the tibia. Administered first aid – splints, etc. Will haul him to Whitefish & telegraph for ambulance to meet the train to Sudbury.

Kindly advise me as to the probable time of your next visit to the camp.

Wishing you a happy new year.

Yours sincerely,
H.N. Bethune

No other letters have survived from Bethune's early manhood or from the first months of his marriage to Frances. The first of what we have was written in 1925. After two years of marriage, Bethune and Frances found themselves constantly arguing over serious matters such as money and less weighty ones like food and literature. In the fall of 1925, she left him and visited a friend in Nova Scotia. The separation seemed only to heighten Bethune's love for her.

411 Selden Ave
Detroit
Oct. 20, 1925

My dearest –
That looks rather curious and cold written by type but as I have just acquired my typewriter I simply must use it. First of all let me hasten to assure you that I still love, worship, and adore you, my dearest. I am missing you frightfully but paradoxically, wouldn't miss missing you for worlds. So please stay away a little longer. Of course when you do return you must bear with fortitude the accumulated affection of these ages. (So far this has taken me fifteen minutes and as it is now 9:45 p.m. and past my bed time I will bid you, sweet, goodnight.)

The next morning.
No letter from you today. Curses. Very cold. Ben has been and gone, washed the dishes and done all the floors. My typewriting seems to be improving. One progresses. This is a cheerful and stimulating thought. In fact I am rather bucked with myselph. This last word looks rather queer but then it may be just my fancy.

Yes, I am able to share with you your delight in being back once more on Canadian (for want of a better) soil. I think with you that we simply must move. At times this place overpowers even my stout spirit and what it must do to your soul my darling I can only conjecture with feelings of mingled despair and admiration. Patience and fortitude; these rather old-fashioned virtues have stood you in good stead. Any other women I have known, would have chucked the whole business long ago.

Evening.
I have just come in from my gymnasium class. You didn't know that I did gymnasium? Well I do. I was simply disgusted with my lack of condition. I am stiff and sore but, in the language of this country, I'm a 100% better man. Hurrah. No smoking and bed at 9:30.

The first letter from Nova Scotia arrived this afternoon. It does me good to know that you are happy. My poor dear I only wish that I was able to make Detroit a possible place for both of us. But the more I see of it the more I long to escape. But I'm not downhearted!!!!!!!

Good night my own sweet one, I do love you truly, and you only. I kiss your dear lips.

Your own, your Beth

In the summer of 1926, Bethune began to weaken and tire easily, and a medical examination revealed him to have tuberculosis in both lungs. Temporarily, he went to rest at the Calydor Sanatorium in Gravenhurst, Ontario, for what he thought would be only a brief interruption of his career. His letter from there to Frances reflected a continued optimism.

Friday night at the Calydor
[Fall 1926]

Three letters today! Perfectly lovely to have such masses of correspondence from you darling, even the suicidal-intent one.

I refuse to look at the dark side of things. My health insurance is $8.00 a day plus $12.00 (for 2 months) while I'm in hospital, so that will be alright. Dr. Newfield [Bethune's replacement at his Detroit practice], if he can't make it go can get someone else to go in at 411 [Selden Ave, Detroit] as it *is* a gold mine if properly attended to, but thank god, I'm out of *that* shaft.

Send Goodfellow a cheque for balance of the amt. of the paint job (I have already given him $25.00 you remember).

I wept over one of the letters you wrote me – darling, don't go home if you feel so bad about it but come to Toronto and get a job so at least we can be near each other.

Goodbye, darling,
Your Beth

With Bethune ill, he and Frances separated, and she returned to Scotland to her family. The reckoning, Bethune knew, would not be a pleasant one, as he acknowledged in letters to her.

Calydor
1 Oct., 1926

You are you, and a self-contained self-sufficient entity like a well-buttressed little island that needs no connections with the external world to maintain its life and content ...

What I give these people is nothing really – just a few handsprings for the children and a shadow show on the wall.

But darling, you're all I've got in the world I care a rap about and for you I will do anything – and the first thing is to make you financially free from worry and I know that away you are sufficient unto yourself to conquer dragons.

I do hate your coming combat in Edinburgh – the useless explanations sexplanations – all inexplicable without the pre-knowledge of the attending necessity (or what appeared to be necessity). This reminds me of Samuel Butler's aphorism that man is born with two illusions – one of necessity and the other of happiness. I wish I could help you. Would it do any good for me to write your mother our whole history?

Our marriage has been wonderful for me. If I had to go over it again I would still want *you* for *my* side, my darling ... *Keep a stiff* upper lip – we, you and I, will beat them yet. The thought of you to fight for makes me strong.

Goodbye, goodbye darling,
Beth

Calydor
Saturday morning

My dear girl, don't worry or fuss. You can tell your people that I took
your money, wasted it and left you stranded, and beyond calling you a
fool for your action and I knave for mine what's to be said?

You have done nothing wrong except to have consigned yourself and
your money to a man who did not appreciate the one and was careless
of the other.

But let me get up! Get well first and I will repay!

*Bethune did not get up immediately. Indeed, his emotional state began to
decline as he contemplated a lengthy battle with tuberculosis.*

Calydor Sanatorium
Gravenhurst, Ontario
Nov. 8/26

My dear Edward –
I had meant to write to you before but had unfortunately mislaid your
address, but searching today found it happily.

News? – Well, I am still in bed and will be perhaps for another month.
It is curious how, after the initial rebellion, one acquires a form of living
– I mean, a mode, not a form, of course, – which is, or was up til now,
repugnant to what one considered as one's temperament. This is a most
vague and misused word – it really means one's more or less habitual
reaction to fixed externals – a mood, a resultant reflex higgledy piggledy
jumble out of which the strongest hig or pig emerges triumphant –
porcus victorieux.

Well, I am a new pig but a useless one at times. Too much the product
of my generation to conceive my situation as tragic – there has been no
tragedy since the war – I am forced to regard the situation, if not with
grimness, then at least with a shrug of my shoulders for an entirely farcical and futile world – myself as an entirely farcical, futile figure in it.
Unable to force back on the merciful but mysterious ways of a Hidden
Purpose in life, and having entirely abandoned the anthropological idea
of God, there is but little comfort in the conception of a Vital Force, one
is reduced to the consolation of similar sufferers and one's friends
become elevated to the altar like a ceborum [*sic*].

Well, enough of this – I am feeling well and they tell me I am improving. I will get well of course, but the internal is worrying.

I have read a lot – some profitably, others wastefully.

I am going to take up French for my amusement – I feel I should read something 'serious,' 'something worthwhile' – but I have no heart for didactics – fiction is as true as solemn as treatises on life and on most facts, too.

Well, I must stop this depressing and pessimistic letter, but write me and tell me little things about yourself and what you are thinking about.

Best regards to your mother and father.

Yours affectionately,
Norman Bethune

From Calydor, Bethune went to Trudeau, where his condition appeared to improve. Bethune then returned to Detroit to attempt to re-establish his medical practice. From there he wrote to assure Frances of his continued love and to urge her to rejoin him. (This letter has been copied by Ted Allan. The ellipses are his, indicating his inability to read Bethune's writing.)

411 Selden
Detroit
March 27, 27
Sunday evening 7:30

Darling Frances –
Thank you, my dearest for your last nice two letters. I mean the serious one and the one about coming. I left Trudeau on Thursday and spent Friday and Saturday in Hamilton – & had all my meals (except breakfast) with my poor dear parents. Father looks frailer but is better as he had a transfusion last month – rather irritable but all in all remarkably cheerful. Mother (although I know it's nothing to you) is just the same – a very interesting woman!

I came into Detroit this afternoon – crept in – how dirty this place is! Awfully squalid – terribly so. The people look as vulgar and brutal as ever. I do wish they didn't but they do. Then up to the door – nobody in and the janitress let me in with loud cries of welcome. I had the place to myself for an hour – and thought of nothing but you, you, you – a thousand memories of your pale and hopeless dear face before me.

Do you remember the nice room with its ... parapets of books – oh, you must & not all your memories are bitter are they dear?

I am writing now sitting up in the little couch in the electrical room where I put in those nasty last days with my toothache and it seems just yesterday and nothing has happened. Nothing *has* happened except one thing – to me I mean – that I can see you clearer and more definitely and love you more.

I know you don't want me to love you but I do. I don't care what you say or do to me – I love you more than I ever have.

I've had a *perfect* 6 months away from you and enjoyed every minute of it – that's a terrible thing, I know but it's true, & because of it I love you a thousand times more. Now I want to see you. Now I think I can talk with you and understand you and *you* me, perhaps. I would like just to see you tonight and hold your hand for an hour in a garden.

Tomorrow I start work. I will write you later in the week and tell you all. I will be careful with myself for you depend on me – I don't worry like I used to about your depending on me – I like it now.

You silly Billy, I'm not contagious, infectious, catching or anything & never was! Not 1–1,000,000,000.

Good night, my dear one. I will answer your serious letter some time – we aren't far apart.

I am sending you some books.

Your Beth

Bethune's ardour seemed to drive Frances even further from him. In June 1927, she initiated divorce proceedings. To make matters worse, his health began to fail so dramatically that he was forced to return to the Trudeau Sanatorium. Death began to preoccupy him. On about twenty metres of brown wrapping paper spread around the walls of his cottage at Trudeau, he drew a mural with accompanying inscriptions, which he called The T.B.'s Progress. *It was modelled on Hogarth's* The Rake's Progress *and portrayed the life of a tuber-culosis sufferer from the womb through to his final embrace by the kindly Angel of Death. In the journal* The Fluoroscope, *on 15 August 1932 (vol. 1, no. 7), Bethune described the mural images and his captions for each image (his description differs from the actual mural in certain details). Although fear of death had greatly darkened Bethune's mood, his poetry (some of it doggerel) showed that he had not lost his sense of humour.*

The T.B.'s Progress

Attacked as he is so frequently in early manhood, when the future is beckoning with alluring smiles, the first reaction of the tuberculous to the realization of his disease, is often one of utter despair. Tragedy stares him in the face. Life seems ruined. Crashing down over his ears is the wreck of his future plans and expectations. Doubts and uncertainties fill his days and nights with depressing fears. Many of these fears are unjustifiable, as he will discover later, but the nervousness of many tuberculous patients can only be partly attributable to the disease process, as a large part is caused by worry over financial conditions, the dependence on others' support, the laying aside of long-cherished plans and the uncertainties of a clouded future. The young man who is suddenly told that he has tuberculosis and must stop work and enter a sanatorium, in most cases regards his life as a tragedy with only one possible ending. He begins to realize after a time that this view of his life and his disease is wrong. Hope re-enters his heart when he sees his friends returning to the outside world and taking up their normal lives again. In the sanatorium, perhaps for the first time, he has the opportunity to think. Contemplation becomes a substitution for action. The result is a deepening of his intellectual and spiritual life. Realities change their nature – the unimportant becomes the important and the formerly essential becomes the superfluous. It is only the dull and unimaginative who can lie in a bed in a sanatorium for six months or a year and fail to rise a better and finer person. Life should be enriched and not impoverished by this retreat from the world.

I came down with active pulmonary tuberculosis in 1926 when just starting off, in what I had reason to believe, would be a successful medical practice. I fought against the realization of my disease just as many of you have done, but increasing loss of strength, cough and positive sputum, forced me at last to stop work. A large cavity was found by X-rays in one lung with some disease in the other. I was put to bed for a year. On exercise, the cavity began to increase in size. Doubts and fears for the future began to cloud my normal optimism. Then I was given artificial pneumothorax and improved immediately. In a dark moment while taking the early air injections, I drew for the amusement of myself and my cottage mates, the allegorical story of my past life and what I thought the future would be.

The small cottage called 'The Lea,' in which five of us lived, was one of the oldest in the sanatorium and sat back on the hill behind

Dr. Trudeau's first cottage, 'The Little Red.' The interior was panelled in yellow pine, now darkened by the years. There were four doors and three windows. The continuous coloured drawing, five feet high and sixty feet long, ran around the walls, fitting in the spaces between the roof and the wainscotting, the doors and windows. The title of the drawing was 'THE T.B.'S PROGRESS, A DRAMA in one act and nine painful scenes.' Below the drawing were bits of poetry (so-called!) describing the scenes. The cottage was torn down last year and the drawings transferred to the Fluoroscopic Room of the Tuberculosis Unit, University Hospital, Ann Arbor, Michigan.

The first scene or drawing was a picture of my pre-natal existence. The womb was depicted as a dark cave, with the infant already being attacked by the tubercle bacillus which is represented throughout the drawings as a red pterodactyl – a sort of prehistoric reptile with a long beak and sharp teeth and bat-like wings. Although, for scientific accuracy, the theory of inter-uterine infection is highly improbable, for the sake of artistic design it was too good an idea to neglect! The legend accompanying this was:

> Look, O Stranger, at the danger
> To our hero, embryonic.
> T.B. bats, so red, ferocious,
> In the breast of our precocious
> Laddie, do him in just like his daddy.
> His dark cave no barrier knows,
> Against this worst of mankind's foes.

The second scene shows my entrance into the world; I am being carried in the arms of a beautiful angel with brilliant iridescent wings who is clothed in long, white flowing robes. Facing her, seated on a sort of throne, is a male angel (the Angel of Fate) who unrolls in his hand a scroll on which is inscribed my future. Incidentally, this theory of pre-destination is probably a relic of my Scotch ancestors. Looking over his shoulder are other angels who, as they read my future, turn away weeping. The legend below this is:

> The angels at his birth,
> Foreseeing all his years,
> Restrain not, nor should we,
> The tribute of their tears.

Detail from Scene II

Drawn in what appears to be oil pastels on brown wrapping paper encircling the walls of his residential cottage at the Trudeau Sanatorium, *The T.B.'s Progress* vividly conveyed the dimming of Bethune's hopes under the threat of death by tuberculosis in 1927. The images and verse ('so-called' poetry, he admitted) portrayed the life of a tuberculosis sufferer from the womb through to his final embrace by the kindly Angel of Death. Although fear of death greatly darkened Bethune's mood, his work showed that he had not lost his sense of humour. Selected images from the mural are reproduced here.

Scene III

The third scene is my childhood. It is depicted as a dangerous journey through a thick wood where lurk various wild animals. Childhood diseases are shown as cruel terrifying creatures, the ideas of which I took from old medieval illuminated manuscripts. The Measle is a sort of spotted tiger; the Mump, the Whoop, the Dipth, and the Scarlet are various other wild and weird animals, which either lurk behind the trees, or fly in the sky ready to pounce down on the child. This child is shown being attacked by an enormous dragon, called the Dipth and is being defended by a knight in shining armour whose long bright sword kills the dragon. The name of this knight is Sir Schick, referring to the Schick protection against diphtheria. The legend reads:

> From Dragon Dipth, Sir Shick defends,
> From other foes he cannot save.
> The wounds and scars of their attack,
> He'll carry to his grave.

Scene IV

This refers, of course, to the predisposition which we think childhood diseases sometimes give for tuberculosis.

The fourth scene describes my early manhood. I am out of the woods of childhood and have set sail across the Sea of Adolescence. I start off happily on a great ship like a Spanish galleon – 'Youth at the Prow and Pleasure at the Helm.' Everything seems propitious that my journey will be fine and successful, but half-way across, my ship comes near a rocky coast, and, like Ulysses, the Sirens sing their songs and lure me off my course. I land from the ship as the beauteous creatures (Fame, Wealth, Love and Art) point the way up the rocky cliffs to a splendid castle on the top called the 'Castle of Heart's Desire.' Just as I am about to enter I am attacked by swarms of T.B. bats who strike me down. The legend below reads:

> On Adolescence's troubled seas,
> The sails of argosy are set,
> Alas, he hears the Sirens' song,
> His course is changed, his bark a wreck.

The fifth drawing shows my fall into the Abyss of Despair. I fall head over heels from the high mountain, pursued as I fall by swarms of T.B. bats. As I fall, I look back and see that the Castle of Heart's Desire, which once looked so magnificently substantial from the front, is actually only a Hollywood set. At the bottom of the canyon is flowing a dark red river, representing a haemorrhage. The poetry under this reads:

> Down, down he falls from that high mount,
> Success so near at hand,
> His foes triumphant see him reel
> Down to that bloody strand.

The sixth drawing shows me as I lie in the depths looking upward and seeing, on a high mountain, another castle flying the Red Cross flag. This is Trudeau Sanatorium. Outside the gates is the bronze statue of Trudeau himself. The battlements of the castle are defended by different warriors, the doctors of that place – Dr. Lawrason Brown, Dr. Baldwin, Dr. Heise, Mr. Sampson of the X-ray department, and Miss Amberson, the Superintendent of Nurses. I climb slowly up to this castle where I gain entrance and protection from my enemies. There is a gas filling station (Pneumothorax apparatus) just inside, and music and laughter come through the gates. The little cottage of Dr. John Barnwell, now head of the T.B. Unit, University Hospital, Ann Arbor, is shown under the trees just outside the castle gates. Coming out through the windows are the notes of an old song we played on the gramophone, which will

Scene VI

always remind me of the happy times we had together. The poetry under this is:

> On Pisgah's Heights stands Trudeau strong,
> Bright sanctuary high,
> Where Heise, Brown and Amberson
> His enemies defy.

Pisgah is the mountain that Trudeau Sanatorium is built against.

The seventh drawing shows my return to the city. Here is where my mistaken pessimism enters. The city is drawn as a rather modernistic impression of skyscrapers seen from above and the people are like little black ants on the street. The air is filled with T.B. bats who attack me again, and I have a relapse of my disease. The poetry underneath this:

> Lured by that Siren, Spurious Fame
> Who had no heart nor pity,
> Our hero strives to win a name,
> In the canyons of the City.
> Temptations flourish thickly there,
> But T.B. bats are thicker,
> They swarm about the fetid air,
> While he grew sick, and sicker.

Scene VIII

The eighth drawing shows me starting off to the South-west in pursuit of Health and Happiness, which are shown as two lovely female forms on a bright cloud, with the sun shining above them as they beckon me across the desert. This, of course, is nothing but a mirage. Our hero is very thin and weak and has a small sputum cup strapped to his cadaverous body. With a staff in his hand, he stumbles out across the plain over which are scattered the wrecks of the old-fashioned covered wagon days. The legend under this reads:

> Once more laid flat upon his back,
> Our victim pulls a boner;
> Instead of back to Saranac
> He's off to Arizona.
> And so the plains got his remains

Scene IX

For his disease deceased him;
He coughed and spat, lost all his fat,
Kind death at last released him.

This, of course, is rather morbid and entirely imaginative, and from what has occurred since, quite untrue!

The ninth and last drawing shows the Angel of Death holding me in her arms and looking down on me with a kindly and benign expression on her face. She is not a dark angel but just as beautiful and bright as the other angels at my birth. In the foreground is a small churchyard with the five tombstones of the men who lived with me in the cottage. The poetry under this drawing is:

> Sweet Death, thou kindest angel of them all,
> In thy soft arms, at last, O let me fall;
> Bright stars are out, long gone the burning sun
> My little act is over, and the tiresome play is done.

Two of the men who thought they would die in the time we agreed upon (and they helped me suggest the time!) have done so. My own death I put down to occur in 1932. How wrong I was, unless, of course, something happens in the rest of this year. But my natural expectations are to last much longer than that!

My life was saved by artificial pneumothorax and phrenicectomy [cutting the phrenic nerve to a tuberculous lung, forcing it to remain inactive], and hundreds of you will be like me in this regard. Looking back I can see how my fears and hopeless attitude in regard to the future were wrong. Fear is the great destroyer of happiness, and most fears are unjustifiable. It can be said that man lives by hope alone. Under modern methods of treatment and early diagnosis, nearly every tuberculous patient has a great chance to recover if he is careful and follows the advice of his physician. Never despair, but be cheerful and quiet in your mind; follow the rules and play the game out to the end.

Even as he was creating scenes in which he forecast the imminence of his own death, Bethune began the artificial pneumothorax therapy which would save his life. And it would do so with astonishing swiftness. He began the treatment on 27 October and, health restored, left Trudeau in early December 1927. His physical battle against tuberculosis was over. His medical war against it was just beginning.

3

Crusader:
Montreal, 1928–1934

With the New Year in 1928, Norman Bethune began his second life. In part it was a physical rebirth, certified by his release from Trudeau Sanatorium, his tuberculous lung stabilized. It was also a psychological and moral rebirth. The new Bethune was now an evangelist – not, to be sure, in the mode of his Christian father, with whom he strongly disagreed. No, his was a crusade against tuberculosis and the social conditions that caused it. His distaste for his father's vocation, however, did not blind him to the fact that in his campaign to eradicate tuberculosis he had, after a fashion, followed in his father's footsteps: 'I know I'm always in a hurry but I come by this trait honestly. My father was a Presbyterian minister who joined the Moody and Sankey evangelical movement. Their slogan was "the world for Christ in one generation," and that is my slogan, whether people like it or not.'[1]

Bethune surpassed even his father in ambition, and he used every means available in this crusade to make the world free of tuberculosis. He employed a new medium, the radio, writing a play for it on tuberculosis treatment. He gave entertaining speeches which pointed the finger of blame for the disease at several sources – landlords whose cramped apartments forced unhealthy crowding, conservative doctors and sanatorium officials, and governments for failing to provide financial support to those stricken by the disease. Many in his audiences were impressed and amused; others were affronted. No less controversially, he wrote a sparkling, some said blasphemous, parody of the Apostle's Creed, which he called 'The Compressionist's Creed,' in which he vigorously advocated pneumothorax collapse therapy.[2] He dismissed the critics of pneumothorax as 'Cranks whose patients are dead and buried.' At the time, rest – not collapse therapy or surgery – was the routine treatment for pulmonary tuberculosis. Like a sinner who has been reborn as a Christian, he could say he had tried both remedies. So his dismissal of minimal intervention carried the ring of personal and medical authority.

His activism in the fight against tuberculosis also extended to diagnosis and public education. He opted for the use of X-rays as a diagnostic tool rather than the time-honoured but more passive methods of inspection and observation through surface percussion and stethoscope.[3] He also worked to transform the prevailing attitudes towards tuberculosis and illness more generally. Disease was not blind, natural, inevitable. It was discriminating, choosing the poor over the rich. Its effects were more likely to be fatal for those with less wealth. And its incidence could be greatly reduced, if not ended entirely, by preventive techniques, which required devoting more funds to public health. These concerns drove him on, especially in the midst of the 1930s Depression, propelling him to the forefront of the small army of activists who argued that radical change was necessary to address profound social and health problems. His dissatisfaction with existing tuberculosis treatment began to stir in him a new political conscience, although its full development was still a step away.[4]

Bethune's zeal also extended to many of the surgical instruments then in use. His rages at poorly designed equipment – expressed even as a patient lay split open before him on the operating table – were legendary. Beginning about 1930, he assiduously set to work reconstructing his tools. Within the space of a few months, he invented, or devised replacements for, much of the equipment he would come to rely on in the operating room. Linking up with the Pilling Company of Philadelphia, Bethune soon saw his name inscribed on much medical apparatus. (Characteristically, he granted Pilling the right to manufacture and sell his designs only in the United States; he reserved the Canadian rights for a Mr Masters, the Royal Victoria Hospital mechanic who built the equipment for him in Montreal.)[5] The Bethune Pneumothorax Apparatus, with its foot pump, dubbed 'The Nurse's Friend'; the Bethune Scapula Lifter and Retractor, nicknamed 'The Iron Intern'; the Bethune Rib Shears; the Bethune Rib Strippers – all came to prominent and common use in operating rooms, some of the equipment being employed for decades after it was designed. Bethune's procedures, such as the use of maggots for treating lung infections, and pleural poudrage (blowing talc into the pleural cavity in order to ensure that the lung remained fixed during surgery), were also considered very innovative.[6]

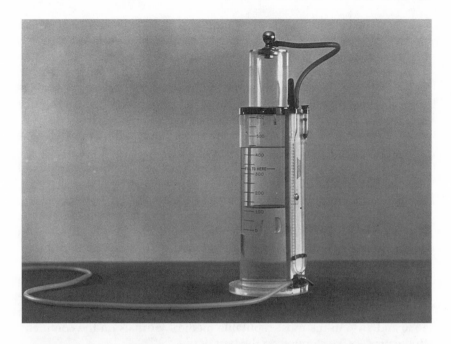

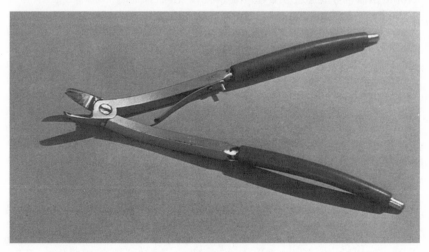

Two of Bethune's most enduring creations: the Bethune Pneumothorax
Apparatus, with its foot pump, dubbed 'The Nurse's Friend,' and the Bethune
Rib Shears.

It was Bethune's luck to be seized by this dedication just as an opportunity presented itself for him to commit himself to tuberculosis research and surgery. About the time that Bethune emerged from the Trudeau Sanatorium, Dr Edward Archibald, one of the North American pioneers in the struggle against tuberculosis, began to develop a tuberculosis research centre. In 1928 he was appointed chief surgeon of Montreal's Royal Victoria Hospital, just 150 kilometres from Saranac Lake. Learning of Bethune's qualifications and ambition, Archibald invited him to become his first assistant.[7]

Bethune worked with Archibald from 1928 to 1932. Since Archibald was the father of pulmonary surgery in North America, it was a coup to be taken under his wing. At thirty-eight, Bethune was at an advanced age to be starting a new career. But that deterred him not a bit. He entered the battle against tuberculosis with a vigour renewed by his scrape with death and the reflection enforced by his stay at Trudeau Sanatorium.

His Montreal years were among the most productive of his active life. In just eight years, he rose to the peak of his profession, gaining renown for his work, speaking at numerous national and international conventions of surgical professionals, and publishing fourteen articles between 1929 and 1936 in the most reputable medical journals on the continent. In the process, he stepped on the best of toes.

Bethune had an incurable compulsion to afflict the comfortable, especially in his own profession, and he did so with manifest delight and skill. Unfortunately, Archibald, his director at the Royal Victoria Hospital, was offended by this impertinence. After a time, the two men began to clash over their greatly divergent views on surgical methods and strategies as well as their different assessments of the balance between the risk of surgery to a patient's health compared with the risk from non-intervention. Bethune often criticized his cautious colleagues who operated only on patients who would have recovered anyway. He thought they merely condemned patients in the high-risk category to a slow death. Bethune often went ahead and operated, with the result that the incidence of death climbed higher than Archibald thought proper.[8] Another problem was that although Bethune greatly appreciated being able to serve under Archibald, he was not a man who would remain under anyone's wing for long. Together, these factors led to a rift between the two. By the fall of 1932, their personal and professional differences had become too glaring to ignore, and Archibald effectively fired Bethune.

Once again Bethune faced an uncertain future and financial difficulty.

But, in November 1932, it was his good fortune to be appointed chief of thoracic surgery and bronchoscopy at the Hôpital du Sacré-Coeur (Sacred Heart Hospital) in Cartierville, just north of Montreal. No longer an assistant constrained by the conservative hand of his director, Bethune flourished in the new environment, and his reputation and that of the hospital both grew.[9]

His complicated relationship with his former wife, Frances, remained troubled. Their divorce in 1928 had not stilled their powerful attraction for one another, and after his appointment at the Royal Victoria Hospital, he wrote her in Edinburgh asking for a reconciliation. Her fascination with him was equal to his ardour, and on 11 November 1929, not long after she joined him in Montreal, they were remarried. But they soon reverted to their destructive pattern of interaction. In April 1933 they divorced for the second time and Frances married a friend of Bethune's, A.R.E. Coleman.

Bethune's first months in Montreal provided a refreshing contrast to the previous two unhappy years. He liked his work with Archibald, and he was optimistic about the future. Even his hopes for a second life with Frances were revived when she finally agreed to correspond with him from Scotland, where she had returned after their divorce. From his residence in the Faculty Club of McGill University, he wrote her in the autumn of 1928. (The first page of this letter has been lost, so that the salutation and date are missing.)

My job here is a combined clinical one in the Royal Victoria Hospital – in the chest clinic and part research work. I told Archibald a couple of months ago I would be forced to leave as I couldn't live on my income. He was keen that I should stay and offered me this fellowship at $1500 a year. I will stay one year I think and then Archibald will be able to place me somewhere. He is the outstanding figure in chest surgery in America and a most charming fellow.

Fortunately I was able to bring to the clinic some new ideas as a result of my Ray Brook research. [Bethune had studied biochemistry at the New York State Hospital for Incipient Tuberculosis in Ray Brook, New York, in early 1928.] He has told me he can't hold out any hopes of a hospital appointment here – my appointment is in the university [McGill] – but I told him I was indifferent to that – all I wanted was a thorough training in chest work – then I can go anywhere. I have been thinking of England next year in a sanatorium.

I have also a tentative offer from Shanghai, China – but not for the immediate present – for next year.

I am in excellent health – have lost a lot of weight this summer and am now down to 164 lbs. I go to bed every afternoon from 2–5. The work is really very light. My pneumothorax is holding well and I have no cough, expectoration or fever. The insurance comes to hand regularly. I feel confident it will hold for another year – and then the future must take care of itself.

I will never return to general practice and am getting prepared to do nothing but chest work – both medical and surgical combined. The way will open out, I'm sure.

I can scarcely tell you, my darling Frances, how glad for your sake this fellowship has turned up. That happiness of yours, is, to me, the most desired thing in the world. If it were not for my doubts I would say at once – 'Come here. Marry me. Why should we be separate who love each other.'

I can be happy with you – but you not with me.

I was thinking that if you came here this winter – we could meet just as friends, living apart. In any case, whether you marry me or not, that is, I am sure, *our* only way.

Montreal pleases me. I am happy here.

I miss you dreadfully but I don't want to snatch at you ever again. I want you to be just Frances Penney – [indecipherable] the Frances Penney I knew in Edinburgh – self-contained and undistorted.

Goodbye, darling, for the present, you are ever in my thoughts.

Your affectionate lover
Beth

Montreal
Jan. 5 [1929]

Darling Frances –
Herewith the usual.

I spent Christmas with my family in Toronto. Shortly, Father and I had our usual hate together – especially heated as he is gambling on the stock market (made $500 last year!) and I refused to drink a scotch and soda in the bath room and had it in front of him. What hypocrites these professed religious are ...

Work goes on as usual. I must look for a job in the States, I think, in the summer. I shall dislike leaving Montreal, but feel my life's rhythm is a determined and pre-destined irregular one, so I accept it. It is very pleasant here – very gentle and quiet and I am a different soul.

Very clear and cold today. Sun shimmering on the snow and the sparrows making a great racket outside my windows. I wish you were here. I am glad you are relatively happy and well, at least more so than when you lived with my petulant irritability.

God bless you,
Beth

Another letter to Frances from early 1929 painted a similar picture of his life, suggesting a mellow, even reserved Bethune. (The original of this letter is not extant. The fragment below, including ellipses, is what Ted Allan copied from the letter supplied to him by Frances Coleman.)

I get up at nine, and have coffee, toast and marmalade, and walk to the hospital (25 minutes along Sherbrooke Street) and then clinical work til 1. Lunch at the hospital. And research from 2–3. Then home to bed until six. Up and make dinner. Then bed again at 11 or 12, after an evening of reading. Once in a while I go to pictures or a hockey match ...

Last Sunday, having been in bed for a week with a bad cold, I got very tired of the flat and took the train at 8:35 in the morning with my skis for the mountains. (40 miles north.) Skied six miles – lunch in the woods and then back to the station and home again at 9 and so to bed.

Today (Monday) I feel perfectly wonderful. It stopped my cough! It was lovely up in the Laurentians – like Switzerland. The train was just like the trains in Vienna, do you remember when you and I used to go into the country – the same lovely young people eating sandwiches out of paper bags and going to sleep on each other's shoulders coming home. My skiing was bloody awful. I fell all over the place ...

My health is excellent. I had an X-ray today and it shows no disease or cavity present, except healed scars ...

I've often thought I'd like to surprise you by waiting at the corner of the street for you one morning as you walk down for the car. I'd just say, 'Hullo – let's go for a walk.'

And did we love each other in your dream – were we in each other's arms again?

Bethune's letters had the desired effect on Frances. She agreed to join him in Montreal, and they were married again on 11 November 1929. But their happiness was brief. Already by 1931, as the following letter indicates, they were separated and discussing divorce. Bethune was in the southern United States on a lecture-study trip.

Grand Canyon National Park
Arizona
Nov. 30/31

Darling Frances –
Thank you for your two letters which were waiting me on my return from Tucson.

I have no desire to force you into marriage with R.E. [Coleman]. Believe me, I will never force you to do anything your heart is opposed to, ever again. I love you and always will, however, much you may hurt or wound me – and now all that is left for me to show you I love you is to help you to gain what you want. I can do that best by keeping you supplied with money, I think – for as some one has said 'religion knows no peace comparable to that supplied by good clothes.'

But I do think, my dear, the honourable thing is that if you are not going to marry R.E. is to tell me so –

1. I will not obtain a divorce
2. Although it is not for me to dictate, nor will I now, do you think it is fair to keep him as a lover?

However, that's for you to decide – but, Frances, it makes *me* feel such a rotten cad – the complacent husband. Well, I will say no more – I will even bear this if it makes for your happiness.

I enclose $200.00 for December.

$100 – yourself
$25 – to rent
$25 – odds & ends I left in the shops
$50 – for your Christmas present

Present these cheques *at once* to the bank. They are worth about 10% more in Canadian currency ($20.00).

I am going down to Phoenix on Dec. 3–4–5 to address a medical meeting. I flew down over the desert to Tucson and back, then drove up here. You would love this – like a tremendous super-Switzerland – quite the most amazing sight I have ever beheld.

Send all mail *including cheques promptly on the day they arrive* to Prescott, where I will return after Phoenix. I can go direct to Reno in December if you wish to marry R.E. but I must know at once.

Beth

Bethune became more willing to seek a divorce when he met a woman in Alabama whom he hoped to marry. This relationship, however, was short-lived.

The Cawthon
Mobile, Alabama.
Dec. 31/31

Frances dear –
I have been travelling for a month and have not received any letters from you with the exception of the last in which you acknowledged my Christmas presents and told me you had started to work again.

If you remember, you begged me not to force you to marry R.E. and my reply that I would do nothing to put you in such a position against your own desires. I also wrote you that since you apparently did not at this time want to marry R.E. and since I had no inclination to marry again myself, that I would not divorce you, but we would be separated only. Well, my dear, the unexpected has happened as usual. I have fallen in love and want to marry this girl that I feel sure I can be happy with. It was love at first sight with both of us. She is a most charming American, 26, the granddaughter of a famous Alabama physician who Osler has written about in his 'Alabama Student.' Her name was Zarna Bassett Boynton and she is now married to a Dr. Mott Rawlings of El Paso, Texas. We have told her husband we love each other and she is going to divorce him. I will go ahead with our divorce as soon as I can raise the money necessary.

Darling, let us give up trying to reconcile our irreconcilable natures. As you have said so often 'Breakfast, dinner and bed are not for us two.' Our only kinship is a 'spiritual affinity' and this, alas, is not enough at our time of life and age. We have never been at ease with each other such as you and R.E. feel in each other's company and such as Bassett and I feel together. Instead of torturing ourselves with mutual recriminations let us quietly acknowledge the fact and live apart as friends – true friends. We can and will. The affection I feel for you and have felt for you in the past is unique – I can never feel it again for any one – I am not sure I want to.

You will love Bassett. You are both much the same – the same qualities in you attracted her to me in the first place – her lovely spirit and mind with the soul of a poet.

Will you write her?

Mrs. J. Mott Rawlings
714 Baltimore St., El Paso,
Texas

I am going up to stay with John Barnwell, University Hospital, Ann Arbor, Michigan for a couple of weeks. Please write me there. Then I will come to Montreal after staying a day or so in Hamilton.

Since I love and am loved I have lost all the bitterness I felt towards you, darling, and my heart is filled with the warmest affection and regard.

Your friend,
Beth

Obtaining a divorce in Canada in the 1930s was neither simple nor pleasant. Couples often resorted to staging an adultery in order to satisfy the courts. Bethune and Frances went through the same ritual, although it was the cause of conflict between them, as Bethune's cryptic letter to her revealed.

City of Detroit
Herman Kiefer Hospital.
Sunday, July 10/32

Darling
Thank you for your long-awaited letter. That was a lovely thing, that bit of pure poetry. I am sending you a couple of articles I cut out. Please send them back to me as I want to keep them. The piece on modern poetry is very acute.

Now some of the things in your letter.

1. I never led the legal dog a dance. What would you think of a man who would travel 600 miles to see me and call me up 200 miles away on long distance to see if I would be in town 4 hours later? I was just going out of the door for an appointment at Northville [Michigan] (25 miles away) and of course told him he could see me there. As it happened

when I arrived in Northville, John Barnwell called me up and wanted me to see his brother who is to be operated on the next day. I left word the [indecipherable] chap could follow me – another 17 miles. He talked with me for 5 minutes only. He left me no card. I didn't know his name. He promised to write me reference Toronto affairs which he failed to do. In short, he showed himself to be a bungling ass. I was perfectly willing to go through the Toronto business.

2. In regard to Toronto he again showed himself a fool. I was down on the program to read a paper at 12 noon on Wednesday, June 22. He could have met me there. Again on Friday I spoke in the discussion on bronchiactares. He could have easily found me – a hundred people knew me by name or appearance. No *rendezvous* was appointed by him. I acted as I always act, simply and without indirection.

3. In regard to witnesses. There were 3 people at least – employees of the hotel who saw me and my companion. In addition, we had breakfast. We were the only people in the hotel.

Of all the squeamish, squelchy oily people refer me to the legal light and their ilk. They are the rounded and complete fools.

I regard with horror the arrangement made for Toronto. I would certainly have refused had I known of it beforehand. I would never have consented to your being a part of it as a denouncing witness. That would have been too ghastly. I see you are being badly advised by Coleman. If this mismanagement goes on much longer, I shall get a Mexican divorce. This is recognized in Michigan. Then you may do as you please. I can see now that your mind is made up. Well, so be it.

Beth

Despite the messiness of their divorce, Bethune was able to maintain a sense of humour about the ordeal. On news of their second divorce having been granted, Bethune wrote to Frances.

Royal Victoria Hospital
Montreal
April 12/33

Frances darling –
I enclose a letter of Millar, Horne & Hanna, the official hangman. Well,

Bethune painted this portrait in oils of his wife, Frances Penney, in 1933, the year they divorced for the second time.

they may think they have done the job but how surprised the Senator & Horne would be to know that all their mumblings and posturing have left the 2 principals – like 2 naughty reprimanded boys – sniggling behind their backs.

God bless you. I love you.
Beth

The first five articles he published in medical journals, four of them in 1929 alone, were scholarly ones based exclusively on his research on tuberculosis. But in 1932 his articles began to propose more active measures to eradicate tuberculosis. In the following excerpts from 'A Plea for Early Compression in Pulmonary Tuberculosis,' published in the Canadian Medical Association Journal, *vol. 27 (July 1932), Bethune's argument was still couched in formal language, but his commitment to action was nonetheless apparent.*

A Plea for Early Compression in Pulmonary Tuberculosis

Tuberculosis can be cured, not only clinically but often anatomically, if properly treated in its early acute stage ... The treatment of pulmonary tuberculosis involves two problems. The first is that of the infected individual, regarded as a whole, acting and reacting in his social and physical environment, and the second, the reaction of that individual's body, and more particularly his lungs, to the presence of the tubercle bacillus. The tubercle bacillus may be considered, as it truly is, just another factor in the environment of man, impinging on him, causing certain changes in his body and modifying its behaviour. The first problem then becomes chiefly an economic and social one, and the second, a physiological and immunological one. In the final analysis they are mutually reactive and inseparable. [Dr Edward Livingstone] Trudeau well said, 'There is a rich man's tuberculosis and a poor man's tuberculosis. The rich man recovers and the poor man dies.' This succinctly expresses the close embrace of economics and pathology. Any scheme to cure this disease which does not consider man as a whole, as the resultant of environmental strain and stress, is bound to fail. Tuberculosis is not merely a disease of the lungs; it is a profound change of the entire body which occurs when man, regarded as an organism acting under the dictation of, and the product of, his environment, fails to circumnavigate or subjugate certain injurious forces acting on his body and mind. Let him persist in continuing in such an environment and he will die. Change these factors, both external and internal, readjust the scene, if not the stage, and he, in the majority of instances, will recover. The sanatorium with its bed rest, fresh air, and good food, is such an external environmental change. The second requirement is to alter the local environment of the tubercle bacilli, and this change is most quickly and effectively obtained by collapse therapy. In the case of a man acutely infected with the tubercle bacillus, activity in his daily struggle to adapt himself to his social and economic environment is almost invariably followed by a coincidental activity of the disease. Rest in the first direction is followed by arrest in the other.

Tuberculosis is commonly regarded as a chronic disease. This only means that the tuberculous takes an unconscionably long time in dying. Did the lung, alas, not 'suffer in silence,' but did it protest more vigorously, tuberculosis, like syphilis, would be treated in the first acute stage with a high hope of cure, and we would not await the development of the second or third stages, when a satisfactory result is difficult and sometimes impossible. These early lesions are not infrequently missed by a physical examination and a stethoscope. They will be discovered through a careful history and an X-ray film.

Early pulmonary tuberculosis is of all so-called chronic diseases the easiest to cure. The remedy is rest. Dr. John Flinn has well called this the 'specific treatment.' Pulmonary tuberculosis shows an inherent tendency, a willingness for recovery, which when considered beside chronic heart, kidney or liver diseases, which show little or no tendency to cure, makes it unique among the diseases of long duration afflicting man. Given half a chance, pulmonary tuberculosis will meet the physician half-way towards recovery. Our sanatoriums are filled today with the incurable sequelae, the deplorable after-results, the uncollapsible cavities, the avoidable complications of what was once, for many patients, an entirely curable disease in the early stage. The incurable tuberculous who will fill our sanatoriums for the next five years are now walking the streets, working at desks or machines with early curable tuberculosis, and coming into doctors' offices with loss of appetite, loss of weight, tiredness, and are getting bottles of medicine for their stomach complaints or tonics for their fatigue. They eventually will come to the sanatorium with moderately or far advanced disease with cavitation. We, as a people, can get rid of tuberculosis, when once we make up our minds it is worthwhile to spend enough money to do so. Better education of doctors, public education to the point of phthisiophobia, enforced periodic physical and X-ray examinations, early diagnosis, early bed-rest, early compression, isolation and protection of the young are our remedies.

We, as physicians, can do but little to change the external environmental forces which predispose to re-infection. Poverty, poor food, unsanitary surroundings, contact with infectious foci, overwork, and mental strain are mostly beyond our control. Those essential and radical readjustments are problems for the sociologists and economists. We produce in a sanatorium, for a few short months, a new and harmonious environment and attempt to counteract years of disharmony and maladjustment. All the more reason, since the time is so short, to take advantage of these months by actively altering the local environment of the bacillus in the diseased lung by collapse therapy. Rest, either physiological or so-called mechanical, will not by itself cure the disease; it merely induces local conditions favourable for the re-establishing of the body's defensive mechanism, those mysterious and incalculable elements, the sum total of which are called resistance. Once resistance has been built up it must be carefully protected. This preservation of resistance is the chief problem of rehabilitation and its watchword is 'The Fatigue Conscience.' It is thus seen that there are three acts to the drama; the first, the predisposing environment and the onset of the acute re-infection; the second, the temporary change of this injurious environment in the sanatorium, with an active attempt to enforce lung relaxation; and the third, the readjustment to the external environment after the sanatorium. The first and last are the important ones and the most difficult problems in the treatment of this disease.

Until that happy day breaks when the immunologist and serologist solve the problem of how to prevent invasion and, once invaded, to destroy in vivo the tubercle bacillus, the phthisiotherapist is forced to adopt the mechanistic viewpoint in the treatment of this disease. This is no new idea. It was suggested by William Carson, of Liverpool, in 1821, who said in part – 'It has long been my opinion that if this disease (phthisis) is to be cured, and it is an event of which I am by no means disposed to despair, it must be accomplished by mechanical means, or in other words by a surgical operation.' He urged artificial pneumothorax and other collapse procedures. While this mechanical viewpoint is a confession of failure to treat this disease directly, while some of the procedures advocated are clumsy, crude, and often dangerous, yet lung relaxation and lung compression must be accepted to-day for want of something better. That partial or complete respiratory immobilization will hasten absorption and induce fibrosis in a lung invaded by the tubercle bacillus faster and more surely than any other procedure is the outstanding fact we know about the treatment of this disease. The treatment of pulmonary tuberculosis to-day is the treatment of neglected cavities. The remedy is earlier diagnosis and earlier compression.

...

More and more, rightly or wrongly, and I believe, wrongly, we are regarding pulmonary tuberculosis as a disease of a lung instead of the entire body. It is truly a form of scientific despair which will seem absurd when immunology and serology come into their own. Yet, that narrow and empirical viewpoint of the mechanical mind, with its eyes fixed on practically nothing but the local pulmonary lesion, has contributed more to the successful treatment of this disease than a hundred years of forced feeding, fresh air, vaccine and chemicotherapy, change of work, or intermittent rest with exercise.

Who can regard the millions of money lost in earning capacity each year, the high cost of sanatorium upkeep, the poor results of short-time hospitalization, the drain on the patient's, his family's, or his country's purse, the years wasted in curing, and the lives lost, without thinking that sanatoria and short bed-rest are not worth while? The day of the sanatorium as a sort of boarding-house is past. The modern sanatorium is a hospital for active treatment. No sanatorium to-day can call itself modern which does not have at least 50 per cent of its patients under some form of collapse therapy, a distribution of say 30 per cent pneumothoraces, 15 per cent phrenicectomies, and 5 per cent thoracoplasties or extra-pleural wax fillings, etc. Compression saves time, saves money, and saves life. The patient with early tuberculosis who, through economic pressure, can afford to spend less than two to three years in a sanatorium must have mechanical pressure. Lack of time and money kills more cases of pulmonary tuberculosis than lack of resistance to that disease. The poor man dies because he cannot afford to live. Here the economist and the sociologist meet the compressionist on common ground ...

Learned medical journals are seldom a forum for fun, and in many of Bethune's fourteen scholarly articles he abided by convention. But even in some of these, he could not entirely resist stirring things up with humour. One such article was 'A Phrenicectomy Necklace,' in which he described an operation he performed on the Hollywood actress Renée Adorée. Bethune's task was not just to perform the surgery, but also to find some way to conceal the resulting scar on her neck. By 1931, when the operation was performed, Adorée's career was in decline, and indeed she would die of tuberculosis. But she wrote a poem to Bethune thanking him for the operation. Published in the American Review of Tuberculosis, *volume 26 (September 1932), the article won Bethune a bet. He had argued with a colleague that most editors of learned journals were so in awe of 'experts' that they would publish virtually anything by them without regard to the article's merit. He submitted 'A Phrenicectomy Necklace' to prove his point. In a later article, he would acknowledge the spoof.[10] Still, it developed a serious theme to which Bethune would often refer – the surgeon as artist, a role that Bethune increasingly saw himself in.*

A Phrenicectomy Necklace

The practice of surgery has been called an art, and it may be considered so, if that term is not defined too closely. In all its essentials, however, it is a craft, and the surgeon a craftsman, an artisan, a plastic mechanic.

Bound by the rigid and inexorable laws of his medium, the human body, the surgeon is permitted but few of the liberties his fellow craftsmen may take who work with stone, wood or metal. He is a master of makeshift, a ready compromiser, denied, as in no other craft, the relief of substitution. A *tour de force*, although occasionally successful, is more apt to be disastrous. His critics are harsh, unforgiving and of distressingly long memories. He is not allowed the exhibition of playful fancies, wit or humour, which other craftsmen enjoy in their productions. But, for all that, our craftsman often has the soul of a creative artist, although the nature of his plastic medium restricts the free play of his artistic nature. Like most other men, his creative force is confined to one channel and allowed but one escape.

The modern introduction of anaesthesia has liberated the craft from the hurried expediency of the past to the more leisurely procedures of today. Modern surgical craftsmanship with its new leisure and, as an immediate consequence, its new precision, permits and encourages the artistic sensibilities of the operator. These artistic desires and their approximate satisfaction are contained, to a large extent, in what is known as 'surgical technique.' Still, for all the remarkable transition from butchery to bloodlessness an operation scar still remains a scar, and, regarded artistically, can never be considered else but an aesthetic affront to the human body. Some of these insults may be concealed by clothing, rearrangement of hair or other artifices; those others, beyond concealment, must be borne with whatever resignation their sufferers can command.

The powerful combination of the patient's vanity and the craftsman's artistic urge has produced the cleverly hidden scar of the 'face-lifter,' the dubious buttonhole incision for the appendix, the transference of the smallpox-inoculation scar from the arm to the thigh (this last representing a well-intended misdirection), the crease-hidden thyroidectomy incision, artificial teeth, the toupé, the glass eye, the artificial nose and many otorhinolaryngological and orthopaedic operations. Therefore, little apology is offered in presenting another suggestion for the satisfaction of both the patient's and the surgeon's harmless aesthetic vanities.

Since the vertical phrenicectomy incision has been abandoned the scar of the transverse approach has become less noticeable. Yet, even in the same hands, the transverse scar will show slight variations of position from patient to patient: here, a little too far out; here, a trifle too low; here, a half-inch too high; and in others, a trifle too long. Now the ideal scar should run neither transversely nor vertically, but obliquely downward and inward to the sternoclavicular joint, and lie in a normal crease of the neck. It should be three-quarters to one inch in length, although an additional half-inch is sometimes allowable.

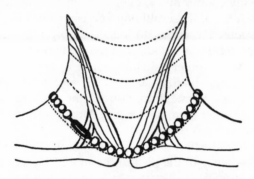

FIG. 1. DIAGRAMMATIC SKETCH OF PHRENICECTOMY NECKLACE IN POSITION
The lower end of the bar rests on the edge of the clavicular head of the sterno-mastoid muscle. The scalene muscle (not shown) should be felt below.

To disguise the scar of this incision, the common practice is to place it in a crease of the neck; but with the head turned sharply to the side, as in the operating position, creases are apt to be obliterated. In many young subjects no creases can be seen. Correct anatomical placement and the future ease with which the scar may be hidden may both be obtained by using an ordinary bead necklace. This, of course, must be rolled away to draw on the skin a line in which it lay. Not infrequently, when the beads are replaced, this line drawn freehand, is found to be just a trifle out of position. This may be avoided in the following way:

Take an ordinary bead necklace of the 'choker' type (a 10 ¢ one from Woolworth's is excellent) and, after removal of a few beads from the string, introduce a thin, slotted, flexible, silver bar, ½ inches long and ¼ inch wide. A short link of silver chain, 5 inches long, is placed at one end of the string of beads so that the clasp may be adjusted to give a total length of necklace from 12 to 16 inches. This range will accommodate all but the thinnest or thickest necks. The flexible silver bar can be easily bent to fit the neck as snugly as the original beads. This bar has a slot

1 inch long and $\frac{1}{8}$ inch wide. The necklace, after being sterilized by boiling and after the skin has been prepared, is placed in position with the patient sitting upright, head to the front. The beads should lie easily and naturally on the neck and the lower ends cross the sternoclavicular articulations. The adjustable clasp is fastened and the bar is then placed in the correct position by palpating the anterior scalene muscle which is felt below. With a small applicator (a toothpick is useful) dipped in mercurochrome, one then can draw a line on the skin through the slot in the bar, without disturbing the beads. The necklace is then removed and the patient placed in the operating position. The incision is made through the red line. After the operation the patient is informed that a necklace of such and such a length (say 14 inches) will hide the scar from view.[1]

Strange to say, this seems to fill the female breast with the most profound gratitude.

In late 1933 Bethune tried his hand at a different type of writing – a radio play. The result, 'The Patient's Dilemma; or, Modern Methods of Treating Tuberculosis,' was highly didactic, reflecting Bethune's own zeal to conquer tuberculosis. Moreover, 'The Patient's Dilemma' sounds embarrassingly stilted to today's ear. Still, it's useful to recall that this type of stuffy, instructional form was common in radio programs and advertisements until the 1950s. To the contemporary observer, Bethune's play also displays elements of a 'doctor-knows-best' superiority, especially with regard to female patients and nurses. And curiously, given all we know about Bethune's growing sense of outrage at the lack of adequate government financial aid for public health, the play presents a remarkably sanguine view of the facilities available for tuberculosis sufferers.

Hôpital du Sacré-Coeur
Montreal
Dec. 17, 1933

Dr. John Wherrett –
I'm enclosing the little play for the radio for the Christmas Seal campaign. The time is 15 minutes. I will advise you tomorrow approximate cost of production here. You might approach the Can. Radio commission for *gratis* time over their system.

I'm prepared to write a number of these little dramas on tuberculosis

1 This necklace was made by Pilling and Son Co., Philadelphia, Pennsylvania.

if your C. Inst. Assn. will sponsor them. Another series can be written on cancer, heart disease, gastro-intestinal disorders etc. I think you will agree with me that the radio has never been exploited to its fullest extent in the education of the public – & the general practitioner.

Yours sincerely,
Norman Bethune, M.D., F.R.C.S.
Chief of Division of Thoracic Surgery and Bronchoscopy

A Play for the Radio
THE PATIENT'S DILEMMA
or
Modern Methods of Treating Tuberculosis

AUTHOR: NORMAN BETHUNE

Scene: Doctor's Consulting Room or Pulmonary Clinic

ACTORS
1 / **The Doctor**
2 / **The Nurse** – Miss Jones
3 / **Patients:**
1. Miss Wilkinson
2. Miss Owens and mother
3. James Kirk
4. Mrs. Peterson
5. Arthur Smith

Telephone rings.
Nurse, answering telephone – Yes, I am expecting the doctor at two o'clock. You may have an appointment at two-thirty, Mrs. Owens.
Doctor enters – Good afternoon, Miss Jones. Many new patients this afternoon? Are the X-ray films of yesterday's new patients developed and have the sputums been examined?
Nurse   Yes sir, there is one new case and four old cases waiting. Here is a list of the sputum examinations.
Doctor takes the list and reads aloud – Miss Wilkinson, positive, James Kirk negative, Mrs. Peterson negative, good, Miss Ericson positive, Humph!

Nurse   Miss Wilkinson.

Doctor   Good afternoon, Miss Wilkinson.

Miss W.   Good afternoon, Doctor.

Doctor   Your X-ray film taken yesterday is ready, and the sputum you sent has been examined. How do you feel today?

Miss W.   I feel rather tired, doctor. I woke up at seven o'clock this morning and my pajamas were so damp with perspiration I had to get up and change them. I took my temperature as you asked at four o'clock in the afternoon, at eight at night and again this morning. Here it is.

Doctor, reading – Humph! – 99.8 at four, 100 at eight, 98 this morning.

Miss W.   I was glad you didn't find any signs with your stethoscope yesterday, doctor. That means I haven't got tuberculosis, doesn't it?

Doctor   By no means. Two out of three early cases show no signs that a doctor can discover in examining the chest. However, the X-ray will show the disease. Here is your film. (Points out X-ray film to patient.) Look, you see those little white fluffy marks? That means that you have a small tuberculous lesion in the apex – that is, the top – of the left lung. In addition, your sputum is positive.

Miss W.   What does that mean?

Doctor   It means that your sputum contains tubercle bacilli, the germs that cause tuberculosis.

Miss W.   Oh doctor, then I've got consumption, haven't I?

Doctor   Consumption was the old name given to a very rapid type of tuberculosis of the lungs. We don't use the word now. It meant of course, that the patient was losing a great deal of weight – was being consumed by his disease. It is not a good term because loss of weight may not be noticed in tuberculosis, although it is true, it is a common symptom. Now this film (pointing at the X-ray) shows that there is in your lung what we call a small area of infiltration just below the clavicle – your collar-bone, or on a level with the upper part of your shoulder blade behind. This is what is giving you the pain between the shoulder blades you told me about yesterday.

Miss W.   Well, it's not really a pain, doctor – it's more like a dull burning sensation or sometimes a little stab.

Doctor   That means that the pleura is involved. The pleura is the covering of the lung and is very sensitive to inflammation. Unfortunately, the lung itself is quite insensitive and does not feel pain. That is why some people may have far advanced tuberculosis without enough pain to drive them to see a doctor. Fortunately you came to me because you were losing weight and had a cough, isn't that so?

Miss W.   Yes doctor, I lost five pounds in one month and felt so tired all the time.

Doctor   The tiredness is an indication that you were being poisoned by some infective process in your body. The X-ray of the chest shows that this poison is coming from the disease in the lung.

Miss W.   Oh dear, what shall I do now?

Doctor   I am glad that you have asked me that straightforward question. It means that you have acknowledged your disease and are ready to reconcile yourself to it. There is no use fighting tuberculosis – if you oppose it, it will defeat you in the end. The only way to conquer it is to acknowledge its presence and act accordingly. You must go into a sanatorium for at least six months or better, a year, for complete bed rest.

Miss W.   Why a sanatorium, doctor?

Doctor   Because there you will learn how to cure yourself. You will learn discipline. Through discipline you will conquer your disease. Come and see me tomorrow and we will talk about the arrangements. You will find it is not expensive, and if you cannot pay for it yourself the government will do that for you. It will be a new revelation of living to you.

Miss W.   Then I can be cured of my disease?

Doctor   You have an excellent chance to be cured and to lead a perfectly normal life in the future. I would say that your chances are nine out of ten of being made well in two or three years, but do not deceive yourself – two years of rest is the minimal time you will need. Goodbye – come and see me tomorrow.

Miss W.   Thank you doctor. I feel much better. Even though you have told me I have tuberculosis, the very fact my diagnosis is made and I know definitely what my disease is and how it can be cured relieves my mind tremendously.

Doctor   Goodbye Miss Wilkinson. You will be a good patient I see.

Nurse   Mrs. and Miss Owens.

Mrs. O.   Doctor I have brought my daughter Margaret to see you. She is nineteen years of age and is going to college. I have been rather worried about her lately.

Doctor   Why have you been worried, Mrs. Owens?

Mrs. O.   Well about two months ago, she caught a cold – quite an ordinary cold, I thought, like a bronchitis, but the cough has kept up ever since.

Miss O.   Why mother, I don't cough!

Mrs. O.   Yes you do, my dear. You may not notice it yourself, but often in the mornings I can hear you give half a dozen little coughs. Then too, I am sure you have lost weight lately, and you are not eating well. Don't you remember that only yesterday you said you had no appetite, and were having some stomach trouble? While last night doctor, she went to a dance, came in at one, and told me this morning that she felt so tired that she could hardly get up out of bed at ten o'clock. That is quite unlike her.

Doctor   Do you expectorate, Miss Owens?

Miss O.   Oh no, doctor. I'm quite all right, I know. Perhaps I have a little cough, now that mother mentions it, but it is probably due to cigarettes. It's true I get tired more easily, but then I'm working hard at college. (she coughs) There, that's all the cough I've got.

Doctor   Do you smoke much?

Miss O.   Oh, about five or six cigarettes a day.

Doctor   Well, that's quite moderate, and should not cause a cough in a person accustomed to them. Are you sure you did not feel any secretion or moisture in your throat just then and instead of spitting it out, swallowed it? That is very common among girls and women who have been raised to think that expectorating is unclean and unaesthetic and who consciously or unconsciously swallow sputum raised from the lungs rather than spitting it out. Mind you, I'm not blaming you, but I think I saw you swallow just now some sputum that the cough cleared from the bronchial tubes. Please let me examine your chest. (rings bell and nurse enters)
Nurse, please take Miss Owens into the examining-room. (To Mrs. Owens) I will examine your daughter with the stethoscope and under the fluoroscope.

Mrs. O.   What's a fluoroscope, doctor?

Doctor   It's an instrument using X-rays, but instead of taking a photograph like an X-ray film through the chest we can see if there is any disease present in the lung. It must not be relied upon to detect a very small early amount of disease. Whether or not the fluoroscope will show any trouble, your daughter's symptoms are sufficient to have an X-ray film taken. We will do that also this afternoon. Let us go into the examining-room as they are probably ready for us now. (They enter examining-room)

Doctor to **Miss O.**   Please take this piece of gauze in your right hand, and cover your mouth lightly with it. I will first percuss the chest – that is the term we use for the method to find out if there is any change from the normal sound that the chest and the lungs within it give out when struck lightly with the finger. No, there is no marked change except that it is a trifle duller on the left, just between the edge of the shoulder blade behind, and the spine. I will now listen with the stethoscope to the breath sounds. I want you to give two little coughs and take a deep breath afterwards like this (illustrates method of coughing). Please continue like that until you are tired. (She coughs as instructed.) Yes, there are a few small rales over the same dull area we found on percussion.

Mrs. O.   What is a rale, doctor?

Doctor   A rale is a small moist sound which we hear with the stetho-scope. It may come from the small air cells in the lung, or from the bronchial tubes. The smaller, finer, and more moist it is, the more likely that it comes from the lung itself. It is the most important sign in early tuberculosis. If you think of the breath sounds as heard with the stethoscope as the wind blowing past your windows, then the rales are like the rain falling on the window-pane. In the lungs, the wind is the noise of the air as it passes through the bronchial tubes, and the rain on the window-pane is a small clicking sound that fol-lows on at the end of a deep breath after coughing. These rales are often the only sign of disease that we can detect and should always be listened to after a cough. They may not be heard at all during quiet breathing. Well, the rest of the lungs seem normal. Now let us exam-ine you under the fluoroscope. Please stand facing me in front of the machine. Do not be alarmed – you will feel nothing whatsoever. I must turn out the light now to get my eyes accustomed to seeing in the dark. (Steps on the switch.) Yes, just as I thought. You have a small amount of disease extending down from the top of the lung as far as the third rib. The rest of the lung is clear. We will take an X-ray film to be absolutely sure.

Mrs. O.   Oh doctor, how awful!

Doctor   Not at all. The disease has been discovered early and with proper attention can be checked. We will decide after the X-ray film is taken whether or not we should start you on pneumothorax treat-ment.

Miss O.   Why, what is that doctor?

Doctor   It means putting a cushion of air between the lung and the chest wall. The lung then collapses, and the progress of the disease is halted. In most cases the tuberculous process is slowly absorbed or heals with scar. I suspect you have a small cavity also, and in that case these air injections are all the more imperative. The operation of giving air injections is so simple that it can hardly be called an operation at all. It is quite painless and is done every week or two with a small needle. Of course, ordinary bed-rest treatment is carried on at the same time. I think it would reassure you if you could talk with some of my patients who are having this treatment. Let me see – yes, there is a patient outside who has come today for a refill – that is another air injection. I will bring her in and you can talk with her. You will then be initiated into the great family of the tuberculous, and I'm sure there is a feeling of companionship in this great fraternity quite unlike any other company on earth. Eugene O'Neill, the dramatist, has often commented on this kinship as being unique among people suffering from a common disease. He knows this well, as he, like many other great characters in history, has had tuberculosis himself. The lives of tuberculous individuals have a much greater significance to others suffering from tuberculosis than the lives of what I might almost say, were ordinary individuals. (Goes to the door and calls.) Nurse, please send in Mrs. Peterson. Mrs. Peterson two years ago came to me with much the same symptoms as yours, and I found then in her very much the same amount of disease as you have.

Mrs. P. enters – Good afternoon, doctor.

Doctor   Let me introduce you to Mrs. and Miss Owens. How are you feeling today? I haven't seen you for about two weeks.

Mrs. P.   Oh doctor, I feel perfectly splendid. I have no cough or expectoration and have gained fifteen pounds in the last three months.

Doctor   Good. Do you mind telling Miss Owens what your experience has been in the last two years? You see, she is a newcomer to the great army of the tuberculous.

Mrs. P. to **Miss O.**   Have you got tuberculosis too? Well, do not be afraid. I know exactly how you feel. I felt just awful when the doctor told me first. You see, I had just been married three months and we were so happy. Then I had a small haemorrhage and that frightened me, I tell you. The doctor found a small cavity with the X-ray, and sent me to the sanatorium, where I was given air injections immediately. I was bringing up about two ounces of sputum a day, and running fever too. My poor husband was quite broken up I can tell you, and I was too, for I thought I was going to die just when life was beginning for me. But the sanatorium taught me a lot. It was the most cheerful place I have ever been in. I always thought sanatoriums were so sad and depressing, but I don't think so now. First of all my fever fell to normal, and my cough and sputum stopped. After a year the doctors said I could go home. Now I am doing my own work around the house.

Doctor   I hope you aren't lifting heavy weights.

Mrs. P.   Oh no doctor, I'm very careful. I only do my housework in the morning, then I cure all afternoon and am in bed by nine o'clock at night.

Mrs. O.   Well Margaret, the outlook doesn't seem so dismal after all, does it my dear? I am glad we had your tuberculosis discovered so early. Tell me, Mrs. Peterson, what do you mean when you say you cure in the afternoon?

Doctor   Well Mrs. Owens that is an expression we tuberculous people use when we mean complete rest, lying in bed or in special reclining chairs. There are a lot of other special words Margaret will learn in time, for example, to get gas or to have a refill is to have an injection of air into the chest, to have a film means to have an X-ray of the lungs, fever is called 'temp' or temperature, a thermometer is called a temp-stick, an operation on the phrenic nerve is called a phrenic, etc. You will learn all these in good time. Before you go, we will take an X-ray film and ask Miss Jones for a sterile bottle on your way out, and try and bring me any sputum you raise. Then come and see me tomorrow afternoon and we will talk over a plan of campaign. Do not feel too depressed that you must drop your college course. We must think how you are going to be in the next ten or twenty years from now, and not about a relatively unimportant thing such as a university diploma.

Miss O.   Yes, I suppose you're right doctor, though it does seem a bit hard.

Mrs. O.   Let me thank you, Mrs. Peterson, for what you have told us about your experiences in curing your disease. Really, no one would ever think that you had ever been ill a day in your life – you look so well.

Doctor   Goodbye. Come and see me tomorrow, and speak to the nurse on the way out. She will have your X-ray taken. (To Mrs. Peterson) Now, Mrs. Peterson, let us see you under the fluoroscope before you have your refill of air. (Noise of the machine) Good. Your lung is collapsed 75% and I can't see the cavity. Now for the injection. Please lie down on the table on your side. I see by the record that you had 500 last time.

Mrs. P.   Yes doctor.

Doctor   There – just a little needle prick. I will give you another 500 today. There – it's all over. That didn't hurt, did it?

Mrs. P.   Oh no, doctor, I hardly felt it at all.

Doctor   Now let us look again under the fluoroscope. (Noise of the machine) Yes, the lung is now collapsed 90% – there is no fluid. How do you feel? Can you walk?

Mrs. P.   Oh yes, doctor, I feel perfectly all right. The air injections don't bother me at all. I'll go home in the street-car. Goodbye doctor.

Doctor   Goodbye. Come and see me in two weeks. You are doing well, and your lung is healing nicely. Keep up with your air injections for another year, and then we will begin to think about letting the lung expand. Goodbye.

Nurse   Mr. James Kirk.

Doctor   Good afternoon, Mr. Kirk.

Mr. K.   Good afternoon, doctor.

Doctor   Well, Mr. Kirk, you had your phrenic nerve operation last month, didn't you? Have you noticed any change in your symptoms?

Mr. K.   Oh yes, doctor. My cough is much less and I am gaining weight. I still don't quite understand how that operation works.

Doctor   Well, what we did, was to cut the phrenic nerve, which is the nerve running down from the neck to the diaphragm. You know the diaphragm is the big muscle in two parts that runs across the lower ribs from side to side, and divides the chest cavity from the abdominal cavity. It moves up and down like the piston of a motor car when you breathe. After cutting the nerve, half of this muscle is paralysed and doesn't move, and so the lung above it on the same side doesn't move so much either. This gives it rest, and rest is what cures tuberculosis. Let me look at you under the fluoroscope. Yes, your diaphragm on the left side is raised about two inches higher than on the right. This rise has relaxed the diseased lung above it, and closed the cavity that you once had. Keep on curing, be up for only one hour a day. You are doing well. Come and see me in a month. Goodbye.

Mr. K.   Thank you doctor, goodbye.

Nurse   Mr. Smith.

Mr. S.   Hello, Doctor, I just dropped in as I was passing on my way up to the river on a fishing expedition over the weekend, from the office, just for old-time's sake, you know.

Doctor   Well, well, Smith, you're certainly looking well. I haven't seen you for six months. You're getting fat – how is business?

Mr. S.   Business is not so good, but I couldn't feel better myself. I work eight hours a day when there's any work to do.

Doctor   How is the cough?

Mr. S.   Why, I haven't any cough. I haven't had any cough or expectoration for two years, since my thoracoplasty operation. Good Lord, when I think what a specimen I was then, and compare myself today, I can hardly believe it's the same person.

Doctor   You certainly look fine. If I didn't know that you had had most of your ribs taken out of one side to collapse your old cavity I could never be persuaded that you have ever had an operation on your chest. You carry yourself so erect, and there is no sign of any deformity. However, since you're here there is no harm in running over you. Let me examine you. Yes, the disease seems healed completely. Better have an X-ray anyway. Remember, this goes for twice a year for the rest of your life.

Mr. S.   O.K. doctor, just as you say. I know we old TB.'s are apt to get careless when we feel so good. But looking back, I can never feel too grateful for your advice to have that rib operation. When you couldn't give me air injections on account of adhesions between the lung and the pleura and that large cavity of mine which wouldn't close in spite of two years in bed, why I thought I would never be able to get up and go places. But for that rib operation I would still be lying on my back, instead of going on a twenty mile fishing expedition. I only wish more people knew about modern methods of treating tuberculosis, and especially that they would come to the doctor early, before the disease gets too far.

Doctor   Yes, Smith, many cases are missed because they don't have X-rays of the chest or put off going too long to a doctor who specializes in this disease. The outlook of the public towards tuberculosis must be educated by modern means. It is no longer a life sentence to be told that you have tuberculosis. Begin treatment early and most patients have an excellent chance to recover as you have done, by one or other of the modern methods we possess. Well, have an X-ray to check up and drop in and see me again in six months' time. Goodbye.

Doctor to Nurse   Well nurse, that's the lot, I think. I must go off to see my patients in the sanatorium. Did I tell you that Mrs. Pretty has had her baby and both are doing well?

Nurse   You don't mean Mrs. Pretty who was so sick two years ago and got air injections?

Doctor   Yes, she is completely cured and I told her last year it was now

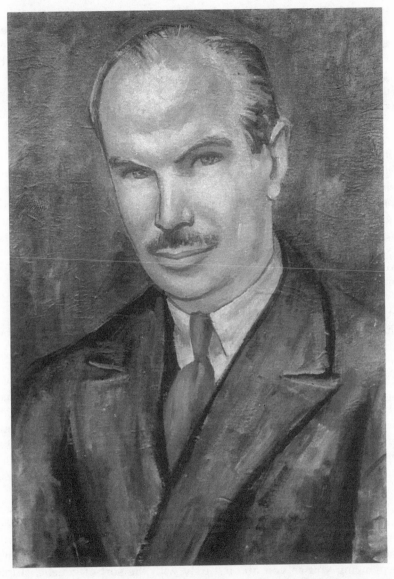

In 1934 Bethune presented himself, in this self-portrait in oils, as an intense *bourgeois gentilhomme*. Chief of thoracic surgery at Sacré Coeur Hospital, he was at the height of his influence as an authority on tuberculosis and its treatment. The birth of Bethune the communist maverick was still a lifetime away – 1935, to be exact.

safe for her to have the child she and her husband wanted so much. The child was born perfectly healthy, and as she is cured she will be able to nurse it without the slightest fear that she will ever give tuberculosis to him. This really is the great triumph for the new methods of treating this old disease, isn't it nurse?

Nurse   I am so glad. Goodbye doctor.

(15 minutes)

After their second divorce, Bethune continued to exhibit a possessiveness towards Frances, telling even new acquaintances, 'I do not give my wife, I only lend her.'[11] His attitude must have caused concern to A.R.E. Coleman, Frances's new husband, and Bethune wrote the following letter to Frances so that she could show it to Coleman, to prove to him that the passionate relationship between Bethune and Frances was ended.

[Montreal]
Sunday, Feb. 11/34

Frances –
Thank you for your letter. I see your confusion of mind, body and soul and since, within the past 3 months, my ideas have clarified, today I think I may be able to put into words what I believe to be the truth.

Truthfully and sincerely I believe I want nothing more from you. Not I as a man, physically nor as a soul – spiritually. I believe we have had all the profitable commerce between us that is possible, and nothing more is to be gained by prolongation of our relationship. It never at any time completely satisfied either of us – let us make no more attempts. I regret nothing of the past that has happened between us except one thing – my essential masculine stupidity on the non-recognition of reality – and my fumbling attempts to change a fantasy into a fact.

Forgive me, if you can. I am truly sorry for the unhappiness I have caused you. I was like a clumsy, and furious gardener, hacking away at a tree, a living tree, in an attempt to make it conform to a preconceived and fantastic design of his own. I tried to bend you, to re-make you, not recognizing you as you are, but only with the sort of genetic, stupid male idea of you as woman. Any woman – and not as *a* woman, a special kind of woman called Frances Campbell Penney. I know now you must be taken only as you are. You are not to be changed. Either a man must take you as you are or he will destroy both you and himself in the attempt to change you.

Well, I am not going to do that. Because of my love for you. I am not going to do that. I believe you must be left alone and then you will flower in peace and quiet and give peace and quietness to those about you. But no persuasion, no aggression of others, and on your part, most important, no attempt to change yourself to please another.

There would be no need for us to part completely if R.E. [Coleman] would abandon his suspicions – suspicions of both you and I. I am not the cause of the disharmony between you two. I am no rival. He has nothing to fear from me. He has only to fear himself. He said at your marriage he accepted the idea of the spiritual relationship between you and I. He must accept it, or it will destroy him. He must accept what you and I have been to each other in the past. It does him no harm. Only egotism forbids acceptance of this.

And you must spend your life acting in the true, internal, deep compulsion of your own spirit. You must give up trying to conform to another's idea of you. Do as I do – if I can say that – be yourself and *don't try to please people*. For you that only results in self-mutilation. If they do not accept you as you are – remove yourself, let them go – or go yourself. Only live with those who respect the spiritual and physical necessities of your nature.

The tragedy of it all is this – that between the two of us – R.E. and myself – two men who protest they love you – we have torn you, violated you and will, if we persist in our present course, distort or destroy one of the sweetest natures that God ever made. Well, I will do my part – I will leave you alone.

I accept gratefully what you once gave me, and now ask you nothing more. That is the only way I can show I love you. I can do nothing for you except leave you alone, entirely. We must die to each other. For peace between you and R.E. you and I must die to each other. Let us remember it only as a dream.

Good-bye, my sweet Frances. I loved you once and to prove it, I will leave you now. Let us part. Good-bye.

Beth

P.S. Show this letter to R.E. I have written it as truthfully and sincerely as I am able. A truthful and sincere soul would accept it as such.

His relationship with Frances was also sometimes testy.

Montreal
June 7.34

Frances –
You may do me one service – be silent about me. I have just heard, indi-
rectly, that you are talking about me – still. Between you and your husband's chatter you both have done me irreparable harm in Montreal.
Why do you persist in analysis – grotesque and tragic – of the ruin of
what you & I tried once to create? Say to those negligible people, those
priers & peepers – 'Yes. I knew him once. I did him an injury and prefer
not to talk about it.' I will do the same – I who never mention your name
to anyone. I have asked little of you – will you do this?

Beth

*In August 1934, John Barnwell, Bethune's friend from their time together at
the Trudeau Sanatorium in 1927, wrote to Bethune inquiring about his health
and advising him about the fate of his mural* The T.B.'s Progress. *It had been
kept in its original form, but now a Miss Young at the University Hospital at
Ann Arbor, Michigan, where Barnwell worked, wished to preserve it by cutting
out the panels and framing them under glass.*[12]

Hôpital du Sacré-Coeur
Sept. 5, 1934

Dear John –
Simply delighted to hear from you again. Yes, I had a spontaneous trau-
matic pneumo on my 'bad' side. Entirely OK now, no blowing up of the
smouldering embers, no stirring or growls from the tigers, no rattle
from the dead snakes and dragons. I guess they're all dead.
    Yes, by all means preserve the murals by any way Miss Young sug-
gests. Frankly I don't think they're worth glass. I didn't get the photo of
the Creed. Did you forget to enclose it?
    Have had a lovely summer. Cape Cod, then I've taken a cottage (with
5 bedrooms) in the mountains 86 miles north for the winter & will live
there 3 days a week & work in town 4. Will you all come for Christmas?

Love to the entire family.

Beth

Sorry I missed the Collers. Have you Roger's Cleveland address?

On 8 September Barnwell wrote to Bethune again, asking him to design a medal for student nurses who finished their course without developing a positive tuberculosis reaction. 'I think that you could design a simple emblem embodying the proper sense of humour, as well as the kind of patience that should represent such an accomplishment,' he wrote. Barnwell also enclosed a copy of Bethune's work 'The Compressionist's Creed,' the first version of which Bethune had composed about 1932.

Hôpital du Sacré-Coeur
Sept. 12, 1934

Dear John –
Thanks for the photos of the Creed. This was the first, 'unrevised' version. I had forgotten!
    I like your idea for a nurse's medal, a *croix de guerre* – farewell to arms, sort of thing, but don't quite understand. Have your nurses been given tuberculin – a course of tuberculin? Were they positive to start & end with a negative or *vice versa*?
    I'm off to Saranac Lake this weekend & will deposit a small but costly wreath on the steps of the Robbins Cottage – perhaps even break a beer bottle in the bathroom of hallowed memories.

Beth

Hôpital du Sacré-Coeur
Oct. 9/34

Dear John –
I enclose a suggestion for a medal –
    The ribbon is scarlet.
    There are 2 clasps – suggestion of the double barred TB cross
    1st *AVE ATQUE VALE* (Hail and farewell)
    2nd *AUX ARMES* (To arms)

The Compressionist's Creed

I believe in Trudeau, the mighty father of the American Sanatorium, maker of a heaven on earth for the tuberculous; and in Artificial Pneumothorax; which was conceived by Carson; born of the labors of Forlanini; suffered under Pompous Pride and Prejudice; was criticized by the Cranks whose patients are dead and buried; thousands now well, even in the third stage, rose again from their bed; ascending into the Heaven of Medicine's Immortals, they sit on the right hand of Hippocrates our Father, from thence they do judge those pthisiotherapists quick to collapse cavities or dead on their job.

I believe in Bodington, Brehmer, Koch and Brauer, in Murphy, Friedrich, Wilms, Sauerbruch, Stuertz and Jacobeus, in the unforgiveness of the sins of omission in Collapse Therapy, in the resurrection of a healthy body from a diseased one and long life for the tuberculous with care everlasting.

Amen.

Wishing you a very good collapse
and a happy pneumothorax
Norman Bethune
Noel 1935

Sacre coeur Hospital
Montreal

I do not pity the wounded person — I become the wounded person
Walt Whitman

Bethune's 'Compressionist's Creed' (*left*) was a plea for the use of pneumothorax collapse therapy, the radical procedure which aided his recovery from tuberculosis. Inez Fisher, the wife of Bethune's long-time friend Lincoln Fisher, recalled seeing Bethune 'dash off his Compressionist's Creed one evening between glasses of Habanero and it seemed to me his mode of expression was nothing short of a gift from the gods.' Bethune combined the Creed with the 'Filling Station' cartoon (*above*) to create his 1935 Christmas card.

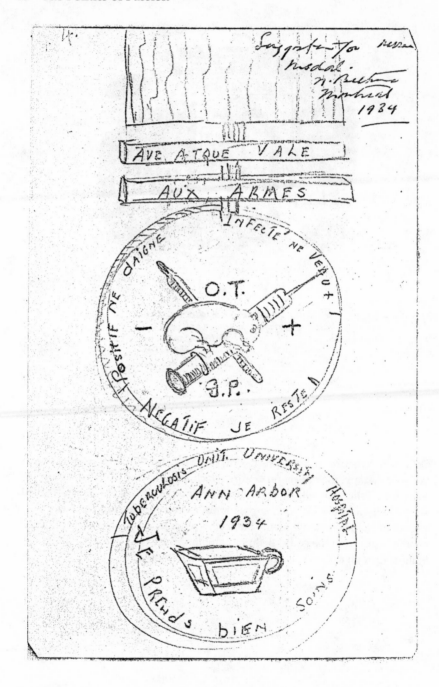

The medal face has a white guinea pig; couchant, on a field of blood, [left] –, [right] +, superior, O.T. (Old Timer), inferior, G.P. (guinea pig, or general practitioner). Two arms supporting – tuberculin syringe & a thermometer.

The inscription is a paraphrase of the motto of the ancient French family of Rohan of the time of Henry of Navarre.

Prince, ne daigne	To be a prince, I do not daigne [*sic* – deign]
Roi, ne veux	King, I do not want to be
Rohan, je suis	I am a Rohan.
Positif, ne daigne	To be positive, I do not daigne [*sic*]
Infecté ne veux	To be infected, I have no wish
Negatif je suis	Negative, I remain
or	
reste	

On the obverse side of the medal is a sputum cup. Above is Tuberculosis Unit, University Hospital, Ann Arbor, 1934.

Below: JE PRENDS BIEN SOINS – (I take great care)
The whole should be done in coloured enamel.

Best of love,
Beth

PS   This work of art(?) is done in collaboration with Dr. Margaret Cameron, Royal Edward Institute, Montreal. If it goes through, she should have one!

On 4 December Barnwell replied, 'We have all had a great deal of fun out of your design for the medal. From last reports, it is to be made by the inmates of Jackson penitentiary. If Maggie has no objections, I shall ask the warden to send one directed to Dr. Margaret Cameron.'[13] No copies of the medal have been located.

4

Convert:
1935–1936

The years 1935 and 1936 made the Norman Bethune we know today – *enfant terrible*, advocate of socialized medicine, communist. In the space of mere months, both his political sentiments and his career were remarkably altered. Our contemporary image of Bethune is so wedded to him as a communist that we assume he was always a confirmed Bolshevik. On the contrary, in the years up to 1935 Bethune was anything but a leftist. For the first forty-five years of his life, Bethune showed no inclination to join the political fray.[1] He was a communist for only his last four years. The stormy transition from individualist to communist is evident in his writing of these two years. As late as 8 October 1935, contemplating an offer to become the head of the Friends of the Soviet Union group in Montreal, Bethune expressed his doubts about 'this modern religion,' and, in a letter of 28 October turning down that position, he wrote, 'I am not, as yet, perfectly convinced that communism is the solution to the problem.' Yet so volatile were the times and his mood that he would join the Communist Party the next month.[2]

Events gave him no opportunity to reverse course politically. On 18 July 1936 the Republican government of Spain was attacked by its own military, led by fascist general Francisco Franco. Just three months later, Bethune was bound for the arena in which he believed the 'real issues of our time are going to be fought out.'

In 1935 and 1936 Bethune also transformed his view of medicine, abandoning any pretense he might once have had about business as usual being good enough. Judging only by accolades and honours, his career star was on a swift ascent. In 1935 he became a full member of the American Association of Thoracic Surgery and was elected to the association's five-person council. The next year, he became an associate fellow of the Montreal Medico-Chirurgical Society. He published five articles in prestigious medical journals between February 1935 and December 1936. He was often invited to speak at medical conferences, where he delighted in tweaking proper medical noses. But he was becoming increasingly exasperated with his colleagues, prodding them to 'discuss more often the great problems of our age.' He set out to do that, and more, in the autumn of 1935, when he invited a number of physicians, nurses, and social workers to join him in examining the impact of the Depression on people's health and the role of health professionals in the midst of this crisis. Bethune envisioned the group studying and discussing the problem, but also taking some action to address it. The result was a landmark declaration setting out the need for dramatic changes in public health. The group proposed several models of public health care, all involving a much more comprehensive state system than existed at the time. The plans were contained in a public statement issued over Bethune's name as secretary of the Montreal Group for the Security of the People's Health. This manifesto and his public exhortations that governments and doctors abandon private funding of health care, which had proven so ineffective in the Depression, made him the object of considerable scorn in medical circles. Always an iconoclastic practitioner, he now became a shunned one.[3]

What caused such a revolution in his outlook and practice? The volatility of the Depression decade accounts for much of it, and his visit to the Soviet Union in August 1935 turned his attention to communism as a solution to the social inequality made obvious by the Depression. But he was also deeply challenged and inspired by a new love, Marian Scott. Bethune was accustomed to having women in his life; he was frequently in the company of females, including very beautiful ones. Scott was that, but she was also much more. She was artistic, political, and, regrettably, married.

Scott was a painter, and to Bethune art was one of the highest human callings. He greatly enjoyed the company of artists, and regarded himself as a kindred soul. Bethune and Scott met through a common interest in art – an evening gathering at the home of Corrine and John Lyman. The latter, with Scott, was a founding member of Montreal's Contemporary Art Society. Scott later recalled, 'He seemed to me essentially the pioneer, impatient with the travelled road – with things that had been done before – but then that is just another way of saying he was an artist, isn't it?'[4]

Scott's influence helped inspire him to produce a small but vibrant collection of oil paintings and watercolour sketches in these two years. In the spring of 1936, he brought her and her art closer to him in another way, when he convinced Scott to join him and an artist friend, Fritz Brandtner, in opening a children's art centre at his apartment at 1154 Beaver Hall Square.[5] Emotionally, Scott also aroused a passion in Bethune which evoked an outpouring of poetry addressed to 'Pony,' his affectionate appellation for the recipient of his verse.

Scott was active in left-wing politics; Bethune, too, was increasingly drawn in that direction. After their first meeting, their bond was cemented when they found themselves travelling to England together by ocean liner in July 1935. He was en route to the Soviet Union to see firsthand the revolutionary upheaval that no thinking person could ignore. Scott and her six-year-old son, Peter, were bound for a vacation in England with her relatives. She later reminisced that he read William Blake to her from the *Oxford Book of English Verse*, but they also 'did a lot of talking on many things.'[6] Foremost among the 'many things' they discussed on that transatlantic crossing must have been politics. Returning in August, Scott recalled him being 'very impressed with much that he had seen' in the Soviet Union.[7] In subsequent months, Bethune would seek counsel from Scott on a variety of political topics – and, true to form, would offer some of his own as he came to embrace communism.

Scott was also challenging to Bethune because she was unavailable, and conspicuously so. Her husband was Frank Scott, a poet of some prominence and also a law professor at McGill University, a crusading civil libertarian and founder of the League for Social Reconstruction (LSR), the intellectual instigator of the Co-operative Commonwealth Federation (CCF). Married in 1928, Frank and Marian Scott were sufficiently established that any public relationship between Marian and Bethune was out of the question. Marian acknowledged later being 'deeply fond of him,'[8] but acted with complete discretion. Although Bethune's letters were tinged with both temptation and concern that she was feeling stifled in her marriage, the intense affection between him and Scott remained bound in a vault of paper and ink.

Loving the wife of Frank Scott, a CCF stalwart, posed serious problems – for Bethune and for Marian. Although he consorted and argued with people of varied political persuasions, and described himself as a member of the LSR, his political attachment was rapidly shifting toward the Communist Party. Adversaries on the left, the CCF and the CP were bitter public enemies. Peter Dale Scott recalls that this led to 'some tension' between his father and Bethune. Frank Scott and Bethune were also rivals at a more visceral level than politics. 'My father liked to be the male in the room. Bethune also was the commanding male.'[9] Bethune alluded to this contention when he sent Marian his self-portrait in November 1935, telling her that if Frank did not want her to hang it she could return it.[10] The unspoken friction caused Marian some anguish, her son believes. As an artist not so centrally involved with the CCF, she could afford to be more open to left-wing rogues like Bethune, but she obviously had to respect her husband's partisan adherence to the CCF.

This turbulence in his political and personal life was compounded by the economic and political discord he saw about him. In the October 1935 Canadian election, opposition leader William Lyon Mackenzie King campaigned on the slogan 'King or Chaos!' For Bethune, the unrelieved unemployment and poverty at home and the advancing threat of fascism abroad must have suggested that chaos had won the day. To Marian Scott, he wrote, 'I feel a tremendous impulse *to do, to act*.' His impulse would soon lead to action. And he may have had a premonition that this action would take him away from Canada, for in May 1935 he obtained a passport, after a decade of having journeyed no farther afield than the United States.[11]

Bethune's departure for Spain in October 1936 ended his settled life in Canada. He would return a year later for a speaking tour to raise funds for the Republican cause in Spain, but it was merely a temporary sojourn. Increasingly feeling the need for political action, irritated by the resistance to change in Canada's political and medical systems, and thwarted in love, Bethune left home forever in 1936. In going, he ceased to be a Canadian national and became an internationalist, a citizen of no country, his only home the anti-fascist cause.

As he concentrated on surgical problems at the Sacré Coeur Hospital in Montreal, Bethune's brilliance as a medical innovator blossomed, and his reputation spread. He was frequently asked to help resolve difficult cases at other hospitals. In articles for a variety of medical journals, he described solutions to challenges of considerable range, from preventing haemorrhage to holding open the ribcage while performing chest surgery. During 1935–6 he published four such articles, and typical of them was the following explanation of an unusual use of maggots to clear chronic chest infection. Maggots were usually regarded as evidence of a lack of proper antiseptic procedures. But having read medical literature about introducing blow-fly larvae to clear wounds, Bethune experi-

mented with their use in a sixty-year-old man with a chronic chest infection. In an era before antibiotics, Bethune found the procedure effective. Sixty years later, with bacteria becoming increasingly resistant to antibiotics, medical science has begun again to look favourably on the method.

A Case of Chronic Thoracic Empyema Treated with Maggots

By Norman Bethune, M.B., F.R.C.S.(E.)
Division of Thoracic Surgery and Bronchoscopy,
Sacré Coeur Hospital, Montreal

The observation of Ambroise Paré (1509–1590) that neglected wounds containing maggots healed remarkably well has been confirmed many times since. It was William S. Baer,[1] of Baltimore, who put these historical observations into actual practice by the deliberate introduction of the larvae of the blow-fly into the open wounds of chronic osteomyelitis. Following the publication of his work in 1931, Dr. Dudley Ross, Surgeon of the Children's Memorial Hospital, Montreal, began to use these maggots in a similar fashion, obtaining the blow-flies from Baer. The fly after being hatched produces eggs in four to seven days; the eggs hatch in four to twenty-four hours, the larvae turn into pupae in five to seven days and the adult flies emerge in seven to ten days. These flies were fed and housed according to Baer's procedure and the eggs sterilized after his method.

Case Report

(No. 80732). E.G., a male, aged 60 years, was admitted to the Royal Victoria Hospital on March 7, 1932. The history showed that he had had a former admission in October, 1930, with acute empyema [accumulation of pus] on the right side, which had been drained by rib resection, and he had been discharged in December of the same year with a healed wound. The diagnosis of right basal bronchiectasis had been made at the same time, but no treatment for this underlying condition was suggested, on account of the patient's age. On discharge the sputum was about six ounces a day. Following discharge he was fairly well, apart from occasional pain in the right chest, but in March, 1932, complained of a very severe pain over the old scar and the clinical examination con-

---

1   Baer, W.S.: Treatment of chronic osteomyelitis with maggots (larva of blow-fly), *J. Bone & Joint Surg.*, 1931, 13: 438

Night Operating Theatre was painted as a challenge, after Bethune boasted that he could create a piece which would be accepted at the spring 1935 exhibition of the Montreal Museum of Fine Arts. Bethune was not a trained artist, but the work he produced – completed in just two afternoons, according to his wife – was deemed worthy to hang in the show. The oil-painting depicts the operating room at the Sacré Coeur Hospital, where Bethune worked. The original today hangs in the medical library of the Royal Victoria Hospital in Montreal.

firmed by thoracentesis disclosed a recurrence of the empyema. Five hundred c.c. of foul greyish-green thick pus was aspirated. Bacteriological examination showed streptococci and slender Gram-negative bacilli, large numbers of fusiform bacilli, but no spirochaetes or tubercle bacilli. The dark field showed no spirochaetes. Cultures gave a streptococcus; no growth of anaerobic culture. On March 9th a partial Schede operation was done, with resection of five inches each of the eighth and ninth ribs from their angle forward, and excision of very thick fibrotic

partially calcified costal pleura. The empyema pocket ran up underneath the seventh rib, but the upper limit could be reached with the finger upwards and forward to the anterior axillary line. The capacity was
500 c.c., measured with saline. A dry dressing was applied. Histological
examination of the pleura showed no evidence of tuberculosis. March
10th, dressing changed; the discharge was very foul.

March 18th, no chemicals having been introduced into the wound
since the operation, but, it being merely washed out with saline, a test-
tubeful of maggots, kindly given me by Dr. Ross, was put into the
wound, the edges being bound with adhesive and a screen put over the
top. An electric light was suspended near the screen, with the object of
driving the maggots into the depths of the wound.

March 19th, the discharge was much more profuse, but much thinner
also; the maggots were lively. March 21st, the maggots were still active,
but less so. They seemed larger and appeared to be nearing the end of
their life cycle. The discharge was less and thinner, not so foul. March
22nd, maggots dead; the discharge was now quite thin; healthy pink
granulation tissue was seen covering the lung. Culture – streptococci
persisting. Direct smear showed a few streptococci, a Gram-positive
micrococcus, but no fusiforms. March 24th, more maggots applied.
March 28th, discharge was now negligible and granulation tissue extensive in formation. The whole wound looked very clean, pink and
healthy. March 30th, maggots dead; washed out with saline. The capacity of the cavity was 100 c.c. April 5th, the patient was up; April 19th discharged; wound practically healed; the cavity was filled in with
granulation tissue, with the exception of the skin edge separation. The
patient was completely unaware of the nature of his treatment.

This case was followed for two and a half years, with no recurrence of
the empyema.

Comment

The noteworthy thing was the extremely rapid formation of granulation
tissue and the rapid reduction in the size of the empyema cavity, not
produced exclusively by expansion of the lung. It is believed that this is
the first case to be reported in the literature of the use of maggots in
chronic recurrent empyema.

*In July 1935, travelling by ocean liner to Britain en route to the Soviet Union,
Bethune found himself in the company of Marian Scott. An intense relationship*

blossomed on board, which continued upon their arrival in London. There, Marian and her son, Peter, stayed with her aunt at 63 Eccleston Square, where Bethune visited them before proceeding to the USSR. 'Pony' remained Bethune's affectionate nickname for Scott.

Lost.

In the NEIGhborhood of Eccleston Square, on July 17ᵗʰ, a Canadian bred Pony, accompanied by foal. Stands about five and half hands high. White face, gentle disposition ×

Was the companion of a small boy who is inconsolable over his loss. Any information received leading to her recovery will be handsomely rewarded.

Address — Beth. ℅ Canada House.

Copy of a hand bill
Printed .London. July 25ᵗʰ.1935

Back from the Soviet Union, Bethune confronted the pain of his love for Marian Scott, a love which he recognized must remain unrequited. The original of this

letter is not available, and I have had to rely on Ted Allan's transcription
of it. Ellipses indicate places where Allan found Bethune's handwriting indeci-
pherable. Allan speculated that Bethune was drinking – to the point of
intoxication – as he wrote it.

Ritz Carlton Hotel
Montreal
Sunday Aug 31/35

Pony.
It is pleasant to sit and think that you are near me, close beside me, only a few streets away. I am very conscious of your presence and happy because of it – yet sad too, darling, because of the knowledge that you and I are bound together, to work out some part of our lives together – for good or for evil – we seem to be bound.

Perhaps this is a presumption of my part – but I think not. And if your glance, your touch, your hands & lips are not mistaken, unreal or mis-read – you feel it too.

Do you remember the girl in *Farewell To Arms* saying with that myste-rious foresight of love 'Let us be good to each other. We are to have such a strange life together.' And her lover comforts her sad heart as best he may, not knowing or understanding. But she knew the dark paths ahead.

Well, my sweet, I know it too.

Let me persuade you to stop now.

Go back. Put away this small child of our love you are holding so qui-etly and tenderly in your cupped hands – now, when it can be put away without agony & tears – before it has grown in stature & strength & threatens to destroy all you hold precious in life – your home, your hus-band, your child.

And I say this because I am persuaded there is something fatal and doomed and pre-destined about myself. (& I know it.) [The last four words were crossed out.]

But again I think – no. Let us go on into the future together – heads up & with a smile on our lips. If we are true to ourselves, the future may not be happy (O Pony I'm afraid, so afraid for you) – but no real harm or injury can touch us – nothing can come from without to destroy us. This is the way I try to persuade myself & you.

...

It is because I love you I write like this, so darkly, lest I injure you with my love & do you a harm. In the name of love & life instead of bedecking you with jewels I load you with chains.

Beth your sad lover

To Pony

Hand clasped
Look, see us stand, with eager upturned faces
Lit by the rising sun of our new love,
Whose gentle light touches so tenderly
Eyelids and mouth.

O, my sweet, I am afraid
That soon, perhaps, his mounting rays
Now roseate and kind
Will, in the high noon of passionate desire,
Strike down, with shafts of molten fire
Our bared, defenceless heads,
And neath those blazing beams, we languish and despair
Too eager then his course should run
Into the west and harm us once again
In the cool shade of well-remembered trees,
Alone and separate.

Dare we hold high our unprotected heads
Or, warmed by the memory of other dawns
Behind us, smile gently, part & go our ways,
Across the waste land of the years
Carefree and undisturbed.

Or stay instead and unafrighted, cry
Come light of love and life, shine down,
STRIKE, if strike you must
But warm us first, 'twas better so to die
Beneath your fierce flames than perish in the shade,
Cold and alone.

Perhaps a miracle as happened once, should come again
That golden globe were made to stand

And never sink and never leave the land
Desolate and dark.
But stay, suspended overhead,
High, serene and clear
Perpetuate.

Beth
Aug. 31, 1935
Montreal

Bethune returned from the Soviet Union in August 1935 favourably impressed with that country's pioneering efforts to improve its people's health standards. Although he admitted that his comments about the new state were not always complimentary, they were sufficiently sympathetic that he was asked to chair the Friends of the Soviet Union Committee in Montreal. Ill in bed with jaundice, he wrote to Marian Scott, asking her advice on taking up a cause about which, he admitted, 'I don't think I know enough.' He included with the letter a watercolour painting of himself lying in bed and – with typical Bethune humour – brushing up on Marx.

1237 Guy
Montreal
Oct. 8, 1935

Pony –
I was approached today by the Executive Committee of 'The Friends of Soviet Russia' with the offer of the chairmanship of that association for the coming year.

It would appear that Sir Andrew MacPhail [professor of medicine at McGill University, who had ventured to the USSR earlier in 1935] had spoken about or
recommended me. Why, I can't say for since my trip, my expressions have not been entirely complimentary in some quarters (depending of course on my audience! – enthusiastic to the reactionaries, minimizing to the radical).

Now, it is rather a question to me whether or not I can conscientiously take such a position. I explained my attitude frankly to Mr. [Louis] Kon – saying definitely that though in theory I am entirely in agreement with the ideology of this modern religion, yet I was disturbed – and

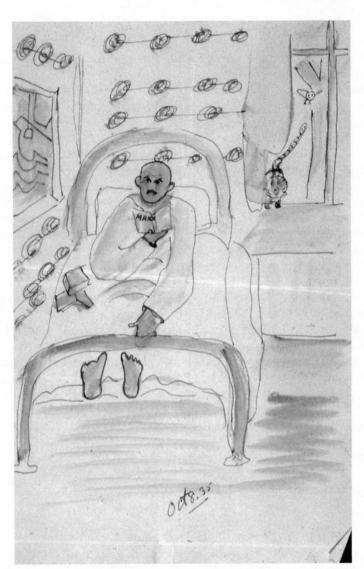

Bethune included this watercolour sketch of himself, ill with jaundice and brushing up on Marx, in his letter of 8 October 1935 to Marian Scott. On the left wall hangs his painting *Night Operating Theatre*. Black-and-white reproduction does not do justice to this sketch. Its humour derives from the fact that Bethune's face, hands, and feet are bright yellow from jaundice.

rather deeply disturbed – in some of its aspects in practice. In short, that I did not believe that communism as practised in Russia today was a suitable technic for the Anglo-Saxons (predominately Anglo-Saxon, at heart) of this country in their attempt to discover some method of herd living suitable for their new concepts of equality and justice in a machine age. But that basically – not imitatively, *in detail*, I was in deep sympathy with Russia. To my surprise he agreed with me.

I added that I was *profoundly* distrustful of social democracy and of the C.C.F., in their non-realization of the absolute inevitability of the use of force and force alone as the only true persuader.

Moneyed people will never give up money and power until subjugated by physical forces stronger than they possess. Democracy will come again, as it will come again in Russia, only after the people are conditioned, as they are being conditioned, to their new manner of living, but democracy at first is shiftless, careless, ignorant and willful. Only when the course is set can it be permitted to guide the ship.

Well, what shall I do? Do you think I can conscientiously take this job? I don't think I know enough. I feel very ignorant. Yet I feel a tremendous impulse *to do, to act*. I hate to be thought one of the intelligentsia who talk and talk and talk and behind their words you feel their hearts are cold and it's only an intellectual conundrum, a game.

You must remember my father was an evangelist and I come of a race of men, violent, unstable, of passionate convictions and wrongheadedness, intolerant yet with it all a vision of truth and a drive to carry them on to it even though it leads, as it has done in my family, to their own destruction – as it did my father.

Beth

P.S. Don't come and see me, Pony. Write me.

After some reflection, Bethune decided that he could not accept the honour, although he offered to speak to the group about his visit, which he did on 30 October.

October 28, 1935

Dear Mr. Kon –
I am extremely obliged to you for your kindness in lending me 'Moscow

Dialogues.' I am finding it extremely interesting as the philosophy underlying communism had never been explained to my satisfaction, outside the rather idealist and grandiose flourish of the 'right yeoman' etc. etc. I hope you will let me keep it a little longer.

Now in regard to the other matter of the chairmanship, I will be perfectly frank with you so you will understand my position exactly.

I do not feel able to accept for two reasons. The first is that I am not, as yet, perfectly convinced that communism is the solution to the problem. If I were, I assure you, I should not only accept your offer but would become a member of the Communist party. What stands in my way of non-acceptance? This – my strong feeling of individualism – the right of a man to walk alone, if that's his nature – my dislike of crowds and regimentation. Perhaps all these fears are illusionary and do not necessarily conflict with the practice of communism, even though they seem to be solved in its theory, but I am afraid.

This being so I must read more, think more about this problem. In short I am not yet ready.

Second – such being the case, to jeopardize the only position – economic and professional – I possess, by even associating with a communistic-leaning association such as yours would be senseless. *If I felt* as strongly and as purely towards communism as perhaps I should, such jeopardization of my means of livelihood would not be an obstacle in the way. But the ironic and ludicrous picture of a half-hearted convert, reluctantly being burnt at the stake for his half-hearted, feeble convictions, rises in my mind.

So it all hinges on this – I am not ready as yet to throw in my lot with you.

Yet I belong to the League for Social Reconstruction even though I feel that they are following a will-of-the-wisp and theirs is not the right way. At the same time I am filled with despair towards the smugness and passivity of the oppressed workers and bourgeois of this continent, but until they accumulate in their hearts a far greater certainty of their own doom than they at present possess, then it is useless to impose on them from without the will to rebellion. It seems they must go still farther down into the abyss before they will rebel. The last election shows they are not ready.

I would be glad to address your Union on some impressions of my very short trip to the U.S.S.R.

Yours sincerely,
Norman Bethune

By 1935, Bethune and Frances were twice married and twice divorced, and after their second divorce Frances had married A.R.E. Coleman. Nonetheless, Bethune retained great affection for her and continued to see her socially.

Sacré Coeur Hospital
Montreal
Oct. 31, 1935

Dear Frances:
Would you care to come out to see my new place next Sunday morning and stay for lunch?

There are nice country walks.

Take the street car to Cartierville, then a taxi (25¢) ask to be driven to Mr. Tiphan at the Sacré Coeur.

Could you come about 10:20 or so?

Don't rush.

Have a good sleep!

Beth

Yvette Patrice was a ten-year-old tuberculosis patient in November 1935 when Bethune performed a risky right total pneumonectomy on her, removing the entire lung. Operations of this kind gave Bethune a reputation in some circles as a surgeon who gambled with patients' lives, and sometimes lost. He argued that conservative surgical policy was no more likely to save lives, only to prolong the agony of tuberculosis sufferers. Bethune's belief that surgery was a creative challenge, like art, was expressed in this letter to Marian Scott.

Sacré Coeur Hospital
Montreal
Nov. 6, 1935

6 P.M.

My child is well.

It was a very beautiful operation.

I felt very happy doing it.

The entire right lung was removed – the first time this has been done – in a child of 10 – in Canada & the 45th operation of its kind ever done in the world. Isn't that nice?

Yes, I will sleep deep tonight – last night was a 'nuit blanche' – not whether I could do it but whether I should. I decided I must at 4 a.m., slept till 7, felt refreshed & 'tight' and went at it like a canvas – my picture full in my mind.

Good night, my sweet,

Beth

In November 1935, recognizing the impossibility of a romance between them, Bethune attempted to reconcile Scott and himself to separation. His letter confirmed the depth of the emotional bond between the two and alluded to Scott's sense of being stifled in her marriage. In a frank discussion of his own emotional character, Bethune inadvertently pointed to a conflict between his heart and his head: the supreme individualist writing to Scott was also the man who would join the Communist Party the same month.

Cartierville
Nov. 21/35

Pony –
These are some of the things I have been thinking since I received your letter this morning.

I, this person you love, am nothing. Understand that firmly. I am nothing in myself. I represent and symbolize an emotion emanating from yourself – of your own being. I am merely an externalized part of your own vital self.

We could have gone a long way together thru this maze if we had held each other's hands.

I have been robbed of jewels.

The tyranny of love, of old love, is holding you. Your emergent and evolutionary spirit is being blackmailed by the past. 'The bonds of love are ill to lose.'

You need more children. You need an altar to immolate yourself upon – a glad, burning sacrifice to a living God – you ask to be consumed – to rise again like a phoenix from the ashes of your own glad destruction – clean, pure & free – with wings.

Security – 'Prenez Garde' – these are the whimpers of weaklings – or the already defeated.

I'll make no effort to urge you. Be sure of that. You must do what you must do. Acting under the urge of an inner compulsion, your motives and actions must be pure & direct.

Do not wait to be forced into an action but anticipate it. This is part of freedom.

Can you ever be free – perhaps not! Only thru another who respects you as much as himself and who also anticipates the inevitable & is ruthless, kind & cruel.

You are essentially – like myself – monogamous – physically but an intellectual wanton and débauché.

F. [Frank Scott] can only keep you – as a free woman – by letting you go. I did this to Frances. Ron Coleman! What ghosts he has to contest. They have defeated him. But in the process I have found *myself* free – free of her and of even me.

I was sad, yet glad when you left on Monday. I saw you as a wall closing in again on me – a loving wall! – & I raised my head, restless. Oh, God, I said to myself must I go thru it all again – the ecstasy & agony of love.

I am a solitary, loving privacy, my own satisfactory aloneness. I saw you as a threat to this. I didn't *need* any woman, or any man. That's what so shook Frances. She was seduced by Coleman's plea that he 'needed her.' She discovered too late that this is the universal plea of all weaklings. Their cry comes from a realization of their own structural weakness. It is a cry for external support. It is made to the strong. And the strong are very susceptible to this cry. It is an appeal to their vanity.

No human should ever make that cry to another. Only to God should such a cry arise and there only can it be answered. But a straight glance, a firm hand – a plea – 'I love you, I want you' – is what a man or a woman should make to his mate. Otherwise he has merely shifted his position physiologically and anatomically and not spiritually – from the womb, from the breast, from the arms – back to arms & breast again – the eternal child – chronic infantilism.

And women find this plea hard to accept – are easily moved by appeals for succour. But it is not treating a woman fairly to do so. It reduces them from the mate of a man to his nurse.

Your hidden – and not too deeply hidden complaint is – lack of life – lack of the opportunity of the full employment of yourself as a living dynamic person. Your complaint against people is only against them as representing obstacles against the deep drive within you. You turned to

Bethune sent this self-portrait in oils to Marian Scott in November 1935. Despite his concern that Scott's husband – poet, lawyer, and political activist Frank Scott – might object to its being hung in their home, it did find a place on the walls of the Scott household, although perhaps not until after Bethune's death. In 1971 Marian Scott donated it to McGill University, and the university in turn presented it to the People's Republic of China.

me as an instrument upon which to play your song of songs – your life song of love – then found you didn't want to sing!

Your painting shows this intense almost painful sense of joy & awareness of all living matter – plants, trees & flowers. You desire to animate (& do) even the dead – your still lifes.

As far as I am concerned, I am the only person alive in the world. Other people – men & women, are to me canvas, interesting animated 'things' – but not more important or not readily distinguishable from rocks, trees, wind, rain, sun & water. (I could *swim* in you.) In there I live & have my being – turning my enforced attention like an obedient but impatient child – to people, to 'life,' to 'the world.' So I don't need you (except to bathe in & bask in!). I want you as a man wants a woman. I like you too. I like you rather like I like myself – with reservations! You are my sister – we think alike, act alike & feel alike. I am merely the masculine edition of yourself.

You are the *first* woman in the world I have met about whom I have felt *no doubt* that we could live together, physically & mentally & spiritually mated. This has never happened to me before & is important.

We might have been a co-operative of 2 free souls – yet each, the other, going about his & her own mysterious business – proud, humble yet untouchable.

I am glad now we did not take each other physically. For me it would have meant that I would not have left you, as I am leaving you now – so nobly! so generously! so sweetly! No. I should have behaved with most unseemly vigour, & lack of manners, shouts and clamours. And for you, it was as well too. You have now the exquisite sense of virtue preserved, of moral rectitude which is so sustaining. You are still a faithful wife. And if you had, what then – for a thirst appeased, a hunger satisfied, but with your conflict, your essential problem unchanged, so for you no serenity, no peace, no quietness of soul. And because I would know this instantly, neither for me either, serenity, peace or quietness.

Yes. I understand you, my own, my darling. The great question – 'what do you do with your old loves'?

Well, Pony, my sweet, all this is to say I love you, I want you & I respect you.

I am here if I can be of any use to you at any time. And that's all one man can say to a woman. *Au revoir.*
Beth

P.S. – I am sending you my portrait. If you don't like it (I don't know if it is good or not but there's a lot of *me* in it) or can't hang it or don't like to hang it or F. objects to it – why, send it back. I would like one of you for my birthday – our birthday.

Beth

Bethune's confidence in parting, however, was not long sustained. Brief notes followed which affirmed his deep attachment to Scott.

Dec. 20, 1935

Oh Pony, Pony – it was false. I do need you.

Beth

Dec. 26/35

Pony, darling, I adore you. Come & take tea with me Friday afternoon.

Beth
who loves you

After his return to Canada in August 1935, Bethune spoke publicly several times about his observations of the Soviet Union. One such occasion was on 20 December 1935, when the Montreal Medico-Chirurgical Society invited four city doctors who had attended the International Physiological Congress to present their views. Drs Hans Selye, J.S.L. Brown, and David Slight offered relatively objective assessments of medical practice in the USSR and the course of the congress. Bethune's address, typically opinionated, was a pragmatic but poetic assessment of the Soviet revolution which acknowledged both its problems and its potential. His comments were later published in the March-April 1936 edition of the Bulletin of the Montreal Medico-Chirurgical Society.

Reflections on Return from 'Through the Looking Glass'

My position as the last speaker of this evening was of my own choosing. I had decided to take the opposite position to that of my fellow Lenin graduates. I felt fairly sure they would be unanimous. If they depreciated Russia, I would praise her and if they praised, I would diminish her. This would not be done in a spirit of pure perversity, but from a concern for truth which appears to me to consist, not infrequently, in the conjunction of apparently irreconcilable aspects of reality. Whatever one says about Russia is true – relatively true and not in any absolute terms, of course.

All accounts of returned travellers from strange lands and foreign shores are essentially self-disclosatory and unwittingly autobiographical in character. Criticism becomes a critique of the critic. This is traditionally true of all returned travellers, from those Biblical gentlemen who reported Palestine to be a land flowing with milk and honey – when it was nothing of the sort – to Marco Polo, Christopher Columbus and Baron Munchhausen. What you are hearing tonight is an account of four men in terms of one country.

Now, I did not go, like these others, to Russia to attend a physiological congress. I went to Russia for much more important reasons than that. I went to Russia primarily to look at the Russians, and secondarily, to see what they were doing about eradicating one of the most easily eradicable of all contagious diseases, namely, tuberculosis. I happen to possess some very definite ideas on how this might be done, given the necessary courage and currency. I shall not say anything tonight about what they are doing in this way. I will also say nothing about the congress, since I only attended one session – the opening one – being far too busy swimming in the Neva, walking about unhindered in the streets, looking into windows, making the round of the picture galleries and markets and shops – a combination of Walter Winchell, Peeping Tom and Innocent Abroad.

The title of my talk would lead one to suppose that I was about to draw a comparison between Looking-Glass Land and Russia. It would be easy enough to parody that fairy-tale or write, with one's tongue in one's cheek, an article entitled 'Malice in Blunderland.' Derision and denial are interesting psychological phenomena, and are essentially protective in nature. It is easier to deride than praise. But it should be remembered that in calling Russia a land of topsy-turvy, as it has been called, a reasonable doubt may arise that it may not be the things one sees upside down in Russia, but that this disturbing optical illusion may also be obtained by an observer standing on his head and seeing normal things in their proper position. Certainly, over the portals of Russia should be inscribed 'Abandon old Conceptions all Ye who enter Here.' To seek comparison of the White Knight, the White Queen, the Red King, Humpty Dumpty, the Mad Hatter, Tweedledee and Tweedledum, would be entertaining and occasionally true. As an example, Stalin, who is universally acknowledged to be the greatest living statesman, might be given the role of the Walrus, and Lenin as the Carpenter and the NEP men as the Oysters who were taken for such a disastrous walk down the Beach in 1921. Also, to take without benefit of context some of the sayings of the characters in 'Through The Looking Glass' as being applicable to Russia today would also be interesting; such as, Russia might be compared to the Looking Glass room which Alice found looking so like her own drawing room, only the things went the other way, and the books were like her books, except the words went the wrong way. Tweedledum and Tweedledee might be parodied as Diddleyou and Diddleme, the ridiculous, contradictory, fat little men of the Intourist Agency. That it's 'Jam tomorrow and Jam yesterday but never Jam today,' might be taken as the complaint of those workers who are impatient of what they may think is the slow progress of improvement in living conditions, and the White Queen's remembrance of things which happened the week after next, as an example of the unlimited optimism and the faith that the Russians have in their own future. And it would also be true of Russia today to use the White Queen's reply to the protest of Alice, who said: 'Oh, I can't believe that.' 'Can't you?' said the Queen. 'Try again; draw a long breath and shut your eyes.' Alice laughed – 'One can't believe impossible things.' The Queen: 'I dare say you haven't had much practice. Why I sometimes believe as many as six impossible things before breakfast.' Then there would be much truth in Alice's delighted exclamation, when she found the fire in the fireplace was real. 'So I shall be as warm here as in the old room, warmer, in fact, because there will be no one here to scold me away from the fire.' And when she looked down from a little hill and saw the whole country as a huge chessboard and life itself as a game of chess, which was being played all over the world, and said: 'I shouldn't mind being a Pawn if only I might join, although, of course, I should like to be a Queen best.' To this the White Queen replied: 'That is easily managed, you can be the White Queen's Pawn, if you like, and you are in the second square to begin with, and then when you get to the eighth square you will be a Queen and we shall be Queens together, and it will all be feasting and fun.' And that statement would be the faith and hope of communism in a nutshell.

Isadora Duncan, in the story of her life, describes her confinement, 'There I lay a fountain spouting blood, milk and tears.' What would a person think, watching for the first time a woman in labour and not knowing what was occurring to her? Would he not be appalled at the blood, the agony, the apparent cruelty of the attendants, the whole revolting technique of delivery? He would cry, 'Stop this, do something, help! police! murder!' Then tell him that what he was seeing was a new life being brought into the world, that the pain would pass, that the agony and the ugliness were necessary and always would be necessary to birth. Knowing this, then, what could he say truthfully about this woman as she lies there? Is she not ugly – yes; is she not beautiful – yes; is she not pitiful, ludicrous, grotesque and absurd – yes; is she not magnificent and sublime – yes. And all these things would be true. Now, Russia is going through her delivery and the midwives and obstetricians have been so busy keeping the precious baby alive, that they haven't got around as yet to cleaning up the mess, and it is this mess, this ugly, uncomfortable and sometimes stupid mess, which affronts the eyes and elevates the noses of those timid male and female virgins suffering from frigid sterility of the souls, who lack the imagination to see behind the blood the significance of birth. Creation is not and never has been a genteel gesture. It is rude, violent and revolutionary. But to those courageous hearts who believe in the unlimited future of man, his divine destiny which lies in his own hands to make of it what he will, Russia presents today the most exciting spectacle of the evolutionary, emergent and heroic spirit of man which has appeared on this earth since the Reformation. To deny this is to deny our faith in man – and that is the unforgivable sin, the final apostasy.

Bethune's emotional poems to Marian Scott continued into 1936.

A Poem to Pony

My pony is a bird in my hand
Fluttering,
Beating her wings,
Not to be held.

My pony is a tree in the wind,
Dancing,
Bowing and swaying
Not to be broken.

My pony is a wave in the sea
Sweeping

Across the deep wastes
Not to be hindered.

My pony is a gleam in the dark,
Shining,
A dart, a flash of sun
Then done.

My Pony is not for love,
Invulnerable,
Yet her I love
or no one.

Beth
March 11/36

[Untitled]

My pony is a bird,
You find it strange that
Hooves should beat, like wings,
The sky?

My pony is a flower
'Tis odd, is't not,
Her eyes should shine
Like stars?

My pony is a cloud
How strange her feet should be
So firmly fixed in
The deep earth?

My pony is all of these –
And none – so strange a flame.
Myself – my own – unknown
My sister and my bride.

To Pony
from Beth
March 20/36
after seeing her

Remembrance

I can't pretend
I think of you every hour. Why
Some dull days I'm not aware of you at all,
Any more than the beating of my heart. Then,
a young tree in the wind,
A white flower in the grass,
A quick bird in flight,
A breath of sun-warmed air,
And the whole world is emptied of delight
Like a cup turned upside down
And I am hollowed and sick for my love.
But I can't pretend
This happens every day
My pony

Beth
March 29/36

The turmoil of Bethune's journey to communism during 1935–6, coupled with his unrequited love for Marian Scott, was reflected in his fiction. 'Encounter,' one of just a handful of his short stories still extant, was sent to Marian Scott on 31 March 1936. It presented the quintessential Bethune – by turns combative, whimsical, philosophical, and preachy, yet always poised to deliver the unexpected ironic twist that flouted convention. As with his visual art, Bethune's self-taught fictive technique demonstrated an intuitive artistic strength that made for memorable literature. The editors of New Frontier, *the Communist Party's cultural magazine, however, thought the story not up to its literary – or perhaps its political – standards. Undeterred, Bethune handed out copies to his friends, inscribed 'refused by* New Frontier.'*

Encounter

I don't think he had any doubts about me at first. He really thought I was, what, at first glance, I appeared to be – so unguarded, so confident was his approach. Everything about him said – 'Why, hello, I know you.' Of course, it was rather late, the night was dark, but even so, there was little excuse for his mistake. Well, anyway, this is what happened.

I left my cousin's about one, after a furious, interminable argument about communism. Just to look at these complacent capitalists makes me extraordinary actionary [sic], much less to talk to them. As usual we got nowhere. It was like an argument between two men, one blind, one deaf, about music – say an orchestra and we had slugged at each other all evening with clumsy club-like words. Of course, we had had a lot to drink and that hadn't made it any better, in fact worse, because, as time went on, we appeared, each to ourselves, as the sole-remaining, heroic and desperate defender of our separate citadels of Truth and it became more important than anything in the world, that the God, who was articulate in us, should defeat the Antichrist in the other. I left, licking my wounds, feeling very angry and frustrated. The cool air was a benediction on my head. Quiet and withdrawn, the deserted street stretched up the hill into the night.

He must have watched me coming, for his advance from across the street had a sort of prepared gaiety. At least I didn't take him unawares. He came towards me very friendly-like, very much in a friend-prepared-to-meet manner. Now, I don't know why I did it. Perhaps it was just a continuation of my mood, the last dregs of my anger. I wanted to shake him also out of his too easily accepted assumptions. I certainly didn't do it because I disliked him. In fact, truthfully, I did it because I really loved him. When he was about ten feet from me, I suddenly crouched down on all fours, glared at him and said in a fierce, truculent way – 'Wow.'

He stopped. I would have stopped too, I expect. In an uncertain, yet with a rising nervous tone, he repeated my salutation. His very nervousness was an incitement to attack, and I advanced towards him slowly, the snow very cold, like little, broken-up diamonds beneath my bare hands. Well, that certainly took him aback. He half-turned and retreated to the opposite side of the street and stood there regarding me, trying to readjust himself, his mental conflict so plain to read, I could have burst out laughing. I can quite understand his mixed emotions, can't you? After all, it was rather late, the street was deserted except for he and I, he had mistaken me for an acquaintance, and I must have looked very curious with my head down, glaring at him. Why had not I simply said, 'Sorry, you've made a mistake?'

So he half-backed, half-turned to the opposite side and stood looking at me in bewilderment. Probably nothing more would have happened, if I hadn't taken up the offensive and, without a sound, in an ominous and intimidating silence, advanced towards him on my knees and hands. He stood his ground bravely for a short time, but my attitude was so menacing, that finally his courage broke. He turned and ran – actually fled – between a purple cottage and a white stucco garage and from there he shouted at me. Yes, shouted. I suppose he thought he was safe. I let him think so, got up erect on my legs, returned to my own side and started down the street, not very fast and watching for him out of the corner of my eye. He must have cut around behind the houses, for he suddenly reappeared a little ahead of me, talking to himself, and probably to me, in a low jittery fashion. I couldn't make out all the words, but 'what the hell' and 'I'll be damned' were quite clear at least. Well, we went through the same performance again, the advance, the challenge, the doubt, the retreat, the reappearance. Each time his uncertainty mounted and his perplexity increased. After half a dozen reenactments of this ridiculous performance I got rather tired of it and instead of walking on as before, after one of his disappearances, I hid behind a telegraph pole. It was a big pole, bigger than I was, in the shadow of a house, and from my hiding place I could watch him unseen. He reappeared and stood gazing eagerly up, then down the empty street. No one. Fearing a trap, he walked slowly over to my side, very excited yet very much on guard. Where could I be? When he was about six feet from my hiding place, I pounced out, advanced a step and threw myself at him, shouting loud enough to rattle the windows – 'Grrrrrrrrrr.'

With a cry of mingled terror and supplication he fled precipitously straight up the street. I watched him go with the bitter ironic smile of the misunderstood. 'Fool,' I flung at him, then turned myself and walked away. After fifty feet I turned again to see what he would do, and what he did persuaded me that I had finally, yes, even against his will, convinced him, for he came back to the pole behind which I had hid, walked slowly around it, smelt carefully every inch within reach of his nose, then ceremoniously pissed against the place, where I had leant.

Yes, I think now his doubts were dissipated. That young, credulous Airedale pup was finally convinced he had met at last that fabulous creature, the Man-Dog of canine mythology. To him had been granted the terrifying yet ineffable bliss of a visitation from the past, a glimpse of the reincarnated One, the Living Legend, the long-awaited, the desperately desired, the ever-to-be-hoped-for One, who could explain, and only He, the hithertofore unexplainable feelings of sympathy and adoration in his heart for that mysterious superdog, Man, so like himself in life, love and the pursuit of shadows, in his fine courage, his slavish cringing, his unconquerable gaiety, that some mutual Origin, some common Ancestor must be postulated to explain their kinship. He had seen Him, the old dogs' tales were true, there was a Santa Claus, and never again would he regard with easy familiarity a man as just a man, but in every encounter, any day or night, he might meet the One again. Perhaps tomorrow. Life can be very exciting, can't it, when there is hope?

But I am the one who is afraid to meet him again.

In the fall of 1935, Bethune invited a group of doctors, nurses, and social workers to discuss the health problems of a Canadian population suffering in the grip of the Depression. He was both its founder and its 'leading spirit, always with a new idea,' according to Libbie Park, a member of the group.[12] Bethune envisioned it undertaking study and discussion, but ultimately turning this work to action. His goal was to set out a comprehensive plan for a Canadian medical system that would help the millions of people who were deprived of health care. The group of about fifteen met regularly through the winter and spring, often in Bethune's apartment. The Montreal Group for the Security of the People's Health, as it came to be called, would not issue its first formal statement until July 1936. In April, however, Bethune made use of its accumulated information when he accepted an invitation to appear before the Montreal Medico-Chirurgical Society. His address, later published in the Canadian Doctor *in January 1937 under the title 'Take Private Profit Out of Medicine,' was a frank condemnation of the Canadian health-care structure. But more radical still, Bethune announced that the only way to repair this defective structure was 'to change the economic system which produces ill-health.' His target was no longer just medicine, it was also capitalism.*

Take Private Profit Out of Medicine
Symposium on Medical Economics
Discussion
Montreal Medico-Chirurgical Society, April 17, 1936
Norman Bethune

General Approach
Tonight there has been shown the most interesting case ever presented to this Society. It is the case of 'The People versus the Doctors.' We are

acting both as defendant and judge. This behoves us to apply our minds with the utmost objectivity to this question. This case is an ethical and moral problem in the field of social and political economics, and not medical economics alone. Medicine must be envisaged as embedded in the social fabric and inseparable from it. It is the product of any given social environment. The basis of any social structure is economic. The economic theory and practice in this country is termed capitalistic. It is founded on individualism, competition and private profit. This capitalistic system is undergoing an economic crisis, commonly called the depression. This is not a temporary illness of the body politic, but a deadly disease requiring systemic treatment. Systemic treatment is called, by the timid, radical remedies. Those palliative measures as suggested by most of our political quacks are aspirin tablets for a syphilitic headache. They may relieve, they will never cure.

Medicine is a typical, loosely organized, basically individualistic industry in this 'catch as catch can' capitalistic system operating as a monopoly on a private profit basis. Now, it is inevitable that medicine should undergo much the same crisis as the rest of the capitalistic world and should present much the same interesting and uncomfortable phenomena. This may be epitomized as 'poverty of health in the midst of scientific abundance of knowledge of disease.' Just as thousands of people are hungry in a country which produces more food than the people can consume (we even burn coffee, kill hogs and pay farmers not to plant wheat and cotton), just as thousands are wretchedly clothed though the manufacturers can make more clothing than they can sell, so millions are sick, hundreds of thousands suffer pain, and tens of thousands die prematurely through lack of adequate medical care, which is available but for which they cannot pay. Inability to purchase is combined with poor distribution. The problem of medical economics is a part of the problem of world economics and is inseparable and indivisible from it. Medicine, as we are practising it, is a luxury trade. We are selling bread at the price of jewels. The poor, which comprise fifty per cent of our population, cannot pay, and starve; we cannot sell, and suffer. The people have no health protection and we have no economic security. This brings us to the point of the two aspects of this problem.

The Patients' Predicament

There are in this country three great economic groups, 1st: The comfortable, 2nd: The uncomfortable, 3rd: The miserable. In the upper bracket are those who are comfortably well off, rich or wealthy; in the mid bracket are those who are moderately uncomfortable and insecure; and in the lower, those vast masses, not in brackets but in chains, who are living on the edge of the subsistence level. These people in the lower income class are receiving only one-third of the home, office and clinic services from physicians that a fundamental standard of health requires. Only 55 per cent, as shown by the Committee on the Cost of Medical Care, of as many cases are being hospitalized as an adequate standard would prescribe, and only 54 per cent of as many days are being spent in hospital as are desirable. The only exception are those surgical cases hospitalized, which is approximately normal for both rich and poor. In short, one has to suffer a major surgical catastrophe to have even approximate adequate care. The Committee's report also showed that 46.6% of people whose income is less than $1200 a year received no medical, dental or eye care whatsoever in a year. If this is combined with those whose incomes are $10,000 or more (13.8% of such persons received no similar care), we are faced with the appalling fact, that 38.2% of all people, irrespective of income, receive no medical, dental or eye care whatsoever. What is the cause of this alarming state of affairs? 1st: Financial inability to pay is the major cause; 2nd: Ignorance; 3rd: Apathy; 4th: Lack of medical service. So we see that in the United States, with a population of 120 million people in 1929, only 48 people out of 100 had the care of a physician during the year; only 21 people out of 100 visited the dentist once a year; only 1 in 17 had hospital care; only 1 in 26 had their eyes examined, and only 1 in 9 had health examination, vaccination or immunization. Yet morbidity figures for this group of people show that they suffered 844.5 illnesses per 1,000 persons in the same year. If Canada is taken, as it well may be, as part of the American scene, the figures for this country would not show very much variation.

The Doctors' Dilemma

Enormous accumulation of scientific knowledge has made it practically impossible for any one man to have an entire grasp of even the facts, much less their application, of the sum total of medical knowledge. This has made specialization imperative and group practice a necessity. Individual specialization predicates concentrated centres of population. The general practitioner, unsupported by specialists, knows that he cannot give the people their money's worth, yet the financial cost of specialization bars many from proceeding to such fields. The necessity to make money after a difficult financial struggle to pay for medical education drives the young doctor too often into any form of remunerative work however uncongenial it may be. There he is caught up in the coils of economics, from which not one in a thousand can ever escape. The fee-for-service is very disturbing morally to practitioners. The patient is frequently unable to correctly appraise the value of the doctor's service or dis-service. Perrot and Collins, in 1933, in an investigation of 9,130 families in America, found the depression poor had a larger incidence of illness than any other group. Also that 61% of all physicians' calls to such a class were free, that 33% of calls to the moderately comfortable were free, and that 26% of calls to even those comfortably well off were not paid for. If $3,000 net be taken as an adequate income, 40% of all physicians in the United States made less money than that. If $2,500 net be taken, 33% of all physicians had inadequate incomes. If $1,500 net be taken, then 18% of doctors had inadequate incomes, and 5% of all physicians were unable to meet their professional expenses from gross receipts. The very interesting comparison with the salaries of physicians attached as full time workers in the army, the navy and hospitals and public health services showed, that only 13.2% had incomes below $3,000.

However, quite apart from this, it was the opinion of the Committee that the existing medical system with all its ramifications could not supply service in quantity or value to the fundamental standard of service prescribed. The tremendous expansion of the Public Health services is urgently needed, and instead of $1 out of the $30 per capita, which is the cost of medical care, at least $2.50 would be desirable. However, our politicians in this regard have raised the cynical indifference of their attitude towards public health, especially the indigent, to the dignity of a doctrine.

Where Do We Go from Here?

Permit a few categorical statements. Dogmatism has a role in the realm of vacillation.

1.) The best form of providing health protection would be to change the economic system which produces ill-health, liquidate ignorance, poverty and unemployment. The practice of each individual purchasing his own medical care does not work. It is unjust, inefficient, wasteful and completely out-moded. Doctors, private charity and philanthropic institutions have kept it alive as long as possible. It should have died a natural death a hundred years ago, with the coming of the industrial revolution in the opening years of the 19th century. In our highly-geared, modern industrial society there is no such thing as private health – all health is public. The illness and maladjustments of one unit of the mass affects all other members. The protection of the people's health should be recognized by the Government as its primary obligation and duty to its citizens. Socialized medicine and the abolition or restriction of private practice would appear to be the realistic solution of the problem. Let us take the profit, the private economic profit, out of medicine, and purify our profession of rapacious individualism. Let us make it disgraceful to enrich ourselves at the expense of the miseries of our fellow-men. Let us organize ourselves so that we can no longer be exploited as we are being exploited by our politicians. Let us re-define medical ethics – not as a code of professional etiquette between doctors, but as a code of fundamental morality and justice between medicine and the people. In our medical society let us discuss more often the great problems of our age and not so much interesting cases; the relationship of medicine to the State; the duties of the profession to the people; the matrix of economics and sociology in which we exist. Let us recognize that our most important contemporaneous problems are economic and social and not technical and scientific in the narrow sense that we employ those words.

2.) Medicine, like any other organization to-day, whether it be the Church or the Bar, is judging its leaders by their attitude to the fundamental social and economic issues of the day. We need fewer leading physicians and famous surgeons in modern medicine and more far-sighted, socially-imaginative statesmen.

The medical profession must do this – as the traditional, historical and altruistic guardians of the people's health, let us present to the Government a complete, comprehensive programme of a planned medical service for all the people; then, in whatever position the profession finds itself after such a plan has been evolved, that position it must accept. This apparent immolation as a burnt offering on the altar of ideal public health will result in the profession rising like a glorious Phoenix from the dead ashes of its former self.

Medicine must be entirely reorganized and unified, welded into a great army of doctors, dentists, nurses, technicians and social service workers, to make a collectivized attack on disease and utilizing all the present scientific knowledge of its members to that end.

Let us say to the people not – 'how much have you got' but – 'how best can we serve you.' Our slogan should be 'we are in business for your health.'

3.) Socialized medicine means that health protection becomes public property, like the post office, the army, the navy, the judiciary and the school; 2nd: supported by public funds; 3rd: with services available to all, not according to income but according to need. Charity must be abolished and justice substituted. Charity debases the donor and debauches the recipient; 4th: its workers to be paid by the State, with assured salaries and pensions; 5th: with democratic self government by the Health workers themselves.

Twenty-five years ago it was thought contemptible to be called a Socialist. To-day it is ridiculous not to be one.

Medical reforms, such as limited Health Insurance schemes, are not socialized medicine. They are bastard forms of Socialism produced by belated humanitarianism out of necessity.

The three major objections which the opponents of socialized medicine emphasize are: *1st: Loss of initiative.* Although the human donkey probably needs, in this state of modern barbarism, some sort of vegetable dangled in front of his nose, these need not be golden carrots but a posy or prestige will do as well. *2nd: Bureaucracy.* This can be checked by democratic control of organization from bottom to top. *3rd: The importance of the patient's own selection of a doctor.* This is a myth: its only proponents are the doctors themselves – not the patients. Give a limited choice – say of 2 or 3 doctors, then, if the patient is not satisfied, send him to a psychiatrist! Sauce for the goose is sauce for the gander – the doctor must also be given his own selection of patients! 99% of patients want results not personalities.

4.) Our profession must arouse itself from its scientific and intensely personal preoccupation and becoming socially-minded, realize the inseparability of health from economic security.

Let us abandon our isolation and grasp the realities of the present economic crisis. The world is changing beneath our very eyes and already the bark of Aesculapius is beginning to feel beneath its keel the great surge and movement of the rising world tide which is sweeping on, obliterating old landscapes and old scenes. We must go with the tide or be wrecked.

5.) The contest in the world to-day is between two kinds of men: those who believe in the old jungle individualism, and those who believe in cooperative efforts for the securing of a better life for all.

The people are ready for socialized medicine. The obstructionists to the people's health security lie within the profession itself. Recognize this fact. It is the all-important fact of the situation. These men with the mocking face of the reactionary or the listlessness of the futilitarian, proclaim their principles under the guise of 'maintenance of the sacred relationship between doctor and patient,' 'inefficiency of other non-profit nationalized enterprises,' 'the danger of Socialism,' 'the freedom of individualism.' These are the enemies of the people and make no mistake. They are the enemies of medicine too.

The situation which is confronting Medicine to-day is a contest of two forces in Medicine itself. One holds that the important thing is the maintenance of our vested historical interest, our private property, our monopoly of health distribution. The other contends that the function of Medicine is greater than the maintenance of the doctor's position, that the security of the people's health is our primary duty, that we are the servants, not the masters, of the people, and that human rights are above professional privileges. So the old challenge of Shakespeare's character in Henry IV still rings out across the centuries: 'Under which King, Bezonian, stand or die!'

A small group of doctors, dentists, nurses and social service workers, to study the present-day position of private and public health and its relationship to the State, has been founded in Montreal. I would be glad to give information to any one who may be interested in such a Group for the study of schemes for the security of the people's health.

The following appeal was one of several put forth by the Montreal Group for the Security of the People's Health leading up to the provincial election of 17 August 1936 in Quebec. Attached to the letter was a statement about the group's survey of medical conditions in the Montreal region, along with a discussion about possible medical-care plans. It was a draft form of the manifesto of the Montreal group, which was circulated to political candidates in the week before the August 17 election. The group's call for a mass meeting of the medical, dental, and nursing professionals of Montreal generated little enthusiasm. The gathering that occurred was not a great success, according to Libbie Park.[13]

July 13, 1936
Dr. Grant Fleming,
Dean of Medical Faculty,
McGill University.

Dear Doctor Fleming:
The following open letter, which is being sent to the various medical,

dental and nursing associations of the city, expresses the convictions of
our study group. We beg you earnestly to give your support to the proposal to call a mass meeting of the three professions, for discussion of
these suggestions. This is a critical time for both the profession and the
people.

We feel strongly that we must present a United Professional Front to
the political parties seeking power. Only in such a way can we obtain
for the underprivileged and unemployed the benefits of modern medicine to which they are entitled, and for ourselves, the recognition by the
state of the proper remuneration which is our due.

We must be on guard also, against the advice of certain lay representatives of wealth and privilege whose interest and interference in the
problems of medicine in Montreal, has been disclosed before with such
humiliating consequences.

If the Montreal Medico-Chirurgical Society is not inclined to sponsor
such a mass meeting, we, as a group, are determined to go ahead and
make the appeal ourselves by circularizing the professions directly.

We hope this will not be necessary. We hope the move will be initiated by the English speaking medical society.

Very sincerely,
N. Bethune,
Secretary
Montreal Group for the Security of the People's Health

*The manifesto of the Montreal Group for the Security of the People's Health
was issued just one week before the provincial election. It was a wide-ranging,
hard-hitting, and prescient document. In part it was a condemnation of the provincial and federal governments' refusal to alleviate unemployment and poverty. It also offered proposals for various forms of socialized medicine and
suggested ways to improve the operation of the Montreal city government's
recently created Medical Relief Commission. Given the tenor of political criticism of the day, it was not surprising that the group's proposals focused on
resolving public health problems by injecting state funds and imposing government planning. But there were also two other significant themes woven into the
document. One was the need for unity, political involvement, and democratic
governance within the various medical professions; the second was the value of
communal self-help among the unemployed. Proposals such as communal kitchens and child-care centres were similar to experiments going on in the Soviet*

Union, which Bethune might have observed on his visit the previous year, and about which other members of the Montreal group would have been familiar. Blunt criticism and proposals for radical social reconstruction were scarcely what politicians or the medical societies of the day were likely to wish to hear, and the manifesto must have won few converts among those to whom it was sent. Although the manifesto was the work of several people, Bethune had a guiding hand in it, and it reflects his thinking on the issue.

An Open Letter to All Political Candidates Seeking Election in Montreal

August 10, 1936

Dear Sir:
The enclosed are the proposals made by the Montreal Group for the Security of the People's Health to the various political parties in the coming election. We earnestly urge you to give them your deepest consideration for inclusion as a health plank on your platform. These proposals have been drawn up after considerable study by a large group of Montreal doctors, dentists, nurses, statisticians and Social Service Workers. Would you be good enough to send us a written reply in regard to these proposals.

We ask you to bring up the question of state responsibility for the maintenance of the People's health in all you public meetings and addresses to the electorate, so that the medical, dental and nursing professions may know your stand in this tremendously important matter.

Very sincerely yours,
Norman Bethune
Secretary,
Montreal Group for the Security of the People's Health
1154 Beaver Hall Square
Montreal, P.Q.

Medical Care for the People of Montreal and the Province of Quebec
Proposals submitted for discussion and amendment to officers of all Medical, Dental and Nursing Societies and Associations in the Province of Quebec; to members of the professions; to Hospitals; to Social and Charitable Agencies; Public Health and Government Officials; Montreal Unemployment Commission and Representatives of the Church
by

The Montreal Group for the Security of the People's Health
1154 Beaver Hall Square
Montreal

The Montreal Group for the Security of the People's Health is a non-political organization of physicians, surgeons, dentists, nurses, social service workers and statisticians formed in the winter of 1935–1936 to study the relationship of present day medicine to the people and to the state, in all the civilized countries of the world, with particular attention to the Dominion of Canada and the Province of Quebec.

The reasons for the urgent necessity of such a study were drawn up by the group in its fundamental platform.

1. There is an underlying feeling that medicine, as now practised in this country, does not serve adequately either the patient or the physicians.

2. Our civilization in recent years has undergone and is undergoing profound socio-economic changes which have altered both individual and group relationships. Although medical science has made tremendous progress, yet the application of these advances has not been fully utilized either to the benefit of the people or the profession.

3. The cause of this incomplete utilization lies in the uneven distribution of the products of scientific knowledge and research, with a lack of purchasing power of the people.

The doctor is a producer. The doctor is a commodity producer; the commodity he produces is the application of his knowledge of health and the means and measures he takes to combat disease. He, like the rest of society into which he is closely interwoven, is suffering today because he can find but few consumers able to pay for his product. In short, 'production relationships,' in terms of political economics, between producer and consumer are maladjusted and distorted. Medicine as a part of modern society presents the same contradictions in miniature as affects the whole. These contradictions may be characterized as poverty of purchasing power in the midst of plenty.

4. There is a growing realization that the adequate prevention and cure of disease has gone beyond the capacity of individual practitioners or charitable institutions, and that it demands the recognition by the state of the following principle – the maintenance of the health of the population is one of the fundamental functions and duties of the state and should be undertaken by the state under the same necessities as it has taken over public education, the police, the army and fire protection.

5. What's wrong with our practice of medicine at present?

A. *Patient's View.*

1. The vast majority of the population (based on sociological division of three groups) cannot pay for adequate medical aid.

2. Even such medical aid as supplied by charity is inadequate, unless in cases of extreme illness requiring hospitalization.

3. There is an appalling lack of provision for preventive and hygienic measures in the community.

B. *Doctor's View.*

1. Individualistic general practice of medicine cannot supply the full benefits of modern science owing to the high degree of specialization demanded by advancing knowledge.

2. Preventive medicine in the real sense of the term is not practised, being non-remunerative.

3. Since the vast majority of people cannot even pay for inefficient service which the doctor is willing to render, the demands made on the physician's charity are beyond those of any other social group. This produces an accentuation of the economic crisis of medicine which leads to a lowering of altruistic principles and high morale of the profession; the doctor is enslaved by drudgers' work, his relative poverty prevents post-graduate work and vacation, his economic security is precarious, and the incidence of early death is well known.

The state has already recognized in part its obligations to its citizens by taking over certain medical functions, e.g. the care of contagious diseases, inspection of school children, food inspection, pre-natal care, etc. Should it not extend these activities to cover the entire field of prevention and cure of disease for all classes of society?

In view of the coming Provincial Elections in this Province, it would appear to be a most opportune time to put forward some definite plan or plans to the political parties seeking election, expressing the collective demands of the allied medical, dental and nursing professions.

The recently instituted Unemployment Medical Relief Commission in Montreal is a step in the right direction. At the same time, other plans should be presented by the organized professions (the English and French doctors, dentists and nurses) to embrace the entire province.

The following suggestions are made –

1. It is the grave duty of the combined professions to point out to our politicians the present deplorable, yet remediable, condition of the health of our citizens. Our knowledge of health and disease places this moral responsibility firmly on our shoulders.

2. From each political party, demands should be made that, as a

prominent plank on their respective platforms, State responsibility for the health of its citizens – whether employed or otherwise – is a primary principle. A man should not lose his rights as a citizen because he loses his job. The Honourable Norman Rogers in the House of Commons, March 30th, 1936, said 'The welfare of its citizens is the prime duty of the State.'

3. That on no account an attempt be made after the election, on the false ground of economy, to abolish the present medical relief for the unemployed in Montreal.

4. That, if alterations in the present set-up of the Commission be contemplated in the future, they should tend towards increasing the amount set aside for the Commission's functioning. This is 25¢ a month per person on relief. An increase to 50¢ per month (as the Ontario Government has found advisable in certain districts) should be demanded.

5. That, in view of the possibility of a reduction in the monthly accounts of doctors under the Commission, such reductions should be strenuously opposed unless a proportionate reduction be made in the accounts of the other recipients, i.e. the druggists. Here the principle that the doctor (precisely as the druggist) is selling a commodity, should be rigidly maintained. This should be the end of the exploitation of the medical profession. It has been carrying the burden of the unemployed and low income groups for years.

6. If the proposed proportionate distribution of funds to doctors (80%) and to druggists (20%), dentists nil, nurses nil, on the basis of 25¢ a month allocated for each unemployed, be found to be, in practice, out of all proportion to this, that the municipalities should set up three or more city drug dispensaries to take the excessive profits out of filling pre-scriptions, and furnish drugs to its unemployed citizens at cost price.

That such an event of uneven distribution is not beyond possibility, the experience of the Municipality of Lachine, in 1935, may be quoted –

To drug stores	$ 9,224	equals	60%
To doctors	$ 4,918	"	32%
To dentists	$ 1,263	"	8%
Total	$15,405	"	100%

Under the present Montreal Commission, the distribution proposed would have been as follows:

To drug stores	$ 3,081	equals	20%
To doctors	12,324	"	80%
To dentists	Nil	"	Nil
Total	$15,405	"	100%

7. That in the event of a marked reduction of doctors' monthly accounts for service to the unemployed being made (for example, 25% to 50% of their total) on the plea of the Commission's inability to pay, that the following plan be substituted. The factual basis of the following plan is founded on the figures of the Montreal Relief Commission for March: –

Heads of families (men or women) unemployed	65,785
Dependents of the above	102,122
Unemployable	2,269
Total on Relief	170,176

At 25¢ per month, the yearly income of the Commission for medical relief for distribution to doctors and druggists is 170,176 × .25 × 12 equals $510,528.00. Of this amount, the doctors' share will be 80% equals $408,420.00. Of the 1200 doctors in Montreal, 800 have registered on the Commission's list. This would permit an average of $500.00 odd per year for each registered doctor. If the 170,176 persons on relief would be evenly divided, each of the registered doctors would have 212 patients. The proposed plan, in the event of the probability of the breakdown of the present scheme, is as follows –

8. A City Medical Planning Board be formed by representatives of the English and French doctors, dentists and nurses. Any registered doctor in good standing in his medical society (this would be necessary for proper disciplinary control) may register with the Board and practice under this scheme. He might be allowed to accept a maximum of 500 patients on his list. The patients should have the right of choice of doctor and also right of change at certain fixed intervals. For these doctors accepting relief patients, abolish entirely the antiquated system of fee-for-service and substitute a per capita payment for an all-in service. It would cost no more than the present system ($3.00 a year for each patient). It would do an end with padding accounts, dishonest calls, dishonest prescriptions. It would reduce the overhead of the commission. An Appeal board should be set up to deal with patients' and doctors' complaints.

9. *Additional Medical Relief.*

Not only must the present medical relief be maintained, but it must be expanded and increased to include surgical dental treatment, home nursing and proportionate payments to the hospitals for the use of the outdoor departments.

10. The outdoor departments of our Hospitals would be utilized as consultant departments. A staff fund to be distributed equitably among doctors, interns, and nurses should be allocated to each Hospital treating the unemployed, both in indoor and outdoor departments. Doctors treating relief patients urgently require the service of the outdoors for special investigation and advice and the hospitals should be paid for this service. An additional $3.00 per capita per year would cover this essential service.

11. The present hospitalization plan under the Q.P.C.A. to continue, but amended to eliminate the property-owning clause.

12. Thus, an additional 25¢ per month bringing medical expenditure per capita for those on relief to 50¢ per month, instead of the present 25¢ would cost approximately $1,021,056.00 a year, or $6.00 per capita on relief a year (based on the March 1936 figures of 170,000). The suggestion is made that the additional 25¢ per month be paid by the Provincial Government.

13. Resistance should be made to the appointment of 'Relief Doctors' on salary. The English experience of this system is unsatisfactory.

14. A City Nursing Planning Board should be set up to unify the activities of the County Health Unit Nurses, Welfare Nurses, School Nurses and Victorian Order of Nurses, and work in close conjunction with the City Medical Planning Board. There is much wasteful re-duplication of administration and there should be a marked extension of all the above mentioned groups, each autonomous in their individual field but under central control. The Home Nursing Service for the Unemployed should be paid for out of the additional 25¢ per month.

15. That the Central City and Provincial Medical Planning Boards set up a Medical Commission to study the effect of the depression and continued unemployment with the low subsistence food allowance under relief. Malnutrition, predisposition to deficiency diseases, tuberculosis, etc. should be studied. This group of nearly 200,000 people should be thoroughly investigated from the physical, psychiatric, racial, sociological, occupational points of view. The present situation presents a unique opportunity to collect a mass of invaluable data and must be seized.

Routine inspection of school children in 1935 found that over 50% were suffering from various defects. Half of the defective had dental caries (due to lack of minerals and vitamins) and 8626 (14%) were suffering from malnutrition. The effects of undernourishment may not show themselves for years as Dr. G.C.M. McGonigle, medical officer of health for Stockton-on-Tees, England, in his recent book *Poverty and Public Health* has shown. It is true those on relief are not starving to death – they are merely starving.

16. To educate the wives and daughters of men on relief in the purchase and preparation of a more evenly balanced diet than they are at present obtaining, it is suggested that the Relief Commission set up a number of model kitchens in each ward (vacant stores can be utilized) where expert dieticians will give practical demonstrations of the preparation of balanced meals, even on the present low relief allowance for food. The church and press should be urged to give these demonstrations wide publicity. The Montreal Light, Heat and Power Commission should be enlisted to furnish gas stoves, and other commercial firms, utensils, etc. The cooked food so prepared could be sold at cost price to those on relief, so that eventually a communal centre with communal kitchens (especially for the single) would be set up with co-operative pooled resources. This might be extended to include 'Infant Parking' for exhausted mothers, free movies and occupational therapy shops such as a co-operative shoe-repair, carpentry, dress-making. The result of unemployment is gradual deterioration of physical and mental morale. We must actively combat this deterioration.

17. A physical examination of every unemployed man or woman, put to work with the proposed Bouchard Plan, should be demanded. Continued under-nourishment under the present relief food allowance combined with inadequate clothing (a single man now has $1.80 a week to feed himself and 15¢ a week for clothing) will most certainly predispose many such men and women to serious illness if forced to work under unfavourable climatic conditions.

18. That, following the resolution passed by the Ontario Medical Association at their last meeting, favouring experimental programmes under the auspices of the local medical societies, the following plans be tried in carefully selected localities in the Province of Quebec. These four plans are typical of the large number now under discussion all over the world and could be used as controls to each other in a proper scientific manner.

19. *First Plan – Municipal Medicine.*

This would be an amplification and extension of the present full-time health unit system of the Public Health Service of the Province. A full-time team of doctors, dentists, nurses, including all specialities such as surgery, gynaecology, obstetrics, paediatrics, etc., should be selected (*not* politically appointed) by a Provincial Medical Planning Board (to be set up by the medical, dental and nursing societies) and placed in a given municipality, provided with a small modern hospital (a new one to be built or an older one to be modernized). They would take over and control the health, prevention and cure of disease for the entire population, irrespective of economic or social grouping. All such members of this combined medico-surgical, dental, nursing group should be placed on salary. Such a team of active, keen and highly trained men and women could be easily recruited from among the younger and more energetic members of these professions. A high sense of social responsibility would be essential for appointment. The total costs of such a plan to be borne by municipal taxes and assisted by provincial grant. The Life [Insurance] Officers Association should be approached to offer their services (as they offered them in British Columbia) to work out the cost of such a scheme and place the whole on a firm actuarial basis. This is also necessary for the second plan.

20. *Second Plan – Compulsory Health Insurance.*

Select a municipality which presents a fairly homogeneous economic pattern of income-level groups, and where relief recipients are at an irreducible minimum. No exclusion must be made, but all wage-earners and those gainfully employed must be included, irrespective of income. Only in such a way can true mutualization of insurance be possible. The actuarial figures will determine the premiums to be paid.

21. *Third Plan.*

Voluntary Hospitalization of Health Insurance in a selected urban municipality of from five to ten thousand people.

22. *Fourth Plan.*

Care of the unemployed on a fee-for-service basis covering the entire province based on the Essex (Ontario) County Model, with consideration of province-wide plans to include the low-income groups.

23. The necessity of a province-wide plan is made evident by the Speech of the Honourable Norman Rogers, on the National Employment Commission (official report of the House of Commons Debates) in March, 1936.

The relief situation in Quebec –

		% of Dominion Total
Employable	104,220	31.37%
Dependents	146,410	29.4%
Unemployable	23,510	48.71%
Farmers' families	72,350	22.15%
Total	346,490 equals 12% of population	

Percentage in relation to Dominion-wide relief (1,233,390)

$$\frac{346,490 \times 100}{1,233,390} = 28\% \text{ of Canada's unemployed}$$

The % of unemployed on relief in Quebec is the highest in Canada and comprises 48.71% of the total unemployable in Canada. Such an appalling figure demands immediate investigation.

24. *Conclusion.*

That in view of the emergency of the situation and the necessity for planning for permanent poverty, a congress of French, English doctors, dentists, nurses, social service workers, Public Health officials, representatives of the Trades and Labour Council, the Unemployed, the Federated Charities, the Relief Commission and the Church should be called, sponsored by the French and English medical, dental and nursing societies to formulate plans for action. Only through the demands made by such a United Professional front will the politicians be made to realize the potential force which the 10,000 members of the allied professions in Quebec represent.

Unless we, the combined profession, formulate and implement some plan or plans to give adequate medical service to the unemployed and the low-income groups, we may have to accept what may be forced on us. An additional plan should be prepared for consideration of Public Medicine on the same basis as Public Education, Fire Protection, the Army, and the Police Forces. Medicine must be controlled by medicine. Action should be immediate, united and decisive.

25. *Doctor, Dentist, Nurse and Social Service Worker!*

Join your local society, urge unification of French, English doctors, dentists, nurses and social service workers. Fight racial and professional isolation. We must unite in a common cause – health security for our people, and economic security for ourselves.

Circulated to candidates in the Quebec election, the report written by the Montreal Group for the Security of the People's Health had some impact. In a letter to Marian Scott, then at her summer cottage at Lachute, Bethune informed her of the responses to it from the leader of the Union Nationale, Maurice Duplessis, and the incumbent Liberal premier, Adélard Godbout.

Aug 13/36

Dear Pony –
    We are getting there!
    Duplessis has acknowledged publicly – Godbout privately!
    Herewith a copy of a letter to Woodsworth sent tonight.
    Use your discretion in showing it to Frank.
    Is the water still cool & dark,
    the sands still curving white
    And are you still so beautiful?
    I long for you – being none of all these.

Beth

Written in Montreal in October 1936, just weeks before his departure for Spain, 'Red Moon' showed the extent to which Bethune had been affected by the Spanish struggle. The poem was subsequently published in Canadian Forum *in July 1937.*

Red Moon

And this same pallid moon tonight,
    Which rides so quietly, clear and high,
The mirror of our pale and troubled gaze,
    Raised to the cool Canadian sky,

Above the shattered Spanish mountain tops
    Last night, rose low and wild and red,

Reflecting back from her illumined shield,
　　The blood bespattered faces of the dead.

To that pale disc, we raise our clenchèd fists
　　And to those nameless dead our vows renew,
'Comrades, who fought for freedom and the future world,
　　Who died for us, we will remember you.'

Norman Bethune

In late October 1936, just before leaving for Spain, Bethune wrote a simple will providing for the people and causes he cared deeply for: his former wife. Frances, and the Children's Art Centre, based in his apartment. To take care of Frances, Bethune sold his prized Ford roadster to Hy Shister, who in turn was to pay Frances $25 a month for a year. He also left her control of his apartment at 1154 Beaver Hall Square, which for the previous six months had been both his home and the site of the Children's Art Centre. His artist friends Fritz and Mieze Brandtner moved into the flat, thus maintaining it as a creative hub. At age forty-six, when many doctors would have been comfortably established and looking forward to a life of ease, Bethune had pitifully few possessions, and what little he had he was throwing aside, to embark on a path both arduous and dangerous.

1154 Beaver Hall Square
Montreal, Oct. 28/36

The flat in 1154 Beaver Hall Square with all its contents belongs to Frances Coleman for her disposal at any time or in any way she pleases.

　　The account in the Royal Bank, St. Matthew St. branch also I turn over to her. I have given her power-of-attorney to dispose of any money there, also to enable her to make contracts, etc. in my name. The sum of $300.00 to be paid by Dr. H. Shister at $25.00 a month for 12 months also belongs to her.

　　The children's art centre is to be financed (at a limit of $25.00 a month) for a period of 4 months. By that time, if this is no longer self-supporting, or if the Committee founded by Marian Scott, Sonia Apter and Frances Coleman and others have not found a sponsor for the movement, I will not commit Frances Coleman to continuing it. If

'Viva Espana.' Just days before leaving for the Spanish Civil War, Bethune visited the Toronto workshop of painter Charles Comfort and wrote his own epitaph: 'Born a bourgeoise [*sic*]. Died a communist.'

F. Brandtner can not pay the rent after 4 months, she may sub-let the flat to another tenant.

N. Bethune

To Fritz Brandtner.
It is understood that Frances Coleman is the sole owner of the lease of 1154 Beaver Hall Square flat and all its contents. The rent for such a flat ($42.50 a month less 50¢ weekly for garbage disposal) is to be deposited with her on the last day of each month. She will then pay this rent to the National Trust Co. herself.

If for any reason, she wishes to dispose of the flat, the agreement between her and yourself is to be terminated by 1 month's notice.

She is not bound to any contract to sub-let this flat to you beyond 1 month's notice.

I agree to acknowledge any responsibility as founder of the Children's Creative Art Centre to contribute to its support for 4 more months beginning Nov. 1, 1936. If this is not self-supporting after that time or has not found another supporter, I do not engage myself to continue my support. I hope and trust that the applications you make to Frances Coleman for any month's subsidy should not exceed $10.00 or $15.00.

The increase in your revenue from private adult and children's classes should take care of your slightly increased expenses in this studio.

I have authorized her to expend $10.00 on advertisements for the above named adult and children's pay classes.

Norman Bethune

5

Anti-fascist:
Spain, November 1936 to May 1937

Much about Bethune in Spain remains shrouded in mystery or controversy. There is still argument over what took him there, what forced
him to leave, and what he accomplished. Perhaps only the surface data
are agreed upon.

Bethune departed from Quebec City for Spain on 24 October 1936 and
arrived in Madrid on 3 November, just days before Franco's right-wing
forces unleashed a savage offensive on the Republican capital. The city
was saved by the hastily organized Spanish militia, the Communist
Fifth Regiment, and the first units of the International Brigades, anti-
fascists who, at the peak of their strength, would number thirty thousand, including thirteen hundred Canadians.[1] As a skilled surgeon,
Bethune had the option of joining a military hospital in Madrid or working at the International Brigades training centre in Albacete, but he
rejected both. Instead he quickly devised a plan to create a mobile blood
transfusion service for the front. Having cleared the idea with Spanish
officials and the Committee to Aid Spanish Democracy (CASD) in Toronto, he sped to London to immerse himself in the intricacies of blood
transfusion and purchase the necessary equipment. Back in Madrid on
12 December, Bethune, Hazen Sise, and Henning Sorensen set up the
transfusion unit in a fifteen-room apartment allocated to them by the
Socorro Rojo Internacional (SRI), the main Spanish medical and humanitarian relief agency. The flat had previously been occupied by the legal
advisor to the German embassy and was just below the office of the SRI.
The location, 36 Principe de Vergara, was close to downtown Madrid
and the front on the western fringe of the city, but it was also safely
secluded in a wealthy district – 'the Westmount of Madrid,' Sise called it
– so Franco's military declined to bombard it.[2] By 17 December, Bethune

could report back to Canada that 'we are now completely organized and settled in for work.'

For the next three months, Bethune and the team of Canadians and Spaniards in the transfusion unit improved the service and extended it to the shifting fronts in the war zone. It was a momentous accomplishment, and the Spanish government paid tribute to Bethune's role in it by making him an honorary military *comandante*, a major, the highest rank held by any foreigner in the medical service.[3] (The title was honorary because the Canadian government tried to prevent Canadians from assisting the Spanish Republicans by banning them from serving in the armed forces of a foreign state at war. Such service was made illegal by the 1937 Foreign Enlistment Act. In fact, the Canadian government specially graced the blood transfusion unit by amending the Foreign Enlistment Act to ban participation in humanitarian agencies which did not assist both sides in the civil war.)[4]

The month of April 1937, however, brought to a boil what had been a simmering conflict within the transfusion unit. On 19 April 1937, Bethune resigned as head of the team. Remorseful yet bitter, Bethune left 'the centre of gravity of the world' on 18 May. He had been in Spain just six months, time enough to make himself revered and infamous.

Probing beneath surface details, it is clear that the very process of his going to Spain was marked by personal drive, political intrigue, and a little chance. Indeed, there is a measure of irony in how Bethune's medical mission to Spain originated. The idea sprang from Graham Spry, a stalwart of the Co-operative Commonwealth Federation (CCF). Like fellow CCF member Frank Scott, Spry was partisanly anti-communist. In the summer of 1936, he proposed to the CCF that it raise money to send a hospital to Spain as a way to counter the public respect swinging to the communists because of their calls for assistance to the Spanish Republic. On 26 September the 'Spanish Hospital and Medical Aid Committee' was still 'a figment of my imagination,' he admitted, when he announced the plan in the CCF newspaper, the *New Commonwealth*. 'To my delight and alarm, Dr. Norman Bethune responded almost immediately. When Bethune arrived in Toronto, I had to confess that there was neither an organization nor the money to send him to Spain.' That did not deter Bethune. He sailed for Spain using a steamship ticket that Spry cajoled from a friend.[5]

Ironic, too, was the fact that in sending Bethune and his medical equipment, Spry actually facilitated a long-standing communist project – to 'force the CCF into a united front' with the Communist Party, a

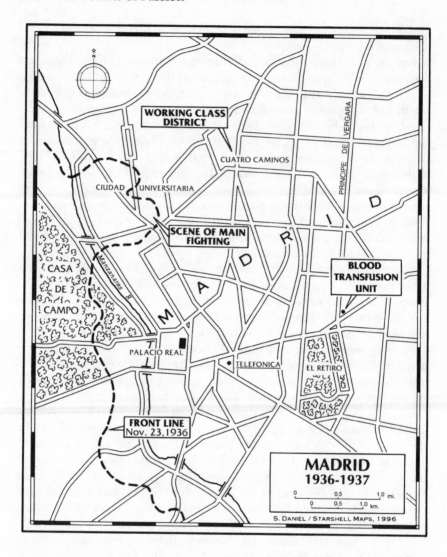

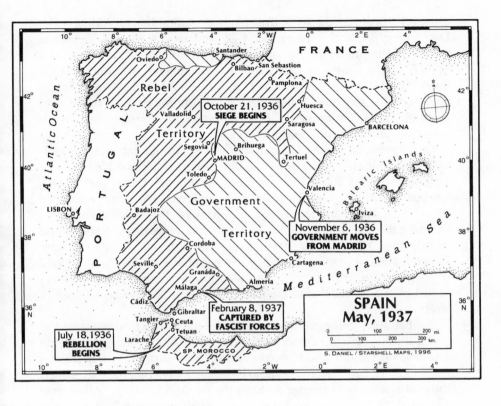

SPAIN
May, 1937

S. DANIEL / STARSHELL MAPS, 1996

prospect Spry viewed with dread.[6] The Committee to Aid Spanish Democracy, with the respected CCF member Reverend Benjamin Spence as chairman but with communists Tim Buck and A.A. MacLeod as two of the four vice-chairmen, was the only significant CP-CCF united front effort in Canadian history. Spry could not have been happy about another outcome of Bethune's departure for Spain, namely, that sending him, a communist, as head of the medical mission immensely raised the profile of the Communist Party.

Yet in going to Spain, Bethune was acting out of characteristic individualism, not on instructions from the Communist Party. He had been a member of the CP from November 1935, although this affiliation was not openly known. The Canadian party followed the directives of the Communist International. Based in Moscow, the Comintern began debating the possibility of sending volunteers to assist the Republic on 26 July 1936. But the idea was not publicly endorsed by Soviet leader Joseph Stalin until 15 October.[7] By then, Bethune was already well along in his departure arrangements and would sail on the *Empress of Britain* in just over a week. Bethune waited on no man, not even the man of steel.

For Bethune, going to Spain brought him to the flashpoint of the world conflict between democracy and fascism. But in joining the democratic ranks, Bethune also hoped to take the issue further, to help spark a revolutionary outburst. In his radio broadcasts from Spain, he described the civil war as 'the opening battle of the world revolution.' Adventure and the thrill of danger also attracted him to Spain. Hazen Sise, who was a driver in the blood transfusion unit from its inception, confided to his diary in December 1936 that Bethune was strongly motivated by a compulsion to aid the anti-fascist cause, but that he was also 'a little in love with death.'[8]

Another subject of dispute is why Bethune was recalled in disgrace from Spain. This hornet's nest has been prodded again by a remarkable report recently obtained from the Communist International archives in Moscow and deposited in the National Archives of Canada. (See Appendix 1 for a translation of the report.) Before examining it, however, we should set out some of the traditional explanations for why he was ordered back to Canada.

The justification of the day is contained in Bethune's official letter of resignation as head of the blood transfusion unit. In view of the fact that the unit 'is now operating as an efficient, well-organised institute,' he wrote, 'it is clear to me that my function as chief ... has come to a natural end ... If the resignation is accepted I will at once proceed to Canada to carry out propaganda work ...' These clipped, proper phrases, however, concealed a detailed, dramatic, and messy divorce. Two of Bethune's close associates in the transfusion team – Sise and Sorensen – and Ted Allan, who arrived on the scene after Bethune had begun to jump the rails, have all left recollections or written about the incident.

Sise's letters and diaries suggest the following explanation for Bethune's recall from Spain in 1937. There were conflicts with the Spanish staff, especially the doctors, which can be traced to medical, political, cultural, and personal differences. Sise goes so far as to attribute the problems to Spanish xenophobia, exhibited, in particular, by the chauvinistic Dr Antonio Calebras.[9] The Spanish authorities and doctors were dubious of Bethune's expertise in the area of blood transfusion, since he was known primarily as a surgeon. They appear to have regarded him as parasitizing the existing blood transfusion work of Dr Frederick Duran Jordá, whose Barcelona blood collection system was in place before Bethune arrived, although it did not work directly at the front lines, as Bethune's did.[10] For their part, the Canadians questioned the qualifications and practices of the Spanish medical staff. Dr Calebras 'had attached some of his relatives to the unit and they were drawing pay and supplies.' Calebras's sister-in-law was apparently collecting two salaries, which infuriated Bethune. Another irritant was that some family members of the Spanish staff ate meals in the unit kitchen, although such petty abuses of CASD funds were not confined to the Spanish.[11]

Temperamentally, Bethune could be irascible and high-handed, character traits which must have been exacerbated under the pressure, danger, and defeats of the war. Sorensen, his interpreter and an active supporter – probably a member – of the Communist Party of Canada, was sometimes ashamed of Bethune's arrogance. In a Madrid bank, for instance, Bethune demanded that the teller serve him immediately because of his status. Spanish authorities, too, were not spared Bethune's wrath. During an interrogation by the Spanish military, for instance, Sorensen found that he had to soften, in translation, Bethune's hostile replies and considered Bethune fortunate not to have been disciplined.[12]

Bethune's independence and flair for publicity also made some Spanish government officials nervous. A large number of foreigners, many of them news correspondents, congregated at the transfusion unit's headquarters. The constant favourable press coverage Bethune's operation received may have made the Spanish jealous.[13] His innovative idea of creating a film about the Instituto Hispano-Canadiense de Transfusión de Sangre showed typical panache. He convinced the CASD to supply the funds and enlisted the help of a Hungarian photographer, Geza Karpathi (later known by his screen acting name, Charles Korvin), and an American news correspondent, Herbert Kline. Together they produced the film *Heart of Spain* about the transfusion service. But taking pictures and collecting information at the front – both integral to any film project – were deemed by some Spaniards to be highly suspect.[14]

A climate of suspicion and fear of treachery poisoned Republican Spain, and this also helped lead to Bethune's recall. The elected government was always a tenuous coalition of leftist and centrist parties, fractured by internal jealousies. Beginning with the siege of Madrid in November 1936, 'loyalty was everywhere suspect,' wrote Hugh Thomas. Reporters asked fascist general Emilio Mola, at the head of the four columns of troops descending on the city, which one would take it. The 'fifth column' of secret fascist sympathizers inside the city, he boasted. An already edgy world immediately acquired a new phrase for treachery.[15] Despite the fact that no important civilian support for Franco materialized in Republican territory, the Spanish government took Mola's words zealously to heart. The campaign against internal enemies became particularly vicious in the spring of 1937, when an internal war erupted, a war against political dissidents of all stripes and perceived enemies of the Republic. Throughout March and April 1937, the Canadian Communist Party newspaper, the *Daily Clarion*, reported that the Spanish government was 'hitting hard at spies,' with the police breaking up alleged spy rings. Terror gripped Republican Spain, mirroring the purge of 'wreckers,' 'saboteurs,' and 'Trotskyists' in the Soviet Union.[16] In such a climate, even those whose pulse throbbed with hatred for fascism but whose behaviour gave the least cause for doubt fell under suspicion. Bethune, unfortunately, was one such.

The spring of 1937 was also a period in which the Spanish Republican government reorganized and began to take control of the many groups which had sprung up, willy-nilly, amidst the chaos following the war's outbreak. The blood transfusion unit was one of the agencies the government wanted under its command. On 2 March 1937 the unit was incorporated into the Spanish military and placed under a control board of two Spanish doctors and Bethune.[17] But the change contributed to a schism between Bethune and the Spaniards. Feeling constrained and dissatisfied, Bethune reacted irrationally. One sign of this was a bizarre cable on 12 April to the CASD urging the committee to authorize him to withdraw the Canadian personnel and leave Spain.[18] According to Roderick Stewart and Ted Allan, Bethune also took to drinking heavily, and Allan believed he was close to a nervous breakdown.[19]

Reorganized in March, the Spanish-Canadian Blood Transfusion Unit was an efficient team conveying blood to the central sections of the front round the clock. Although it was conceived by Bethune, it became mainly a Spanish operation, maintained primarily by the Spanish staff of doctors, nurses, technicians, and support staff.[20] Allan later commented that he was less than impressed with some of the Spanish doctors. They 'were average human beings ... Some were republicans, some were anarchists, and some were right wing socialists.'[21] Indeed, Allan would subsequently assert that two of the Spanish doctors working at the institute were Franco sympathizers.[22] Dealing with political conflict, managing staff, and ensuring the smooth running of a bureaucracy was scarcely Bethune's forte.

Bethune's inability to fit into this new regime was pointed out by Tom Worsley, a British adventurer who worked closely but briefly with the Canadian doctor as a driver for the transfusion unit in February and March 1937. In a *roman-à-clef* written immediately after his return from Spain, Worsley portrayed Bethune harshly, but showed a keen eye for the conflicts within the organization which forced Bethune's departure. Worsley's fictional reconfiguration of Bethune, 'Rathbone,' was a bombastic empire-builder, holding court for the foreign press, spending money lavishly, and rushing to military confrontations like an ambulance-chasing lawyer. (The importance of the fact that Bethune was the doctor in the ambulance sometimes eluded Worsley.) In February-March 1937, 'Rathbone' was absent from Madrid and the institute for a full month. (Bethune's frequent absences from Madrid were also observed by Allan, and chronologies by Sise and Sorensen confirm that he was away from Madrid from late January until early March 1937.)[23] With 'Rathbone' gone, tensions festered. The Spanish medical staff were partly irate with him, but they were also locked in a feud with his secretary. 'Gretchen,' as Worsley called her, was 'a big, blonde Swede' whose 'striking appearance and warm nature had made her a well-known figure in Madrid.'[24]

'Gretchen' and her relationship to Bethune are subjects until now unmentioned in biographies of Bethune. But some facts about her have recently been unveiled in the extraordinary document which, as mentioned above, has been recently obtained from records of the Communist International in Moscow. This report contains revelations which confirm some of Worsley's observations, and it makes still more serious allegations relating to her, Bethune, and his recall from Spain.

The report should first be put into context. Written by an anonymous figure in the Spanish government, it reflects the state of extreme suspicion ruling the government and its Communist Party ally in the spring of 1937. Its contents suggest that someone in the government had launched a vendetta against Bethune and was ready to raise any argument, specious or not, against him. It also indicates that Worsley's 'Gretchen' corresponds with a Swedish woman, identified only as Kajsa. The report confirms that Kajsa was Bethune's secretary at the institute. Other sources identify her as Bethune's lover, too. In a conversation with me in 1995, Allan indicated that in early 1937 he chanced upon Bethune in bed with a naked young Swedish woman, a liaison confirmed in interviews of Henning Sorensen by Roderick Stewart. Notes by Sise from the time also contain a cryptic reference to 'Kaijsa' and 'language difficulty' at the institute.[25]

Kajsa remains mostly an enigma, but even the partial image we have of her suggests that Bethune must have found her highly attractive. In the only other reference I have found to her – the unpublished memoirs of Kate Mangan, a Briton who worked in the Republican press and censorship office in 1936 and 1937 – Kajsa is pictured as a dazzling woman. Mangan wrote that in every unit 'there was always one Swede. We had Kajsa von Rothman. She was a handsome giantess with red-gold flowing hair ... She had worked previously with Dr Bethune and had started the war wearing trousers and riding a motor-bike. With us she wore flowing, Isadora Duncan garments.'[26]

Spanish authorities stared down their noses at Kajsa, seeing her as a woman of loose morals, a supporter of the anarchists (and hence suspect to the communists), and, more ominously, a spy. Suspicions about the large number of foreigners gathering at 36 Principe de Vergara caused Sorensen to inform the Spanish government. On 4 January 1937 the police arrived and took everyone into custody, Bethune, Sorensen, and Sise included. The three Canadians were released, the report said, but 'not so the rest. Among those detained were a commander, Harturg [Hartung], of Austrian nationality, and one Kajsa. This last one, after checking many things out, was set free. The commander disappeared and they say he was executed.' Kajsa was later at risk of being detained again for asking suspicious questions of a bridge guard, but was saved by the transfusion team's chauffeur. Nonetheless, the report writer remained convinced she was engaged in acts that hinted of spying: 'Currently, and due to Kajsa's initiative, it is said, there exists with the transfusion team a series of detailed maps, similar to military maps.'

The report also contained attempts to implicate Bethune in nefarious acts, although the specific charges are utterly spurious – vague allegations about the disappearance of jewellery and documents from a sealed room at 36 Principe de Vergara – as well as this outlandish bid to portray him as a spy: 'A suspicious fact which should also be considered is that Mr. Bethune openly takes detailed notes of the locations of bridges, crossroads, distances between determined points, journey times, etc., writing it all down carefully.' Such details, of course, were vital information to the transfusion team, which delivered blood across a broad sector of the front day and night. The accusations are important mainly because they illustrate the widespread state of paranoia and, specifically, the extent to which some Spanish officials were prepared to manufacture a case to condemn Bethune.

The report points out one other fact about Bethune's leaving Spain, that the Canadians in the transfusion unit were themselves critical of him and instrumental in having the CASD bring him back to Canada. The Spanish report declares that Ted Allan and Henning Sorensen had written a letter of complaint to the Communist Party of Canada demanding his recall. Notes by Sorensen indicate that already by 18 March the Canadian Communist Party was being advised of trouble with Bethune. On 5 April, according to Sorensen, he, Hazen Sise, and Allen May 'persuaded Beth to leave.'[27] Snubbed by his own comrades, Bethune's exit was inevitable. The transfusion unit continued to operate. The fate of Kajsa von Rothman is, regrettably, unknown.[28]

What Bethune accomplished in Spain is, on the surface, easy to summarize. In his authoritative history of the war, Hugh Thomas declared forthrightly that 'the medical assistance to the Republic brought many advances of military and civilian surgery and general therapy. Of these, the most outstanding were the remarkable developments in the technique of blood transfusion inspired by the Canadian Dr. Norman Bethune.'[29] Thomas was generous to Bethune, but he underemphasized the blood transfusion advances the Spanish government had made in the brief months between the outbreak of the war in July 1936 and Bethune's arrival in November. There was a system in place when Bethune landed in Spain. But it was centred in Barcelona, far from the front lines. Bethune's great insight was to perceive the need for blood *at the front*. Moreover, at his baptism into the horrors of the Spanish war, the front and the blood supply were virtually on top of one another – in Madrid. In the midst of Franco's brutal attack on the city, it was Bethune's genius to rise above the immediate chaos and visualize what would become his greatest service in Spain. It became clear to him that in this battle raging in a major city the two conditions for an immediately successful blood service were at hand – demand and supply. The idea of large-scale, free civilian donations of blood was a breakthrough at the time. The transfusion unit attracted thousands of donors. Bethune noted that donating blood gave Spaniards a tangible way to express their anti-Franco sentiment and their solidarity with front-line fighters. He would later apply the same lesson in China, despite being initially stymied by cultural resistance to donating blood.[30] Bethune's accomplishment in taking blood transfusion directly to the battle front would also save lives after the Spanish Civil War. During the Second World War, the Western Allies studied and learned from the lessons of the Spanish experience in front-line transfusion.[31]

Spain revealed Bethune to be more than just an insightful medical innovator; it also unveiled an intuitive promoter. In Spain he reached the height of his astute grasp of the means to attract publicity. The genius of the Spanish-Canadian Blood Transfusion Institute was not just the precious work it performed but also its propaganda value back home. For reasons of personal ego and national pride, he pressed ahead with a service that put Canada on the map and greatly increased the financial contributions that flowed from Canada in support of the Spanish cause. As Bethune saw it, the Scots and English had their field hospitals and ambulance services. Canada should be no less prominent in the anti-fascist cause. The trucks prominently labelled Servicio Canadiense de Transfusión de Sangre were highly visible signs of international solidarity. But they were also early expressions of Canadian pride, of Canadian nationalism. Canadians in the 1930s were not used to such up-front nationalist swagger. Here was a doctor who pushed Canada into the limelight in the anti-fascist cause, and Canadians – even wracked as they were by the Depression – responded by donating tens of thousands of dollars to the unit. Moreover, Bethune's efforts also aided recruitment for the Canadian contingent in Spain, the Mackenzie-Papineau Battalion. Certainly it was disproportionately large in size for Canada's meagre population. From a population base one-tenth that of the United States, for example, Canada sent about one-third as many recruits.[32] Bethune's prominence and Canadian pride in his achievements are part of the reason for that high enlistment rate.

Bethune's sure sense of publicity and his grasp of the propaganda of the deed had several lasting legacies. The film he conceived of, *Heart of Spain*, was a fitting tribute to the courage of the Spanish people and an effective fund-raising tool for Bethune when he returned from Spain for a North American tour. His broadcasts from Spain and the pamphlet *The Crime on the Road: Malaga-Almeria* are passionate memorials to the great battle waged against fascism.

Perhaps the last word on Bethune's work in Spain should be left to Tom Worsley, who described Bethune's character harshly, but who added that it was

suited to the earlier phase [of the war] into which the virtues of an adventurer fitted. He was really lost when individual dramatics had to be subordinated to a collective discipline. I am sorry that I never saw him at the very beginning, when he arrived headlong in Madrid in November 1936 ... and set about building up the Blood Transfusion Institute. He must have been in his element in those anxious days when Franco was expected in the city at any moment; and when he bustled through the trenches, visiting the boys and cheering them with his optimistic and dramatic outbursts. By the time I arrived that was all over. His work was really finished. His contribution to Spain – and it was very considerable – had already been given.[33]

Spain challenged Bethune and demanded many changes of him. Some of them were profound, some apparently superficial. In an article published in the Communist Party newspaper the Daily Clarion *on 6 September 1937, four months after he left Spain, Bethune recalled one of the transformations he made on arrival in Madrid – he shaved off his moustache. That simple alteration in his appearance, however, reflected political tensions in the Spanish Republic that would ultimately return to haunt Bethune.*

A Bethune Incident
Why the Doctor Shaved Off His Moustache

As Told to Allen May

Canadians who first became acquainted with the features of Dr. Norman Bethune through pictures published by the Committee to Aid Spanish Democracy when he first came to Spain in November will recall that he wore a moustache.

Pictures today show him clean shaven – and thereby hangs a tale.

Bethune likes to tell the story himself because he finds it both amusing and significant.

He arrived in Madrid in November bearing money raised by the workers of Canada, his own medical skill and a commission from the United Front of his fellow countrymen to discover the best means of aiding the Spanish people in their fight for economic and political freedom. He knew not a word of Spanish and his only knowledge of Spain was that it was being threatened by Fascist bullets. His intentions were quite simple and entirely innocent.

The day after he arrived he was having coffee in the cafe attached to his hotel where the proprietor spoke some English. The place was crowded with ferocious looking militiamen all armed. Bethune noticed one who seemed to be examining him very narrowly, but paid no more attention, until he went out into the street and found himself followed by the same fellow.

'I stopped in front of a store and this lad came up to me jabbering in great excitement,' Bethune related. 'He put his hand in his pocket and I knew what that meant even if I couldn't understand his words – I have seen enough tough guys in the States to realize that he had a gun in that pocket. I went back into the hotel and he came right after me.

'I asked the concierge what the man wanted and he told me the fellow thought I was a fascist.

'"Why?" I asked and he said "the man thought I looked like one because I was so well dressed and wore a moustache, besides he had heard me mention the word 'fascist.'"

'"He says you had a funny look on your face when you said it," the concierge told me.

'Then they got into an argument and I went up to my room. A minute later there was a knock at the door and when I opened it there were five – not one or two, mind you, but five – guards with rifles and a young chap with a brief case who said he was from the police and he was very sorry but I was under suspicion and he would have to see my papers.

'All I had was my passport and a safe conduct from the Spanish embassy from Paris and I felt pretty uncomfortable while he was looking through them.

'They seemed to satisfy him, however, because he gave them back and said I was all right. It was quite a relief when he went out the door. He hadn't been gone a second, though, when there was another knock and in walked Henning Sorensen. I was never happier to see anyone in my life. Henning had been in the country for some weeks and I knew he spoke the language.

'I remembered a letter I was carrying for him from Montreal and gave it to him.

'In bounded the police official like a jack-in-the-box and grabbed the letter.

'I must read it,' he said.

'He tore open the envelope and the first word his eye fell on was "Darling." That was good because he merely turned the letter over and looked at the bottom of the last page where he found another good English term of affection.

'He excused himself and explained to the suspicious militiaman who had followed him into the room that we were not spies. They both went out. Henning was embarrassed but I was glad to be out of a tight spot even at the expense of his feelings.

'We weren't arrested but I shaved my moustache off in a hurry, I can tell you. It's not safe even to look like a fascist in this country.'

Two months after leaving Canada, Bethune sent back his first official report to the Committee to Aid Spanish Democracy. Much had been accomplished in a brief time, Bethune could proudly state.

Servicio Canadiense de Transfusión de Sangre
Principe de Vergara 36
Madrid
Dec. 17/36

Dear Ben:
This is really the first time since my arrival in this country that I can give you definite news and detailed information.

I am glad to say that we are now completely organized and settled in for work. As I wrote you before (I hope you received my letter) unless we were able to offer the Government some definite proposal and concrete scheme our efforts would peter out – by this I mean I would simply go into a hospital as a surgeon and that would be the end of the 'Canadian Unit.' Now it seemed better to emulate England and Scotland and establish ourselves as a definite entity. England has the 'English Hospital,' Scotland has the 'Scottish Ambulance.'

So with this in mind and after making several blind starts (such as the two days we spent at the front with the International Brigade) Sorensen and I left for Paris to collect apparatus and car.

No cars are for sale in Spain. I had in mind a Ford station car, as a compromise between a truck and a car. It must carry about 1½ tons of cargo, could be used as an ambulance if needed for such and yet it would be handy enough to transport 4 people in comparative comfort.

I couldn't buy this car in Paris. I had to go to London. Here I was able to pick one up for one hundred and seventy-five pounds sterling and with alterations such as luggage rack on top, built in boxes etc. made a good type of transportation for our purpose so I bought complete equipment for a mobile blood transfusion service.

The idea of mobility was always kept in mind so such apparatus as refrigerators, auto clave, incubators etc. all were purchased to run by gasoline or kerosene and to be independent of electrical power.

The refrigerator is Electrolux run by kerosene and very efficient. The auto clave (for sterilization of solutions, bottles, etc.) is run by gasoline, the incubator by kerosene and the distilled water still by kerosene.

So our four major pieces of apparatus run to about one ton in weight (the auto clave weighs about 450 lbs itself). They take up the major part of the interior.

Then in addition we have 175 pieces of glassware of all varieties and kinds – vacuum bottles, blood flasks, drip bottles, containers etc. We have 3 complete direct blood transfusion sets of the latest English model (Froud syringe) microscope haemocytometers, complete set of chest instruments, 2000 sets of type 2 and 3 blood serum for testing blood groups, hurricane lamps, gas masks etc.

In all, our equipment consists of 1,375 separate pieces. We have enough chemicals to make up solutions for intravenous injections of physiological serums, glucose and sodium citrate to last us for three months, I estimate.

These chemicals are packed in water-tight tin cases and each is weighed out separately so that by adding each package to a given amount of distilled water the proper strength of solution is obtained.

Now we are installed in a 15 room flat formerly occupied by a German diplomat (Fascist, now in Berlin) very magnificent and palatial at the above address. Just above us are the S.R.I. [Socorro Rojo Internacional] head offices. We are working under their protection. They are the best organized and most powerful health organization in Spain and much superior to the International Red Cross (this organization is very suspiciously Fascist between you and I) or the weak Spanish Red Cross.

The S.R.I. was formed before the revolution to care for the political prisoners and their families who suffered Fascist oppression and since the revolution has gradually taken over the majority of the sanitary services of the country. Their work in the rescue of orphans and evacuation of abandoned areas is tremendous. They run about 1,000 orphanages, camps, hospitals, creches etc. in Spain. All their leaders are party people – as everywhere in Spain the people who lead the major services are Communists – they do the hard and dirty work.

Now as to our organization. Through the press and daily over the local radio we broadcast appeals for blood donors. As a result we have thousands of volunteers and are busy grouping them and card indexing them. We have now 800 and in a few days will have over 1,000. There are about 56 hospitals in the City. We have surveyed the entire situation and have a list of them containing the information as to size, capacity, addresses, under what organization, telephone, chief surgeon, type of service etc. A large map of the City (4 × 5 ft.) in our office (the former library, the walls entirely lined by 8,000 books, gold brocade curtains and Aubusson carpets!) gives at once the route to the hospitals.

We collect the blood every day from a selected group of donors types I, II, III, IV. We are running about 1 gallon daily just now. This is stored in our refrigerator. On call from the hospital the blood flasks are transferred to heated vacuum bottles and carried in knapsacks with additional bottles, warm physiological serum and glucose solution plus a complete sterilized tin box containing: towel, forceps, knife, syringe, catgut, group testing serums. We have 15 complete sets of these.

So on arrival we're ready to start work at once. We go to the man and decide what he needs – either blood or physiological serum, or glucose or a combination of these. If blood is needed on account of acute exsanguination we 'group' him at once with our serum. This is done by a prick of the finger, a glass stick and serum and takes 2 minutes, then after grouping we give him the blood of the type needed (type I, II, III, or IV).

If in doubt we can always give IV as this is called the 'Universal' donor. We are not sure how long the citrated blood will keep good in our refrigerators but we are experimenting and hope for several weeks.

We have plans to branch out and give the service up in the Guadarrama Mountains up to a distance of 100 miles from the City later and might need another car but this won't be for several months yet.

Now as to personnel – I, myself am of course director, Henning Sorensen is Liaison officer, Hazen Sise is driver and general utility man (he is a Canadian, the son of Paul Sise, president of the Northern Electric Co. of Montreal, a talented young architect) then we have 2 Spanish medical students, a Spanish Biologist and Mrs. Celia Greenspan of New York (wife of M. Greenspan the journalist) as technician. We have a staff of 4 servants, a cook, 2 maids and laundry man, also a military armed guard for our door. We are all well and happy.

About one quarter of the City is badly damaged and abandoned except by troops. 300,000 people, mostly women, children and aged have been evacuated. Between 7–8 thousand civilians have been killed by bombardment in the last month and many more thousand wounded.

Morale is excellent. Madrid won't fall but will be the tomb of Fascism!

Junker machines (3 motor bombers) came over yesterday at 6 p.m. accompanied by 24 pursuit planes; they dropped several tons of bombs. I took some photos of a hit hospital in the afternoon. Their 100 and 250 kilo bombs make an awful mess!

Just now there is a lull but Franco has declared he will not leave one stone standing in Madrid. Well let him try.

The water is still good. No epidemics have broken out as yet. The electric light is on but the gas is very low and reserved for hospitals. Coal is practically gone and meat is scarce, no milk, butter, sugar but plenty of vegetables and fruit (oranges and apples).

Well, we are here 'for the duration' as we used to say in 1914. I can only say how grateful I am for the wonderful backing of the committee and the people of Canada.

The $1,800.00 I came over with – $1,000.00 went to the Oviedo Miners for Anti Tetanus Serum and the $800.00 was spent in travelling and living expenses for Sorensen and myself in Spain and back to London (incidentally I would have been lost in these early days without his Spanish and French). The $3,000.00 received in Paris and the additional $4,000.00 in London went into the car and equipment ($1,200.00 in duty, *refundable*) leaving a balance of cash in hand now sufficient to keep the unit in this country under present conditions for 3 months more. Of this cash on hand, $2,000.00 is in American Express orders and the balance ($500.00) in Spanish Pesetas and the dollar is fixed by the Government at 11 pesetas or roughly 9 cents. Prices are spiked and there is no inflation.

I am enclosing a photo but will send you a better one next week. This was taken on our arrival last week. I enclose also samples of our stationery. A *Medal* is being struck for our donors with a *Star* for each donation. Will send you next week a photo and a badge also.

This letter is going out with a member of the Scottish Ambulance which is returning to Scotland to be re-organized.

Best of luck to everybody and a Merry Christmas.

Your comrade
Norman Bethune

P.S. This unit is causing considerable interest among the Foreign Press but I am keeping back the story until next week, when I have informed the Press Censor (an Austrian Comrade –!) it may be released as you will probably hear about it before this letter reaches you.

N.B.

Bethune had experience with radio in the early 1930s, having written his radio play on tuberculosis. So when Spanish government short-wave radio stations beaming signals to North America invited him to speak, he readily contributed several broadcasts. These were reprinted by the CASD in Canada as part of a pamphlet which also included broadcasts by the eminent British scientist J.B.S. Haldane and Hazen Sise. The broadcasts are further demonstration of Bethune's skill in conveying the terrors and inspiration of the anti-fascist struggle.

Messages from Madrid

Canada Greets Spain
December 24, 1936

Comrades of Spain. I, and my comrades of the Canadian Blood Transfusion Service, have the honour to be in Spain as the representatives of the Canadian Committee to Aid Spanish Democracy.

This Committee, with headquarters in Toronto, Canada, is formed of workers and intellectuals, of liberals and socialists and Communists. We, the United Front of Canada, join hands with the United States of Spain – the International Anti-Fascists of the old and new worlds.

When we first came to Spain, two months ago, you used to talk to us about your war, your revolution, but now you are beginning to speak about our war, Spain's war, Canada's war, England's war, the war of the workers of the world. And that is a good sign. It is a sign that the causes and consequences of our struggle are deeper and more far reaching than the boundaries of Spain; that they stretch across the Pyrenees, across the English Channel, across the Atlantic and include the world.

World Significance of Spain's Struggle

The revolution of the workers against the economic, religious and intellectual slavery happened to have occurred this year in Spain. It might just as well have happened in a dozen other countries but that you had the courage, the dignity and the audacity to face your problems with more open eyes, firmer lips and stouter hearts than the workers of the rest of the world.

What Spain does today, what you Spaniards do tomorrow, will decide the future of the world for the next 100 years. If you are defeated the world will fall back into the new dark ages of Fascism – if you are successful, as we are confident you will be successful, we will go forward into the glories of the new golden age of economic and political democracy.

Remember we Canadian workers are with you. We have come here as into the opening battle of the world revolution. Your fight is our fight. Your victory is our victory. Ask us how we can help you. You will find us ready to respond.

– Salud

Practical International Comradeship
December 29, 1936

It gives me great pleasure to describe my personal observations regarding the care of the sick and wounded in Madrid. I believe I am competent to do so on account of my experience not only as a doctor who served in the Great War of 1914–1918 but as one who held, up to the time of his arrival in Spain, the post of Chief of Service, Department of Thoracic Surgery and Bronchoscopy, Sacré Coeur Hospital, Montreal, Canada. So what I will say will be based on personal observations.

There are in Madrid today 57 hospitals with a total of over ten thousand beds. They range from huge Military Hospitals, such as the Palace Hotel, each with over a thousand beds, entirely confined to wounded cases, down to small 50 bed special hospitals for cancer, etc. Not only are the usual sicknesses of the civil population being carefully taken care of but the thousands of wounded are receiving expert care and attention.

Madrid Hospital Scene

As an example of this come with me to a large military hospital such as the Palace Hotel. Its operating room, in its great dining room, with tremendous crystal chandeliers and glittering gold mirrors, has eight tables, side by side, each staffed by two doctors, an anaesthetist and nurse. Here some of the most famous surgeons of Spain, the equal, to say the least, of any country in the world, are at work. Each on his own speciality.

This first one is a famous brain surgeon who is now exploring a wound of the head. He once received $5,000 for a similar operation in private practise, now he does it gladly for his $1.00 a day.

Next to him a great abdominal surgeon is sewing up carefully multiple perforations of the intestine of a soldier shot through the abdomen. Notice his movements. They are as quick, as expert, as careful, as those which made him an International figure in his profession. This is his 20th operation today. He is tired and weary but his love of his countrymen, his pride in his art is as high as ever.

On the next table is a German soldier (an anti-fascist) shot through the thigh with a dum-dum bullet – the exit of its passage is large enough to hold one's clenched fist. He must have anti-tetanus serum and a blood transfusion before he leaves the table.

Here is another – a Pole – shot through the shoulder and the bullet has not yet appeared. There is no guess work. Before he comes on the table the X-ray shows exactly where the bullet may be successfully extracted.

The Kind of Help Needed

Now all this is very spectacular. But what is happening above in the wards. Here they lie – row on row – Spaniards, English, German, Italians, French, Belgium, Scotch, Irish, American. The wounded soldiers of the greatest Anti-Fascist army the world has yet seen. They represent the United Front of International Anti-Fascism. They have fought this war for you and for me. They need your help.

'How?' you ask. First they need nurses who can speak their own language. It is more important that a wounded man should be nursed by a woman who can speak his own language than be operated on by a surgeon who may understand nothing more than the technical problem involved. Then they need the food of their home-land prepared by these hands who nurse them.

The delights of scrambled eggs on toast with a cup of English tea would be like a gift from heaven to stomachs not yet attuned to olive oil and Spanish beans. So I see the need for an International Nursing Corps of French, German and English nurses; principally to nurse the sick and wounded of the heroes of the International Brigade.

What Spain Needs

Now this is what is needed in Spain:

1. More physicians who speak French or German, if not Spanish.

2. More brain surgeons, on account of the high proportion of the head injuries owing to lack of proper protection of the skull by steel helmets. The Chief Surgeon of one of the fronts told me on Christmas Day that 70 percent of head wounds could have been prevented by the use of steel helmets – but he added bitterly – 'France and England would not let us buy steel helmets to save our lives against German and Italian bullets.'

3. More foreign nurses to be attached to hospitals treating the wounded from the International Brigade.

4. A convalescent home and club for the German, French, English, Italian and Polish members of the International Brigade. Think of being in a country, say like these Englishmen in a German Battalion, of being wounded and in a hospital and being operated on and nursed by those who could not speak a single word of English – of being discharged and wandering about Madrid lonely, discouraged and sad.

Now who in England will provide these. Here is a project to make happier the lives of some of the finest of young British manhood I have ever had the pleasure to meet. These young men, some of them not yet 20 but most between 20 and 30, are fighting for ideals as pure, as strongly felt, as animated [as] their Anglo-Saxon Ancestors in the Wars of the Crusades. And they are fighting to save this land, this pleasant land of Spain, from the grasps of the Fascist infidel – who denies by word and action belief in the virtue of mankind, his ability to govern himself, freed from political dictatorship and economic oppression.

5. We need more ambulances. More splints. More X-ray films.

Happy New Year

We would also be glad to hear from those who are listening in nightly as we are not sure of the number of our audience. Will you drop me a line?

And now we wish you a Happy New Year.

We are happy here too because we know that 1937 will see the International Fascists driven from this land forever. Spain will be free and the second great fight against the threat of the New Dark Ages of Fascism will be defeated [sic]. All men of good will should not only earnestly desire but must purposefully act towards that end.

– Salud

They Made the Supreme Sacrifice
January 1, 1937

There has been heavy fighting today. As we were working at our job in the hospitals, the staccato tack-tack-tack of machine guns comes through the windows, as if they were firing at the end of the street, so clear is this cold Spanish winter air. In truth, they were nearly a mile distant.

The burst of field gun-fire has been almost continuous, reminding your commentator of the barrages on the Western Front in 1915. To these dangers are added the attacks of Fascist bombers, attended by their fighting escort.

German Plane Brought Down

In today's attack, by 15 German and Italian bombers, five of the escort fighters attacked one solitary Spanish Government pursuit plane. They set him on fire, but, as he fell, overcome in the unequal contest, he charged full-out, head-on, into one of Franco's planes. They fell together, in flames, crashing into a vine covered hill one hundred yards apart. Both pilots were killed instantly.

As I happened to be at a clearing station hospital close by, we walked across the fields to inspect the wreckage. I took from the Fascist machine the plate off its engine and have it in front of me as I speak. The pilot was a young German military pilot.

Made the Supreme Sacrifice

Now within sight of these planes is the cemetery of the International Brigade. Here row on row lie the bodies of those men who died as Anti-Fascists to save Spain from the fate of their own countries. They – these workers, students and intellectuals, who so dedicated their young lives in the cause of Spanish Democracy – are from every country in Europe. They are from Italy, Germany, France, England, Scotland, Ireland, Poland, Czechoslovakia and Austria.

These young men volunteered fully and they travelled, many in disguise, thousands of miles from their native lands, working their way out secretly to escape the police terrorism. They left their wives and families and in the pride of their young strength and fine political convictions, died under this old Spanish sun, on the bare hills, among the vines and olive trees of this beautiful land surrounded by people of whom not more than a handful could speak their own language, facing overwhelming odds of trained mercenary professional troops. Against a military machine dominated by German and Italian Staff Officers, fighting with rifles, some of them dating before the so-called Great War of 1914, against modern German and Italian machine guns, without steel helmets or proper clothing.

From German cities, from Italian towns, from French villages, English farms, Scottish highlands and American plains, these serious, calm-eyed, earnest workmen and intellectuals and students came, thinking not of their personal comfort or safety, fighting not for money (their pay was 10 pesetas – about 50¢ a day) fighting not for King or Country, not at the frantic urging of selfish bank barons or masters of finance, who saw their profits in danger, but fighting and dying for an ideal of human freedom. From that same high motivation spoken of so many centuries ago – 'Greater love hath no man than this that he should lay down his life for his friend.' And that 'friend' was not only the Spanish worker groaning under the cruel heel and iron fist of monopoly capitalism and religious bigotry, but the workers of the world suffering under these same masters in other countries, in your country and in mine.

Unknown Soldiers of Democracy
And here they lie, quietly and still. And see what is written above their heads: 'Volunteers of the International Brigade' – 'Who died as heroes for the liberty of the Spanish people and the happiness and progress of humanity.' Above each grave is written his name, his nationality and the date of his death.

Madrid: Peaceful amid War
January 2, 1937
Madrid is, paradoxically enough, the most peaceful city in Europe.

It is a city at equilibrium within itself, a city without the intense class antagonisms and discords that are called disorder in any other city. That is due to its homogeneous society – the workers, the small shop-keepers and the petit-bourgeois all moulded into one class with one idea – winning the war against the Fascist aggressor.

So, as in a family or clan in which there is internal peace although the family or clan may be fighting against its external enemies. No police are needed to maintain the law. Every member, every citizen, is under the strict necessity of order – self-imposed and conscious.

Private property is respected – confiscated property belonging to the people at large, is equally respected. On large magnificent mansions, which once belonged to the late so-called nobility, one may see signs such as these: 'Citizens, this property belongs to you, respect it.' Note the wording of the sign – not 'Belongs to the State' – the State as an institution superior to and above the people, but – 'belongs to you' – belongs to me. So, if you or I damage it, we are damaging our own property.

There is absolutely no looting. This is clear from one manifest fact – the things which are looted in a war are first of all articles of necessity such as clothing and food. Later come the luxuries – jewels, fur coats, etc. Now the people of Madrid are wearing the same clothes as they wore before the rebellion in spite of the large quantities of fine clothes left by fleeing Fascists and members of the so-called upper classes.

Buying of necessities and clothing is brisk in the shops. I was in a large departmental store today and saw a woman of the so-called middle classes buy a tricycle for her boy of 10 and a large doll for her daughter of 5.

We were heavily bombed from the air today about 12 noon. Twelve huge Italian tri-motored bombers came over the city and bombed not positions of military importance, but a poor quarter of the city called Cuatro Caminos. This is a district some miles behind the front line, inhabited by the poorest people living in one or two storey mud and brick dwellings. The massacred victims were mainly women, children and old people.

Standing in a doorway as these huge machines flew slowly overhead, each one heavily loaded with bombs, I glanced up and down the streets. People hurried to 'refugios'; a hush fell over the city – it was a hunted animal crouched down in the grass, quiet and apprehensive. There is no escape, so be still. Then in the dead silence of the streets the songs of birds came startlingly clear in the bright winter air.

What is the object of these bombings of lowly civilian habitations? Is it to produce panic in the city? Because, if so, it is a completely cruel, useless and wanton endeavour. This people cannot be terrified. They are being treated by the Fascists as if they were soldiers bearing offensive arms. This is murder of defenceless civilians.

No one can realize what utter helplessness one feels when these huge death-ships are overhead. It is practically useless to go into a building – even a ten-storey building. The bombs tear through the roof, through every floor in the building and explode in the basement, bringing down concrete buildings as if they were made of matchwood.

It is not much safer to be in the basement of the lower floors, than in the upper stories. One takes shelter in doorways to be out of the way of falling masonry, huge pieces of facade and stone work. If the building you happen to be in is hit, you will be killed or wounded. If it is not hit, you will not be killed or wounded. One place is really as good as another.

After the bombs fall – and you can see them falling like great black pears – there is a thunderous roar. Clouds of dust and explosive fumes fill the air, whole sides of houses fall into the street. From heaps of huddled clothes on the cobblestones blood begins to flow – these were once live women and children.

Many are buried alive in the ruins. One hears their cries – they cannot be reached. Burst water and gas mains add to the danger. Ambulances arrive. The blackened and crumpled bodies of the still-alive are carried away.

Psychological Effects

Now observe the faces of, not the dead, but those who still live. Because it is the wished-for effect on them which is the motive for these massacres, not just the killing of a few hundred innocent civilians and the destruction of property, but the terrorising of hundreds of thousands who escaped this death. They stand and watch or work themselves at the rescue. Their lips are set and cold. They don't shout or gesticulate. They look at each other sorrowfully, and when they talk of the fascist assassins, their faces express fortitude, dignity and contempt.

These people have endured from the arrogance of wealth, the greed of the church, the poverty and oppression of centuries. This is just one more blow, one more lash of the whip. They have stood these blows, these lashes before and they will stand them to the end. They cannot be shaken.

Wars Contrasted: 1914–18 and 1936–37
January 5, 1937

This is an appeal, if such an appeal is necessary to any scientific or common-sense person, especially to psychologists and those interested in contemporaneous psychological problems, such as war, to come to Madrid and see their theories of 'Masses,' of 'Mobs,' put to the test of reality.

These fashionable theories, too many of those formulated in laboratories or in armchairs or from observation of lower animals, have been accepted by the laity as truths beyond the necessity of proof. But, if some of these theories of the 'mass men,' the 'mass women,' be subjected to the scrutiny of reality, there is a possibility of a wide divergence between theory and scientific observation.

Now what I am driving towards is this: Today the fashionable explanations of the individual are in terms introduced by Freud or Adler – in terms of sexual domination or the will-to-power. 'The instinct of the herd,' as Trotter calls it, the motives which animate the mass or the nation, as a people at war, is defined principally in terms of the defence of property. Now this is true of a capitalistic war, but it is not true of this war.

War Propaganda Methods and Motives

I remember the so-called Great War of 1914–1918 and compare to myself the emotions of the people of say London or Paris then to those of the people of Madrid today. In the former case, in the early days, there was a high-pitched almost hysterical feeling in the air, engendered by propaganda, a hatred of the Germans as beasts of prey against their aggression towards a peaceful people, of their ruthlessness towards the innocent bystander – Belgium. The true issues at stake were never clarified. The truth in full was never told.

Such old methods of propaganda are not seen now in these parts of Spain held by the government. The appeal now is deeper, more profound, more truthful. Franco and his mercenary troops, Moors, Foreign Legionnaires, Germans and Italians, are not only depicted as ruthless, immoral and vicious, but explained as why they are ruthless, immoral and vicious. They are shown as aggressors, against the most elementary rights of man.

It seems to me that such an appeal was seldom or never made – at least from our side, in the last war. And this simplification in propaganda of war motives – from Franco's side, the necessity of keeping the workers in subjection and on our side, the determination to end economic, religious and intellectual slavery, gives to these people in Madrid tremendous unity and power that must be seen to be believed.

A Holy War

It gives this war the aspect of a holy war, a religious war – and by that I mean the union of common sense rationalism with profound subconscious, only partly articulated instincts, one of these instincts is that a man should be – to call himself a man – free from dictatorship and from domination by his fellow man. The Spaniard is not fighting for 'King and Country,' he is fighting for his rights as a man. He is fighting for Spain of course because this is his beloved land, but for more than that.

The people of Madrid may be seen as a unified and consolidated mass of both emotional and intellectual forces. This gives them strength and endurance. Against the daily bombardment of German and Italian air planes, against hunger and cold. Nothing less than this unification of the intellect and the emotions could produce such profound belief in this rightness of their fight against the Fascist aggressor. And this is why the people of Spain are fighting so courageously, so fiercely, against International Fascism.

Here are no imported ideologies, no Moscow gold, no Third International dictatorship, and their motives in the struggle are indigenous to themselves. They arise from the local conditions of economics and religious oppression and by reason of their indigenous source they possess a gratifying growth and strength which makes their success assured.

In January, he sent CASD another summary of life under bombardment and the day-to-day work of the transfusion service.

Madrid Jan. 11–37

Dear Ben:
We have had a very hectic ten days as you may know and I haven't really had the time to sit down and write you a letter but as an Englishman is leaving today for Paris I felt I should take advantage of this and let you know the news.

Frank Pitcairn – author of 'A Reporter in Spain,' promised to write an article on our unit for the 'Daily Worker' of London whose correspondent he is. But as he hasn't turned up today – he stays with us – I expect he has left for another front.

Professor J.B.S. Haldane who stayed with us for two weeks, has returned to London and has promised to send 'The Clarion' an article on us. I think these would be better than one I might write myself.

As you know we have withstood the heaviest attack and the most serious effort of the Fascists to take the City since the first and second weeks of November. Their losses have been terrific – at least 5,000 (our papers say 10,000) Germans have been killed and Franco has taken the Moors away from Madrid and replaced them with fresh German troops. They thought they had a walk-over and advanced in exactly the same massed formation as they did in 1914–1915 in France. Our machine guns simply mowed them down. Our losses were 1 to 5 of theirs.

The International Brigade has suffered badly of course as they are shock troops but large reinforcements of French, German, English, Polish, Austrian and Italians – with some Americans and Canadians are arriving.

We have been having 2 & 4 raids a day for 2 weeks now and many thousands of non-combatants, women and children, have been killed. I was in the Telephonic Building the other day when it was shelled. However, it is very modern and strongly built. No great damage was done – a handful of people were killed only.

You simply can't get these people to take shelter during shelling and bombing!

Our night work is very eerie! We get a phone call for blood. Snatch up our packed bag, take 2 bottles (each 500 c.c.) – one of group IV and one of group II blood – out of the refrigerator and with our armed guard off we go through the absolutely pitch dark streets and the guns and machine guns and rifle shots sound like as if they were in the next block, although they are really half a mile away. Without lights we drive, stop at the hospital and with a search light in our hands find our way into the cellar principally. All the operating rooms in the hospitals have been moved into the basement to avoid falling shrapnel, bricks and stones coming through the operating room ceiling.

Our bag contains a completely sterilized box of instruments, towels etc. so we can start work at once. The man is lying most frequently on a stretcher so we kneel down beside him, prick the finger and on a slide put 1 drop each of Serum type II and type III. If his red blood cells are agglutinated by II and not by III – he is a type III. If agglutinated by II he is a III, if by both he is a type I, if neither, he is a group IV.

So now we know what blood he can take safely. If I, III or IV he gets our bottle of blood group IV (the universal blood). If he is a II he gets blood group II. He could also take IV but as these 'Universal Donors' are about only 45% of the people, we must use II's when we can. Then the proper blood is warmed in a pan of water and we are ready to start. The man is usually as white as the paper, mostly shocked, with an imperceptible pulse. He may be exsanguinated also and not so much shocked, but usually is both shocked and exsanguinated. We now inject novo-caine over the vein in the bend of the elbow, cut down and find the vein and insert a small glass Canula, then run the blood in. The change in most cases is spectacular. We give him always 500 c.c. of preserved blood and sometimes more and follow it up with saline of 5% glucose solution. The pulse can now be felt and his pale lips have some colour.

Yesterday, we did three transfusions – this is about the average daily, besides the blood we leave at hospitals for them to use themselves. We collect 1/2 to 3/4 gallon daily, mix it with Sodium Citrate (3.8%) and keep it just above freezing in the refrigerator in sterile milk and wine bottles. This blood will keep for about a week. We are working on the use of *Locke's Solution* to preserve the red blood cells longer and are making up Bayliss' *Gum Solution*. (Gum Arabic in Saline). Bayliss was (or is!) an English Physiologist who brought out this gum solution for shock during the war of 1914–18.

The International Brigade Hospital needs male and female French and German speaking nurses – not English speaking at present although these may be needed later. Brain surgeons also.

Well, this is a grand country and great people. The wounded are wonderful.

After I had given a transfusion to a French soldier who had lost his arm, he raised the other to me as I left the room in the Casualty Clearing Station, and with his raised clenched fist exclaimed 'Viva la Revolution.' The next boy to him was a Spaniard – a medical student, shot through the liver and stomach. When I had given him a transfusion and asked him how he felt – he said 'It is nothing' – Nada! He recovered. So did the Frenchman.

Transfusion work should be given in Casualty Clearing Stations when they come out of the operating room of the 1st hospital behind the lines and *before* they are sent back to rear hospitals. But as Madrid is the front line, our work is mostly here although we go out 25 kilometres to other parts of the line.

I am sending you the engine plate of a German fighting plane – a Heinkel.

I sent you last month 25 posters and will send more. These posters are wonderful artistic efforts. The whole city is covered with them. They stress as you see – *Anti-fascism, not* Anarchism, Socialism or Communism. More and more every day all parties are becoming united under the realization of this war against international fascist aggression.

I am enclosing some radio speeches. Use them when you think fit. Either singly or I would suggest *together* in the press or journals.

Well I will close now. We all feel enormously encouraged by your grand support. You may rest assured and give our assurance to the workers of Canada that their efforts and money are saving many

Spanish, French, German and English lives. *We will win* – the Fascists are already defeated. Madrid will be the tomb of Fascism.

Salud, Compañeros!
Norman Bethune

P.S.   I nearly forgot to mention the reason you received so little news of me in December was I gave letters to the Foreign Propaganda Chief who was arrested a week ago as a suspected spy. None were sent out! Except one I gave to an English woman going out to Paris. There are too many Fascist spies here.

N.B.

Madrid is the centre of gravity of the world and I wouldn't be anywhere else.
Please send us – Periodicals and papers.
We have seen no papers nor journals since arrival. Was Roosevelt elected?
Please send – Montreal Gazette, Montreal Star – Toronto Star, New Masses, New Frontier, etc.

N.B.

We really know nothing of the outside world.

A working-class residential area in the northern end of Madrid, Cuatro Caminos was a constant target for savage aerial attacks by Franco's bombers. The bombing of a hospital there inspired a Bethune poem.

I Come from Cuatro Caminos

> I come from Cuatro Caminos,
> From Cuatro Caminos I come,
> My eyes are overflowing,
> And clouded with blood.
> The blood of a little fair one,
> Whom I saw destroyed on the ground;
> The blood of a young woman,

The blood of an old man, a very old man,
The blood of many people, of many
Trusting, helpless,
Fallen under the bombs
Of the pirates of the air.
I come from Cuatro Caminos,
From Cuatro Caminos I come,
My ears are deaf
With blasphemies and wailings,
Ay Little One, Little One;
What hast thou done to these dogs
That they have dashed thee in pieces
On the stones of the ground?
Ay, ay, ay, Mother, my Mother!
Why have they killed the old grandfather?
Because they are wolf's cubs,
Cubs of a man-eating wolf.
Because the blood that runs in their veins
Is blood of brothel and mud
Because in their regiment
They were born fatherless
A 'curse on God' rends the air
Towards the infamy of Heaven.

The feverish efforts needed to establish the blood transfusion service were evident from this hurried letter to Hazen Sise, discussing details and personalities.

Socorro Rojo Internacional
Servicio Canadiense de Transfusión de Sangre
Principe de Vergara, 36
Madrid
Continental Hotel
Barcelona
Jan 16.37

Dear Hazen –
After a perfectly hectic 3 (or is it 4) days, the following points are clear –
   1. Impossible to purchase any kind of car in Barcelona.
   2. The blood ampules are O.K. and since it's a patented and compli-

cated process of putting up the blood, it can not be reproduced in Madrid, ergo – we must use Barcelona as a collecting centre for this kind of blood.

3. The manufacture will cost about 3000 pes. a month. I have guaranteed this payment.

4. We propose to start a 'shuttle' service from Barcelona to Valencia, Madrid and Cordova with distributing centres at these other points. Here (at the D.S.) must be installed refrigerators, distribution, staff, etc. That's a problem of the S.R.I. (and us, of course).

5. I have sent a cable to Spence asking them to send out Paterson of Montreal (an Englishman who runs a ski shop in Montreal and who wanted to come out with me at first – he is a first class chap and an excellent motor driver – has his own M.G.). The alternative I proposed was Norman McLeod of Toronto, a splendid fellow – engineer, 30. This man (either fellow) should be, with you, a two-man team on the delivery truck from Barcelona to the Front – a week's trip.

6. Henning and I will stay in Madrid and keep going on our original system plus this new idea.

7. We are leaving for Marseilles this afternoon to buy a truck (1½ ton) and drive it to Barcelona. Here it will be fitted with the following to transform it into a refrigerator car –

1. 2 electro box refrigerators running on 125 volts each (D.C.)

2. 20 batteries

3. dynamo and gas engine to charge batteries

All these are here and ordered and ready to be installed on our return. Your contacts here

1. Dr. F. Duran, Hospital #18 Tel. 35901

He is the originator of the sterile ampule and has a refrigerator car for the Aragon Front. I have left him with 3000 pes.

2. Perez. At General Motors factory who is going over the Ford engine, repainting car, etc., changing oil, etc. etc. Speaks perfect English. G.M. on Calle de Mallorca – street car 49 (2 blocks from Sagrada Familia). He has keys.

We hope to be back in 1 week. Address: American Express, Marseilles

Salud,
Beth

On 8 February 1937, at the peak of the transfusion service's development and

his own success, Bethune triumphantly sent the following cable to the CASD, which was reprinted in the Daily Clarion *of 9 February.*

We have succeeded in unifying all remaining Spanish transfusion units under us. We are serving 100 hospitals and casualty clearing stations in the front lines of Madrid and 100 kilometres from the front of the sector Del Centro.

The new name of the Canadian Medical Unit is Instituto Hispano-Canadiense de Transfusión de Sangre. I have been appointed director-in-chief as a grateful tribute to Canadian workers and have been given the military rank of comandante.

Sise and Sorensen have been appointed captains. We now have a staff of twenty-five, composed of haematologist, bacteriologist, five Spanish doctors, three assistants, six nurses, four technicians, chauffeurs and servants.

Sorensen is an invaluable liaison officer. Sise is operating the refrigeration truck on the southern fronts. We collected and gave ten gallons of blood during January. Expect to increase this to twenty-five gallons during this month.

This is the first unified blood transfusion service in army and medical history. Plans are well under way to supply the entire Spanish anti-fascist army preserved blood. Your institute is now operating on a 1,000 kilometre front.

I must leave for Paris immediately to buy fifty additional transfusion apparatuses. The Madrid Defence Junta has given us two new cars. We now have five cars operating here day and night in this sector.

I have contracted with an English professional photographer to make a movie film of the work of the Institute for the Canadian public.

Madrid is the centre of gravity of the world. All are well and happy.

No Pasaran (They Shall Not Pass)!
Salud Camaradas y Compañeros!

The thousand-kilometre front served by the transfusion unit was stretched even thinner on 3 February 1937, when Franco's forces, assisted by heavily armoured Italian and German troops, along with ships and planes, launched an assault on the southern city of Malaga. By 7 February the Republican defenders and some one hundred thousand civilian refugees were in full flight from the city, driven east on the narrow coastal road to Almeria. Bethune, Sise, and Tom

Worsley had already decided to test their new Renault truck on the longest road available, from Barcelona to Malaga. But reports of the massive Republican defeat also helped convince them to take a load of bottled blood to aid the victims. Just west of Almeria, they encountered the first pitiful refugees. Their desperate condition and huge numbers forced Bethune and his crew to shift their goal from delivering blood to assisting the fugitives. Bethune recorded his passionate recollection of the tragic flight from Malaga to Almeria, published in a pamphlet entitled The Crime on the Road: Malaga-Almeria.

The evacuation en masse of the civilian population of Malaga started on Sunday Feb. 7. Twenty-five thousand German, Italian and Moorish troops entered the town on Monday morning the eighth. Tanks, submarines, warships, air planes combined to smash the defences of the city held by a small heroic band of Spanish troops without tanks, air planes or support. The so-called Nationalists entered, as they have entered every captured village and city in Spain, what was practically a deserted town.

Now imagine one hundred and fifty thousand men, women and children setting out for safety to the town situated over a hundred miles away. There is only one road they can take. There is no other way of escape. This road, bordered on one side by the high Sierra Nevada mountains and on the other by the sea, is cut into the side of the cliffs and climbs up and down from sea level to over 500 feet. The city they must reach is Almeria, and it is over two hundred kilometres away. A strong, healthy young man can walk on foot forty or fifty kilometres a day. The journey these women, children and old people must face will take five days and five nights at least. There will be no food to be found in the villages, no trains, no buses to transport them. They must walk and as they walked, staggered and stumbled with cut, bruised feet along that flint, white road the fascists bombed them from the air and fired at them from their ships at sea.

Now, what I want to tell you is what I saw myself of this forced march – the largest, most terrible evacuation of a city in modern times. We had arrived in Almeria at five o'clock on Wednesday the tenth with a refrigeration truckload of preserved blood from Barcelona. Our intention was to proceed to Malaga to give blood transfusions to wounded. In Almeria we heard for the first time that the town had fallen and were warned to go no farther as no one knew where the front line now was but everyone was sure that the town of Motril had also fallen. We thought it important to proceed and discover how the evacuation of the wounded was proceeding. We set out at six o'clock in the evening along the Malaga road and a few miles on we met the head of the piteous procession. Here were the strong with all their goods on donkeys, mules and horses. We passed them, and the farther we went the more pitiful the sights became. Thousands of children, we counted five thousand under ten years of age, and at least one thousand of them barefoot and many of them clad only in a single garment. They were slung over their mother's shoulders or clung to her hands. Here a father staggered along with two children of one and two years of age on his back in addition to carrying pots and pans or some treasured possession. The incessant stream of people became so dense we could barely force the car through them. At eighty-eight kilometres from Almeria they beseeched us to go no farther, that the fascists were just behind. By this time we had passed so many distressed women and children that we thought it best to turn back and start transporting the worst cases to safety.

It was difficult to choose which to take. Our car was besieged by a mob of frantic mothers and fathers who with tired outstretched arms held up to us their children, their eyes and faces swollen and congested by four days of sun and dust.

'Take this one.' 'See this child.' 'This one is wounded.' Children with bloodstained rags wrapped around their arms and legs, children without shoes, their feet swollen to twice their size crying helplessly from pain, hunger and fatigue. Two hundred kilometres of misery. Imagine four days and four nights, hiding by day in the hills as the fascist barbarians pursued them by plane, walking by night packed in a solid stream men, women, children, mules, donkeys, goats, crying out the names of their separated relatives, lost in the mob. How could we choose between taking a child dying of dysentery or a mother silently watching us with great sunken eyes carrying against her open breast her child born on the road two days ago. She had stopped walking for ten hours only. Here was a woman of sixty unable to stagger another step, her gigantic swollen legs with their open varicose ulcers bleeding into her cut linen sandals. Many old people simply gave up the struggle, lay down by the side of the road and waited for death.

We first decided to take only children and mothers. Then the separation between father and child, husband and wife became too cruel to bear. We finished by transporting families with the largest number of young children and the solitary children of which there were hundreds without parents. We carried thirty to forty people a trip for the next three days and nights back to Almeria to the hospital of the Socorro Rojo

Internacional where they received medical attention, food and clothing. The tireless devotion of Hazen Sise and Thomas Worsley, drivers of the truck, saved many lives. In turn they drove back and forth day and night sleeping out on the open road between shifts with no food except dry bread and oranges.

And now comes the final barbarism. Not content with bombing and shelling this procession of unarmed peasants on this long road, on the evening of the 12th when the little seaport of Almeria was completely filled with refugees, its population swollen to double its size, when forty thousand exhausted people had reached a haven of what they thought was safety, we were heavily bombed by German and Italian fascist air planes. The siren alarm sounded thirty seconds before the first bomb fell. These planes made no effort to hit the government battleship in the harbor or bomb the barracks. They deliberately dropped ten great bombs in the very centre of the town where on the main street were sleeping huddled together on the pavement so closely that a car could pass only with difficulty, the exhausted refugees. After the planes had passed I picked up in my arms three dead children from the pavement in front of the Provincial Committee for the Evacuation of Refugees where they had been standing in a great queue waiting for a cupful of preserved milk and a handful of dry bread, the only food some of them had for days. The street was a shambles of the dead and dying, lit only by the orange glare of burning buildings. In the darkness the moans of the wounded children, shrieks of agonized mothers, the curses of the men rose in a massed cry higher and higher to a pitch of intolerable intensity. One's body felt as heavy as the dead themselves, but empty and hollow, and in one's brain burned a bright flame of hate. That night were murdered fifty civilians and an additional fifty were wounded. There were two soldiers killed.

Now, what was the crime that these unarmed civilians had committed to be murdered in this bloody manner? Their only crime was that they had voted to elect a government of the people, committed to the most moderate alleviation of the crushing burden of centuries of the greed of capitalism. The question has been raised: why did they not stay in Malaga and await the entrance of the fascists? They knew what would happen to them. They knew what would happen to their men and women as had happened so many times before in other captured towns. Every male between the age of 15 and 60 who could not prove that he had not by force been made to assist the government would immediately be shot. And it is this knowledge that has concentrated two-thirds of the entire population of Spain in one half the country that is still held by the republic.

Written in March 1937 but not published in the Communist Party newspaper the Daily Clarion *until 17 July, 'With the Canadian Blood Transfusion Unit at Guadalajara' reflects Bethune's continued faith in the Republican cause. His conviction that Republican Spain represented an international crusade that would destroy the barbarity of fascism emerges graphically in the article. Bethune's sense of loyalty, however, would not prevent the movement itself from reprimanding him and sending him back to Canada just a month later.*

The hospital stood at the top of the hill on the right as we crossed the bridge coming into the town of Guadalajara. It was about eleven – the clear, cold-bright day of March 12. In the Ford was Henning Sorensen, Geysa [Karpathi], and Calebras, my Spanish assistant. I was driving. In the back we had a refrigerator and ten pint bottles of preserved blood packed in a wire basket. We had left Madrid at ten and had made the 54 kilometres in less than an hour, rolling along that fine paved Zaragosa road at well over seventy most of the time.

At Alcala de Henares we had looked for one of our hospitals but found they had moved over night up to the front, leaving behind, in their hurry, their refrigerator. We picked it up and were taking it to them.

All the roads showed the evidence of the battle ahead. We passed truck after truck loaded with young soldiers standing in the swaying cars with bayonets fixed, singing and shouting as we shot past. No more could be seen the old signs they used to paint on the side – no more C.N.T., U.G.T., F.A.I., C.P. – now just the great red five-pointed star of the people's united army.

Tanks ahead – a string of them – like great dinosaurs, you didn't realize until you tried to pass them how fast they were moving on their seeming-clumsy caterpillar wheels – 25, 30, 40, 45 miles an hour – we catch up and pass with a wave of our hand to the unseen driver. Gasoline trucks, bread wagons, donkey carts, mule trains all moving up. Yes, a drive was on. How important? Who are those steel helmeted troops – a shout in German – the famous Thaelmann Battalion going into action. It must be important. They are the feared 'shock troops' of the International Brigade.

The wind was piercing cold as we crossed the plain. Blowing straight down from snow-covered peaks of the Guadarrama range on our left, glittering so near, it made us turn up the collars of our warm brown coats and thank again, below our breath, the generous Syndicate of Tailors of Madrid who had presented us with them the week before. The front left window of the car was broken and had been for a week – hit by the swinging pole of a mule train – no time to lay the car up now for repairs.

Fifty, sixty, seventy, eighty kilometres an hour – God, what a swell road! At this rate we could be in Franco's line in half an hour's driving!

Sharp left turn at the top of the hill and there was the 500 bed hospital. No more red crosses now. Last week the fascist planes tried to bomb it so down came the cross – too easy a mark to hit – 500 wounded helpless men, too good a chance to miss.

The sure sign of an engagement were the long rows of blood-drenched stretchers, propped up on end, leaning against the walls, waiting to be washed.

All was bustle and hurry.

'Yes, go straight up.' So up we go to the operating room. Here three tables are at work, the close air heavy with the fumes of ether. Casting a glance, a nod, a salud to the chief surgeon as we cross the room to the white enamelled refrigerator standing against the wall. The row of empty blood bottles on the top tell the story – three, five, seven empties and inside, only three unused.

'Better leave them six now; must come back tomorrow.' 'All right?' – the chief surgeon looks up for a second from the table. Nods his head and smiles.

'Where are the tags?'

'Here,' says a nurse and pulls a handful of blood-stained bottle tags from her apron. A glance at each – on the back is written the name, the battalion, the wound, the date of the recipient. 'Let's go.' Out of the door, down the long corridor filled with stretcher-men, doctors, nurses and walking wounded to Dr. Jolly's department. His fine, open New Zealand face breaks into a smile as he sees us. We are old friends from early days in Madrid.

'Where's the refrigerator?'

'We have it in the car outside.'

'Good, bring it in, we need it. There's a rush on.'

The room is packed with wounded. They sit on the floor with blood-stained bandages on head, arms and legs, waiting to be dressed.

'Sorry, I must go now. Just operated on an Italian captain, poor fellow.

Shot through the stomach. Hope he will live. Andre wants to see you. He's used up all his blood.'

We feel fine. We feel like a successful salesman who has just placed a big order for goods. This is great! Isn't it grand to be needed, to be wanted!

So we bring the refrigerator in and set it down and plug in. Inside we put our remaining four bottles of blood. Here comes Andre, Jolly's assistant. A young French doctor just out of medical school, his fantastic black, short-cut beard making him look like a young pirate. He shakes our hand and bursts into rapid machine-gun French.

'Can you leave me another two needles? I need another syringe. I broke one last night. Can you give me some more grouping serums?'

'Sure.' His thanks are effusive.

'I want to write my thesis for my master's degree in the University of Paris on blood transfusion at the front. Will you Canadians help me?'

'Sure.' More effusions, more French. Dr. Jolly calls him from the operating room.

'I must go now, but there's a wounded man upstairs from the International Brigade and we can't make out what nationality he is. He can't speak English, French, Italian, Spanish or German. He's been hit by a bomb, lost one hand. We had to amputate the other and he's blinded in one eye. He needs a blood transfusion. We have to operate but I'm afraid he can't stand the shock. Will you give him a blood transfusion?'

'Let's go.'

'Where's the man you can't make understand?' The pretty Spanish nurse shakes her dark head with a sad smile.

'Oh, there's lots of those.'

'He's lost both hands and he's blind.'

'Oh, I know, here, come, this ward.'

Yes, it must be him. He's a big fellow with a great bloody bandage on his head. Must be six feet anyway, close to 200 lbs. His swollen face is covered with caked blood. Half an hour from the line. Still has his old shirt on. It's covered with stiff blood. Where hands used to be are two shapeless bundles of bloody bandages.

'Sorensen, come here.'

At the name, the man turns his head slowly and from his swollen lips a question painfully comes. I can't understand, but Henning breaks into a rapid strange speech. 'Why, he's Swedish. No wonder they can't understand him.'

Yes, he needs a transfusion. Two tourniquets still in place to check the blood flow from both torn radial arteries. Must have lost a couple of quarts from the look of his face and feeble pulse. Five minutes and we're ready – blood heated to body temperature, grouped, syringe all sterilized. I look at the label 'Blood number 695, Donor number 1106, Group IV, collected Madrid 6th March.' Yes, it's O.K. No haemolysis. Let's go – needle in, syringe working smoothly – five minutes and it's finished.

'Feel better?'

Translation. A twist from his bruised lips is his reply.

Henning bends over him with the anxious, distressed air of a father for his only child. They talk. I clean the syringe and pack the bag. Then back.

'What's the pulse?' Yes, one hundred and stronger, colour better. He'll do.

'Come,' to Sorensen. He tears himself away with reluctance, a backward glance at the door, a word, a reply.

'What did he say?'

Sorensen, quiet, mournful and low: 'He said, "Ten days ago I was in Sweden. I have been in Spain three days. This was my first engagement, and now I am no more use to my comrades. I have done nothing for the cause."'

'Done nothing!' We look at each other with amazed eyes. 'Done nothing!' What modesty, what courage, what a soul!

Yet that is the spirit of the International Brigade; of ten thousand determined unconquerable men, with no thought of themselves, with no thought of sacrifice, but simply and with a pure heart ready to lay down their lives for their friends. 'Greater love hath no man more than this!'

These are your comrades in Spain.

To them – salud!

It was not all glorious sacrifice. By March 1937 the Spanish-Canadian Blood Transfusion Unit was a large, complex team conveying blood to the central sections of the front in a round-the-clock operation. It needed a dedicated manager, skilled at dealing with harried, overworked personnel and capable of circumventing political snags. In this, Bethune was out of his element. Conflicts within the unit, and suspicion of Bethune and some of his foreign associates, combined to convince the Spanish government to bring the unit under its control, as part of a broader effort to take command of the war. Learning of the plan, Bethune exploded, dashing off a cable to the CASD dramatically claiming that 'our work as Canadians here is finished,' and demanding that they be recalled. In his call for the committee to 'remember Kléber and the International Column,' Bethune appeared to hint that the government was preparing to act pre-emptively against the communists. General Emilio Kléber was a communist commander in the International Brigades who was reputed to be a naturalized Canadian, but who in fact was a Hungarian by the name of Lazar Stern. In January 1937, Kléber fell afoul of Spanish premier Francisco Largo Caballero, a socialist who feared that Kléber wished to use the International Brigades to stage a communist coup d'état. Kléber was forced to leave his command. Bethune seemed to fear that the Republican government's takeover of the transfusion unit signalled a revived campaign against communist influence.

April 12, 1937
Madrid

Government decrees all organizations in Spain whether Spanish or foreign must come under control of Ministry of War. No independent organizations allowed. The Sanidad Militar have taken over control Canadian Unit. Our positions now nominal. Fortunately transfusion service is well established and can carry on without us. Ninety percent capital equipment expenditure paid out. Strongly urge you act immediately. Authorize me by cable as chief to first withdraw Canadian personnel, second hand over to government cars, refrigerators and equipment, third agree to provide two hundred dollars monthly six months for maintenance institute, fourth return Canada with such Canadians as desire with film for antifascist propaganda. Our work as Canadians here is finished. Remember Kléber and the International Column. Only future cables signed Beth Bethune are from me. Continue collection funds. Many schemes more urgent now than Blood Transfusion. Will inform you later.

Salud

The bizarre message was a clear sign of Bethune's losing touch with both reality and his comrades. In late May, after the crisis evaporated, Sise, Sorensen, and May would cable back to the committee explaining that 'frank expressions [of problems in the unit] withheld for obvious reasons. Due to circumstances surrounding Bethune's departure which he doubtless will explain on arrival [in Canada] we advise against his operating further projects in Spain but believe him very valuable in Canada for propaganda. Advise strongly against reducing blood unit support. Withdrawal would have regrettable political consequences. Cable sent about April ten containing code signature Beth Bethune suggesting withdrawal sent without our consent contained misleading information complications of which we repudiate.' Back in Canada, the CASD puzzled over the strange twist in events. It saw no cause to justify Bethune's rash proposal, and it rejected the idea.³⁴ But it did act on his suggestion to bring the yet unfinished film, Heart of Spain, *back to Canada for an anti-fascist propaganda campaign. With his star on the wane in Spain and ascending in the film, it was logical to extract Bethune from difficulty and bring him back to Canada to conduct a fund-raising lecture tour. Bethune's subsequent resignation letter presented him as the terse model bureaucrat he was not.*

Sanidad Militar
Instituto Hispano-Canadiense de Transfusión de Sangre
Principe de Vergara, 36 – Teléfono 50881
Madrid
April 19, 1937
Jefe de Sanidad Militar

Camarada:
In view of the fact that the Instituto Hispano-Canadiense de Transfusión de Sangre as conceived by me in January is now operating as an efficient, well-organised institute, and as part of the Sanidad Militar, it is clear to me that my function as chief of the organisation here in Spain has come to a natural end. Since I am firmly of the opinion that all services of the Republican Army should be controlled by the Spanish people I hereby offer my resignation as chief of the organisation.

If the resignation is accepted I will at once proceed to Canada to carry out propaganda work in connection with the Institute and in support of the Popular Front.

In view of the necessity of the continuation of financial support of the Institute in Spain from the Popular Front in Canada, I hereby delegate my authority as Chief representative of the Canadian Committee to Aid Spanish Democracy to the following members: Allen May, Ted Allan, Hazen Sise and Henning Sorensen. I would also suggest that the functions of the above members of the Committee should be as follows: Allen May, official secretary and responsable [sic] of the Canadian Committee; Ted Allan, political commissar; Hazen Sise, director of transport;

Henning Sorensen, liaison officer between Canadian representatives and Sanidad Militar.

Also, in view of the urgency of the situation and the necessity of showing our propaganda film as quickly as possible, I would like my resignation to take effect immediately,

Dr. Norman Bethune

With the reorganization in effect, Bethune cabled back to the CASD to burst the crisis he had inflated three weeks earlier. The reference to milk relates to efforts by the CASD to supply children with vital food, with which Bethune was particularly concerned and which he would often mention on his return to Canada.

May 5

Relationship with Sanidad Militar clarified and satisfactory. All Spain organization as planned by me now proceeding. Name Hispano-Canadiense being retained for Madrid sector. Bethune unit operating smoothly and efficiently. All here agree Bethune return Canada with wonderful film now finished for propaganda work. Remaining Canadians to direct disposal Canadian funds [and] aid administration along lines my suggestions. All have civil status only. Spanish military medical officers in charge actual operations. During my absence Canadian committee in charge composed May, directing secretary, Sise, charge transport, Sorensen, liaison with Sanidad. Will advise arrival milk. All representatives content. Signed Bethune, May, Sise, Sorensen. Beth Bethune.

On 5 May, shortly before Bethune's departure, he wrote a letter to Marian Scott (and other friends), which he titled 'An Apology for Not Writing Letters.' It was an attempt to return to their earlier discussions on the relationship between left-wing political activism and the creation of art. Rather than a profound foray into the subject, however, his letter spoke more to the immense turmoil of his life. Bethune wandered over the topic, picking up one idea then discarding it, as though in shell-shock. His writing became concrete only towards the final paragraphs, where he concluded that 'the function of the artist is to disturb ... He is an agitator.'

An Apology for Not Writing Letters

To my friends in Canada:

This is an attempt at an explanation why I, who think of you so often, with love and affection, have not written – or so briefly – since my arrival in Spain.

I had thought to say simply (that is, shortly) – I have been too busy; I am a man of action; I have no time to write. Yet as I look at these words, I see they are false. They simply aren't true. In fact, I have had plenty of time to write you, that is if I had cared to write, but, in truth, I did not care. Now why is this? Why have I not written to those of you who, I know, without illusion, would like to hear from me? Why is it I can not put down one word after another on paper and make a letter out of them?

I will try and be truthful. It is difficult to be truthful, isn't it?

First of all, I don't feel like writing. I don't feel the necessity of communication. I don't feel strongly the necessity of a re-construction of experience – my actions and the action of others – into the form of art which a letter should take. As an artist, unless that re-construction take a satisfactory form which is truthful, simple and moving, I will not, nay, I can not, write at all. I feel that unless I can re-construct those remembrances of action into reality for you, I will not attempt it. To me, a letter, is an important thing – words are important things. At present, I don't feel any necessity to communicate these experiences. They are in me, have changed me, but I don't want to talk about them. I don't want to talk about them yet.

Besides, I am afraid to write you. I am afraid of the banality of words, of the vocal, the verbal, of the literary re-construction. I am afraid they won't be true.

Only by a shared physical experience – tactile, visual or auditory – may an approximately similar emotion be felt by two people without the aid of art. Only through art, can the truth of a non-shared experience be transmitted. To share with you what I have seen, what I have experienced in the past six months, is impossible without art. Without art, experience becomes, on the one hand, the denuded, bare bones of fact – a static, still-life – the how-many-ness of things; or, on the other hand, the swollen, exaggerated shapes of fantastically-coloured romanticism. And I will do neither. I refuse to write either way. Both are false – the first by its poverty, the second by its excess.

So I despair of my ability to transpose the reality of experience into the reality of the written word. Art should be the legitimate and recognizable child of experience. I am afraid of a changeling. I am afraid it would have none of the unmistakable, inherited characteristics of its original, true, parental reality.

I can not write you, my friends, because this art of letters is a second, a repeated form of action. And one form of action at a time is enough. I can not do both – but successively, with an interval of a year, or ten years. Perhaps I can do both. I don't know. I don't think it matters very much.

I think that art has no excuse, no reason for existence except through the re-creation – by a dialectical process – of a new form of reality, for the old experience – transmitted through a man's sensorium – changed and illuminated by his conscious and unconscious mind. Exact reproduction is useless – that way lies death. The process of change from the old to the new is not a flat circular movement – a turn and return on itself, but helical and ascending.

The process of creative art is the negation of the negation. First there is the change, that is, the negation, of the original, the positive reality; then the second change (or negation), which is a re-affirmation, a re-birth, through art, of the original experience, to the new positive, the new form of reality.

Let us take an example from painting – a moving object such as a tree swaying in the wind, a child at play, a bird in flight – any form of action, seen and perceived. This is the positive, the thesis. Reduced from the dynamic positive in time and space to a static form, by representation, (in this case, by paint on canvas) it becomes the negation of action, the denial of action. This is the antithesis. Then by the miracle of creative art, this static thing, (of necessity static, owing, to the medium employed) is vivified, transformed into movement again, into life again, but into a new life, becomes positive again, becomes the negation of the negation, the synthesis – the union of life and death, of action and non-action, the emergence of the new from the old, but retaining the old within the new.

Now the same thing applies to the literary art, the plastic arts, music, the dance or what not – any art form. And unless that fresh emergent form, with its core of the old, is a new thing, a dynamic thing, a quick and living thing, it is not art. It arouses no response except intellectual appreciation, the facile response to familiar, recognizable objects, or admiration for technical skill.

And because I can't write you, my friends, as I should like to write you, because my words are poor, anaemic and hobbling things, I have not written. Yes, I could write, but I am ashamed to write – like this:

'We were heavily shelled today. It was very uncomfortable. Fifty people were killed in the streets. The weather is lovely now although the winter has been hard. I am well. I think of you often. Yes, it is true I love you. Good bye.'

I put them down and look at these words with horror and disgust. I wish I could describe to you how much I dislike these words. 'Uncomfortable' – good god! what a word to describe the paralysing fear that seizes one when a shell bursts with a great roar and crash near by; 'killed,' for those poor huddled bodies of rags and blood, lying in such strange shapes, face down on the cobble-stones, or with sightless eyes upturned to a cruel and indifferent sky; 'lovely' when the sun falls on our numbed faces like a benediction; 'well' when to be alive is well enough; 'think' for that cry rising from our hearts day by day for remembered ones; 'love' for this ache of separation.

So you see, it's no good.

Forgive me if I talk more about art. It must seem to you that I know either a great deal about it or nothing at all. I really know very little about it. I think it is very mysterious, very strange. But it seems to me to be a natural product of the subconscious mind of man, of all men, in some degree. Arising into the realm of deliberate thought, its life is imperilled. A theory of art reminds me of a medieval chart of the then-known world – curious, fantastic and wonderfully untrue. A theory of art is an attempt of the rational mind to impose its discipline and its order on the seeming chaos and seeming disorder of the emotional subconscious. If this is attempted – and it has frequently been attempted, a certain form of art, ordered and neat, arises. By its subjection to the conscious mind, to the deliberate directional thought of the artist and his theory, it lives for a while and then languishes and dies. It can not survive its separation from the great breeding ground of the unconscious. The mind (that alien in the attic) by its dictatorship, destroys the very thing it has discovered.

Most great artists of the world have been – thank Heaven – 'stupid' in the worldly sense. They didn't think too much, they simply painted. Driven on by an irresistible internal compulsion, they painted as they did, as they must paint.

A great artist lets himself go. He is natural. He 'swims easily in the stream of his own temperament.' He listens to himself. He respects himself. He has a deeper fund of strength to draw from than that arising from rational and logical knowledge. Yet how beautifully the dialectical process comes in again, – modified by thought, his primitive unconsciousness, conditioned by experience, reacts to reality and produces new forms of that reality. These particular forms of art arise, satisfy for their time, decay and die. But, by their appearance, they modify and influence succeeding art forms. They also modify and influence the very reality which produced them. Art itself never dies. Art itself is a great ever blooming tree, timeless, indestructible and immortal. The particular art forms of a generation are the flowers of that immortal tree. They are the expressions of their particular time but they are the products also of all the preceding time.

The artist needs, among other things, leisure, immense quietness, privacy and aloneness. The environment in which he has his being, are those dark, sunless, yet strangely illuminated depths of the world's subconscious, – the warm, pulsating yet quiet depths of the other-world.

He comes up into the light of every-day, like a great leviathan of the deep, breaking the smooth surface of accepted things, gay, serious, sportive and destructive. In the bright banal glare of day, he enjoys the purification of violence, the catharsis of action. His appetite for life is enormous. He enters eagerly into the life of man, of all men. He becomes all men in himself. He views the world with an all-embracing eye which looks upwards, outwards, inwards and downwards, – understanding, critical, tender and severe. Then he plunges back once more, back into the depths of that other-world, – strange, mysterious, secret and alone. And there, in those depths, he gives birth to the children of his being – new forms, new colours, new sounds, new movements, reminiscent of the known, yet not the known; alike and yet unlike; strange yet familiar; calm, profound and sure.

The function of the artist is to disturb. His duty is to arouse the sleeper, to shake the complacent pillars of the world. He reminds the world of its dark ancestry, shows the world its present, and points the way to its new birth. He is at once the product and the preceptor of his time. After his passage we are troubled and made unsure of our too-easily accepted realities. He makes uneasy the static, the set and the still. In a world terrified of change, he preaches revolution – the principle of life. He is an agitator, a disturber of the peace – quick, impatient, positive, restless and disquieting. He is the creative spirit of life working in the soul of man.

But enough. Perhaps the true reason I can not write is that I'm too tired – another 150 miles on the road today, and what roads!

Our first job is to defeat fascism – the enemy of the creative artist. After that we can write about it.

Good bye. I do think of you with love and affection. Forgive me when I do not write.

Salud
Norman Bethune

6

Propagandist:
North America, June 1937 to
January 1938

For six months, a man who by habit poured his passion onto the printed page, even in the midst of battle, was astonishingly restrained on paper. Although he was proclaimed as a hero on his return to Canada, and not only in the communist press, his pen inscribed no invective or analysis and only a few letters. In the absence of these clues to his state of mind, we must look to newspaper articles in which he was quoted extensively and which thereby give a hint of his own thoughts at the time.

Why did Bethune write so little during this North American inter-lude? One probable reason was that he was far from feeling like a proud hero. In fact, he showed evidence of mourning his humiliating exit from Spain. On his return, the Committee to Aid Spanish Democracy (CASD) sent him on a three-month continental tour, speaking and showing the film *Heart of Spain*. Some of his reports *en route* revealed a chastened man. For instance, he informed the CASD from Calgary on 16 August that 'all engagements assigned me either by you or the provincial com-mittees since my tour started have been kept by me on time. I have not missed a single date in spite of three and occasionally four speeches a day.'[1] Here was a truant schoolboy humbling himself before his teacher, not the rambunctious Bethune of old. George Mooney, who knew Bethune before he left for Spain, reported that the man who returned to Montreal was dull by comparison. 'There was less of the sparkle to him, less of the beau brummel. His clothes were cheap and unpressed. He didn't laugh the way he used to. The spring in his step was gone ... He was drinking heavily.'[2] Disgraced by his experience in Spain and preoc-cupied with atoning for it, Bethune must have found writing hard to do.

Bethune's avoidance of writing may also have been the result of his being profoundly alienated from North America. The horrors of war in

Spain had stoked his fires of hatred for fascism. This was no longer an abstract ideology, as some in North America imagined. It was the cause of carnage and death, which Bethune had seen firsthand. He must also have missed the frenetic pace of life, and the independence, adventure, and challenge of the Spanish war.

These factors contributed to the absence of writing by him. But Bethune's urge to express himself found another outlet – the public-speaking platform. At first he was unhappy on the lecture circuit. He admitted to Frances that 'this public speaking is not to my liking.' There were good reasons for his dissatisfaction. This was talk, not action – exactly what he had gone to Spain to escape. Moreover, Nanaimo, Prince Albert, and Timmins were far from the front. Many Canadians wished nothing more than to forget the conflagrations raging outside what they thought was the fireproof house of North America. Travelling across the continent, Bethune was forced to look into the face of isolationism and smug contentment, and at times he must have despaired.[3] It was contempt for this political conservatism, along with personal frustrations and the need to act, which had driven him to Spain just a year before.

The CASD also gave him a punishing speaking schedule, requiring him to address several groups each day, then to collect his film and travel on to another town, ready for the next day's presentation. From 20 to 24 July, for instance, he spoke at Winnipeg, Brandon, Regina, Saskatoon, and Edmonton, before setting out for San Francisco and Los Angeles. As he wrote to the CASD, 'Spain will be peaceful after the Canadian publicity tour.'[4] The demanding pace and constant media and public attention might, at least, have tempered any drinking problem Bethune had.

Despite his initial hesitation, Bethune warmed to the tour and proved to be a commanding public speaker. This should not be surprising to anyone who recalled the flamboyant medical lecturer he had been in Detroit during 1925–6 and in Montreal during the early 1930s. The dramatic meetings in Legion halls, arenas, theatres, and hospitals and the adulation of thousands of people could not have failed to move a man so passionate in his devotion to the anti-fascist cause. Newspaper articles noted his vigour and enthusiasm.[5] His excellence as a public speaker is confirmed by the large audiences at his speeches. He began his tour on 18 June before a capacity audience of nine thousand at the Mount Royal Arena in Montreal and carried on triumphantly from there.[6] A total of thirty thousand people attended his many engagements through western Canada from July to September.[7] Bethune's effectiveness on the lecture circuit was also apparent from the gratifying flow of cash that poured into the CASD. In Montreal, Bethune's audience gave $3,000 to the Spanish aid effort, in Winnipeg $1,800. In Vancouver $1,000 was collected from an audience that overflowed the Orpheum Theatre.[8]

Other evidence shows the depth of Bethune's influence during the tour. From May 1937 to March 1938, CASD grew considerably. The high level of support for the Spanish people's struggle also gave birth to a second organization, the Friends of the Mackenzie-Papineau Battalion, which raised money and goods to assist the hundreds of Canadians in Spain. Martin Lobigs, who conducted a detailed study of the Canadian campaign to assist Republican Spain, estimates that public support for the volunteers rose steadily between January 1937, when the first volunteers left Canada, and early 1939, when they returned.[9] Bethune's cross-country tour in the summer of 1937 must have contributed greatly to this growth in public favour. Both secret RCMP reports and personal reminiscences also attest to the influence Bethune's speeches had in inspiring volunteers to join the Mackenzie-Papineau Battalion and fight in Spain.[10]

The heavy political hand of the CASD weighed on Bethune. The CASD executive, including Communist Party leader Tim Buck, insisted on maintaining the public image of the CASD as a united front of several political parties and groups. They contended that potential supporters would be scared off if they got the impression that the committee was just a front for the communists.[11] Why this should have required an individual representative of the CASD like Bethune to deny his political affiliation was unexplained.

For a time, Bethune accepted the committee's tight rein. But in July, on his swing into the Prairie provinces, he kicked off the traces, and in response to challenges about his politics, he boldly declared that he was a communist.[12] This would not have been surprising to anyone with the slightest ear for political nuance. The tone of his speeches made his sympathies obvious to anyone. Bethune denounced the Red Cross for failing to assist the Spanish people, he condemned the Canadian government for throwing obstacles instead of assistance at the feet of the blood transfusion service, and he portrayed the Spanish Civil War as the opening of a great battle between two antagonistic classes in contemporary society.[13] He also waded in to offer candid, sometimes snap, judgments on political events outside of Spain. Fascism was rearing its ugly head in Canada, he asserted, citing such evidence as the federal government's disallowance of the Alberta Social Credit government's banking legislation.[14] The May 1937 coronation of George VI in Britain was just 'a war stunt.'[15] Such remarks stung conservatives. He was taken to task in the pages of newspapers and privately for his controversial comments.[16] In Quebec, Bethune's message was so controversial that Conrad Caumont, the vicar-general of the Montreal diocese of the Catholic Church, approached owners of daily newspapers and radio stations asking them not to publicize his speeches.[17] In Sydney and Halifax, Nova Scotia, radio stations refused to advertise his meeting and censored part of his response to questions.[18]

In his private get-togethers, Bethune was no more capable of holding his tongue. According to an RCMP report, when Bethune was a guest of the British Columbia executive of the CCF in Vancouver in August 1937, he 'scathingly denounced the CCF for harbouring Trotskyites in their organization and for their refusal to co-operate with the Communists during the recent Provincial elections.'[19]

This North American interlude gave Bethune a break from the battle front, but it was a brief one indeed. At his first speech in Toronto after returning from Spain in June 1937, Bethune dismissed talk that world war would break out in the future. 'The world war is on now,' he asserted. And more importantly, 'this battle – this world war – will mean the end of fascism in the world today.'[20] In this historic conflict, Bethune saw himself as nothing less than a front-line soldier. It was not surprising, then, that in the space of six months, Bethune's attention leaped from the European to the Asian arena, from Spain to China. Events themselves conspired to draw Bethune out of the temporary funk into which his quarrels in Spain had put him. On 7 July, speaking in the remote hard-rock northern Quebec mining town of Rouyn, Bethune was probably not aware that his destiny was being forged halfway round the world. Yet he certainly learned very soon that Japan had invaded China, determined to totally subjugate its Asian neighbour. Reports of the brutality of the Japanese attacks on cities such as Beijing and Shanghai were daily front-page fare; even Spain was relegated to the back pages. Bethune soon dispensed with the fiction that he was returning to Spain. China was now his destination, he confided to a group in Salmon Arm, B.C., in early August, a fact the RCMP also reported then. By late October, he was in New York, accumulating the medical equipment, drugs, and supplies he would take with him to assist the communist forces there.[21]

Bethune's new focus on China corresponded to a shift in direction within the Communist Party. It had shown some interest in the struggle there before Japan's invasion of China, but the attack greatly intensified that attention. The Communist Party's newspaper, the *Daily Clarion*, began a campaign to demonstrate, in the words of an article it printed by Mao Zedong, that 'Spain's fight is oppressed China's fight.' The *Clarion* was soon prominently featuring items on anti-silk parades, campaigns to boycott Japanese-produced toys at Christmas, and demands that Canada stop supplying copper, aluminum, and scrap metal to Japan.[22] In the fall of 1937, Bethune read a pre-publication edition of Edgar Snow's *Red Star over China*.[23] It was a stirring testament to the communist belief that if Spain had been round one of the popular resistance to fascist aggression, China was round two. Having personally been knocked out of Spain, Bethune the fighter could not pass up a second crack at the fascist bully.

The first interview printed on Bethune's return from Spain on 6 June found him demonstrating a feisty contempt for the great powers' self-righteous hand-wringing over how to deal with the fascist countries' intervention in the war. This article was printed in the Montreal Gazette *on 8 June 1937.*

Dr. Bethune Pours Hot Scorn on Neutrality 'Poltroonery'
Canadian Surgeon, Back from Madrid Transfusion Work, Scores Cowardice of Democratic Powers

By L.S.B. Shapiro
(Gazette Resident Correspondent)

New York, June 7 – 'What's the matter with England, France, the United States, Canada? Are they afraid that by supplying arms to the Loyalist forces they'll start a world war? Why, the world war has started. In fact, it's in its third stage – Manchuria, Ethiopia and now Spain. It's democracy against Fascism.'

The speaker was Dr. Norman Bethune, Montreal physician who was head of the blood transfusion service on the Madrid front. His thin face was flushed; his lean body quivered and he pounded his fist in emphasis as he fairly shouted the words. Then he paused slightly to recover his composure.

'We in Madrid cannot understand such timidity, such poltroonery on the part of the democratic nations. Supplied with the proper arms, the Loyalists would throw the Franco forces into the sea in one month. The war would be over; the danger gone. But as long as Italy and Germany are openly waging war against the Spanish people, the war will go on indefinitely. And although the Fascists will never take Madrid and they'll never take Bilbao, the lingering Spanish war will surely spread all over the world.'

The Montreal physician, who went to Spain seven months ago to take over the transfusion service with the assistance of Hazen Sise and Henning Sorenson [sic], of Montreal, and Allan May [sic], of Toronto, arrived here today in the Queen Mary, travelling steerage.

(As quoted by The Canadian Press, Dr. Bethune said: 'I wasn't spending the unit's money on first class tickets.')

Accompanied by two photographers who took action pictures on the Spanish war front, he will tour Canada for a brief period before returning to his duties in Madrid.

The tour will start in Toronto next Monday evening, and Dr. Bethune will appear in Montreal on Thursday, June 17. He will spend this week in New York, developing and cutting the films.

Although he spoke highly of the service of his companions, Sise, May and Sorenson, and of the 21 Spanish doctors who make up his transfusion unit, Dr. Bethune waved aside any stories of personal heroism.

'Heroism is taken for granted in Loyalist Spain,' he said. 'The Spanish fighters have my completest admiration. You just can't break the spirit of the people no matter how intense the bombardment of Madrid. Great deeds are routine affairs. Why, one American in the Abraham Lincoln Battalion was wounded six times, and each time insisted on returning to the front. That is an ordinary case, but it is indicative of the spirit of the people.

'I'll tell you this. The rebels will never win Spain. The Loyalists will never agree to a truce. No, not until the last man, woman and child has been killed. They realize they are fighting the fight of democracy against Fascism.'

Here the grim faced, grey haired physician again drew himself to his full height and pounded the words home.

'But they cannot understand, they cannot conceive it: to them it is unbelievable that the great democracies should declare neutrality laws which work against a legally-elected government fighting against rebels and foreign invaders.

Fascist Motives Scored

'Do you think,' and he lowered his voice in a confidential tone 'that Germany and Italy are fighting in Spain because they are against Bolshevism? That is silly. The Communist party is a minor party in Spain. There is no Communist threat. Why, Negrin, the Premier, is a Right Republican. There are only two communists in the Government. There are not more than 250,000 Communists in all Spain.

'No, what Italy is fighting for is a strategic position in the Mediterranean. What Germany is fighting for are iron and manganese mines. They are the rebels. Franco is nothing. The German General Staff is directing the war and there are 100,000 Italians fighting. Why, oh why, can't the democratic nations see this? That's what the Spanish people cannot understand.'

The physician stopped and shook his head as though he, too, were confused by the problems which confound the Spanish people.

'Until Russia sent arms,' he continued, 'the Spaniards were actually fighting with fists, with knives, with scythes. But Russia's help is not enough. We are getting nothing from France, nothing from Britain, nothing from Canada, nothing from America.'

Cash Paid for Arms

Your reporter broke in with a question.

'If we take for granted that Germany and Italy are fighting for their own national motives,' was the query, 'what will Russia's price be in the case of a Loyalist victory?'

The answer came quickly.

'Naturally Russia is anxious to help in any anti-Fascist battle. But their price? Why, they are being paid on the line for every piece of equipment sent. Spain asks nothing except the right to buy arms freely for her rightful fight against rebels and invaders.'

Dr. Bethune recalled the razing of Guernica and the retreat from Malaga. He was on the road from Malaga as thousands of Spanish families struggled along the highway in order to remain in Loyalist territory. He spoke spiritedly of the shelling of Almeria, and the artillery warfare against Madrid which he said was of no strategic value.

'They are getting away with murder. Simply murder,' he said grimly.

Dr. Bethune estimated that there are 250 Canadians fighting for the Loyalists. He is certain that there are none on the rebel side.

'And most of the Canadians are French-Canadian Catholics,' he added. 'There is no religious war in Madrid. The Lutheran Church is

open every day. I attended services there every Sunday. In Bilbao the
Catholic churches are open. They are not open in Madrid because there
has been no demand that they should be opened. The Basque representative in the Cabinet is a Catholic.'

Of the battle of Guadalajara, the physician said it was not a defeat; it
was a rout. The Garibaldi Battalion of Italian anti-Fascists were the happiest people in Spain on that day, he added.

'Before that battle,' he said, 'the Garibaldi Battalion had only one rifle
to every three men. It had no shoes, no coats, no equipment. But the Fascists ran in such a hurry' ... and the physician chuckled as he recalled
it ... 'that after the battle the Loyalist battalions on that front were the
best equipped in Spain. The Italians left everything, even their new cam-
ouflaged uniforms, the first we had ever seen. And in one stage of the
rout, one Garibaldi battalion defeated an entire regular Italian regiment.
It was the most amazing rout you could ever imagine.'

Madrid 'Perfectly Safe'

Of Madrid itself, he said: 'It is safer to live in Madrid than it is in New
York or Montreal. There is no confusion. Everything is orderly. The jewellery shops are open. They display costly pieces in their windows. Life
is normal except during a bombardment and then the people merely
refuse to become panicky. Their spirit will not be broken.'

In the grimness of the struggle, Dr. Bethune found some amusing
angles.

'Do you know what we do with the Italian prisoners we capture? If
they are wounded, we send them to hospital. I myself have given Fascists 15 blood transfusions. After they are better and they know that
Madrid is not full of red hordes, we send them back to Italy. Sure we do.
They'll make plenty of trouble for Mussolini. Plenty.'

He showed your correspondent a banknote he had taken from a
Moor. It was received by the black man as payment for fighting, a 1,000
mark note on the Reich bank dated April, 1910, worth less than the
paper it was printed on.

'Yes,' he repeated grimly, 'with the proper arms, the Spanish people
would beat Franco in a month easily. No matter what happens, they will
never yield. But the democratic nations of the world may suffer for their
sheer timidity in this so-called neutrality policy.'

Touching briefly on the recent *Deutschland* incident and the German
retaliation against the Spanish port of Almeria, he described the shelling
of the port as a 'barbaric crime.' The battleship *Deutschland* was in a

place where it had no business to be, he said. The Spanish pilots who bombed her 'and incidentally it was damn good bombing' said the warship fired on them first. 'Probably it did,' he said.

'But the retaliation against civilians was exactly the same as if the Spanish pilots, instead of striking a warship, had bombed a liner, he declared. Almeria, he said, was a small port of no military importance. Ninety per cent of the victims were civilians.

Morale Higher than Ever

Dr. Bethune said the morale of the Government-held portions of Spain was 'higher now than ever before.' In contrast, he affirmed 'Franco is holding a deserted country.' Dr. Bethune stated that 50 per cent of the civilian population of that part of Spain held by the insurgents had moved into the Government's territory. The reason, he said, was the fact that when insurgents entered a town they immediately shot all able-bodied men between 16 and 60, 'unless they can prove they gave no aid to the enemy – an impossible thing to prove.'

Dr. Bethune said he volunteered his services to the Canadian Red Cross to work in Spain, but the Red Cross advised him it was not sending units overseas.

The Canadian Committee for the Aid of Spanish Democracy then sent him over. Upon arrival at Madrid 'we saw the need for a preserved blood service, so we started it.'

He reached Madrid late in 1936 and got his unit in operation toward the end of the year.

In Toronto, an obviously sympathetic Daily Star *reporter, William Strange, asked Bethune the inevitable question: Are you a communist? For the moment, Bethune gave the line that the CASD demanded: No. But in Strange's article, published on 16 June in the* Daily Star, *Bethune would also emphatically assert, 'I hate fascism.' It would not be long before his professed hatred for fascism would become a declaration of support for communism.*

**Britain Won't Allow Fascists to Conquer, Dr. Bethune Declares
Insists Person Can Be Anti-Fascist and
Roman Catholic at Same Time
Is Boiling Angry
Acknowledges Cheers with Clenched Fist Salute,
but Isn't Communist**

By William Strange

I talked yesterday for at least a full hour to a man whose name ought to figure in history some day. Not for what he may do in the future, either; but for what he has already done. He is a Canadian doctor, not a simple country doctor this time, but a scientific research man who has 'gone practical' because he couldn't stand by and watch people dying like flies under the wheels of the Fascist juggernaut.

He is Dr. Norman Bethune of Montreal, back from Spain – 'thoroughly fit but a bit tired,' he told me – and boiling over with an implacable anger at things he has seen. I'm going to put the last question I asked him first, because it seems to me to give a key to the strong selfless character of this amazing man.

'What induced you to go?' I asked him. 'You must have known it was going to be no picnic. What drove you into the shambles?'

'Oh well, I guess I felt pretty sympathetic for the people,' he said. 'They were broadcasting appeals for help, and especially for doctors and medical supplies. And I ... well, I felt they weren't getting a break.'

'So you went?' 'Yes, I went.'

Simple, isn't it? The doctor just went. He resigned his jobs (note the plural) and departed on one of the most humane and noble expeditions ever undertaken by a member of a humane and noble profession. A measure of the work he has done may be taken from the fact that he has given 700 blood transfusions in Spain since January the first. And he's going back to give some more. 'Oh yes, I'll go back.' He tossed that assurance over his shoulder as he was shaving.

Wants to Warn

He has a very definite perspective in the horror that is modern Spain; and he wants to warn as many people as possible ... the whole world, I should think.

'What hardly anybody seems to realize,' he said, 'is that the world war has started already. It started even before the trouble broke out in

Spain. It began in 1931 in Manchuria. The Fascists won that time. Then it got going again in Abyssinia, and the Fascists won again. Now it's coming out more clearly into the open. It ought to be plain to democratic countries what we're up against now, for the conflict is a straight fight between fascism and democracy.'

'And will fascism win again in Spain, do you think?'

'Not a chance!' was the emphatic reply. 'A famous Spanish writer made that plain enough to Franco just before he faced the firing squad. "You may conquer us," he told the Fascist leader, "but you cannot win."' 'And will they conquer?' 'I don't think so. I don't see how they can, for all the people that matter in Spain are against the Fascists.' 'Will you clarify that a bit?' I requested. 'Exactly whom do you mean by the people that matter?' 'Why, the workers, of course. The real people.' He might have said 'the simple people,' for they are all the people that matter to him.

Is a Socialist

I thought at this point of a picture I had seen of Dr. Bethune taken on his arrival in Toronto and showing him saluting a cheering crowd with the famous clenched fist salute. 'By the way, doctor, are you a Communist?' The question startled him. 'Most emphatically I am not,' he said, 'let's get this thing straight. You can call me a Socialist if you like. I am a Socialist in the same way that millions of sane people are Socialists. I want to see people getting a square deal, and I hate Fascism. The clenched fist is used as a "People's Front" salute. It's used in Spain by everybody who is against the Fascists. That's really all it means – anti-Fascism. Why, Premier Blum of France uses it, and he's no communist. I should describe it as a reply to the raised hand salute of the Fascist.'

So we got that straight; and I'm glad we did, for no reader of this story will now be able to point at this quietly great humanitarian and make pretence that he's some kind of ogre in disguise.

Real Tragedy

'Now here's something I particularly want to ask,' I said. 'How about the civilian population on the rebel side?'

'There aren't so very many,' he replied grimly. 'Franco is ruling over what is not very far from a deserted territory. There isn't much civilian population in his hands. The people knew what fascism would mean for them, so they got out. This accounts for a good deal of the congestion in the loyalist territory.'

'That sounds like tragedy,' I said.

'You're right there. It is tragedy, God knows.'

'Do you know what those devils did?' he asked me. 'They shot every trade-unionist they could lay hands on. They shot every man who had ever been on strike. They shot every mild Socialist. They shot school teachers who had at any time spoken favourably of democracy. Then after a while they went further than that. They rounded up everyone they could find who had worked for the democratic government of Spain – the legally elected government of their own country! And if these people could not prove positively that they had worked unwilling for that government ... well, they shot them, too. This applied to every man from the ages of 16 to 60. My God, Mr. Strange, they've killed them by the hundred thousand!'

How Moors Are Paid

The doctor showed me a most impressive piece of paper money. It was handsomely printed and even fairly clean. It had been taken from a Moorish prisoner and I gathered that it represented a substantial proportion of his latest 'pay-cheque.' Here is what I read on it. 'Reichsbanknote, 1,000 marks, Berlin, den 21 April, 1910.' The doctor told me that Franco promises his mercenaries that this 'money' will be redeemed after the war! Redeemed in what? one wonders. The 1,000–mark bill is worth less than the paper it is written on. When the Moors find out this swindle, may this redemption not be one of blood?

We discussed Bilbao. 'Yes,' said Dr. Bethune gravely, 'the news from there is bad, real bad. But this is something that I want to make a particular point of. It hasn't fallen yet ... and it may not fall at all. Those Roman Catholic Basques will fight to the last man, and the street-fighting is going to be a bitter struggle. So bitter that I have no hesitation in saying that Davila's real struggle has only just begun. By the way,' he broke off for a moment, 'I do wish you'd stress that Roman Catholic business. These people are genuine Catholics, and they won't give up their religion whatever happens. They haven't been excommunicated, and it's hopelessly wrong for people to think that it is not possible to be anti-fascist and Roman Catholic at one and the same time.'

Spaniards Bewildered

I asked what the Spanish thought of Britain's attitude. 'They are completely bewildered,' he told me. 'They have always trusted in Britain and looked upon her as the world's great democratic bulwark. They're not angry but they are terribly puzzled and a good deal hurt. They are like children whose father is letting them take a licking without lifting a finger to help. They simply cannot understand it.'

'And what is your own opinion of the British attitude?' Dr. Norman Bethune is what might well be described as a forceful humanitarian. At this point he got forceful. 'Cynical' and 'hypocritical' were two of his adjectives: but they were not the strongest. 'My own theory about the British attitude is a very simple one. England is an imperialist, capitalist country possessed of enormous vested interests in various parts of the world, and these are loosely held together by a cement of sentimentality. She is determined to have a weak Spain in order to keep clear her trade route to India. Twenty per cent of Britain's oil supply comes down the Iraq pipe lines and through the Mediterranean; 25 per cent of her raw material imports pass through the Mediterranean. And Mussolini is determined to make the Mediterranean an Italian lake.

Playing Deep Game

'If this were to happen Britain would lose control of Iraq, Egypt and India. Now what we believe is this: That Britain knows a clash with Italy is inevitable, unless Italy goes bankrupt. The British government is playing a deep game. It is willing to let Spain fight Britain's battle in the Mediterranean. Britain has nothing to fear even from a Communist Spain, but she will never allow a Fascist victory. If the Fascists came really close to victory Britain and France would intervene at once. Otherwise the war can go on, hundreds and thousands of men and women may die and the British will do nothing as long as their commercial interests are not threatened.'

This was strong meat. 'You're sure that's for publication?' He answered the question with another: 'Do you think we could let this go on without getting up and shouting about it?' So I asked him next if he thought there was any chance of Great Britain, Canada and the United States coming together in an effort to preserve peace and to bring about the betterment of the world.

'Whatever our ideals may be there is no hope for peace until people realize that the causes of war are economic,' he replied. 'Under the present rule of hopeless economic chaos I don't see any chance of eliminating war. It's a matter of international justice much more than one of policemen.'

And there are Canadians there. Dr. Bethune knows many of them – 'wonderful boys' he called them. There are 500 or so, on the Loyalist side. 'And the rebel side?' 'I don't know of any,' the doctor said. 'None that I've heard of.' I think it would hurt him if there were.

Canadians There

'Any Canadian girls there, too?' 'Quite a few nurses,' he said. And he had a word or two to say of Toronto's 'Jimmy' [Jean] Watts. She does a weekly newscast from Madrid. Did he know her? Well, he ought to. 'She lives in our own institution,' he explained with a chuckle.

And a word about that institution. 'Yes, you can call it a great success, at least from the experimental point of view. We've drawn and used 90 gallons of blood for transfusions this year and now it's been taken over by the Spanish military doctors, and it is being extended right through the loyalist organization. And don't say we "can" blood. We are able to preserve it now and use it days after it has been drawn from the donor; but it isn't "canned"!'

Then came something that had a particular meaning. 'I hate fascism.' Those words came early in this amazing tale of a doctor who risked his life (and is going to risk it again) to bring succour to his suffering fellowmen. 'I hate fascism.'

In an article also published 16 June, the Globe *and* Mail *captured Bethune in full rhetorical flight, decrying the iniquities of the British political system. Obviously offended by Bethune's description of the coronation of George VI as 'a war stunt,' the* Globe *raised an imperious eyebrow at Bethune's claim not to be a communist.*

Bethune Sees Coronation 'A War Stunt'
Royal Pageant Was 'Build-Up and Advertisement,' He Says
Is Home from Spain
'We'll Be Asked to Fight for the Empire,'
Doctor Tells Conference

By A. Lorne MacIntyre
Staff Writer, The Globe and Mail

To Dr. Norman Bethune the Coronation is just a big 'build-up' and 'advertising stunt' for the next war. And the spirit of the British Empire is kept alive and fostered, not by the great British democracy, but by Imperial capitalists who exploit it to control tremendous financial reserves.

That is what Dr. Bethune thinks of the Empire and its people. He said so last night when he addressed a conference called by the Committee to Aid Spanish Democracy, a gathering that met afternoon and night in Carlton United Church.

The Montreal surgeon, back for a publicity tour of Canada after establishing a blood transfusion unit in Spain, was naturally the central figure at the conclave. Ninety-five persons, including Comrades Buck, Carr and other Communists, partially filled the hall to hear him tell of his work in Spain that they had financed. He did this in the afternoon – the calm, detached medical surgeon who can operate without a quiver.

'Political Democracies a Sham'

But at the supper hour, as Dr. Bethune, the observer on international affairs, he declared bitterly: 'Political democracies are a shell and a sham.' What, he asked, was the England that was spoken of in international affairs? It was, he answered himself, nothing but a group of capitalists controlling events. And to him the Empire was 'blocks of gold scattered around the world.'

'The Coronation,' he went on, 'is the biggest build-up and advertising stunt for the next war. And we'll be asked to go over there and fight for the Empire.'

He paused dramatically, said: 'Well, we'll fight, yes. But we want to know what we fight for.' Peace, he had told his listeners shortly before, had to be fought for. 'We'll fight for peace, and it's the only thing we'll fight for.'

Wants $1,000,000

As for Spain, Dr. Bethune expressed himself against the evacuation of orphan children from their native land; feared that if they were moved they would 'lose that beautiful revolutionary spirit.' So he urged the committee to broaden out its work. His blood transfusion work was good, but, he declared, it was not enough. He proposed a Dominion-wide campaign to raise a million dollars to help establish homes in Spain for orphans and to maintain such homes. And he advocated that the committee get a good publicity man and pay him $10,000 to $15,000 a year to handle this campaign. 'He'll swing it for you,' said the doctor.

Later, at its night session, the committee undertook to care for 500 orphans in Spain, decided to immediately launch an all-Canada campaign for funds for this. It decided, too, that the blood transfusion unit be maintained. The Spanish Government is willing, Dr. Bethune had said, to take over this business. The committee will supply the funds to keep it going.

Dr. Bethune recounted his work in Madrid, where by 'trying it out' he was able to refrigerate human blood, use it days and even three weeks later for successful transfusions. It was generally believed that a transfusion had to be an immediate operation from donor to patient. But Dr. Bethune extracted blood from donors, processed it with solutions normally used for keeping blood for short lesser periods than he did, filled pint milk bottles, kept them in refrigerators, shipped them out as needed hundreds of miles away to save lives.

This discovery and system of his holds startling possibilities, not only in war but in peace time. As Dr. Bethune said to his audience, 'It is possible to do a blood extraction from you people in this room and place it in Madrid.' In fact an air plane had flown blood into Madrid from Switzerland. But that, in the words of Dr. Bethune, was 'a publicity stunt.'

The surgeon reduced a description of his discovery from technical language to terms that his listeners understood. Said he: 'Blood is comparable to an egg. An egg five minutes old is a good egg. But an egg kept in refrigeration for two weeks is not a bad egg.'

Bethune still corresponded with Frances and continued to see himself as responsible to help her financially, not an easy task given his own lack of income. He recalled that the couple had considered establishing a medical practice in Rouyn, Quebec, when they first moved to North America. (The original of this letter is not extant. The fragment below, including ellipses, is what Ted Allan copied from the letter supplied to him by Frances Coleman.)

South Porcupine
July 7, 37

Dear Frances –
I saw Janet [Bethune's sister] in Kitchener a few days ago and she told me she was going to write you to spend a couple of weeks in Muskoka where she has taken a cottage.

Her girls are now nearly 'grown up' and very charming.

You would enjoy it.

I am enclosing an unused 1/2 return ticket from Montreal to Toronto which, if you accept, will be part of the expenses. Of course draw on your account ... for the balance of what you need.

I am now on my way across Canada and have had very good meetings. Although this public speaking is not to my liking, I will go through with it. Over to Vancouver then down back through the States.

Remember always that if you want to change your life you may count on me for financial support up to what I can do.

For old times' sake,

Affectionately,
Beth

...

Do you remember Rouyn in 1923? It's now a mining town – not of 3 buildings – but of 20,000 people. We could have been wealthy but oh what a life of poverty.

Years after Bethune and Frances's second divorce and her remarriage to A.R.E. Coleman, Bethune and Frances retained the patterns of their earlier relationship, marked by emotional attachment and conflict. As to his future in September 1937, Bethune appeared uncertain about what specific direction it would lead, but he saw well that he would undertake his uncompromising crusade alone.

King Edward Hotel
Niagara Falls, Ont.
14 Sept. 1937

Dear Frances –
Is it not true we might write to each other the remarks of our times and add but little to the poor satisfaction we now possess?

I regret – it is a constant pain in my heart that I have harmed you. I did not intend to harm you.

I was ill-educated (sexually) as you, never forget that.

If I knew how to recompense you I would do so. I do not know that.

My path is set on a strange road, but as long as I feel it's a good road I will go down it. And you must go down yours.

When I said I had no longer respect for you – you, who I once respected – I meant, to me, your life was devoid of dignity. But my dignity and your dignity perhaps do not agree.

Mine is uncompromise; hatred of evil and stupidity, personal uncontamination and uncontact; aloneness. That is all I meant. I see now once more, I have made the mistake to suggest to you a course of action. Forgive me.

Beth

Bethune's tour saw him visit many cities and towns in Canada and the United States. In a speech in Regina, a report of which was printed 22 July in the Leader-Post, *he warned of the dangers of a fascist victory in Spain. It would encourage the fascists to advance elsewhere in Europe, and even in North America, plunging those areas 'into new dark ages of terror.' Apocalyptic as the language sounded in 1937, within five years his prediction proved devastatingly accurate.*

Spain Critical of Britain's War Attitude
Eden Indifferent, Says Dr. Bethune

Outcome of the Spanish civil war will have a greater effect on the world's future than the war of 1914–18. The Spanish people feel that Great Britain and the other democracies of the world have betrayed them. The Red Cross has done nothing toward helping the orphaned children and wounded soldiers in Spain.

Deadly serious is Dr. Norman Bethune, F.R.C.S., Montreal, head of the Canadian blood transfusion unit in Spain, when talking on the Spanish war.

Dr. Bethune was in Regina Thursday, a guest at the home of Dr. Hugh MacLean, 601 The Balfour.

Thursday noon Dr. Bethune addressed the medical staff at a luncheon at the Regina General hospital on recent developments in the work of blood transfusions. At 8:30 o'clock Thursday night he was to address an open-air meeting in Wascana park or in the event of rain the meeting was to be held in Metropolitan church.

Praises Assistant

Dr. Bethune had the highest praise for Allen May, University of Saskatchewan graduate, who joined the blood transfusion unit in February.

'A very, very excellent assistant,' Dr. Bethune called Mr. May. 'I placed him in charge as secretary when I left.'

Two other Canadians serve with the unit, which at present has the cooperation of six Spanish doctors. They are Henning Sorensen, one-time resident of Saskatchewan, and Hazen Sise, Montreal architect.

From Allen May, Dr. Bethune received a telegram Wednesday stating that things were going well and 400 transfusions had been performed during one week of the present loyalist offensive.

5,000 Ready

Dr. Bethune's work had thrown him into close contact with the Mackenzie-Papineau battalion of Canadian volunteers at Jarama, guarding the highway between Madrid and Valencia. About 600 Canadians were now serving in Spain and 5,000 had offered to go.

What did the loyalists think of the British?

'They're completely dumbfounded by them,' said Dr. Bethune. 'They cannot understand why England, known as the defender of democracy, has abandoned them.'

The Spanish people could not understand why Britain had sabotaged the League of Nations nor why she had supported the non-intervention pact which gave every advantage to the rebels.

Dr. Bethune denounced the attitude of Anthony Eden, British minister of foreign affairs. He pictured Eden at the sessions of the League of Nations in Geneva.

Asleep in League

'He yawns and goes to sleep during the presentation of the Spanish case,' Dr. Bethune said. 'He is obviously indifferent.'

Britain's actions were obviously intended to free herself during the next imperialist war from the trammels which would be placed upon her by the league covenant.

'The Spanish cannot understand the indifference of Britain to outrages of international law. They contend the rebels should be treated as pirates on the high seas.'

Dr. Bethune spoke of the 'open contempt' of the Italians and Germans for the international law which forbids the bombing of unprotected towns behind the lines.

'They feel that they have been abandoned by the democracies of the world,' said Dr. Bethune, 'that they will have to fight till the last man and woman is killed to defend Spain against the foreign aggressors.'

Wives in Trenches

'Wives are fighting in the trenches with their husbands,' he said. Their attitude was: 'Better to die than to spend our lives upon our knees in slavery.'

The Spanish people regarded themselves as unconquerable.

Victory was absolutely sure, said Dr. Bethune, if no more German and Italian troops were brought in, if the naval patrol worked and if non-intervention were actually practised.

'How long could Canada defend herself against a highly mechanized army if she were unable to buy arms from the United States?' was a question posed by Dr. Bethune.

'This is the most important war the world has known – even more important than the war of 1914,' contended Dr. Bethune.

It would decide the fate of Europe (and of Canada) during the next five years.

'If Fascism wins in Spain, it will encourage the Fascists in other countries to such an extent that Europe – and then Canada and the United States – will be plunged into new dark ages of terror.'

Victory for the loyalists would mean that Fascism would disappear from the face of the earth.

No Red Cross

What work was the Red Cross doing in Spain?

'The Red Cross? I've never seen them,' he replied.

'If we had waited for the Canadian Red Cross we would never have been sent to Spain.'

Yet, he added, 100,000 orphaned children needed food and shelter, thousands of soldiers needed medical care.

Agriculture was being maintained intensively behind the lines, Dr. Bethune said. The peasants were working hard and a good crop was expected.

In Madrid Dr. Bethune had met Ernest Hemingway and John Dos Passos, noted American authors who are preparing a film of the Spanish war and also had met Martha Gellhorn, American writer of 'The Trouble I've Seen,' detailing the tragic side of relief in the United States.

Dr. Bethune leaves Regina Friday. At the close of his Canadian tour, he will return to Spain to resume his work with the blood transfusion unit.

Speaking before a large audience in Edmonton, Bethune abandoned any pretense of presenting anything but a strictly communist perspective. And, as reported by the Edmonton Journal *on 26 July, some of his harshest words were directed towards the political situation in Canada, where he said fascism had 'begun to rear its head.' His solution was straight from the communist copybook: 'It can be defeated only by a united front of progressive popular parties. Any progressive person who resists a united front is a traitor to the cause.'*

Sees Fascist Ruthlessness Reflected in Spanish War
Canadian Doctor Who Took Part in Conflict Is Visitor
Describes Service

Spanish civil war is providing the world with a grim example of ruthless ambition and greed of Fascist powers, believes Dr. Norman Bethune, Montreal surgeon, founder and director of a Canadian medical blood transfusion service in war-torn Madrid.

Visiting Edmonton under auspices of the Spanish Democracy Aid committee, the middle-aged, bronzed, grey-haired medical volunteer was accorded a rousing reception when he addressed 1,400 listeners in the Empire theatre Sunday evening.

Dr. Bethune was introduced by Rev. J.T. Stephens as a great war veteran, a distinguished surgeon, a former chief medical officer of the Canadian air force and a former consulting surgeon to the department of pensions and national health. Harold Gerry was chairman.

'When the Spanish government called for medical volunteers, I felt it was my duty to go,' Canada's chief medical representative in Spain told reporters before the public meeting.

'I started our blood transfusion service last November in Madrid with the aid of a C.C.F. Spanish newspaper correspondent. Now our staff numbers 24 doctors, technicians and assistants. Supplied with blood by 1,500 unpaid Madrid donors, our service has provided 1,000 transfusions to wounded soldiers and civilians since Jan. 1,' said Dr. Bethune.

Seeking aid for wounded government forces and refugee children and adults on his current lecture tour of the dominion, Dr. Bethune will return to Spain soon to resume direction of his medical corps.

Strongly sympathetic to the government cause in Spain, Dr. Bethune told his audience Sunday evening the Canadian medical unit in Madrid is independent of Spanish support. It is maintained by Canadian contributors. Employees are paid wages on army scales. Their motive, he said, is 'humanitarian.' The audience, which overflowed the theatre, applauded the speaker frequently.

'When we asked the Canadian government for official recognition so we could get equipment across France duty-free, we were refused. Ottawa said we were too radical. I don't think my method of saving lives can be considered too radical,' snapped the surgeon.

The Spanish civil war was begun, he claimed, when 'privileged classes, supported by the army, took desperate measures to prevent workers of Spain, led by a popular front government, from obtaining long overdue educational and economic reforms.'

Fascism is the last support for decaying capitalism, so Germany and Italy aided the rebels, he declared.

'Nine months ago, confident Insurgent leader Franco called a Madrid cafe from suburbs held by the rebels and ordered a table reserved for him for the following day. It is still waiting for him. Unless he obtains an additional 100,000 German and Italian troops, Franco will not conquer the city,' he said.

Hitler's Hand Seen

Commandeered by the Canadian medical unit in Madrid as a centre of operations, the German embassy offered indisputable evidence that Hitler had begun encouraging a rebellion in Spain two years ago, claimed the speaker.

'We found this evidence in the embassy library,' he said.

'The Spanish people thought they had won democracy in 1931 when they abolished the monarchy. But they had not counted upon the deep-seated hate and resistance of the wealthy class and established institutions in their crusade for freedom. These caused the war,' Dr. Bethune asserted.

'Deplorable condition of education in Spain can be judged from the fact that 60 per cent of the government soldiers in Spain are unable to read and write. One per cent of the population owned 52 per cent of the land. The poor people were oppressed and kept in ignorance.

'When the popular front government came to power in February, 1936, it pledged itself to moderate economic and governmental reforms. The government sought authority from nations of Europe to buy arms when war broke out.

Democratic nations led by England drew up a non-intervention pact that prevented the government from obtaining munitions. The agreement favoured the insurgents because Germany and Italy openly violated it to supply the rebels with arms, the surgeon maintained.

188   The Politics of Passion

Many Germans, Italians

In the army of General Franco, there are 125,000 Italians, 30,000–50,000 Germans, 50,000 Moors, 25,000 Portuguese and 100,000 Spanish, he claimed.

Government's 300,000 soldiers are supported by an international brigade of 15,000 volunteers, representing every nation in the world, including Germany and Italy, said the speaker.

In one engagement, 500 Italians in the international brigade defeated 6,000 compatriots sent to Spain by Mussolini.

In Spain, there is no Bolshevism – only attempts to obtain economic and social progress, he maintained.

'Italy got away with its bluff in Abyssinia. It's getting away with murder in Spain. Mussolini is filled with the egomania of a madman. He wishes to convert the Mediterranean into an Italian lake. Both Italy and Germany are in Spain for economic and strategic reasons,' Dr. Bethune asserted.

The speaker concluded his address with a sweeping denunciation of England's policy in international affairs and a plea to progressive parties in the world to unite to fight Fascism.

England Censured

'England wishes, for economic reasons, a weak, bankrupt Spain. Its capitalistic government and diplomats, led by Anthony Eden, are pro-Nazi and admire the Nazi form of government. The real reasons for the Spanish war and a possible ensuing world war are found in economic imperialistic rivalry,' the surgeon stated.

Britain is 'deserting and sabotaging the League of Nations in favour of an empire league of defence.' Workers must resist this trend and demand a reconstruction of the league, he declared.

'Already Fascism insidiously has begun to rear its head in Canada. It can be defeated only by a united front of progressive popular parties. Any progressive person who resists a united front is a traitor to the cause,' Dr. Bethune declared.

Members of the audience made substantial contributions in aid of the medical committee on conclusion of Dr. Bethune's address.

In a Toronto speech, reported in the Daily Star on 16 September 1937, Bethune provided a huge Massey Hall audience with a quick sketch of his political development from apathy to activism.

Spanish Ambulance Permit Turned Down by Ottawa
Dr. Salem Bland, Rev. Ben Spence Considered Too Radical,
Says Bethune
Called Fascism

How the federal government investigated the membership of a Toronto committee which had raised money to send an ambulance to Spain and found the membership 'too radical' to grant a permit allowing the ambulance to pass across France into Spain duty-free was told by Dr. Norman Bethune, head of the Canadian blood transfusion unit at Madrid, before an audience of over 3,000 in Massey Hall last night.

'Dr. Salem Bland and Rev. Ben Spence were members of that committee, yet Ottawa considered them dangerous, and refused us a permit,' Dr. Bethune said, and the audience booed.

He spoke after a motion picture dealing with the Spanish civil war and called 'Heart of Spain' had been shown. Mr. Spence, introducing the picture, said: 'This film has been shown intact all over the United States and western Canada, but it was ordered cut by the Ontario board of censors. They eliminated all references to Hitler and Mussolini.' Jeers and boos followed his announcement. One voice called: 'It's fascism at work.' Another: 'It's like the middle ages.'

'Canada may seem to be a long way from Spain,' Dr. Bethune said, 'yet in Spain in the next two years the history of Canada and the world will be decided. We must choose between democracy or a new dark age of fascism, between slavery and freedom. That is the choice offered the world.

'The conflict in Spain is not just a Spanish war, no more than the Japanese invasion of China or the Italian invasion of Abyssinia concerned those countries alone. Those wars are far more important than that. Two principles are at conflict in the world. The man clubbed by police in a strike at Oshawa, and the girl striker felled by tear gas in Montreal are in the same position as a soldier defending Madrid as far as these principles are concerned.

'The principles are these: Shall we have a government of the people, for the people by the people, or shall we have a dictatorship, control of the people from the top? In other words, shall we have democracy or fascism?

'You middle classes, you intellectuals, you can't take a middle course this time. You must make up your mind, and when you do I know that your place will be on the side of democracy and the working class.'

Relates Call to Service

Explaining how he happened to go to Spain, Dr. Bethune said the story might be called 'The Evolution of a Doctor.'

'Until I was 45, I thought all politicians and parties were the same. I was a doctor, and nothing else. I did not vote. I practised medicine, but without contact with reality, not understanding that environment and the social structure were the cause of the many physical ills I was called upon to treat.

'I changed by chance. In 1935 an international medical congress was held in Moscow, and I attended. It opened my eyes. I learned that man was not just man, but a being influenced by the social structure and conditioned by economic conditions, and that a doctor must study and understand those conditions before he can treat a patient scientifically.'

The profit motive in the practice of medicine must be eradicated, Dr. Bethune said, before the doctor's special knowledge is available to all the people, many of whom are now unable to buy it.

'The health of the people of a country is that country's principal asset,' he said. 'In my practice I hated the two, five and ten dollar bills that came between me and my patient. Many other doctors feel the same way. I believe that doctors should be civil servants and that treatment should be free to the public and paid for out of general taxation.

'That was one of the first things I learned in Moscow. Then I progressed to a conception of the relation of the middle class to the working class. I realized that the war in Spain was a class war – the privileged class against the middle and working class. When the loyalists of Spain appealed to the world for help I felt I must go.'

Dr. Bethune offered his services to a group in Toronto, formed to help loyalist Spain, and was accepted. It was a broad group, he said, comprising every aspect of political thought, but with a common base – a belief in democracy. Dr. Bethune arrived in Madrid in the fall of 1936.

City Bombed Daily

'The population of the city, swollen by refugees, was 1,300,000. The city was bombed daily, yet you could drive around it for hours and never suspect that anything unusual was going on. General Franco and his troops were five miles away, but the stores were open and business was carried on as usual. One of the things that surprised me was that there were no police on duty anywhere, yet the shops were not looted; law and order were observed. Then I realized that the function of police was to guard property of one type only.

'Madrid's buildings were open to the public. They bore signs reading: "Citizens of Madrid – this building belongs to you. Respect it!" Franco was so close at that time that he telephoned into Madrid's leading restaurant and ordered a table reserved for himself and party for the following night. You can still see that table with the reserved sign on it, but someone has added "guest unaccountably delayed."'

In Madrid, Dr. Bethune said he found that only three out of 37 hospitals had blood transfusion service, and that this was of an obsolete type.

'I decided that this was the work Canadians in Spain could best carry out,' he said. 'I went to London and bought an ambulance and other equipment. Then I went to the Canadian commissioner in London and asked for a letter to allow me to take the ambulance across France into Spain duty-free. The commissioner said he would have to ask Ottawa, and the next day I got Ottawa's reply. They said they had investigated the membership of the committee behind the work and found it too radical. Dr. Bland and Mr. Spence are on that committee.'

Boos and cries of 'Shame!' followed his remarks.

Fostered by Nazis

'When we got back to Madrid we chose the German embassy for our hospital,' Dr. Bethune continued. 'And let me say here that we found in that embassy papers proving that Germany had fostered revolt in Spain almost two years before it actually broke out.

'We built up our unit slowly. Now we have five ambulances and a large, well trained staff. We have a list of 1,200 donors of blood in the city. Fifty of them give us a pint of blood each day. It keeps for almost a month without deterioration.

'We are running a glorified milk service. Every morning two trucks carrying blood for use at front line hospitals leave Madrid.

'In the hospitals at the front you will find prisoners of war receiving the same food, treatment and care that wounded loyalist soldiers receive. One Italian Fascist prisoner feared for his life when he was taken to a hospital. But he learned to trust us and believe when we said: "We do not regard you as an enemy, but as a wounded man."'

'In Spain war goes on against the privileged class, aided by Germany, who wants the minerals of Spain, and Italy, who wants Spain to realize her dream of a second Roman Empire,' Dr. Bethune said.

'Here in Canada we have no war, but we must fight against fascism just the same. We must fight against a coalition government which would be against the workingman. We must stop government interference with the worker's right to strike. We must have a popular front here, a united front, even as they have in Spain, if we would keep fascism out. And one way you can do that is to cast your vote in the coming provincial election for the candidates who support the popular front.'

By November 1937 Bethune had set his course on China. As he wrote to a former lover, Elizabeth Wallace, a 'strange and dangerous' road lay ahead. He wished not to see her because he wanted no 'serious emotional engagement. I am through with such things. I feel myself steeled against them.' The letter is also noteworthy because it shows one of Bethune's typical responses to women: conviction that their lives were going astray and that despite his affection he was unable to help them.

Medical Bureau
381 – 4th Ave
New York

Dear Elizabeth –
I really don't know what to – I mean how to write you. I have neglected to do so for this reason – because I don't know exactly how I can say the things I want to say to you. But I will try.

The reason I did not let you know I had returned to Montreal was because I did not want to see you again. By that I mean I did not want to re-open my life to you again. I would have been forced to say – 'You and I have no possible commerce for us to engage in. My life and its pattern does not fit yours any longer – there was a time when those patterns – yours and mine – might have fitted but that time is past.' And rather than do that – for I am truly fond of you, truly worried about your life in the future – I did nothing. Perhaps I should have seen you again. I meant the last time that it would be goodbye. I felt that your life was set on a road which I hated to see you on – and since I could do nothing for you – I thought I should not see you again. And so I did not call you. I feel for you great pity and great affection but I am powerless to help you.

My road ahead is a strange and dangerous one. You can not come with me. I can not take you because since we last met we have gone far away from each other – and what we have in our hands now is just the memory of one summer's disharmony – sweet and bitter-sweet – was it not?

Then too I don't want to attempt, at my time – and in my time left – any serious emotional engagement. I am through with such things. I feel myself steeled against them. And because I pitied you and were fond of you – I feared lest you might – yes the chance – wrap yourself about me once more as you did once. And so my not seeing you was based on this fear – fear for myself that you penetrate my defences once more – as you did once. I know how best I am vulnerable.

Now you can think about me kindly and sweetly. Do so. I loved you once. I have great affection for you now. Remember me as I will you – with quietness and respect.

Beth

Except for his triumphant homecoming in June, reports of Bethune's activities were surprisingly absent from the communist Daily Clarion. *The paper printed no lengthy interviews and only three articles by him in the nine months after April 1937. The following article, printed 22 November, presented Bethune's views on a subject about which he'd previously written little, the problems of young people in the Depression.*

Youth Will Be Freed – Bethune
Views *Class of '29*, Deeply Impressed by Rehearsal

Doctor Bethune, world-famed head of the Canadian blood-transfusion service in Spain, wrote this plea for youth after attending a rehearsal of Toronto Theatre of Action's new play, *Class of '29*, which opens tonight for a week's run at Margaret Eaton hall.
By Dr. Norman Bethune

The young people of the *Class of '29* are not of any particular university in Canada or America. They are universal types of the universities of five-sixths of the world today.

The frustration of normal ambitions, the negation of reasonable expectations, the 'uselessness of it all' when confronted with modern economic conditions, with the indifference, or worse, 'charity,' of that society, is eating out the heart of young Canada.

This truly is the 'lost generation.'

Their elders mouth the fine-sounding words of outworn 'idealism,' of their old-fashioned individualism, of liberalism, of opportunity; of the virtue of courage when, instead of words, words, words, youth wants action, action, action!

So the youth of Canada looks toward the youth of Spain fighting for its chance. The youth of Spain is fighting the cause of youth – for our right to freedom, liberty, independence, for love, life and the pursuit of happiness.

The history of this heroic band of Canadian young men fighting in Spain, will go down to posterity as one of the great epic stories of all man's history.

It is another children's crusade, a youth crusade against forces determined to force youth back into the dark ages of dictatorship.

Youth will be freed!

7

Anti-imperialist: China, 1938

Henning Sorensen observed: 'When I look upon the life of Norman Bethune, it seems to me to be one long preparation for the final period – his life and work in China.'[1] In China, Bethune found a movement and a people that satisfied his ideal of communism. Their communism, he wrote, was 'automatic as the beating of their hearts.' It was motivated at once by an implacable hatred of Japanese militarism and a world-embracing love for all those who sided with them in their struggle. Perhaps more impressive still, the Chinese communists seemed to be devoid of personal vanity and ambition. Yet even as they fulfilled his ideal image of communism, they also gratified his own bourgeois ego – they revered him. In such primitive living conditions, it was physically impossible to satisfy Bethune the sybarite of old, but Bethune's own determination to share every hardship made this unimportant. Still, as he acknowledged, he had a cook, a personal servant, his own house, and a fine Japanese horse and saddle. Under the circumstances, this was luxury indeed.

Once he determined to fight fascism, Bethune showed an unerring knack for locating the flashpoint of the battle. In Spain, he went immediately to Madrid and established a militarily and symbolically critical new service in a militarily and symbolically critical centre. Similarly in China, Bethune got a quick fix on his destination. In the midst of the confusion caused by the barbarous Japanese attack on the country, Bethune remained firm about where he wanted to go. He would not serve the Guomindang, the Nationalist Party, whose patriotism took second place to anti-communism. His place was with the communists. His determination to reach the arena where he could directly assist them was the cause of his rift with the titular head of the Canadian-American

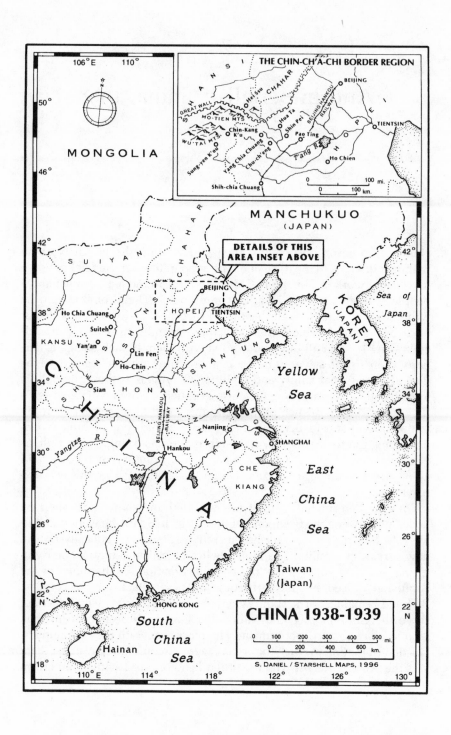

THE CHIN-CH'A-CHI BORDER REGION

106°E   110°

50°

46°

MONGOLIA

S H A N S I

CHAHAR

BEIJING

GREAT WALL   Hei Ssu

MO-TIEN MTS   Hua Ta

WU-TAI MTS   Chin-Kang   Shih Pei

K'u   Pao Ting

Sung-yen K'ou   Yang Chia Chuang   Chu-ch'eng

Shih-chia Chuang

TIENTSIN

H E I

B E I J I N G   H A N K O U   R A I L W A Y

Ho Chien

T'ang R.

H O P E I

0   100 mi.

0   100 km.

42°   MANCHUKUO   42°
                                        (JAPAN)

S U I Y A N   CHAHAR

                              DETAILS OF THIS
                              AREA INSET ABOVE

                         BEIJING

38°   Ho Chia Chuang   HOPEI   TIENTSIN   Sea   of   38°

      Suiteh

KANSU   Yan'an   S   Japan

           Lin Fen   S H A N T U N G

         Ho-Chin

34°   Sian   H O N A N   Yellow   34°

              K   Sea

         I

C   H   N

I   A   Nanjing

      N   Hankou   SHANGHAI

30°   Yangtze R.   East   30°

                      CHE   China

                      KIANG   Sea

26°   26°

                              Taiwan
                              (Japan)

22°   22°
N   N
      HONG KONG   CHINA 1938-1939

      South   0 100 200 300 400 500 mi.
      China   0   200   400   600 km.
18°   Sea
110°E   S. DANIEL / STARSHELL MAPS, 1996

114°   118°   122°   126°   130°

KOREA
(JAPAN)

Hainan

Medical Unit to China, Charles Parsons, an American doctor who decided to go back home rather than trek to northern China. It also led to a separation between Bethune and the unit's third member, Jean Ewen, a Canadian nurse. In seeking out the fighting front, he became one of the very few people in the world who made their way to two centres of conflict between right-wing militarism and democracy in the 1930s.

Bethune's arrival at the front lines in northern China could not have been more fortuitous. The year 1938 was 'China's most bitter hour,' recalled Ma Haide, the American doctor who served with the Chinese communists beginning in the early 1930s. Japan had begun its aggression against China in 1931, and in July 1937 it greatly stepped up the scale of its assault. Now it was aiming at total conquest. With the world community's attention still largely focused on Europe and the war in Spain, the Chinese were left to defend themselves. Seeing in their midst a foreign medical unit must have been an immense psychological boost to them. Their salute to Bethune when he entered Yan'an told it all. Banners across the road hailed the 'Great International Anti-Fascist Fighter,' 'Veteran of the Spanish Civil War,' and 'World Famous Canadian Surgeon and Friend of the Chinese People.' And although small in number and meagre in resources, the unit offered precious expertise. With his experience in Spain, Bethune had the latest practical knowledge of battlefield medicine, including the use of blood transfusions and the need for the earliest possible surgical assistance to the wounded.[2]

Imagine the communists' further delight when Bethune proved to be skilled far beyond medicine. He was also politically conscious, adaptable, inspiring, and seemingly inexhaustible. His writing from 1938 showed that he grasped the nuances of the united front, in which the Communist Party and the Guomindang agreed to set aside their own differences to battle Japan. After an early insistence on building a fixed model hospital to train Chinese medical personnel, a hospital which was quickly destroyed by the Japanese, Bethune came around to the Chinese view that mobility was the foremost characteristic of medical care at the front. Still, he remained his irascible self, speaking bluntly and writing reports that condemned incompetent, shoddy, or ignorant medical practice wherever he saw it. Ewen regarded this as a serious flaw in a man who had to get along in a country in which plain speaking was frowned upon.[3] While it might have been a real barrier to his success in other parts of China, among the communists it seemed to be less significant, especially after the first few months of contact. His obvious desire to improve medical care must have helped to compensate for his manifest impatience. If anything, his frankness and tremendous dedication inspired admiration and gratitude, rather than resentment. And, clearly, he also began to grapple with his impatience.

He had much to teach, but Bethune also had much to learn in China – from both the people and Mao Zedong. Our understanding of Bethune's appreciation of Mao's political and military strategy has rested on two controversial sentences in Ted Allan and Sydney Gordon's *The Scalpel, The Sword*. After his one meeting with Mao in Yan'an in March 1938, Bethune is said to have written: 'The man is a giant! He is one of the great men of our world.' Like significant portions of that book's material about Bethune in China, the quote comes directly from Zhou Erfu's 1948 fictional biography, *Doctor Norman Bethune*.[4] In 1971, considering revisions to their biography, Allan and Gordon argued over the quote. At Gordon's urging, Allan conceded that Bethune probably did not write the lines.[5] Yet what Bethune did write from China, which is reprinted below, shows that he grasped Mao's strategic vision for the anti-Japanese war. More than that, he was deeply impressed with it.

What was it about Mao's thought that swayed Bethune? In the years of Bethune's adherence to communism, the left had not scored many victories. In Spain, there had been much brave talk about defeating Franco, and through the summer and fall of 1937 Bethune reassured Canadian audiences that Madrid would never fall. But reality was quite different. The international embargo on aid to the Republic and divisions among the Republican forces had hamstrung the democratic side, and it was being steadily pushed to the brink. China, too, looked to be another casualty in waiting, facing a wealthier enemy with a far more powerful military. But Mao saw a way to turn the tables on Japan. Circumstances suggest that what Mao and Bethune discussed when they met was, as Allan and Gordon claim Bethune wrote, Mao's ideas about how 'to nullify the effects of the invaders' superior equipment, and to save China.' What Mao probably presented to Bethune were the arguments he would make in a series of lectures from 26 May to 3 June 1938 at a Yan'an conference on the war of resistance against Japan. This was later published as the essay 'On Protracted War.' In it Mao argued that the previous ten months of war had shown the fallacy of two theories: that China faced inevitable defeat and that China would be quickly victorious. In fact, he argued, China could win, but it would be a long war, 'the sacrifices will be great and there will be a very painful period.'[6] Soon Bethune himself was writing that Japan wanted 'a quick war and a quick peace. We want a long war and no peace until the Japanese are driven from China. I put this at a minimum of 4 years.'[7] Bethune had seen the merit of and adopted Mao's strategy for victory. It had several key points: wage guerrilla warfare; allow the Japanese to believe they had control of the country because they held the cities but deny them the vast population in the towns and villages; and build a united front of all patriotic parties and classes.

Looking at Bethune's outpouring of writing from China, one cannot fail to marvel anew at his energy and insight. While travelling half a huge country to join the Eighth Route Army, striving to come to grips with cultural differences and the primitive state of medical care virtually everywhere, operating almost daily in constantly shifting battlefield conditions, and working feverishly to improve medical practices throughout the region north of Yan'an, Bethune wrote endlessly. Reports, letters, speeches, news articles, short stories, and appeals for communication and assistance from North America – all this and more rolled out of Bethune's indestructible portable typewriter. From 1938 alone, we have more than sixty-five thousand words from Bethune, the equivalent of a novella. And he wrote far more than that. Cut off from medical-training resources because of the Japanese blockade, Bethune improvised by writing his own medical textbooks, some twenty in total. Unfortunately, the main textbooks, 'Theory and Practice of Battlefield Rescue in Guerrilla Warfare,' a 150-page manual, and 'Organization and Technique for Division Field Hospitals in Guerrilla Warfare,' have been lost.[8] Even without his staggering medical and organizational duties, Bethune's written output alone during this time was enormous.

Perhaps Bethune's greatest frustration in 1938 was the lack of support from North America. Bethune sailed from Vancouver believing that he was the advance guard of a force of volunteers bringing skills and supplies to the Chinese people. A stream of appeals to the China Aid Council in the United States and other comrades back home failed to rouse this force. More humiliating still, his requests did not even summon up the money for his own modest needs. In June lack of money forced him to try to write news articles for cash. By August he was forced to fall back on the Eighth Route Army itself for funds, although he insisted that these be kept to an absolute minimum.

This frustration aside, his writing from 1938 revealed a man who had recovered a sense of mission following the disappointment of his recall from Spain. Throwing himself into a war fought in supremely harsh conditions, but which he was convinced could be won, Bethune left behind anguish and found satisfaction and new optimism among the communists of China.

Bethune's excitement about going to China lifted the weighty burden of Spain from him. In a letter to Norman Lee, a former member of the executive of the Committee to Aid Spanish Democracy, he showed a renewal of the enthusiasm and confidence which had drained from him with his departure from Spain the previous year.

Jan 8/38
Empress of Asia

My dear Norman –
The 1st North American medical unit to China is on its way!
   Dr. Charles Parsons (American)
   Miss Jean Ewen (Canadian)
   Dr. Norman Bethune
with a completely equipped small hospital. All raised privately – but in 4 weeks time once we are in the country, then the big drive in Canada & U.S.A. should start.
   A.A. MacLeod will notify you re details. I enclose a letter from Agnes Smedley showing the desperate need – far greater than Spain.
   I promise to be a better correspondent!
   Salud (or the Chinese equivalent) to all.

Norman

To Marian Scott he sent this breezy note.

Empress of Asia
Jan 8/38 (en route)

You see Pony, why I *must* go to China.
   Please Read *Edgar Snow*'s book – Red Star Over China. *Agnes Smedley* – Red Army Marches. Bertram's First Act in China.
   I feel so happy & gay now. Happier than since I left Spain.
   Goodbye & bless you

Beth

Bethune continued to provide his former wife, Frances, with money from his own meagre income. In April 1938, for instance, Oliver Haskell, the director of the China Aid Council in New York, wrote to Bethune that the council had sent $200 to Frances, who 'seemed to be in great difficulty and asked for $200 to be sent immediately.'⁹ Bethune's own concern about her situation was evident on his leaving.

8 Jan 38
Empress of Asia

My dear Frances
I am doing what I can for you, for justice & my former love for you. I am giving you what is due you. Please do not consider it in any other way except as that.

It would seem that the time for offering advice is gone but I beg of you to leave Montreal.

I feel so unhappy about you & what you have become and will become. Escape for your life or terrible people will kill everything in you that I once loved.

Goodbye,
Beth

Arriving in Hong Kong in late January, the Canadian-American medical team flew directly to Hankou, some thousand kilometres north. Although it had been the seat of the Chinese National government under the Guomindang Party, it was already under air bombardment by the Japanese. The government had fled west, further into the interior, to Chongqing. Before leaving North America, the team had been told only to make themselves available to the Chinese government. What action to pursue caused a falling out between Bethune and Ewen, on one side, and Parsons. Having met communist leader Zhou Enlai and Dr R.K.S. Lim, the director of the Chinese Red Cross, Bethune was determined to join the Eighth Route Army in Yan'an. But Parsons refused to go north with the communists and returned to North America.¹⁰ Faced with an enforced wait of three weeks before arrangements could be made to escort them north, Bethune and Ewen insisted on being put to work in Hankou. There, on 14 February 1938, Bethune recorded his observations about the state of medical care in the Guomindang-held areas of China. (Ellipses indicate sections of this report that are torn and indecipherable.)

Medical Work among Chinese Soldiers

There are in Hankou a number of organizations rendering medical assistance to wounded soldiers and civilians. These organizations are as follows:

1. The Army Medical Service of the National government, Dept. of War.
2. The Medical Relief Commission of the National Red Cross Society of China.
3. The International Red Cross Committee for Central China.
4. The League of Nations of Geneva.
5. The Canadian-American Medical Unit.
6. Organization for the care of Refugees and Children.
7. North China Women's Partisan Organization.
8. The North-West Women's Joint Salvation Association.
9. Women's National Association For War Relief.
10. The Wu-han Mission Societies.
11. The Chinese Y.M.C.A.
12. The Chinese Y.W.C.A.
13. Buddhist Relief Organization.
14. Relief Organization of the Trade Guilds
etc.

The functions and activities of some of these organizations will now be considered.

1. The Army Medical Service. On the outbreak of hostilities, the A.M.S. was found almost completely unprepared for the deluge of wounded and sick soldiers which followed a heroic stand of the Chinese Army at Shanghai. The organization was very primitive, inadequately staffed and terribly under-supplied with materials of all kinds. These supplies were rapidly exhausted so that now the army is suffering both from a lack of medical officers, and medical materials of all descriptions. First of all, there was no properly speaking Army Medical Corps as known in the English, American, and Canadian Armies, and not even a training centre for officers, non-commissioned officers, men and nurses. What had to be improvised was done on the German-Japanese model. In this system, there are three branches of the service.

Divisional Sanitary Service composed of three Sanitary companies:
First Divisional Sanitary Company composed of ten medical officers,

stretcher-bearers, and nurses with a total personnel of 132. They staff the battalion and regimental aid-posts (a regiment is composed of three battalions of approximately 600 men each).

Second Divisional Sanitary Company staff and operate the Divisional Casualty Clearing Station serving four regiments. Here the wounded are classified and sorted out to either the Divisional Receiving Station (capacity 300 beds) or to the Divisional Field Hospital (capacity 300 beds) for severely wounded.

Both the above Sanitary Companies are controlled by each Division separately. In many divisions, such sanitary companies assist merely on paper.

Third Divisional Sanitary Company. On the line of communication, are operated the station of hospitals and a chain of small Receiving Stations separated from each other by the distance which stretcher-bearers (often civilian, men and women) can carry a wounded man in a day, that is 20–30 miles, on their way back to the base. When possible, and such opportunities are few, trucks, trains, and boats are very occasionally used. Owing to the bad roads, motor ambulances are a practicable impossibility and the wounded must either walk or be carried on stretchers often for hundreds of miles. Even when a hospital is reached, there are more often than not no beds to lie upon, no dressings, no anaesthetics and perhaps no doctors. Practically no provision is made for base hospitals, at present, and owing to the breakdown of the organization of the sanitary companies, only the more lightly wounded who are able to straggle back by themselves ever reach the base. Most of the functions of base hospitals are being done by Foreign Mission Hospitals.

Two or three Divisions comprise an Army Corps. Each Corp Commander is responsible for the medical service of his own Corp. In a Route Army, composed of two or three Army Corps, there is at present no coordinated medical service with the exception of the 8th Route Army. The Army Medical Service has at present about 270 hospitals of various kinds – Station Hospitals on the main line of communication, surgical and general base hospitals. Convalescent homes and camps and special hospitals such as orthopaedic, are unknown. Of the 270 hospitals only ten or twelve are furnished with doctors, capable of performing surgical operations. When it is seen that the line of communication back to the base is often 200–300 miles in length, through a country practically impassible for trucks, cars or carts, the difficulties can be understood. At present, the major defects are the lack of transport and lack of an organization linking up the front line and the rear. The severely wounded fail to reach the rear and even when they reach the head of the line of communication at the Divisional Field Hospital, and Divisional Clearing Station, they die because of a lack of proper surgeons trained in operative technique capable of saving their lives. The medical officers of these hospitals are often inexperienced in surgical affairs. Many are incompetent through lack of training. As a result of the lack of properly qualified doctors, many former orderlies, male nurses and medical students are given the rank of medical officers and their partial training employed as best it may be.

It is not unjust to say that the Army Medical Service is entirely inadequate to the demands made upon it, but there are indications that the problem is being seriously tackled, although these problems are enough to daunt all but the most determined spirit. Such people are coming forward in China and taking things over. We were much impressed by the ability of General Liu, Deputy General of the Medical Service. General Liu was through the fierce fighting on the Shanghai Front and his descriptions of the heroism of the Chinese soldiers made a profound impression on us. These Chinese soldiers dug pits as high as their shoulders and in these, half filled with water, they stood for days under constant artillery and aerial bombardment. The country was flat and muddy. No relief, no food could be brought to the line in daylight, and the evacuation of wounded had to be carried out at night. A bowl of cold dirty rice was all these soldiers had to eat. No medical aid post, no Casualty Clearing Hospitals could be erected, when every tree, every hut was bombed and shelled by the Japanese. None but the lightly wounded ever survived the terrible journey back to the rear when they either dragged themselves or were carried through the mud fields during the dark night, resting in water-filled ditches during the day. Any indication that a hut was used as a hospital was immediately followed by fiendish efforts of the Japanese bombers to destroy and kill the wounded inside. It was dangerous to display a Red Cross flag. Thousands of Chinese wounded were killed in this way and many doctors, nurses, and stretcher-bearers lost their lives.

2. The Medical Relief commission of the National Red Cross Society of China was formed to supplement the work of the Army Medical Service. This commission is financed by worldwide contributions from philanthropists, organizations, and societies, sympathetic to the Chinese people. The Director, Dr. Robert K.S. Lim, F.R.S. (Edinburgh) formerly Professor and Head of the Department of Physiology at the Beijing Union Medical College. He has the supreme control over all medical

relief work under the Chinese Red Cross. His address is No. 1 Ewo Road, Hankou, China. We have had the privilege of many conversations with this remarkable man, and have been tremendously impressed with his organization ability, his vision and drive.

The work of the Commission is to assist the Army Medical Service. It has organized two types of Mobile Medical Units.

1. Operating Surgical units with a personnel of twenty each, composed of five surgeons, 5 nurses, 5 dressers, and 5 orderlies. Only males are employed. They function as Divisional Clearing Stations and Field Hospitals. These are equipped with surgical instruments and all necessary medical supplies. They have a portable X-Ray with their own mobile power plant. 21 of such units have already been placed in the field. At least another hundred are needed if only medical supplies and equipment will be sent in by the sympathetic world.
2. Dressing Units with a personnel of 15 nurses or 14 nurses and 1 doctor. They work on the lines of communication. 37 of such units have been placed in the field.
3. Civilian Medical Relief work. An obstetrical unit headed by Dr. Jean Chiang, daughter of Professor Chiang, late head of the Dept. of Chinese Studies of the University of McGill, Montreal, Canada has been sent up into North-West China.
4. Plague Prevention Units. These are being organized and sent up into the North.
5. I regard the work of this Commission to be of the greatest importance and recommend its support to the entire world as I see that the Commission has the vision and the organization to render the greatest assistance to the heroic Chinese people. Money and medical supplies should be sent immediately. The money should be sent direct to Dr. Lim, No. 1 Ewo Road, Hankou, China, and supplies sent to the Hong Kong Bureau of the National Red Cross of China, Hong Kong. All bills of lading, invoices, etc. should be addressed to Dr. C.Y. Wu, Overseas Chinese Banking Corporation, Hong Kong.

3. The International Red Cross Committee for Central China. This is a branch or sub-committee of the Chinese Red Cross and must not be confused with the International Red Cross in Geneva. This Committee was formed among the foreign residents ... last year to relieve the terrible suffering among the wounded, and refugees of the Central Area. In addition to this local committee, there exists also in other cities, commit-

tees calling themselves International Red Cross Committees, such as those of Canton, Hong Kong, etc. Their only connection with the International Red Cross of Geneva is through the Chinese National Red Cross from which they ... charges.

The International Red Cross Committee for Central China has its Headquarters in Hankou. The Secretary of the Committee is James L. Maxwell, formerly Secretary of the Medical Mission Section of the Chinese Medical Association. His address is Dollar Steamship Line Office, Hankou. The members of the committee are composed of American, English, French, German, Canadian, and Scandinavian foreign residents of the city. This organization is doing very important work. It is being maintained by donations principally from abroad. In a weekly list of contributors, published on Jan. 11, with donations from 12 Canadian and American Rotary Clubs, Sunday Schools, Chambers of Commerce, Educational Institutions, and colleges, Clubs, Churches, Missionary Societies, and individuals. These contributions maintain medical work principally in 150 Mission Hospitals. There is no over-lapping of work or authority between this committee and the Relief Commission of the Red Cross. On the contrary, there is the closest cooperation between these two bodies.

The function of this committee has settled down to supporting mission hospitals principally although refugee camps are also maintained. The Mission Hospitals take in wounded soldiers as well as carrying on their normal work among civilians. In many cases, the staffs are being badly over-worked, but they are cheerfully undertaking this as part of their Christian duty to assist and relieve suffering wherever it is found. They are doing much of the work that in a properly organized military service would be undertaken by base hospitals. To each mission hospital, the government pays $0.20 rice money (roughly 6½ cents in American money) per day per wounded soldier. And the International Red Cross Committee contributes $0.50 (roughly 16 cents in American money) per day for each wounded soldier taken in. The International Red Cross also supplies medical material free of charge. No charge is made by the mission hospitals for operations, dressings, etc. The International Red Cross is now actively engaged in stocking up mission hospitals for 6 months in advance with medical supplies in the event of the possibility of such supplies being cut off in the future. This will only emphasize the extreme urgency for immediate donations of money and medical supplies.

In the Hankou area, there are five Mission Hospitals all taking in wounded soldiers.

1. Church General Hospital (American Church Mission, Episcopal) capacity 212 beds.
2. Union Hospital (London and Methodist Mission) 180 beds.
3. Methodist Mission Hospital, 150 beds.
4. London Mission Hospital, 70 beds.
5. Roman Catholic Hospital, 30 beds.
6. Seventh Day Adventist Sanatorium, 100 beds.

These hospitals are the best equipped, and do the best work in the Central Area of China.

4. The League of Nations has despatched to China a Unit of Doctors, who are engaged in Plague Prevention work in the North-West. The civilian population is being inoculated against plague, typhus, and cholera. This unit is working in the closest cooperation with the Army Medical Services, the 8th Route Army and the Chinese Red Cross. Dr. Borici is in charge.

5. The Canadian-American Medical Unit. This unit is working in the North-West Provinces with the 8th Route Army. It has been sent over by the Canadian and American Leagues for peace and democracy. This composed of Canadian and American doctors and nurses, who are operating a Casualty Clearing Station with the 8th Route Army. Another function of this unit and of the Canadian and American Committees supporting it is to assist the Chinese partisan groups of civilians and their families, living and fighting behind the Japanese lines. This division of the work is headed by Agnes Smedley. A Committee composed of General Yeh Chien-yin and Agnes Smedley has been formed to be responsible for all the money and supplies to be sent to this unit. Her address is c/o The National city Bank, Hankou. All supplies should be addressed to Agnes Smedley c/o Hong Kong Bureau of the Red Cross of China to be forwarded to Hankou. Food, cod-liver oil for children, clothing, socks, gloves, blankets all are urgently needed. The work of the other committees mentioned will be taken up in another following letter.

How can a civilized world help the heroic Chinese nation in their struggle against the Japanese aggressor?

1. Furnish money and supplies, principally medical to any of the above committees, embracing as they do all ranks, classes, religions, and political organizations. This must be done quickly.

2. Maintain a steady political pressure on their governments to the

end, that assistance be actively furnished China in the way of war materials. Only in this way will this war be brought to a successful conclusion which means the driving out of every Japanese from Chinese territory.

3. Boycott of all Japanese goods sold abroad.

Notes for Canadian, American and English Committees

1. Dr. Lim, head of the Chinese Red Cross, strongly advises against single individuals such as doctors or nurses coming to China either on their own initiative or under the auspices of a committee. Such doctors and nurses should be organized in teams as a mobile operating unit capable of undertaking the work of a field ambulance or of a casualty clearing station. They should be fully equipped with motor ambulances, say four to six to each unit, and have a portable X-ray and power plant also portable such as model F manufactured by the General Electric Company of America. In addition of course they should have complete surgical instruments and medical supplies, a list of which supplies recommended by the Red Cross I enclose. Such a unit should be composed of from two to five surgeons, three to five nurses, and also stretcher bearers and orderlies or drivers. They will be given Chinese auxiliary personnel of doctors and orderlies, interpreters etc.

Such units will be used as models or demonstration units and will be under the control and direction of the National Chinese Red Cross. Correspondence in regard to such units should be addressed to Dr. Robert Lim, Director in Chief of Chinese Red Cross, No. 1 Ewo Road, Hankou.

2. In addition to the above, former non-commissioned officers of the rank of sergeant or sergeant-major or warrant officers of the Canadian, American and English army medical corps will be welcomed for the purpose of training personnel. Before coming out they must obtain permission from Dr. Lim also.

3. It is suggested that in addition to contributing money organizations abroad might take upon themselves a definite task such as supplying one hundred to five thousand pairs of woollen socks, or ten to one hundred gallons of cod liver oil for children, or one hundred to ten thousand first aid dressing packages of the U.S. or English army model, or five hundred to five thousand pounds of gauze or bandages or absorbent cotton. All goods so supplied should be put up in packages of approximately 40 lbs in weight each for transportation.

The world is asked to assist China irrespective of their particular national, individual, religious or political beliefs. China is entitled to assistance from the entire civilized world, and this assistance must come quickly.

Norman Bethune

Although Bethune would later complain from northern China that communications to and from North America were not getting through, occasionally his letters arrived quickly. This one, recounting the early part of his journey from Hankou to Sian, was written on 14 February (although the date may be wrong – certainly it does not correspond to the day of the week Bethune thought it was) and arrived in Toronto in time to be printed in the Daily Clarion *of 4 April.*

February 14, 1938
Tungwan, Shensi, China

[No salutation]
Today, I think, is Thursday. We left Hankou (that is, Jean [Ewen] and I) on Tuesday morning at 7:15 a.m. Travelling with a political commissar of the Eighth Route Army – a young comrade of 27 years of age, already 10 years of experience in the army – he had been on the Great Trek. He was wearing a fine Japanese officer's greatcoat, captured it at Tairywan. We travelled third class as all Eighth Army officers do. We had each our own bedding roll consisting of a pad and one feather-filled blanket like a big comforter as we call it. Plenty of food was bought along the way from sellers at each station.

On Tuesday night we arrived at Chengchow, the junction part of the Peihan (Beijing and Hankou) R.R.; this was heavily bombed last week and the city near the station was badly wrecked and 180 people killed. These bombed houses looked very familiar!

The train going west was full so we slept on the benches in an open shed in the station. Everybody is extremely kind and courteous. My boots excite great curiousity! They are one-half-knee-high B.C. loggers' boots. They create great wonder and admiration, and people come up constantly to feel them!

This next day, Wednesday, at 11 p.m., we got on board a train to Sian. This R.R. is called the Lung-hai R.R. On board were a number of missionaries going west (Americans). Travelled all that day and arrived here this morning at 8 a.m. An hour ago we passed a train which had been bombed, machine-gunned and burnt (that thermite bomb certainly does a good job of taking paint off steel).

This is the beginning of the loess country, low hills of 500 feet of mud terraced like staircases. Perfectly treeless, dry and very cold. The roads are always cut deep into the country, and so lie below the surface of the land – sometimes 10–25 feet below the level of the surrounding country.

Yesterday morning we had an air-raid warning and we all beat it out into the fields. The engine was uncoupled and ran 500 yards up the line. A plane (Japanese) came over and had a look but didn't bomb. The line is crowded with military trains.

We were met by Eighth Army representatives and taken to the trenches; here is where we are now. We have just had chow-noodle soup, meat (pork) and eggs. Very good, and tea, of course, rather bitter, no sugar or milk. Watched the Eighth Army troops drilling. They are very young, look about 19–22 and in the pink of condition. Very smart drill and good discipline. Afterwards all played basketball – officers and men together.

Tomorrow we cross the Yellow River by ferry and then a day's trip north (or more) by truck. Our first stop is Tinfen. We are destined to the north-eastern district of Shansi, Wutaishan, behind the Japanese lines, working with the armed partisans, who have no medical attention at all and no supplies. That suits us fine!

I saw three big motor ambulances here this morning, Chevrolet and General Motors double rear-wheeled trucks taking six stretchers. The roads are very dusty – the air is cold and the wind piercing.

We are all in the best of spirits and in good health and looking forward to our work with our comrades of the Eighth Army with high hopes and expectations. Of doing them some service. I will write whenever I can but it may be difficult or impossible. Our address is c/o Eighth Army headquarters, Shansi Province, China.

Norman Bethune

PS Salud to all my friends in the Mackenzie-Papineau Battalion.

Led by Chinese guides, on 22 February Bethune and Ewen set out for Chin-Kang K'u, the communist base in mountainous Shansi Province of northeast China. But what under other circumstances would have been a tiring but manageable journey of 1200 kilometres and several days turned into a month-long

nightmare. Japanese forces were advancing to attack the main rail line going
north from Hankou, forcing Bethune and Ewen to backtrack and abandon train
travel for a trek that found them at various times on a mule train, on foot, and
in Eighth Route Army trucks. Reaching the safety of Sian on 22 March,
Bethune set down the details of the bizarre odyssey in a letter to friends. A
revised version of it was published in 1938 by the Canadian League for Peace
and Democracy as a pamphlet, From Hankow to Sian.

I really don't know where to start to tell you of our exciting experiences
since we left Hankou on the 22nd of February. I think I wrote you on
leaving but whether I posted the letter in Hankou or in Tungwan I have
forgotten. However, I will start from Hankou and retrace our steps.

We arrived at Chengchow at 11 p.m. travelling third class with one of
the soldiers of one of our divisions, who was returning to rejoin his unit.
His name was Chow Tsang Cheng, 27 years of age, 11 years in the
Army. A fine lad, intelligent and as merry and gay as a cricket. I gave
him my jack-knife from Madrid, which pleased him very much.

When we arrived at Chengchow we found the train for Tungwan
completely filled, so after a stroll up the main street to see the damage
which the Japanese had done the week before, we stretched out on the
wooden bench of an open shed and, wrapped in our warm sheepskin
coats, spent a comfortable night. The damage the bombing had done
was bad enough but, as usual, the much proclaimed accurate marksmanship of the Japanese was pretty bad. About this marksmanship
more later, from personal experience! Here their objective was the railway station and round house. They missed both by a hundred yards!

Next morning we left at 11 for Tungwan. This railway is called the
Lunghai Line. The line we were on yesterday was the Beijing-Hankou
railway. The train was jammed with refugees fleeing west. After an
hour's slow travelling the air raid warning was sounded by the engine,
and we all scampered out of the cars and lay down in the fields about a
hundred yards away. The engine was uncoupled and went forward. We
could see the bombers flying very high, but they did not bother us. They
were flying south. It is certain they did not visit Hankou, for we have
since heard that Hankou has not been bombed since the week of the
14th, when eleven Japanese were brought down at a cost to us of six of
ours. This was a wonderful victory for the Chinese, as not a single foreign aviator was flying for them. Incidentally there are no more than a
dozen foreign flyers here, the most of them being Americans. The Chinese flyers feel rather antagonistic to them for the simple reason that the

Americans get 500 gold dollars a month, their lives are insured for 10,000 gold dollars and they get a bonus of 1000 gold dollars for every machine they bring down, while the Chinese aviators receive 250 mex dollars [Chinese dollars, called mex on the international currency market] a month, their lives are not insured and they get only 500 mex dollars for every machine they bring down.

The chief accountant of the Lunghai Line was on the train. He is a graduate of the Walton School of Business, Philadelphia, Penn. Two remarks were interesting – The Anti-Comintern Pact [a 1936 alliance of Nazi Germany, Italy, and Japan] is similar to the Holy Alliance in European history. Both were designed to hide the real intentions of the conspirators. 'The fact that China is united surprises no one more than the Chinese.'

We travelled all day, all night and arrived at Tungwan at 3 p.m. the next afternoon. There we saw for the first time the great Yellow River. We went to the Eighth Route Army barracks and were much impressed with the cleanliness, order and fine discipline of the men. At nine o'clock two Japanese prisoners were brought in. No one could speak their language, but Chow was able to write it. They were deserters who were tired of the war. They said that many of the comrades felt the same. Slept in the office on the floor, six of us. Up at 6:30 a.m. Hot tea, after washing. Breakfast of rice, turnips and pork at nine. Ten porters, with wheel barrows took our luggage (15 cases) down to the river, which we crossed in a junk. Carried ashore by porters, naked to the waist, wading in the ice cold water. The river here is 400 yards wide with a current I would estimate at eight miles per hour. The junks are carried down stream by this current as they cross for as much as a quarter of a mile. They then have to be towed back above their starting point to recross.

As we boarded the train the air raid warning sounded. Immediately there was a great exodus to the hills and the river bank, but we pulled out and did not wait to see what happened. This railway is called the Tung Kau line and runs north through the centre of Shansi to Chang Chia Kou, north of the Great Wall. It is held by the Japanese beyond Tai-Yuan. The train was filled with troops. We were in the postal car which was very comfortable, as we could spread our luggage out and use the boxes as seats. At night it was rather draughty as the entire sides and roof were perforated with bullet holes, the train having been heavily machine-gunned the trip before.

We are going up the east bank of the Fen river. Two ranges of mountains accompany us, one on either side. This is the loess country. These loess are curious low hills or mountains of light, brownish-ochre sand. The hills are cut in terraces which rise, one after the other, as regular as a stair case. I thought at first these terraces must have been made by man, so regular are they, but when one sees them for hundreds of miles, and often far from human habitation, one realizes that they are a natural formation. We travel very slowly. The weather is fine and warm with a clear blue sky. At every station there are vendors of food, hot millet soup, noodles, tea, fried hard, wheat rolls and steamed buns, and hard-boiled eggs. Many trains are coming down, packed with refugees, sitting on the tops of the carriages, on the engine, anywhere to have a foothold. The river on our left looks very low. There are literally thousands of ducks flying overhead. The land parched, practically treeless, except for a few low cedars.

On Saturday, the 26th, we arrived at the station of Linfen at 3 p.m. There we learned for the first time that the Japanese were only a short distance away and the city was being evacuated. The station itself was jammed with humanity – civilians, men, women and children, carrying all they possessed, their bedding, rolls, a few pots and pans, wounded soldiers, arms, hands and heads wrapped in bloody, dusty bandages. Flat cars loaded with mules, rice and munitions. At four o'clock the Japanese bombers came over and machine-gunned us. We took to the trenches dug in the sand about the station. Only four men were wounded.

The Headquarters of the Eighth Route Army was moved and no one seemed to know where it was located. A train on a siding loaded with stores of the Eighth [Route Army] was preparing to leave. Back to Tungwan! With a heavy heart we climbed aboard a box car filled with bags of rice to the roof and slept fitfully till 3 a.m., when we were awakened by the silence. Our train had gone off and left us on a siding, having brought us only 25 miles. We were the last train from Linfen.

The name of this station was Goasi. Here we stayed all day, while our commander, Major Lee, was making arrangements with the surrounding villagers to unload the trainload of rice, reload it into carts and start off on the 200 mile march back to the Yellow River. A fine hot day. We lay in the sun and looked up the railway line, expecting the Japanese any hour to come around the bend. No soldiers, no one but a hundred or so wounded men walking down the line. We have 400 bags of rice – very precious. It must not be captured. We walked up to the village close by. It is practically deserted except for a few old people. Jean Ewen asked an old woman why she was staying. Her reply was 'What is the use, I can not be worse off than I am now.' All day long we hear explosions down the line. We hear the Japanese planes overhead but are not bombed. Bought a quarter of a pig – $1.40. The commander told us that we are not going back to Tungwan, but that we will cross the river into Shensi and make for Yan'an, about 300 miles west, crossing two rivers and a range of mountains. This seemed nothing to the comrades of the Eighth.

On the 28th we left Goasi with 42 carts, pulled by 3 mules apiece, two in the lead and one between the shafts. We were forced to abandon half the rice and the winter uniforms. It was a brilliant fine day. I walked ahead of our caravan for two hours enjoying the clear dry air. Every town we would come to the gates were closed and no one would answer our call, so we were forced to go around the walls, to pick up the road beyond. At about 4 p.m., having been on the way for four hours, I, who was walking alongside the leading cart, saw two bombers going south about half a mile to our left. As we watched them I saw the second of the pair who was trailing the leader, begin violently to waggle his wings. I recognized the signal and knew that we had been seen and were in for it! We must simply have made the Japs' mouths water – 42 carts stretched out over a quarter of a mile, not an anti-aircraft gun within two hundred miles and not a Chinese pursuit plane in the entire province! We were sitting birds asking to be knocked off! And this they proceeded to do to the best of their ability. They were flying at a height of about one thousand feet. They turned sharply off their course, and while one stayed high the other came down to 500 feet and flew our line looking us over very closely. We were all lying out on the flat ground, not a tree or a stone to protect us. There were fifty of us, drivers, men and boys, with five old rifles between us.

After passing down the line, the bomber turned and flew back to the head, then diving on us so that he was only 200 feet above us, dropped four bombs on the leading section. His aim was so bad that even at that height he missed the leading carts by fifty feet. I would be prepared to bet that had I been in the plane I could have hit those carts with a baseball! As a matter of fact, he was as close to us lying out in the field as he was to the target he was trying to hit. After bombing the leading carts he returned and repeated the performance on the last section with another four bombs. Here his aim was a little better – the bombs dropping about 20 feet away. Jean, who was riding on the last cart, had a narrow escape, a soldier lying beside her getting a piece of bomb in his back and the driver a fracture of the right arm by a piece of steel passing through and coming out under the arm pit. They were lying on the ground 150 feet away from the carts. The bombs exploded immediately on striking and made only a small hole in the ground. In this way they are more effective, as the steel sprays out flatly instead of burying itself in the ground. I observed wounds on the legs of the mules and horses reaching no higher than two feet from the ground, which were received at a distance of 100 feet away. One is really not safe unless one is in a trench. Our total casualties were 15 mules killed, 12 wounded, 3 of which had to be killed, and 4 men wounded.

Jean Ewen showed great pluck and fortitude under her first baptism of fire and immediately after the bomber had passed started to dress the wounded and arrange for their transportation to the nearest village a quarter of a mile away, so that by the time I had walked from the head of the line to the rear where the men had been wounded, she had already applied dressings to the most serious ones.

The wounded driver was only concerned about his mules and wept to hear that all three had been killed. The Eighth Route paid promptly for the killed animals – 100 dollars each (a Chinese dollar is about 30 cents). No wonder the peasants welcome them – this is one army that does not take advantage of the poor and defenceless.

We cut out the dead and wounded animals from the wrecked carts and after 4 hours resumed our way, our caravan now reduced to 20 carts, travelling all night, sleeping on top of rice bags, as the mules pulled us along over the uneven road. The night was dark and overcast. At 5 a.m. we stopped on the bank of the river Fen, and on the hard clay top of the k'ang (sleeping oven) of the village inn, lie down again until roused at 9 for breakfast of hot sweet fermented rice water with an egg beaten up in it – very good.

Opposite us on the far bank is the city of Kiangchow. I can see the twin spires of a Roman Catholic Mission church – typical French architecture – rising high above the roofs of the one and two storied tile-roofed houses and looking very incongruous and out of place. We hear that the Japanese have taken Linfen and are coming down the railway rapidly. We are the rear of the rearguard – we and the hundreds of walking wounded whose infected wounds are covered with dirty blood-stained, sand-caked bandages that have not been changed for a week or more. We hear the Japanese planes bombing the railway line ahead of us. Their cavalry cannot be far behind us. The river here is two hundred yards wide and, it being low, reaches only up to the waist – but at that is too deep for our mules and low carts. We must unload.

The ferry junks and the overhead cable line were burned by Chinese to obstruct the Japanese advance. They certainly obstructed our retreat! While our commander is making arrangements for our stuff to be taken over, I crossed over, being carried piggyback. The current is about six miles an hour of brown muddy water. I was much amused to see the efforts of 20 Chinese coolies trying to get two camels on their feet who had obstinately lain down in the shallow water and refused to move. The crowd alternately burst into roars of curses and laughter, all to no avail. To the best of my knowledge they are still there, unless the Japanese have some secret of how to move camels!

I climbed up the hill, through the city, to the church. The city is practically deserted except for a few shopkeepers and beggars. These two classes are all that remain – the propertied and the propertyless. The first will await the coming of the Japanese with some fear and trembling, but their goods are more important than their fears. They are the typical bourgeoisie the whole world over. They regard this war as just another battle between professional soldiers. They are politically illiterate. Their only concern is their individual welfare. The poor beggars could not be worse off under any other master. This also applies to the poorer peasants. If they leave they will starve, so they remain.

At the mission, the compound of which was completely filled with the families of the church members taking refuge, I had a very pleasant talk in mixed French and English with Father T. Van Hamert, O.F.M., missionaire apostolique, Shansi meridional, a bearded Dutchman, and with Father Quint Pessers, O.F.M., Praef. Apostolique. They opened a bottle of red wine and gave me a good cigar. They told me that the mayor and the police had fled the city two days before, and that they were expecting the Japanese in 36 hours. What would happen to them? Would the Japanese respect the French flag on the church spire? A shrug of the shoulder. Yes, some missionaries had already been killed. They would stay and try to protect their parishioners. I admired their courage. In discussing the Japanese atrocities (the rape of Nanjing and the brutal murder of 8,000 men, women and children will go down in history as an unforgivable crime of the Japanese army), they were of the opinion that the Japanese officers had little or no control over their men, and that this would be the main danger. Both were calm and smiling as I bid them goodbye. Their last words to me were, as we parted, 'I hope we meet again on earth, if not, then in Heaven.'

The next day our rice was carried over the river on the backs of porters. The river had risen during the night so that it was now up to the breasts of our porters, who, completely naked except for a folded jacket on their shoulders, carried us over sitting on chairs carried by four men. I was standing on the north bank waiting to cross, when I heard a great shout of laughter from the opposite side. I looked up to see Jean go over backwards, turning a perfect summersault in three feet of water. One of her bearers had slipped or stumbled. Of course this accident delighted the crowd!

We left Kiangchow at 1:30 p.m., feeling glad to get the river between us and the Japanese, as we heard this morning that the enemy are only 25 miles away and their cavalry even less. It is a cold, heavy day with a bitter wind. We push ahead with two carts, leaving the commander behind to superintend the transport of most of the rice sacks, as not enough mule carts can be found, the army which is ahead of us having commandeered the supply. The villages we pass through are deserted, no workers in the fields, all the culverts torn up. We covered 60 li (20 miles) by 7:30 that evening, walking all the way. Stayed the night at a little village called Chi-Shan. With my jack-knife I opened the carotid artery of a wounded mule with a broken leg (his ears and tail blown off by an air plane bomb the day before) and who had been left in agony for a day by the side of the road. The soldiers refused to shoot it, saying that the owner might claim damages. I took a chance on that and put the poor beast out of its misery. Off the next day early. No soldiers to be seen but the poor walking wounded.

Of the hundreds of wounded we have seen in the past few days, we have not seen a single case of a serious leg wound, only one head injury (a bullet through the jaw). The wounds are all of the hands and arms, many of them being multiple. All the other wounded have either died, been killed or captured. In the four days since leaving Linfen we have not encountered a single army medical officer or seen an ambulance. We have seen only two wounded being carried by stretcher-bearers and one man in a bullock cart who had a great wound in the thigh, which had not been dressed for ten days. Our first-aid bags became rapidly exhausted, but we were able to buy in the larger towns small quantities of gauze, cotton and some crystals of potassium permanganate. With these and our morphine tablets the wounds of all we came across in each day's march were dressed.

These exhausted, dust-covered, gray-faced men and boys, abandoned by their officers, endured without complaint the heat of the day, the bitter cold of the long night (none had blankets or bedding rolls) the pain of their undressed, suppurating wounds, lack of food (to many we gave money to buy rice) all of this without complaint. It was marvellous to see such fortitude. I only wished that I had some of their medical officers in front of me to tell them what I thought of them. None of these men were of the Eighth Route Army. I was to learn later from Professor [Herman] Mooser of the League of Nations Commission [head of an epidemic-prevention unit of the Epidemiological Commission of the League of Nations] in Sian that the only seriously wounded he had seen in military hospitals in China were in the Eighth Route Army. All other hospitals were filled only with those men who could make their way back to the rear by their own efforts.

As I walked along ahead of the carts, I saw a young lad ahead of me stopping to rest every once in a while. On coming abreast of him I noticed that he was very short of breath. He was only a child of 17. There was a great old dark blood stain on the front of his faded blue jacket. I stopped him. He had been shot through the lung a week previously. There was no dressing on a badly suppurating wound of the upper right anterior chest wall. The bullet had gone through the lung and came out at the back. There was fluid in the pleural cavity up as high as the third rib in front. The heart was displaced three inches to the left. This boy had been walking in this condition for a week. If I had not seen it myself I would not have believed it possible. We put him up on our cart where he lay coughing painfully as the mule cart moved slowly along over the rough road, enveloped in clouds of dust. We only made 20 miles that day.

The sensation of having no one between us and the Japanese is a decidedly draughty one! We know that they are gaining on us as their cavalry is capable of doing twice our distance in a day. It is a race between them and us who will reach the Yellow River first. Not until we cross that great stream will we be out of danger. What a humiliating thing it would be to be captured before even joining the Eighth Route Army, after having come half way cross the world to do so!

On the 3rd of March we came to the city of Ho-Chin. It was filled with the provincial troops of General Yan Shi San. We have caught up to the Army!

That night our commander arrived, having walked day and night from Kiangchow, a distance of 75 miles. He was able to trace us by following the print of my rubber soles in the sand! We heard that the American Presbyterian Hospital left the city a month ago. A week later 500 wounded men arrived from the north. There was no hospital of any kind for them to go to. I went to see the only doctor in the city. He is a combined doctor, dentist and druggist. That is to say he is a quack. His shop was filled with wounded waiting dressings. He is charging $1.00 a dressing. He charged me $4.00 for a small roll of gauze worth 50¢.

There seems no organization whatever among the troops. We learn that some refuse to obey their officers. Some of the officers have been accused of cheating the soldiers over their pay. Their pay in the field is $6.00 per month, with food and uniforms. It is said that some of these troops have not been paid for months.

Walked in the town. Live carp in water buckets for sale; black pigs with big floppy ears; barkless dogs, white paper windows; lousy k'angs.

My birthday – 48 – last year in Madrid. Dressed six wounded soldiers (arms and hands) nothing but neglected minor injuries – all others have died on the way back.

On March 4th we left Ho-Chin for the village of Shan-Chien-Chen on the east bank of the Yellow River. We hear that the Japanese have burned the village we passed through the day before yesterday. At 9 p.m., in the pitch dark, we march down to the river banks. Here was an unforgettable sight. Lit by a dozen fires, five thousand men were collected with trucks, carts, mules, horses, artillery and great piles of stores waiting to cross the river into Shensi. The light of the fires was reflected back from the steep wall–like mountain side. The river rushes between two high cliffs. The swift current (12 miles an hour) carries great floating ice flows, which clash against each other far out on the dark surface. The whole scene is wild and fantastic.

Lying on top of rice bags we finally sleep at midnight. The man next to me has a hand grenade in his belt, and as he turns in his sleep it sticks into my back. At 5 we are awake, a cold overcast dawn. There are only four junks. It will take four days to carry us all over. We hear that the Japanese are only ten miles away. The Chinese officer in charge of the ferry puts us on the first junk to leave the bank. The boat is about fifty feet long and twenty-five feet wide. There is 100 on board with field artillery, mules and baggage. As we are swept down stream we see that the wounded (about 1000 of them) are being collected in one spot and are being sent over first. We go down with the current for half a mile, then with long sweeps manage to get out of the main stream. A naked boy leaps overboard and with a pole-anchor slows down our progress. Then the men on the sweep slowly manoeuvre us to the bank, assisted by a back wash current behind a bend. Many troops on the west bank, which is to be strongly fortified with good trenches, dugouts. Several batteries of field guns. Machine-guns on mule back. Troops in dusty-faded uniforms the colour of the soil, which has stained them for months. Equipment good. Many automatic rifles, both light and heavy machine-guns, stick hand grenades.

We march to a nearby village and occupy a deserted house. Open two cans of chipped beef for our midday meal. The last sight I remember as we crossed the river was the great red horse belonging to Zhu De which he had loaned to Captain [Evans F.] Carlson, the U.S. Military Attaché, who had been inspecting the north Shansi front some time ago. Carlson rode the horse down and it had been left in charge of our commander to return to Zhu De, who was reported to be very fond of it. It had been captured from the Japanese and was a grand, big animal with a fine red colour. We hear that the Japanese are in Ho-Chin, the city we left yesterday. Well, we beat them to it!

The river is rising. The high bitter wind makes the shallow broad beamed junks unmanageable. I am afraid that many men will be captured tomorrow on the east bank when the Japanese come down to the river. Ho-Chin is only 5 miles away. This afternoon many Chinese troops crossed from west to east from Shensi into Shansi. That is very encouraging. We are expecting a battle on the river bank. It is raining and cold.

March 6th was cold, a high wind filling the air with dust. The Japanese cavalry arrived on the east bank across from us at 4 p.m. I had gone down to the river with a party of men who were carrying back our supplies from the beach. We were machine-gunned, the bullets striking the water a hundred yards away. We scrambled up the bank into a trench and from there could plainly see the enemy on the opposite side. Walking along the trench out into the river bank we were forced to leave it finally and make a dash across a piece of open land. Here they fired on us again. We threw ourselves down on the ground, the bullets kicking up the dust uncomfortably close. I raised my head and, to my horror, saw that we were lying in front of one of our field-guns 50 feet away. As soon as the Jap turned his attention elsewhere we spent no great amount of time in getting out of that particular spot.

I will say this for the Japs, their accuracy of range was excellent, as the distance was about 1000 yards and the light by no means good. They were firing up at us. We hear that the Japanese force is 20,000 and consists of four to five hundred cavalry, several batteries of field guns and infantry. Most of our supplies have got across, but no news of the red horse of Zhu De.

We moved into a cave tonight, much more comfortable than a house. Dressed many wounded men. Have seen no army doctors. Two of our men have left to get mules and carts. A cold night with two inches of snow the next morning on the ground. We pity the poor troops lying out on the ground without protection. Our cave is fine and warm. Nothing to eat in the village but millet.

In the morning the Japanese artillery arrived on the opposite bank and shelled the west bank all day, the noise of the explosions echoing back and forth between the mountains. Ours reply. This goes on for three days. A Japanese shell blows the top off a house 300 feet away, but they can't hurt us in our cave, which is dug in the side of a hill and 40 feet underground.

We have found a supply of drugs abandoned by some scoundrel of a medical officer – bottles of Tinc. Camph. Co., Digitalis, Adrenalin, silk sutures, syringes, ampules of cocaine.

Woke the next morning to hear one of our Chinese singing the Marseillaise. A fine clear day with a sharp wind. A child with convulsions – terrified mother, soap stick enema – cure! During the convulsion the mother rushed outside the cave and called the child's name loudly. This to bring back his soul which had temporarily left the body (reminds me of the Scotch 'bless you' when one sneezes).

On the 9th we set off for Sian on foot – 225 miles away. Lee, Jean and I set the pace. Jean is out to show some of our sceptical young comrades that she can take it! It is a fine warm day, and the country looks very well with the wheat up about four inches. Shansi, which is denuded of trees, never looked as good and prosperous as this province, which is more fertile (at least in the southern part) and with much more trees. We keep the Yellow River on our right. Lee, a former rickshaw man in Shanghai, arrives at Hanchang comparatively fresh. He has legs like trees. He is a splendid chap about 32 years of age and was on the Great Trek [Long March], so that a mere 25 miles a day is nothing. The only English he knows is 'damn fool.'

As we came in sight of the city of Hanchang, I for one was not sorry. We enter the city at five in the afternoon, through the west gate of the high city wall. We passed many students on the road from the University of Linfen. The students (3,000 of them) all were scattered west and south, some had been killed, some had died in the mountains of cold. Many were eager to go to the University at Yan'an in Shensi run by the Eighth Route Army.

In the city of Hanchang we stayed a week, waiting for trucks to come from Sian. To describe all our week here would be too long. I was besieged with civilian patients, pulmonary tuberculosis, ovarian cyst, gastric ulcer. Here was a Chinese military base hospital in a temple. After a few days the chief surgeon and the entire nursing staff offered to come with us up to Yan'an. Of course we could not take them!

On March 19th we left for Sian 200 miles away. We made this in two days, and here we are now. The first thing we did was to go to the bath house. The ineffable bliss of a hot bath – the first bath in a month! We found that we had been lost and no one knew whether or not we were alive or dead, or captured. We are now waiting to go north to Yan'an in four days' time.

In Sian, Bethune learned that the team was to be joined by another Canadian, Dr Richard Brown. Brown was an Anglican missionary whose home base, the mission hospital in Kweiteh, Honan, had been overrun by the Japanese. Journeying to Hankou to renew his passport and transact hospital business, Brown met the persuasive American journalist and activist Agnes Smedley and decided to join the Eighth Route Army. Although they shared an occupation, the two doctors held fundamentally different views on religion and politics. Brown was a devout Christian who obtained permission to preach to Eighth Route Army troops at a special Easter service.[11] Bethune was a communist and an atheist with a healthy contempt for his evangelical father. (Bethune was infuriated when Jean Ewen once dared to chastise him by saying, 'You are nothing but a bloody missionary!')[12] Nonetheless the two doctors found common cause in providing for the medical needs of the Eighth Route Army. Christians in Canada were less charitable. The Anglican Missionary Society in Toronto was far from happy to see Brown chasing around China with the communists and expressed its misgivings in a letter to him, cutting short his work with Bethune. On the other hand, Zhu De, the commander-in-chief of the Eighth Route Army, publicly declared that 'the 8th Route Army has no prejudice against missionaries. On the contrary, we welcome them and wish to co-operate with them.'[13] Bethune, in fact, looked forward to having Brown's help and had him in harness even before he arrived. Moreover, he could not resist noting the propaganda coup presented by Brown's arrival. In a communication to the China Aid Council on 23 March, he crowed about announcing to the world that the communists had found an unusual ally. 'Think of the tremendous publicity value of having a medical missionary in charge of a combined Canadian and American Medical unit to the Communist Red Army. The terrible bandits! It's simply perfect.'[14] In the following report, he described various medical organizations working with the Eighth Route Army, although only his comments on the Canadian-American Medical Unit are reproduced.

The Canadian-American Medical Unit in the 8th Army. This unit is composed, at present of 3 Canadians – Dr. Richard Brown, Miss Jean Ewen and Dr. Norman Bethune. One American doctor, Dr. Charles Parsons, accompanied this unit as far as Hankou but has now returned to America. It was designed as a mobile operating unit for the front. Not having as yet arrived at its final destination it is not possible to be more precise as to its ultimate form.

Possibilities – 1. a front line mobile operating unit for the seriously wounded, with additional personnel (Chinese) of only stretcher bearers, helpers, etc. In such capacity its location should be in an area not more than ten miles behind an engaging force. 2. As the members of one of the already existing 8th. army base hospitals. Here its function would not only be technical but instructive and educational to the at present inadequately trained staff. (Comment – This proposal sounds quite attractive, but the amount of instruction capable of being absorbed, in war time, by the Chinese from foreign doctors, some of whom can not speak the language, is very doubtful.) This is not only true for medicine and surgery but to lesser extent for nursing. My own impression is that such a proposal is, for foreigners, not a practical one. On this, as on other proposals, I do not take any dogmatic stand, but am willing to try the experiment and to be guided by experience. 3. Working with the hospital to be set up by the National Government in northern Shensi, and staffed by Chinese doctors and nurses. I am opposed to such a plan. 4. Working with one of the Operating Units of the Chinese National Red Cross. I am also opposed to such a plan. Such units are already adequately staffed with trained personnel. 5. Working (with auxiliary Chinese trained assistants) as one of the Operating Units of the Chinese Red Cross, and being maintained and supplied by the Red Cross. Objections – Under the control of the Red Cross and might be sent to any part of the country. Would tend to lose our national character. 6. (*Confidential* and projected only.) Maintaining with the Field Hospital (50 beds) of the League of Nations, which is being sent up to Yan'an next week, a Special Surgical hospital, for the more seriously wounded. Dr. Mooser and I have had many confidential talks on this project which presents so many attractive sides. The 50 bed hospital equipment which the Commission brought out from Geneva has not been used as yet, and within half an hour, after meeting Dr. Mooser he offered this equipment to me! Officially, of course, this is highly irregular, as this hospital equipment is only to be used for civilians, but Dr. Mooser knows the need of the 8th. army and being of the most advanced liberal and left wing tendencies and in addition, being in complete charge in China, is able to do very much as he wishes. If questioned, by Geneva, why the hospital of the League is being used by and for the 8th. army, his reply will be that the wounded soldiers in the League's hospital all were suffering, not only from wounds but from typhus, and as such, it was his duty to isolate them! This will give you some idea as to the wonderful luck it was for us to find such a man in charge here. The equipment contains full surgical supplies, operating instruments, ward supplies etc. – at least ten times the amount of materials we brought out from America. Accompanying this hospital will be Dr. Winzler, the medical officer of the Commission who has had surgical training. Dr. Mooser has told me we can take this hospital anywhere we please – to Wutaishan, if we like! We intend to go up to Yan'an in the course of the next 4 days, and lay the whole plan before Mao for official approval. We are taking the hospital equipment with us in one of the League's trucks. As soon as our plans are settled I will write you on this and other matters with also an analysis of the medical situation from firsthand personal inspection.

This scheme has so many advantages that they outweigh any objection which we or the Canadian or American Committees or as far as I can see, the 8th army might raise. What is causing us, that is Mooser and myself, sleepless nights, is to think of a 'formula' so that your Committee in America and in Canada can use the wonderful fact of the actual co-operation of the Hygiene Section of the League of Nations, with its worldwide reputation, with your Committee! As a publicity factor it is of the highest importance that we use it yet on the other hand without this 'formula' would involve the League, Dr. Rajchman its Hygiene Director and Dr. Mooser in the most serious consequences, both in China, with the National Government and in Geneva, with the League.

More of this matter later.

The medical supplies we brought from America are still on the way and although it is now a month since they left Hong Kong, Dr. Mooser tells me not to worry as his stuff took just as long to come up as far as Sian, from Hong Kong. In the meantime, I have been buying what I have been able to lay my hands on for our dressings and drugs, having spent on this material on our retreat from Linfen, the sum of 100 dollars (Mex) or about 30 dollars gold. I have now 70 dollars (Mex) left of the 200 dollars (Mex) which Agnes Smedley handed me on the morning we left Hankou – Feb. 22. The difference (30 dollars Mex) has been spent on food, cigarettes and donations to starving soldiers. I understand Jean has just about the same amount of money left and in addition has 200

(Mex) dollars given her by Agnes Smedley for Dr. Brown. Dr. Brown has not caught up with us as yet, but yesterday a telegram came through from Hankou that there was another doctor there – a foreigner who was coming up to join us. This may be Brown who left to go to his mission to clean up some matters there before joining us or it may be an Englishman we heard was on his way out.

...

I am carrying on in the capacity of the head of this unit until I am relieved. My plan is to appoint Dr. Brown in charge as soon as he arrives in the north. I will do this on my own responsibility, without waiting for your approval. If you want to send over another man instead of Brown to take charge why that will be O.K. with me. But consider this seriously – think of the tremendous publicity value of having a medical missionary in charge of a combined Canadian and American Medical unit to the Communist Red Army. The terrible bandits! It's simply perfect.

Bethune

Bethune continued to plan how the Canadian-American team could make a substantial contribution to the Chinese. (Portions of the original letter are torn and indecipherable, and are not reproduced.)

8th Route Army Barracks, Sian
March 26, 1938
Agnes Smedley
Hankou

Dear Comrade –
...

In a rather full letter I have sent to the Communist Party (Canada and America) in addition to a description of our little trip north – 'See Shansi First' – I have made an analysis of the medical situation here. In this report I have made several tentative proposals, to be confirmed later after arrival and checked at Yan'an. The proposals were based on the information I was able to collect, principally from Professor Mooser of the Anti-Epidemic Commission (He has given me a copy of the official report of Professor Jettmar on medical conditions in Yan'an, which was sent to Geneva) from Dr. Kiang, Chief Medical Officer of the 8th R.A., from Dr. N.Y. Yang, Chinese Delegate on the Commission (recently

returned from a visit to the north and to Mao), and from the Local Direc-
tor of the Medical Relief Commission of the Chinese National Red
Cross, which as you know, maintain 2 operating units in northern
Shensi and the obstetrical unit by Dr. Jean.

The principal proposal I made was as to the form of activity that the
Canadian-American Medical Unit should take. There are exactly 6 possible ways for us to be used, but of them all the one suggested by
Mooser is by far the most attractive as it eliminates many of the disadvantages of the others and includes one or two major advantages that
the others do not possess. In brief, it is a proposal that our unit and the
League of Nations Commission should establish, *in collaboration* (note
this word very carefully) a Special Hospital in the North. The phrase,
'working with' may also be used but not 'joined with.' Geneva will be
officially informed that an Isolation Hospital for the care of typhus,
typhoid etc. has been set up and, as the Canadian American Unit's work
is on the treatment and control of pulmonary tuberculosis in the same
area, it has been found advantageous to 'collaborate' (an ambiguous
word!) with them. Actually what Mooser proposed and offered to do is
this – He has brought from Geneva the full equipment of a 50 bed Surgical Field Hospital. This was done with the approval of Dr. Rajchman,
Director of the Hygiene Section of the League, to be used in emergency,
for the wounded, although, as you know, officially they have been for-
bidden to do so by Eden and the French. (But Geneva is an awfully long
way from Sian and Mooser is in full charge east of the Lake of Lucerne.)
Now within half an hour after meeting Mooser, he offered me his entire
surgical equipment, and his Medical Officer, to take to the North for the
unqualified use (no tags!) of the 8th Army and its wounded! This hospital can be taken anywhere – to Wutaishan, if the army wants it there!
This Mooser is a quite exceptional fellow, as you can see, and has the
needs of the 8th army very much at heart.

Our plan is to segregate the tuberculous wounded from the others,
and to fill the remainder of the hospital with the more serious cases
which are beyond technical abilities of the inadequately trained medical
staff of the army to render proper treatment to.

Think of the publicity value, in Canada and America, of 'collaboration
with' the League of Nations! Why it makes a lady out of Lizzie! It can
easily be the start of an International Hospital.

Mooser has the Equipment but has no money to run it. That's where
the Canadian-American Committee comes in. We will need something
like 1000 (mex) a month for maintenance in addition to lots of other
things, such as cars, portable X-Rays, instruments, power plants, etc. A

rather full list, and another will follow from Yan'an (we leave for there tomorrow) has already been sent by me to America [*sic*].

(For Lenin's sake, don't buy Pectoral Cough Balsam. Who, on earth advises you on this? The stuff is practically useless and I can make up such a mixture for about 25 cents a gallon instead of the 20 dollars you were charged. There are much better ways of giving iron.)

...

Both Jean and I are well. There is no typhus vaccine here. Mr. Etter, Sanitary Engineer of the Commission, has contracted it here in Sian.

I have been given 500 dollars (mex) by Lin here. I enclose a duplicate expense account – the original of which has gone to America.

With comradely greetings,
Norman Bethune.
(temporarily, in-charge, Canadian-American Medical Unit)

P.S. I propose to appoint, on my own responsibility, Dr. Brown, as Director and Chief Surgeon, when he arrives. Such appointment will have the most important effect in America, for its publicity value. For my part, I will be perfectly content to do the major part of the more important surgical operations and assist in advising, if I am asked, the military organization of a modern army medical service.

March 26. Later –
Please send us over books, papers and don't forget to write! Why not send over a Goodwill Delegation! And if they come, to bring with them, a Kodak developing outfit for our Rolliflex Camera, more films, printing paper and a good enlarger. Also a repeating 22 long rifle for shooting ducks, pheasants etc. with which the country is filled. About 2 thousand rounds of ammunition, to go with it. I need some wool socks (light weight, not the hand knitted ones). We need coffee too. There's not much to eat here except millet and carrots! We should have a movie done (36 mm. size). But I will write you from Yan'an more about our requirements.

The coffee and socks can be got in Hong Kong but there is one lesson to be learned – always travel with your luggage in China – never leave it to be sent!

Goodbye for the present. We are well and happy.

With Comradely greetings.
Norman Bethune

Bethune and Ewen left Sian in late March and arrived in the unofficial commu-
nist capital of Yan'an at the end of the month. Towards midnight on the day
they arrived, they were summoned to Mao Zedong's cave dwelling. The meet-
ing has been etched in the minds of millions through paintings and postage-
stamp images of the two communists. Missing from the pictures, of course, are
Mao's secretary and Ewen, providing essential translation service for two men
who shared a common internationalist vocabulary, but knew nothing of the
other's language. Bethune explained the plan to establish an improved hospital
at Yan'an with the assistance of the League of Nations epidemic-prevention
group and the Chinese Sanitary Corps. But Mao argued that the need for medi-
cal services was far greater at the front. In October 1937 the Eighth Route
Army had begun building the Shansi-Chahar-Hopei anti-Japanese base area in
the border region between Shansi and Hopei Provinces. Also known as the
Chin-Ch'a-Chi region, it had its centre in the Wutai mountain range, offering
protection for partisans. Bethune agreed to lead a team there. While the expedi-
tion was being prepared, Bethune and Ewen worked in the Yan'an hospital.

Brief Review of Medical Work in Yan'an

Early April 1938

From conversation with Dr. Chen Wen Kuei.

Yan'an or Fushih is a *hsien* town about 350 km due north of Sian. It is
the political and training centre of the former Red Army.

The town itself is flat, surrounded on all sides by cliffs and hills. The
former population before the occupation by the Reds was about 3,000,
but within the last year due to the great influx of students from all parts
of the country, especially from the North, Hunan, Canton and Szechuan,
this figure has increased to about 10 times. The problem of accommoda-
tion and food and epidemic, becomes a particularly acute one. The average age of the students range from 12–25, chiefly middle school or
college students, with 10% women.

In order to relieve the congestion and also as an anti-air-raid measure,
the population has been dispersed to the surrounding hills. Inhabitants
are divided into groups and each group is ordered to dig their own cave
for shelter. Owing to the peculiar formation of earth in this region and to
the severe cold these caves have proved to be ideal for the location. In
fact, they have been used by the local people for a long time and some of
the caves are historical. They may be the size of a large room, at the farther end of which there is a *k'ang* built of brick and under which a small

Mao Zedong. Bethune was an accomplished photographer and took photos in both Spain and China. This one was sent back to Canada in 1938.

coal stove can be inserted for heat in the winter. This serves as a warm
bed. The entrance is sheltered by a door, covered with white paper. This
allows for light and the poor carpentry allows for ventilation. Some are
whitewashed in the inside. The temperature outside at this time is about
10°C – and that inside of the caves is usually 0° C. Most people prefer to
live in caves, because they are cooler in the summer and warmer in the
winter than houses there. These caves not only serve as lodgings but
also as offices and hospitals. At night kerosene lamps are used for candles. These can now be purchased locally, and kerosene is produced
from wells in Yenchang about 50 km away.

Everyone in the community is given equal treatment no matter what
rank. There is an excellent spirit of diligence and friendliness. Each person is given one suit of grey cotton wadded uniform, officers are
allowed to have a cotton wadded overcoat. A few uniforms of brown
wool are seen, but these have been captured from the Japanese. Each
man is allowed a ration of $0.04 per day for millet, vegetable – chiefly
turnip and cabbage, both of which are procured fresh locally. Students
are allowed $0.08 as well as soldiers at the front. This enables them to
get mutton or pork occasionally. Meat costs $0.40 per catty. The best
food is enjoyed by the Japanese captives, who have meat everyday and
this is a source of complaint among the people. The average diet is
therefore quite deficient in fat and fat-soluble vitamins and protein. The
majority of people being young and healthy and partly because they
have not been under this diet for a long period, seem thriving and
strong, but a small group of about 1% of weaker constitution who are
unaccustomed to the extreme cold and privation are suffering from malnutrition, and some have developed TB. There was an attempt to screen
out the weaker ones at Sian, but the zeal of these young enthusiasts was
so great, that many of the young girls refusing to be sent back, have
packed up their bundles on their own backs and made their way by foot
to Yan'an, sometimes walking for 10 days.

The only means of transportation is by motorbus from Sian. The 8th
Route Army owns some and others are owned by private commercial
firms. The usual load is 2–2½ tons and the buses accommodate 20–24
people with their personal baggage. A round trip requires 90 gallons of
gasoline, and usually $280 are paid to the private company for each trip.
The road is rough and traverses small rivers with shaky bridges. In the
winter time there is practically no rain, so that except in case of heavy
snow fall, buses can go at any time, but in the summer months the roads
may be impassable for four months due to continuous rain. Usually

three days are required to make the motor trip up to Yan'an, with stopping over at night in the caves of villagers. When the group is small they may be invited to share the family *k'ang*. Most caves are heavily infested with fleas and lice.

Water is supplied from wells. This is usually hard and salty. Drinking water is usually carried up the hills from the Yen Shui, a tributary of the Yellow River. Sewage disposal is also very primitive, consisting of a shallow pit, which is usually covered up when full and a new one dug. This will be a source of fly breeding in the summer.

Medical work is divided into two parts. 1. Training of personnel and medical services.

Training courses are not organized and there are no classrooms. Students follow the physicians, and instructions may be given anywhere, in the open air or at the bedside. Formerly the training of physicians was from 8 months to 2 years. It is chiefly done by apprenticeship and no diplomas are given. At the present time there are about 50 medical students working in the various hospital units in the caves. Each hospital unit has attached to it a nursing student.

There is a great need for medical personnel in Yan'an province. The medical chief is Dr. Fu, a graduate of a mission hospital in Tingehow, Fujien who has been with the Red Army for about 10 yrs. He was with the Army in the Long March. Although physically weak, he is very energetic and works very hard. Another Dr. is a Turk trained in Geneva. Aside from this there are 2–3 other doctors who were graduates of Cheeloo, and former captives of the Red Army. Some have been inspired by the spirit around them and have become members of the Communist Party.

Medical services include the Field Medical Unit and the Base Medical Unit. The former takes care of the Army and follows it. Headquarters are situated in Lin Feng, Shansi. Attached to this unit are several physicians. They are assisted in their transportation and care by the local villagers, who carry them into their homes and take care of them there, or evacuate with the wounded when the enemy approach. Nursing care of these is carried on by young boys of 12–16 with practically no training.

The Base Hospital is between Yenchang and Yan'an. About 200 beds in Yenchang and 100 beds in Yan'an. There are very few wounded in Yan'an, but practically all in Yenchang. These patients are cared for in caves. In Yan'an services are given to civilians. The cases are chiefly medical and obstetrical. Clinics are held daily with about 100 cases seen, chiefly medical upper respiratory infection, frost bite, minor surgery and trachoma. Among the civilian population there is a great deal of syphilis. All medical services are given free. No record kept of cases.

The Sanitary Corps has established a division in Yan'an and they have set up a diagnostic laboratory and also plan to construct a de-louser. The 9th unit of the Red Cross have also been recently sent up.

Special needs of Yan'an:

1) *Food*: Some supplement must be given to supply protein and fat. The authorities should be advised to give meat at least once a week. For the malnourished, tinned eggs, or condensed milk and cod liver oil would probably be the best. The latter are comparatively more difficult to transport than extracts, but are much cheaper and would also supply fat, besides vitamins.

2) *Clothing*: At least 100 suits to be worn when delousing. Warmer clothing, or money to buy locally made felt socks. Hospital blankets for sick.

3) *Drugs and equipment*: Codeine, morphine, arsenicals, copper sulphate, bleaching powder. [There follows a lengthy list of needed supplies, which has not been reproduced.]

While in Yan'an, Bethune also wrote a lengthy article about the innovative university established there by the Communist Party. Although the exact date he wrote it is uncertain, it was published in the Daily Clarion *on 2 August 1938.*

This is the story of what must be the most unique university in the world – a huge college, with an enrolment of 3,500 students, situated 225 miles from a railway, where one can hear, on its 'campus' (the courtyard of an ancient temple) every language in the world spoken, and whose students have come to it from the palaces of millionaires, the cloistered walls of famous colleges, from the slums of Canton, from the windswept deserts of the north, from the trenches in Shantung – sons and daughters of Guomindang generals, peasants, industrial workers, writers, cinema actresses, soldiers of the old Red Army not yet 20 years of age, with 10 years of practical fighting experience behind them, officers, girl students, Boy Scouts – every class, every profession, every trade in China is here represented.

Their classrooms are in the temple 500 years old, in the open fields, in cool, deep caves dug into the hills. Here they work, study, sleep, eat, and sing. They come here for six and a half months, then graduate, and return to their cities, their villages, to the trenches and to the shops to spread among their friends and fellow soldiers and fellow workers the lessons they have learnt, the knowledge they have acquired in this centre of learning.

I have seen many universities, in many lands, old and new, but I have never seen one like this before. I know the universities of Canada, from the University of British Columbia, on the west, to Dalhousie in the east. Their pattern is much the same – the only difference is one of age. I have seen the great universities of America – Harvard, Yale, Princeton, Johns Hopkins, Columbia, University of Chicago, Stanford. They are much the same – the same pseudo-antique gothic or Norman architecture, the same underpaid staffs teaching the same subjects, remote from life, divorced from the realities of contemporaneous events, their eyes fixed on the past while the whole world trembles beneath their feet.

I know the universities of England and Scotland – Oxford, Cambridge, London, Edinburgh and Glasgow. I have visited those of Paris, Madrid and Vienna.

The students of these colleges, in whatever country, in whatever continent, are not very different from those in another. They come to these universities to learn the accumulated knowledge of the past, its science, history, literature and art.

And with that knowledge they go out into the world to improve their economic condition. Only a small percentage of these students leave with the object of concentrating their lives [on] raising the standards of living, improving the lives of those less fortunate than themselves.

This subject has not been taught them, it is not on the curriculum. They are thrown out into the world without a knowledge of that world in which they live and millions like them must live.

Then their education really beings. And that education is the education of every adult – the adjustment of himself to his time, the integration of his personal problems to the problems of the world at large. It is for many a long and painful process, made all the more difficult for the necessity to unlearn, to forget much that he has learned.

For much that he has learned, tested by his own experience, placed up against present world events, he finds is either useless or misleading.

But in this university, every subject is taught, every new acquisition of knowledge is tested, proved and criticized before accepted as truth.

'Is this true now, is this true for China, for the China of today?'

'Let us see how such and such a theory works – not how it worked a thousand years ago – but now, today, in our lives.'

The past is used only to interpret the present, and to predict the future.

This, then, is a university for the study of that ever-changing, dynamic, in-process-of-becoming stuff called life, and for the teaching of a technique for its manipulation and control by man, and for man's betterment.

Its name is The Anti-Japanese University of Yan'an. It is an outgrowth and extension of the former Red Army College, founded over eight years ago in the Chinese Soviets, for the education of its own soldiers and political workers. It has maintained its existence through years of hardship and almost insurmountable difficulties.

Not even during the Great Trek, that epic march of 25,000 li, a march comparable to and surpassing the historic marches of Hannibal, Alexander, and Napoleon – did it disband. The soldiers of the famous Red Army fought and taught – a book in one hand, a rifle in the other. Then the classes numbered 500 – now they run into thousands.

Once the students came only from the Red Army, now they come from every province in China, from every class in society. Now the officers of the Guomindang come to the university to learn how and why the Red Army was able to defeat every effort made to conquer it.

Former enemies sit side by side, sleep on the k'ang, play basketball on the same team. And the Red Army tells its secrets of victory. These secrets of tactics, of guerrilla warfare, of the organization of the peasants – how long it has taken the Guomindang to learn that no war can be successful if fought by soldiers alone, without their support!

All the accumulated knowledge and wisdom of 10 years' successful campaigns is placed at the disposal of the students to the one end in view – the defeat of Japan.

In addition, they are taught that it is not enough to defeat Japanese imperialism if, after the war, the social and economic life of the people remains where it has been for centuries. These subjects are not studied exclusively from books, never as theory, but from experience, from life, as the instructors have lived it, seen it, and know it.

So in this university there are two faculties, and all students attend both. There is the military section and the political section. There is no sharp dividing line between them. Military tactics are seen in their proper relationship to political ideas. By political ideas are meant the complex, inter-related factors of economics, sociology and philosophy, welded together into an inseparable whole by the basic concept of democratic government – 'Government of the people, for the people, and by the people.'

Yan'an, in northern Shensi, is a small town cupped in the hills which rise, bare and treeless, from the edge of its ancient walls. The normal population is less than ten thousand. It is a poor town – the surrounding country barely supporting the scattered peasants who till, with incredible toil, brown, steep slopes and narrow valleys. On the hill tops are the remains of temples.

From my cave, as I write this, I can see across the roofs of the city to the opposite hill, on which stands a Buddhist temple, stranded in time and space, significant in both its decay and its isolation (was its decay due to its isolation?) of that out-moded religion.

Yet this poor region, one of the poorest in China, has become for millions the most important area in the whole of this vast land. To thousands of students it is the Mecca of their dreams, to millions of oppressed peasants and workers it represents the hope for a new and better life.

Yan'an, in miniature, is the future China, young, eager, brave, and gay. I have seen hundreds of other towns and cities in China before I came here, and what I noticed was that this town is the most cheerful, the cleanest, the busiest, the poorest I had ever been in. I believe it is the only city in China without beggars.

It is the only city in this northern area of Shensi and the vicinity of the front without wounded soldiers hobbling about the streets or sitting mournfully on the stones nursing their bandaged hands and arms.

It has street lights (the lamps are taken in during the day) and traffic cops. It has more latrines to the block than cities 10 times its size. The streets are swept every morning.

It is gay with banners and posters. The news bulletins are up-to-date – not only, as in other towns, chronicling the Chinese war, but describing events in America and Europe.

Outside the classrooms of the university are the wall newspapers – drawings, poems, criticism and comments. The students are everywhere – girls in their teens, gay or serious, stroll hand-in-hand down the street, dressed in the faded blue cotton trousers and jacket, cap and belt of the army.

Mixed with them are the veterans from the front in their patched, padded winter uniforms, the officials of the government in their darker blue, the burnt-faced mule drivers, the pale-faced shopkeepers, the 'little red devils' (an affectionate term given those young boys not yet old enough to join the army and who are employed to carry messages).

From the playgrounds come the shouts of basketball players, from the parade grounds the fierce yells of the recruits practising the 'big sword' or bayonet drill. Everybody is busy. Everybody laughs a great deal.

At any time of the day and up to 10 at night one can hear mass singing coming from some classroom or meeting ground, rising up in a great wave of sound, fierce, brave, and free. And over all shines down the hot sun in a cloudless sky.

So what does it matter that there was only millet and carrots for lunch and the same for dinner too? What does it matter that they get one dollar a month allowance, that they sleep 10 in a cave on a hard brick *k'ang*, that they get up at six in the morning and study all day long, with only Saturday off to see their friends, that there are no movies to go to, and only candles to read by?

Why, it doesn't matter at all. They didn't come to this university to play. There is work to be done, there is an enemy to be fought, there is a country to be saved. Their lives now have a purpose, a significance they never had before.

And in the light of that purpose, their lives become good, and fine and free, and everything else is nothing. The faces of the young are not made for disguise. The faces of these students show they are happy and content. They, and they alone, are the hope of China.

In the military faculty of the university are taught the subjects in which the Eighth Route Army are universally acknowledged to be masters, namely guerrilla warfare, night fighting, armed organization of partisan detachments, hand-to-hand fighting.

Other subjects are tactics, strategy, topography, anti-tank and anti-airplane defense, trench construction, etc. This department has various grades of students. All the soldiers [students?] are officers, ranging from company commanders to generals in charge of divisions.

To look at them it is difficult to tell which is which. Both are dressed in the same faded many-times washed blue uniform. None of them wear any distinctive badges of rank. None are called captain, or major, or general – all call each other by the same name of 'Comrade.'

One does not salute an officer because he is an officer. Private soldiers salute each other in the same way they salute an officer – as a sign of comradely greeting. All look astonishingly young. That one over there, whom you might think was a boy of 20, is a famous regimental commander, with eight years of constant, active service behind him. He has been wounded four times. His regiment in the past has defeated the best troops of the Guomindang Army. Sitting beside him is an immaculately-dressed officer in khaki. He is a graduate of the Wangpu Military Academy. He knows a great deal about why he is here. And while he is here he will learn something about imperialism in general, about political economy, about social science. When he leaves and goes back to the [Guomindang] Central Army, he will have a clear insight into the meaning of the united front and the purpose of these serious, determined men and women called by some 'The hope and salvation of China.'

Of all the soldiers enrolled in the university, one out of six are from the Eighth Route Army. All are officers. All have been wounded, many several times. One student – an army corps commander – has been wounded 10 times. He is 22 years of age. Many of these officers were peasants, with little or no formal education. Here, they will learn, or begin to learn, those subjects which up to the present they have had no time for.

Of the officers not belonging to the Eighth Route Army but to the Guomindang Central Army, some have been sent by their superior officers, others have resigned to come, failing to obtain permission. Many of them are graduates of the best military academies in China. One is a graduate of St. Cyr, France. The main idea of these officers is to learn what the Eighth Route Army teaches its soldiers to give them such wonderful morale and to learn how the Eighth Route Army gains the support and confidence of the people. They learn how these things are done. They learn how partisans are organized, and a thousand other 'secrets.'

Many of these officers know more about classical military tactics than their instructors. Their book learning must be reorganized in the light of the practical experience of the Eighth Route Army.

There is no other army in the world with its history of 10 years of repeated successes against many different armies. Such an army has gained the respect of friends and foe alike. And now that army is willing and eager to show its former foes how those brilliant successes were achieved.

Five-sixths of the students in the university are from other universities and schools. Every province in China is represented, even Sinkiang on the borders of Tibet.

One out of seven of the students are girls. Most of these girls are from well-to-do families. The son, the daughter, and the daughter-in-law of a high divisional commander all are students here. They stood not only the ordinary hardships of all students, but dug their own caves in addition.

The daughter has now graduated and returned to do political work among her father's own soldiers. The son graduated last term. His father has offered him a high military position in the North Western Army, but he prefers to stay with the Eighth Army. This curious attitude of these three made the relatives of the general very curious, so curious that they came, in mass, to see what it was all about. Four stayed to enter the university as students.

Many of these young girls are very pretty, all are intelligent. They are taught military tactics along with the soldiers. Why? After they graduate, these young girls are given different kinds of work.

Some will go to the front to work organizing the peasants. Some will go behind the Japanese lines to organize partisans. They must be familiar with military tactics, as they are with organizational ones. The average girl of their age, in Canada or America, is still thinking of dates, dances, and the movies.

A famous movie actress from Shanghai is a student, with her mother, in the university. This girl, a few months ago, was the pampered pet of thousands, living in luxury. She could still do so if she cared. Now she eats what the other students eat – millet and carrots – sleeps on a hard brick *k'ang* with eight other girls in a cave, has no lipstick, no rouge, no perfume.

She receives, as do all the other students, the magnificent sum of one dollar a month to buy soap and toothpaste. Is she happy? She must be, she's as gay and as mischievous as a squirrel.

After she graduates, she will enter the Art Academy here, and from there will go with a company, either to the front, presenting plays to the soldiers or will tour the provinces, into the small towns and villages, many of which have never seen a theatre. Their plays will be written by themselves. They will make all their own stage scenery. And they will walk on foot.

Their plays will show the danger that threatens China, how Japan can be conquered, and how the peasants can gain for themselves democratic political rights, economic security and a way out of their poverty to a happier life. Will it be propaganda? Of course.

Ninety per cent of the good art of ancient or modern times is propaganda for some idea or other. Propaganda is the instillation of ideas, is the awakening of the imagination, is the stimulation to action. And the better art it is, the better propaganda it is. All truth stated clearly and concisely is propaganda. Art itself is the quickest and surest way to convey the truth from one person to another. That is the function of art, but it is the only one which gives it dignity and significance. Only by regarding art in this way can the artist really justify himself as a useful member of human society.

I asked one girl to tell me about herself and why she came to the university. She told me she was eighteen years of age and her father was a magistrate in Honan Province. There she was a student in a girls' middle school (preparatory to the university). She read about the Soviets and about their college and became determined to go. Theirs was the only college which taught how to raise the living conditions of the people. And that seemed to her to be the main thing that China was waiting for.

So she came, with three of her friends. They walked – like most of the students from Sian – a long 225 miles. It took them two weeks. She likes it here and is happy. Does not mind the hardships. Likes this school much better than her old one. Why? 'We learn from actual experience here, not just out of books. In my other school we learnt only about the past. Here we learn the realities of the present.'

Michael is my interpreter. He is a graduate of the university who is going on with further studies. I asked him why he came up here. He was a student of the Medhurst College and intended to be an electrical engineer. He lived in Shanghai and was a member of the Boy Scouts. He had first-hand experience of the Japanese, as he stood on a bridge with his friends and saw workers shot down by machine-guns as they left the factories rather than work for the Japanese.

This made him determined to fight for his country, so he came here to learn how best to do that. He first entered the North Shensi public school, then the university. He wants to be an airplane pilot.

The Eighth Army has no training school for pilots, but sends them away to other centres. Michael must wait awhile, but to wait when one is 18 is very hard.

In the political department the students study the principles of political economics, of social science, of dialectical materialism, of the technique of organization of the trade unions, of the peasants, of the students, and spend a great deal of time on the united front – how it is to be consolidated and extended.

All studies are practical, e.g., the students who return to the villages are impressed that the way to gain the confidence and following of the people is to study what the people need in that particular locality and how best they can be assisted in satisfying those needs.

Local conditions vary; local needs vary. The situation as presented locally must be carefully studied and analysed. There must be no separation of theory and fact. The theory must fit the fact, and not vice versa. Only in this way will political theory be understood and believed by the workers.

Every village presents a specific problem; the villages of the north vary from the villages of the south. The relationship of the landlords to the poor peasants varies from place to place.

In one location the exploitation of the peasants by rent is the outstanding fact, while in another, where the peasants are more independent, the exploitation by taxes is the chief feature to contest. A village more to the rear must be approached from a different angle.

The organization required in one is different from that in another. In the village close to the front the workers are told about Japanese barbarity, and they will be organized into anti-Japanese peasant unions to assist the army, bring it food, carry back the wounded, and volunteer for active service. Here, too, are organized the Self-Defence Guards.

In the rear the work will be different: assisting the mobilizing of recruits for the army, raising subscriptions for war bonds, drilling the workers for anti-Japanese activity, and in every way possible arousing the people to a realization of their danger and how that danger can be met.

The principle to be kept in mind always is: 'We must pay the closest attention to the material interests of the workers, assist them to improve their lives and raise their standard of living. Where rents are too high, we must help to get these rents reduced; if working conditions are bad, assist them in getting them improved; if taxes are too high and conditions in factories are bad, advise, lead, and educate the workers in their struggle.'

Now all this sounds serious and rather intense. Yes, it is; they work hard, but when they play, go to their own theatre and roar with laughter at their comrades on the stage, or, sitting in a great circle, sing together the ancient songs of their country – with new words! – then one sees their faces are the faces of immemorial youth, gay, serious, optimistic, clear-eyed, and serene.

They know their future – dangerous and uncertain. But in all its dark personal uncertainty there shines the bright, unquenchable light of their faith in the future, of the New China, and their steadfast purpose to dedicate their lives to the national salvation.

Such youth as these will be the saviours of their country, their spirit will animate millions to follow them, wherever they may lead.

These are the dangerous enemies of Japan, and it is such as these as will bring her to her knees.

Dr Richard Brown arrived in Yan'an about 20 April, and on 2 May he and Bethune set out for the front in the Wutai Mountains of Shensi Province. Despite her protests, Ewen was urged to return to Sian to buy vital medical

Bethune, General Ho Lung, and Dr Richard Brown, at General Ho's headquarters in North China, May or June 1938. Although Brown was an Anglican
mission doctor, Bethune thought highly of him, writing, 'This Dr. Richard
Brown is a fine fellow – speaks Chinese like a native.'

supplies.[15] *Trekking north to the front, Bethune described the worsening conditions. (The addressee's name was deleted, perhaps by the Canadian Communist
Party.)*

Suiteh, North Shensi
May 3, 38

Dear –
I really feel guilty towards you and it is this very uncomfortable feeling
I have about you that drives me to this letter. I know perfectly well I
should have written you long ago, but my fatal procrastination in letter
writing is to blame – you see it's not me, the real me, that hasn't written
you, and many times – it's this Other Fellow who lives in me who constantly puts Me off. But I've beaten him – and this letter shows it!
    We are *en route* to the front again. In the last day and a half, we

travelled 100 miles north from Yan'an, by truck. Tomorrow we set off on foot – our hospital equipment on packhorse – 150 miles still north to Pan Tang, on the west side of the Yellow River. Here, we are told, are 600 wounded men, with no doctor with a higher rank than nurse. We are going to 'clean up' this hospital then go to Wutaishan, to work behind the Japanese lines. There are the partisans.

This country is very wild, bare and treeless. It's hot.

With me is a Canadian missionary doctor – Dr. Richard Brown, of Toronto. We call it the Canadian-American Medical Unit, but that just to let the Americans get their money's worth – all 3 of us are Canadians!

I will write at more detail later – if I can get the better of this Other Fellow.

With all my love to both of you, and with the happiest memories of your kindness to me both in Montreal and New York,

Yours aye
Beth

Bethune's ambition to establish a hospital based on finances from North America was slain by lack of assistance, remoteness, and primitive conditions. In a letter to Canada, he described the humiliation of being forced to turn to the Chinese themselves for assistance.

May 3

Dear Comrades –

We are now *en route* to the front, having left Yan'an yesterday. This city is approximately 100 miles north of Yan'an. We came here by truck. The only truck that will stand up to these mountains and roads is a really big job like a Dodge. Our medical stuff, now collected at last – valuable lesson learnt, never to be separated from your baggage in China – completely filled the truck, and with a dozen soldiers and guards, we were heavily loaded. The road from Yan'an to Yen Chuan is pretty bad, from Ching Chien to Suiteh is good (I mean good for this part of the country). All roads are packed dirt with a hard surface. The only reason that better time can not be made on them than is now possible, is that they are not graded and scraped down. There is one very long and high mountain between Ching Chien and Suiteh, called Jui Li San (the 9 'li' mountain). The country gets steeper the farther north one gets, there are

8 rivers to ford – no bridges. In the rains, this road will be impassable to cars. At Yen Ping are two oil wells – one at least, is working. Kerosene is made here. All the way up, along the road, are open seams of coal. This coal is a high grade of anthracite. It is simply dug off the open seam and carted away on donkey back.

At (or rather near) Yen Chuan, is a military hospital of 300 beds. This is the hospital that I have written to the American Committee about and had Smedley send a cable asking for $1000 a month for our Unit to operate as a model hospital. In view of the fact that there has been no word from the Committee – I have not received a line from this Committee since I left America – I was forced to tell the Medical Service of the 8th R.A. that it seemed useless to expect financial support of our unit from America, but that in spite of this, we were entirely at their disposal and would go anywhere they cared to send us, but that, of course, we had no money of our own, refused, in addition, to work with or under the direction of Smedley, and would have to be supported by the 8th R.A. This the Chief of Staff assured us would be fine. Acting on this, we drew $100 on April 12. That is Jean Ewen and I received from the 8th R.A. $50 each for our current living expenses, on that date. You must understand that this step was taken with extreme reluctance, on our part, but we were absolutely broke, no word had come from America in spite of our telegrams, cables, and letters from us, written weekly at least.

We have not, at any time after the outfitting of this Unit – the last items of which were added in Sian – needed much money, but Yan'an is an expensive place to live. We needed money not only for food, but there are always other expenses; developing and printing the photograph films cost $4 to $5 a week. Charcoal is expensive – $3 a small load. This is used not only for cooking, but for heating our cold caves. There is always 4 to 6 for dinner, of the foreigners in the city. I am only mentioning these housekeeping facts, to give you an idea of the conditions here.

Well, since the model hospital was off (it must be carefully kept in mind that all schemes, even the tentative ones proposed were fully discussed with responsible officials) the Chief Medical Officer of the Medical Service of the Front (Dr. Chiang) decided last week we should go to Shen Mu, in the extreme north, near the Great Wall, as soon as our American supplies arrived. All the American material arrived safely and in good condition. Nothing was lost. You can imagine our joy! We embraced the panniers! But before the stuff arrived in Yan'an, we got word that it had come to Sian, so Jean was sent down to bring it up personally. The stuff arrived but no Jean! I sent her two telegrams but received no reply – the last one saying that Brown and I were leaving for the front in 4 days' time and to return. We left word in Yan'an, that when she arrives she is to follow us.

At Ching Chien we met the Chief Medical Officer of the Front, who told us that owing to the changed military situation – owing to the Japanese withdrawing from a large part of the territory they held in Shansi, that the wounded were coming into Shensi by another route, and that he intended to send us to Pan Tang. This town now has 600 wounded according to last reports, and no doctors above the rank of dresser.

We, that is Brown and I, have agreed to go to Pan Tang at once. At the same time we told him of our desire to go to Wutaishan. He has asked us to 'clean up' the hospital at Pan Tang first and that later, if they need help in Wutaishan, that he will send us there. This 'cleaning up' process will probably take a month.

So that is the situation at present.

Our address for books, magazines and papers (you seem determined not to send any letters) is Dr. Ma Haide, Yan'an, Shensi, China. He will forward. If you change your mind about giving additional medical assistance to the 8th R.A., send all money direct to Mao Zedong, at Yan'an. The 8th R.A. and nobody but the 8th R.A. should be the recipient of money from abroad, directly.

Six days on foot to Pan Tang. Off tomorrow, all our supplies on pack ponies.

Salud,
Norman Bethune

P.S. This Dr. Richard Brown is a fine fellow – speaks Chinese like a native. Unfortunately, he only has 4 months leave from his hospital. When he leaves, Dr. Haide will come north to replace him. But I could use a half dozen more Canadian or American doctors. Where is Dr. L. Fraad? Send him over immediately. Send a spare tube for the X-ray and a generator.

From Suiteh they continued north to the base hospital at Ho Chia Chuang. Here Bethune wrote a lengthy report to Mao Zedong in Yan'an describing his activities to date and making recommendations for improvements in existing conditions. Adding a note to 'Canadian and American "detail men"' – those in North America preparing the fresh troops he hoped would soon arrive – he provided a lengthy list of equipment, personal supplies and clothing that should be brought. For example: 'Chinese chairs (up here, at least) are uncomfortable – nothing is as comfortable as the canvas folding chair sold by A. and F. [Abercrombie and Fitch in New York. Each member should have one – and bring one for me!' Some sections of this lengthy report have not been reproduced here.

Ho Chia Chuang, Northern Shensi,
May 17, 1938

Mao Zedong
Yan'an

Dear Comrade –
The following is a brief, introductory report on medical conditions in this hospital, with some recommendations for your consideration.

We left Yan'an on Monday, the second of May. At Er Shi Li Pu, we stopped to pick up some supplies and to leave others. Of the supplies we asked for, Dr. Sung gave us only a small part. We asked for 50 lbs. of ether, and received 10; for 25 lbs. of gauze, none; for 10 lbs. of refined salt, for intravenous use, a handful; for a small barrel of Plaster of Paris, for fracture work, none. I may say that all these supplies were out at Er Shi Li Pu, as we saw them there. In view of the amount of work that we were asked to do, and the long distance we were to be away from supplies, and especially as there was an increasing amount of supplies coming to Er Shi Li Pu, this refusal was very regrettable. At the same time it should be remarked that the people there leave valuable drugs unpacked. We were never able to see an inventory of supplies on hand. It is suggested that shelves be erected, all drugs and supplies unpacked and put on them, that inventory be made, stock books kept. In addition, the place is over-staffed.

At Chang Chien, we met Dr. Chiang, who joined us on our trip north. Ten days before he had asked us to go to Pan Tang, where he said there were six hundred wounded. He informed us that the hospital in Pan Tang had been moved to Ho Chia Chuang and we were to proceed there. After a 2 day stop at Mi Shih to repack our supplies, we set off with 13 mules, on May 6th, arriving here on the 11th.

At Yen Chuan, there are no wounded, only sick; at Mi Shih, only 20 or 30 of the 8th Army wounded. We were not asked to see these. At Chia Hsien all the wounded belong to the Shansi Provincial Army, and none to the 8th R.A.

In this hospital, instead of the 600 we expected to find there are only 175 wounded of the 8th R.A. Of these 35 are very serious. All have old neglected wounds of the thigh and leg – most of them incurable except by amputation. Three of the 35 are lying naked on straw-covered *k'angs*, with only a single cotton quilt. The others are still in their old, unwashed cotton-padded winter, dirty uniforms. They are, without exception, all anaemic, underfed and dehydrated. The surgical care they receive is to dress the wounds – discharging sinuses leading down to the diseased bone. They are dying of sepsis. These are the cases we are asked to operate on. They are all bad surgical risks.

May 22, 1938
The first three days were spent in preparing an operating room and post-operative ward. This was difficult on account of the lack of material – such as cotton cloth, pails, gauze, etc. Mattresses had to be made to cover and enclose straw as otherwise it becomes wet and unusable. There was only enough cotton cloth to make 10 mattresses. The patients were evacuated from two adjacent rooms, opening one into the other and these were used as operation and recovery rooms, after as thorough a cleaning as it was possible to give them. Sheets, towels, gauze squares, mops, masks, glove cases, all were cut from our remaining cotton cloth, sewn and sterilized in the autoclave.

We had, after examination of the 35 serious cases, divided them into classes 1, 2, or 3 depending on the emergency of the case. Class 1 required immediate operation, principally on account of abscess formation complicating bone infection. Class 2 could wait a short time, and Class 3 were those in which operation time was not important. All these cases are completely bedridden ...

Our Plans for the Immediate Future, of the Canadian-American Mobile Medical Unit

We (that is Dr. Brown and Bethune) are working in the closest co-operation both in practical everyday work, and in round table discussions with Dr. Chiang. Some of our conclusions are as follows:

1. It is unpractical to think that this Unit of 2 surgeons can go into hospitals such as this and do all the work which needs being done. In this hospital alone, there is enough work to keep us both busy for six months. We can't do it for two important reasons: 1. the present nursing staff cannot give, with their limited experience and equipment, the proper after-operation care, even though we do operate. 2. the operations are the least important part of treatment – after-care the most important. So, the most

we can do here is to operate only on such cases as require the smallest amount of after-care; amputations and minor cases.

2. The great need to get to the front and, by instruction, prevent many such cases as we see here from getting into such conditions.

3. The very short time that Dr. Brown has left before he must return to his own hospital, and the necessity that he should inspect the entire front (including partisan territory, such as Wutaishan) to be in a position to describe, from firsthand information, the medical needs of the 8th Route Army. His report will be a most valuable piece of work, for publicity.

4. It would be unwise to split the Unit at present, until a doctor can be found or trained to replace Dr. Brown. Dr. Bethune, with his ignorance of the language, in addition to a partially trained Chinese, would be placed in a position in which his work would be seriously hampered. In the interval before Dr. Brown leaves, every effort will be made to find Dr. Bethune an assistant.

5. It is planned to form a permanent Mobile Operating Team, after Dr. Brown's departure and in the meantime, to train such a team. It will be composed of the following:

1. Personnel – Dr. Bethune, Surgeon; Chinese doctor, Asst. Surgeon; Chinese nurse, Operating Room Nurse; Chinese nurse, Post-Oper. Ward Nurse; Chinese, quartermaster; Chinese, secretary; 4 *Hsiao kwei* [assistants]; 3 grooms for horses; cook.
2. Equipment – The present American equipment, supplemented by additional medical supplies.
3. Cost – (to be entirely borne by the American and Canadian Committees) ... $1250.00 [monthly].
...

With the above plan in mind, we are leaving this hospital on a tour of the various Divisional Hospitals in Shansi. We may go to Wutaishan. If so we will return for more supplies and if Bethune does not, then Brown will.

We leave on the 27th of May. Our first stop is Hsing Hsin, in Shansi. An Operation Room is being prepared for us there now, in the Divisional Hospital.

We will close this report with a list of the medical and surgical supplies needed, as far as we have seen them, up to the present.
...

Note: This unit themselves possess more instruments than the rest of the entire medical service in the 8th R.A. combined. Yet the instruments of the Unit, brought from America, are no more than adequate to do general surgery.

This list will give enough to go on with. All the above supplies can be purchased immediately with the assurance that they are desperately needed. This list will undoubtedly be added to the future. Do not be afraid that all this material will not be used to save lives. Delay means life or death.

Additional list. Not of necessities, but of things to make our patients in hospital happier.

1. Radios ... – 6
2. Gramophones. Records in Chinese – to be bought or donated in China – 24
3. Books – plenty of illustrations – to be bought in China – 1000
4. Games, foreign or Chinese – lots
5. Coloured pictures, posters to hang on the walls of the wards – hundreds.

Anything else that occurs to you to brighten their lives.
   With greetings,

Dr. Norman Bethune
Dr. Richard Brown
(Canadian-American Mobile Medical Unit, 8th Route Army)

P.S. Please send us Dr. Ma Haide as soon as possible ...

   Note to Canadian and American 'detail men' ...
I am beginning to doubt whether or not you have received all the letters I have sent you. I have kept copies only of those written since I left Hankou – as previous to that I did not possess a typewriter. I will give you the dates: March 22, Sian; April 14, Yan'an; April 17, Yan'an; April 8, Yan'an; April 13, Yan'an; April 20 Yan'an; May 3, Suiteh.
   ...
   Two cables have been sent – one by Jean and I from Shanghai demanding the recall of Parsons, and the other, through Smedley, appealing for $1000 a month for medical aid. No reply has been received to either. In addition, while we were in Hankou, Smedley sent 3 cables but as far as I know (and I would have known) received no reply.
   I have exhausted every means in my power to try and get a word

from the American Committee. I give it up – after 5 months. You people in America can cable us – why, I can be reached by wire in 24 hours from New York, even up in this little village, in the wilds of Northern Shensi. We have a direct telegraph line to Yan'an – a military line. But Yan'an has a commercial wire to the outside world. Send the cable to Mao Zedong with a request it be sent on to me. Is this too much to ask of you? We have no money to cable you and even though we had, our experience in the past has been so disappointing that I don't feel like asking the 8th Army to give us the money to try again.

Have you received a single letter I have written? [Only one had been received.] Perhaps not. Perhaps the American Committee has not received any of my letters, cables, and appeals. If such is the case, I beg of you and them to forgive the anxious, irritable and angry tone of my letters. Acting on this assumption, I am asking Mao Zedong to send this letter not to you directly – nor to Tim [Buck] – to prevent possible interception.

I have sent the American Committee enough material for publicity and press to fill a paper. The only reply was a letter from the mail clerk of the American League for Peace and Democracy, asking me if Yan'an was my correct address! But not a line from any one else.

Well, I will close.

We are happy and content in our work.

With comradely greetings,
Norman

On 23 May Bethune wrote to Tim Buck and other Canadian comrades complaining about losing track of Ewen after she returned to Sian to search for the supplies the unit had brought from America. On the trip back to Sian, she passed the trucks carrying the equipment to Yan'an, carried on to Sian, and then returned to Yan'an. Bethune and Brown had already left for the front. Although clearly without enthusiasm to rejoin Bethune – whom she found domineering and dogmatic – she followed them north. At the town of Ching Chan, she was delayed, and she never saw Bethune again.[16]

The Village of Ho Chia Chuang, on the Sha Ma Ho, Northern Shensi, May 23, 1938

We have started work here in this little village of about 50 houses. We are 20 li (6½ miles) west of the Yellow River, and about 75 miles south of the Great Wall. We came here on May 11th, walking all the way from Mi Shih – the end of the road for trucks. It took us 6 days to cover the 265 li. The country is wild and mountainous. Our best day was 75 li (25 miles). We had 13 mules for our supplies. The weather was warm and even hot. We all wore straw hats for the sun. The country is practically treeless except in the bottoms of the valleys, where a few willows grow.

There are 175 wounded here, scattered among the houses. It would make your heart bleed to see them – lying on the hard brick *k'angs*, with only a little straw beneath. Some have no coverlets – none have blankets. They are crawling with lice. They have only one uniform and that they have on. It is filthy with the accumulated dirt of 9 months' fighting. Their bandages have been washed so often they are now nothing but dirty rags. Three men, one with the loss of both feet through frost bite gangrene, have no clothes at all to wear. They lie huddled up under a single cover – and this in a country so cold at night that we are glad to have our feather-filled sleeping bags to sleep in.

Their food is boiled millet. All are anaemic and underfed. Most of them are slowly dying of sepsis and starvation. Many have tuberculosis.

Canada must help these people. They have fought for the salvation of China and the liberation of Asia. I know we are poor. I know Spain needs our help, but Spain never needed help as these uncomplaining people do. For five months now the American Committee in New York has been completely silent – not a word from them – in spite of my repeated telegrams and letters. I can give no explanation to Mao Zedong – I am ashamed. If the American Committee has ceased to function, surely the Canadian can help, in addition to supplying the personnel of the first mobile operating unit in any army in China. Cannot Canada alone raise the money to keep our Unit from being an expense to the hard-pressed 8th Army? As you will see in my reports, I have calculated the monthly expenses of our Unit to be $1250.00 (Chinese dollars) a month. At the last rate of Exchange this could be less than $400 (Canadian).

I don't know what has happened to Jean. On the 20th of April she left for Sian to bring back our American equipment which had arrived there. I asked her to wire and to keep in touch with us and to return as soon as she could as both Dr. Brown and I were anxious to get away to the front. This she promised to do. She left in good spirits, leaving her personal belongings behind. Two days after all our supplies arrived, but no Jean. Hearing that she was staying at the Sian Guest House (in spite of the request of Dr. Haide not to do so, as it looked so bad not to stay in

the 8th Army Barracks) I sent her 2 telegrams asking her to return immediately as we were leaving for the front. To these telegrams there was no
reply, so that Dr. Brown and I decided to leave without her. This we did
on May 2. We told Dr. Haide that when she returned she could take her
choice as whether or not to follow us or to work in Sian. On our march,
both Dr. Brown and I commented that she would not have been very
happy walking up and down the mountains we crossed. Up to the
present she has not turned up here and as we have received no letters or
telegrams since leaving, I don't know where she is.

Lord! I wish we had a radio and a hamburger sandwich.

Norman

*Preoccupied as he was by the desperate state of medical care in the area, Bethune
did not neglect the need to explain the anti-fascist struggle in China to the outside world. In the following article, written in June 1938 and intended for the
Manchester Guardian, Bethune presented a detailed analysis of the politics and
social forces in the regions defended by the Eighth Route Army. It is a work of
insight into the nature of guerrilla war, the Communist Party's United Front
strategy, and the reasons why the apparently powerful Japanese invaders would
be defeated. But the overwhelming volume of detail and the bureaucratic language conspire to hide Bethune the writer. If it was received by the Guardian,
shaping it into a meaningful article for a Western audience would have been
difficult. The article is noteworthy because it arose partly from Bethune's dire
poverty. He hoped this would be the first of several articles for foreign newspapers for which he would be paid, relieving the Chinese of the burden of
supporting his unit. (Portions of this lengthy article have been omitted here.)*

The Chin-Ch'a-Chi: The Boundary Region of
Shansi-Chahar-Hopei:
Its United Front Government and the Role of the
8th Route Army and the Chinese Communist Party in
Partisan Warfare

28 June 1938
Here is a region, in the interior of North China, completely surrounded
by the Japanese Army, which holds all the railways and the main lines
comprising its roughly-shaped 100,000 square miles of territory with its
population of 13,000,000 people. It has the first United Front Govern-

ment in China. Because it is the presage of the future development in Government of China, it becomes of the greatest importance that its history, and the story of its formation be known, not only in China, but to the world at large. It is of special importance that the role of the Communist Party in its formation and present functioning be understood, since this role is not merely one of meeting the local situation with an extemporized expediency, but, on the contrary, follows strictly the international line laid down by the Comintern as applicable to the present world-wide situation.

History. After the Japanese invasion and the start of the major Sino-Japanese war on July 7th, 1938, eastern Hopei province and Beijing were captured. The enemy drive is to the west and south. They were soon in possession of the principal railways of Hopei, Chahar and later of Shansi provinces. The Provincial troops of these provinces were either defeated or retired. The local provincial and municipal government officials soon followed suit. The government was disorganized. The principal cities on the Beijing-Tientsin line (the Pei-Ning Lu), the Beijing-Shih Chia Chuang (the Ping-Han Lu), the Beijing-Ta Tung (the Ping-Sui Lu), and the Ta Tung-Tai Yuan (the Tung-Pu Lu) Lines were in possession of the enemy. They held also the towns along the motor road from Shih Chia Chuang to Chang Chow. Within this square, beyond capturing and burning the villages and towns within a few miles from the railways, they did not penetrate deeply. Their highly mechanized army, was of necessity, restricted to rail and motor roads. But, placing garrisons in these cities and towns, they continued their drive to the south. They were apparently undefeatable. They openly held the Chinese troops in contempt. The spirit of the Chinese soldiers was one of pessimism – of despair. Then a Chinese victory of the greatest importance occurred – the victory – the first victory of the war – of the 8th Route Army, under Lin Biao, at Ping Hsing, in northeast Shansi. Here was demonstrated the fact that the enemy could be defeated. It is not an exaggeration to say that this brilliant engagement, resulting in massacre and rout of the Japanese forces in this region, will go down in the history of this war as one of the turning points in the ultimate Chinese victory. Its effect, not only as a crushing defeat of the Japanese army, but as the needed stimulus to the desperate Chinese, can not be overestimated, even though the news of this battle was almost completely suppressed by the Guomindang and is only now becoming generally known.

While it is true that the majority of the Government troops (the term Provincial Troops is really only historically correct, as they were organized under the Central Government) retired, some did not. One army, that under General Mung Kwo Chen, about 4,000 strong, still remained in Hopei province, south of Beijing. This was the 7th Route Army. After the retirement of the majority of the Central troops, this army changed its name to the People's Army, and, enlarging its forces with the partisans, engaged in independent activities. Another division which remained in eastern Hopei was that under General Sung Tien Ying formerly with Feng Yu Hsing, the vice-Chairman of the Central Military Council of the Guomindang. Still another, was the army under General Lu Cheng Tsao, the Manchurian. This army, mostly Manchurians, remained in Mid-Hopei, east of the Ping-Han Railway. His force was approximately 3,000 troops. All of these forces were however, mainly inactive except for a type of guerrilla warfare – the raiding of railway stations, tearing up tracks, etc. They acted independently of each other. There was no central military command. Their effectiveness suffered as a result. The 8th Route Army came into eastern Shansi and western Hopei immediately after the war started. They, instead of retreating, advanced towards the enemy. Their defeat of the Japanese – employing the same tactics which they had formerly found so successful against their late enemy – the Guomindang – followed. So can be seen, that in the fall of 1937, the Chinese troops in mid, eastern and western Hopei, northeastern Shansi and Southern Chahar, on the boundary of Hopei, were composed of widely scattered and independently acting units to a total strength of probably 25,000 men. They were cut off from each other and were only nominally under the control of the Central Government.

Just as it is true that the military had mainly retired, also that the Government officials had done the same, still as in the former case some remained. Those that remained were almost invariably minor officials – municipal and local governments of *hsiens* (counties) and towns. Some *hsiens*, after the flight of their magistrate, elected their own (this was an innovation as formerly all magistrates, who held the highest authority in the *hsiens*, were appointed by the provincial Governor). An example of this is the magistrate, Chang Soo of Wei Hsien in southern Chahar.

Some of the officials who remained were such as the magistrate of Fu Ping, in western Hopei Chow, Yu Wen; Sung Shao Wen, Chief Political Officer of the Northeastern District under Governor Yen Hsi Shan, of Shansi Province. These officials were, like the military, isolated from their former governments. After the fall of Tai Yuan, there could hardly be said to be a government of Shansi province.

The 8th Route Army had sent a division into eastern Shansi, in September. This division was under the command of General Nieh. This army and its political leaders immediately set about the task of mobilizing the people in partisan detachments, to operate in the rear of the enemy and on his flank. This was the beginnings of the most extensive organization of partisans in China today. It must never be forgotten that it was the 8th Route Army and the Chinese Communist Party who were the leaders in this work. Not content with this, the 8th Route Army leaders approached the remaining government officials and asked for their cooperation in this work and in the establishment of a stable government for this region. It was suggested that this government be a United Front Government based on the common aim of the defeat of the Japanese and the improvement of the lives of the people. General Nieh of the 8th Route Army, accompanied by Shung Shao Wen, travelled to Fu Ping and, in conference with the magistrate of that *hsien*, Cho Yu Wen, and with Chang Soo, magistrate of southern Chahar, on December 20th, 1937, decided that a United Front Government be established to maintain the integrity of this region. A telegram to this effect was dispatched to Yen Hsi Shan. He approved. The result of the discussions was the decision to form a committee to prepare the plans for such a government. This committee was formed on December 29th, 1937. It was composed of 5 members. It decided to summon a Conference of all people's organizations and of military forces in the region. This Conference was to be representative of all the people. This now famous conference met at Fu Ping on January 10, 1938.

Here, for the first time in the history of China, there sat down together, government officials, both of the provincial government and the Guomindang; military leaders of Central Government troops and the 8th Route Army; delegates of workers; mass organizations; peasants' unions; unions of women and of youth and representatives of the Communist Party. To the conference came 146 delegates. It was a true democratic parliament. Now was seen the work among the people of the 8th Route Army and the Communist Party from September on. Without this work, such a representative conference of all the people would never have been possible. Instead, just as in the old days, a handful of men would have decided the future form and manner of government of 13,000,000 people. Now these same people decide this themselves. What were these organizations? The Peasants' Union, the Workers' Union, the People's Self Sacrifice League, the Union of Women, the Union of Youth.

The Peasants' Union is a mass organization with 2 million members.

It is a federation of District Unions. Its aim, is, like all mass organizations sponsored by the Communist Party, the bilateral one of irreconcilable opposition to Japanese Imperialism – its military side, and the other, of equally irreconcilable opposition to poverty, ignorance and undemocratic Chinese feudalism – its social side. Its object is to mobilize the people to save China – to arm the people, to organize the People's Army, to improve the livelihood of the peasants, to decrease rents and raise wages, increase the number of schools.

The Workers' Union with 600,000 members. The workers so organized are handicraft men, mine workers (coal and gold), rickshaw men and coolies engaged in non-agrarian work.

The People's Self Sacrifice League has had an interesting history. Organized in 1936 on the 5th Anniversary of the Japanese invasion of Manchuria, by Yen Hsi Shan, its ostensible purpose was to organize the people into fighting Japan. All the organization was in Shansi. Its membership was 700,000. How did it propose to save China? Its avowed aim was to mobilize the people, to arm the people. Yet the people were never armed in Shansi. Of the arms possessed by the partisans of the Boundary Region at the present time, none have come from those owned by the peasants and workers formerly. Why did they not possess arms, like the peasants of the Hopei province? The answer is that Yen Hsi Shan, although proclaiming that only the armed people of China could save China, did nothing to further this. He feared, as all autocratic political authorities do, the combination of an enlightened and armed people. Still, there was a certain amount of general political education done among the Shansi troops and there was also an improvement to the provincial government's administration.

The Union of Women. Its members number 200,000. It was organized by the Communist Party. It has mobilized the wives and daughters of workers, to the end that they in turn will educate their men. Its main work is to take the place of the men fighting, to work in the fields, to make clothes and shoes for the troops, etc.

The Union of Youth is an organization of intellectuals, of university students, of mid and lower schools, of teachers, young government officials. It was organized by the combined Communist Party and the Guomindang. Its purpose is propaganda and the education of the people to the realities of the war.

Mobilization Committees. After the fall of Tai Yuan, and before the organization of the present Regional government, Governor Yen Hsi Shan and the 8th Route Army established local committees to maintain order. At this time many local municipal governments were disorganized. These Committees were temporary and transitional. There were about 40 of such Committees formed, in as many *hsiens*.

All these local Mobilization Committees sent delegates to the Conference. The military delegates were representing the 8th Route Army and the Partisan detachments operating with the 8th Army; delegates from a division of Yen Hsi Shan's troops in eastern Shansi; delegates from the mid-Hopei troops of General Mung Kwo Chen; from General Sung Tien Ying's troops in east Hopei, and from General Lu Cheng Tsao's Manchurian troops lying east of the Ping-Han Railway.

The Conference passed a number of resolutions. Some of the important ones were (1) to establish a United Front Government of this region. The form of this government was to be according to the regulations of the Guomindang, as laid down by the Central Government. (2) military forces were to be enlarged by mobilization of the people into partisan and volunteer forces. While, at this time no proposal of a United Command (that has come later) was made, the resolution stressed the necessity of united aims. (3) to establish a Regional Bank and print its own notes, to issue War Bonds. A number of other resolutions bearing on the finances of the Region were passed also.

At this conference, the members of the Government were elected ... Two only of these [9] men are members of the Communist Party.

How is this a democratic form of government? A delegation of representatives from all the people's organizations meets the Government every two months. These delegates are elected – that is chosen – from the monthly meeting held in each district, of those same organizations. From every village, in each district, the people's organizations, at their own irregularly held mass meetings, delegates are elected to attend these monthly district meetings. The government passes no regulations, issues no laws, without the approval of the bi-monthly people's delegation. As a result, there exists in this Region a People's Government. It is the only People's Government in China.

...

How are the partisans and troops in this isolated area supplied with arms? The Central Government has given them none. Its arms have come from 5 sources – (1) the arms possessed by those troops of the Central and Provincial Governments which did not retire on the Japanese advance. (2) Those arms abandoned by the Central and Provincial troops when those troops did retire. (3) arms possessed by the people themselves, principally in Hopei province. (4) manufactured arms –

small in number – about 100 rifles a month, besides a more considerable number of bombs. (5) Those captured from the Japanese – principally by the 8th Route Army ...

When one considers that there are between 100,000 and 150,000 soldiers of the various armies, partisans, and volunteers to arm, clothe, feed and hospitalize when sick and wounded, it is little wonder that 90% of the income of the government is spent on the army. The cost of the government is probably the lowest in the history of Chinese governments – the Chairman, for example ... receives the magnificent sum of $20 a month. The pay of the soldier ... is $1 a month, that of the general in command of the entire Region, $5 a month. These sums should be compared to the pay of the soldier of the Central Government – $9.00 a month and that of a senior officer, from $250 to $500 a month.

Partisan warfare – There are two kinds of fighting going on in China against the Japanese – one, that of large bodies of regularly trained troops engaged in mobile or so-called 'positional' warfare, and the second, that of partisan warfare or the so-called 'guerrilla' fighting. The tactics are entirely different. In Central China, the troops of the Central Government are engaged in the former fashion, while in this Region, the principal activities of the troops are in the latter. These types of fighting complement each other. The Japanese can only engage in one manner, that of positional warfare, unless they are able to buy, by money or promises, the troops of adjacent or conquered countries to engage in guerrilla warfare also against the Chinese. This is one of their principal objectives in Manchuria and Mongolia. Such armies are called 'puppet armies.'

What is a Partisan? He is a worker – in uniform. He is usually a peasant farmer. He is strong, tough, accustomed to hardship and little or no food for long intervals; exposure to all kinds of weather since childhood has made him indifferent to heat or cold. He has been made aware of the danger to his beloved country by stories spread from mouth to mouth throughout the villages, since he cannot read or write and lives far from great cities. He is told of the destruction by the enemy, of the burning of towns, of the massacre of thousands of workers such as himself. He hears from another worker, this one usually in the uniform of the 8th Route Army of the necessity of fighting Japan. He hears for the first time such strange words as 'imperialism,' 'democracy,' 'War of Aggression,' 'feudalism,' 'Workers of the World,' 'nationalism.' He is told how he can help. The causes of the war are explained to him. The causes of all wars are explained to him. He is urged to unite with his fellow workers. He joins a mass organization. He hears about the bravery of his country's soldiers. He wants to fight too. But how? He may join the Volunteer Guards and be given an old rifle or a rude spear, and set to patrol the roads, to guard bridges and keep a sharp eye open for suspected traitors. In such a unit as the Volunteer Guards he will not leave the district in which he lives. He may even carry on part-time work. Or, on the other hand, he may go directly into a partisan detachment. He is given a military training, a uniform and arms. His pay is the same as that of a regular soldier although his role is a different one. He is instructed by officers of the army or by experienced partisan fighters. He is given a combined military and political training. The detachment to which he belongs may number 10 or 1000. Such a detachment, made up as it is of men of his own or neighbouring villages, operates in its own *hsien* or county as a rule. Here such a detachment has the valuable advantage of knowing every inch of the country, every tree, every winding mule track over the mountains, every stream and ford. They are as elusive as fish in a deep pool, as difficult to corner and surprise as birds in the air. Little wonder that the Japanese keep to the railways and motor roads, with such an enemy to ambush them if they leave those wide tracks. It is these partisans which have completely foiled the Japanese attempts to consolidate or even to put profitably to use the country which they proudly proclaim to have 'conquered' and now 'control.'

The total effect of partisan war is not, nor ever can be, decisive, in terms of final victory. That victory can only be achieved by large armies, in positional warfare. But their role as complementary troops to the army, is an all–important one. They make the armies' tasks easier. They tie up, by their ceaseless activities, large numbers of the enemy's troops. They camouflage, by their attacks, the movements and striking point of the regular army and its concentration of forces.

As a result, although the Japanese hold, with garrisons, 25 large towns or cities on the fringes of this Region, the partisans have been successful in preventing them from utilizing the resources of the countryside. The Japanese make sorties, in full strength, from these cities, raid the neighbouring village, burn, kill but as quickly return to the protection of the high walls. Why do not the partisans attack in force these large walled towns? It is not considered worth the loss of life they would have to pay for their capture. As it is, the enemy must garrison them and this removes large numbers of troops from 'active service.' Many Japanese soldiers sent to these garrisons from the 'front,' find to their dismay that life here is just as unpleasant. He is shot whenever he goes on sentry duty, ambushed when he leaves the town. He never knows when he may be attacked, or how or from what direction.

It is the partisans with their political training, who by their presence and educative activities among the peasants, have prevented the spread of Japanese political influence among the Chinese of North China.

Partisan warfare is of fundamental importance in this war. It is becoming of increasing importance. Now with a unified military command in the Region, with partisans working in and with the Army, the whole strategy of the troops in the Region has become a part of the military policy of the General Military Council. To this, the 8th Route Army has given wholehearted support. Not only in military policy but in political policy, the Government of this Region is in closest alignment with the Central Government. The needs of China as a whole are seen in relationship to the needs of the region. There is no thought of merely protecting this area of the country simply because it is their own homeland. How this Region can best assist China as a whole in meeting the efforts of Japanese imperialism to conquer the nation is the foremost thought here.

Although the Japanese have occupied the principal cities and lines of communications, their political authority has not spread over the hinterland. It is the Japanese hope to spread their political power outwards from the railroads, thus enabling them to exploit the territory economically and to use North China as a base of operations for penetrating the rest of China and as a base against Russia. Here too they are attempting to build up a traitor government to oppose the Central Government. The growth of partisan warfare is preventing the spread of Japanese authority and thus directly defeating the Japanese plan to use North China man power and materials against the rest of China.

This opposition to the penetration of Japanese political power is the chief function of the partisans. The other subsidiary functions of the partisans are to do their best to prevent the advance of the Japanese troops southward by destroying communications and harassing the enemy's rear; to destroy Japanese political authority by attacking all representative bodies of the traitor government and to prevent the further spread of traitor organizations. To do this, this region must be guarded and enlarged. There are no more Central Government troops which may be diverted from the south for this purpose – this work must be done by the partisans.

Japan tries to use Chinese to fight Chinese. She encourages Chinese factionalism. She fears the United Front. She attempts in every way possible to split off and separate small or large political groups from the Central Government. Thus she misrepresents to the world and to the Chinese the sincerity of the 8th Route Army and the Communist Party in their all-obvious cooperation with the Guomindang. This attempt to foster political disunity is one of her most powerful weapons. She also wins traitors by money and terrorism. She has not been unsuccessful. Already she has established a broad traitor base. She is also seeking to enlarge and use the racial conflict within China such as the Mongol-Chinese question. To border nationalities, her slogan is 'you are not Chinese, we only oppose the Nanjing armies not the regional troops.' Another of her slogans was 'We only oppose the Red Army, not the other armies.' At times, the Japanese soldiers in the occupied cities hold mass meetings for the Chinese, give food to the poor, and candy to the children. This is only one side of her strategy, which also includes the burning of villages and the raping of women.

The role of the 8th Route Army and the Chinese Communist Party in this Region – It must be clear that the mass movement has been organized in this region on broad United Front principles. Thus, the cooperation of the local governments, and the Guomindang was always appealed to first before the organizers entered a district. There is no communist 'propaganda' preached or what could be called 'Communist' except by reactionaries. The three principles of Sun Yat Sen abandoned by the Guomindang since 1927 is the base of the combined Communist-Guomindang program. Here we see the interesting phenomenon of the Communist Party insisting on the establishment and actual employ-ment of the ideas of the founder of that very same Guomindang party, which has been making serious efforts to exterminate the Communists for the past eleven years. These principles of democracy, nationalism and improvement in the people's livelihood, become, by re-definition, political liberty, control of government by the people's representatives, the fight against imperialism (at present Japanese imperialism), destruc-tion of the feudal system and a wide social program to increase wages, lower taxes and rents, improvement in health and establishment of schools to liquidate illiteracy. No effort is made to confiscate property, to collectivize the land, to abolish the capitalistic system. The proletarian revolution is deliberately shelved – the bourgeois-democratic revolution must first be made. If it is Communism to advocate the abolition of ignorance and illiteracy, to restrict money usurers, to reduce rents, to raise wages, to give the people's organizations a voice in the manage-ment of the country, to fight Japan to the death – then communism is being preached here, and the Government of this Region is a Communist one. But if none of these things are communistic but merely the barest rights of man, then there is no Communism here. This is not a Soviet but a United Front Region. In the Primary and mid-Schools, all, by the way, being maintained, at full strength and increased in numbers, Nationalism and the Social Sciences are stressed. The only places that Marx-Leninism is being taught as a theory and as a practice, is in the 8th Route Army and the Party Schools. In the Military Academy there are 700 seasoned army and partisan fighters back from the front after a year of fighting. Their subjects are military and political sciences. Political science comprises economics, nationalism, the United Front of China. In the Party School close by is a class of 300 studying Marx-Leninism. They are students, workers, peasants, university professors. They will graduate and go out among the people. With their firm theoretical background, mass organization work becomes easier. They will not teach 'pure' Communism – they will teach anti–imperialism against Japan, democratic rights of the workers, the necessity of unity, the need and way to social security.

The only person proclaiming 'pure' Communism and the Proletarian Revolution in China today is the Trotskyite – that isolated and pathetic figure – as unrealistic as the idealists he denounces are realistic.

In the seventeen years of its existence, the Chinese Communist Party has struggled for the independence of China. In that struggle, it has gone through the fire and emerged Bolshevised. In 1927, the Central Executive Committee of the Guomindang drove the Party members out of the organization. Following this expulsion, the Party led the Soviet Revolution for nearly ten years. That period has ceased. There are no longer any Soviets or Soviet Regions in China. Today, according to the changes in the domestic and international situation, the United Front of all progressives, has completely taken the place of this former policy. The wholehearted aim of the Party is to associate all forces for the prosecution of the Anti-Japanese war. In the past year of war, all China has had to acknowledge that the 10 point program of the Party, is the only one that can possibly save China from her enemy. This program has been accepted by the Central Government with all but a few reservations. Leading Communist members such as Mao Zedong, have been invited to rejoin the Guomindang. Why? Is it because the Central Government has gone Communist? Such an idea is laughable. It is because the Party Program has had such enormous support from all classes, is so articulated with reality, that the Central Government has been forced to agree with its principles. So, today, all China has accepted the 10 Point Win-the-War Program of the Party.

In this region, it is universally acknowledged, that the 8th Route Army and the Communist Party's influence was so strong that it would have been comparatively easy to have established a Soviet had the Communists cared to do so. It was not done. Instead, the Communist Party and the 8th Route Army insisted on a United Front Government here. In the Government are only two members of the Party in a total of nine. The party expresses its aims through the people's mass organizations. It doesn't matter to them who 'runs' the government as long as the people express their will. They are content to take a back seat – and they do. Their political influence here is very great. They are the leaders in Anti-Japanese activities, land reforms, union organizations. On the military side, the 8th Route Army is the backbone of the partisan fighters.

Not only does the 8th Army teach the partisans the tactics which made it invincible in ten years fighting the Guomindang, but more important still, it teaches the political principles which steeled it during the Soviet period. They are taught to fight Japan and save China that they may enjoy their country for themselves. That China belongs to the working class. They are fighting for their own class benefit. Now, the Chinese are a very practical people – no people in the world are less influenced by philosophical idealism. So the good old slogans 'glory,' 'victory,' 'honour,' 'for your King and country,' etc., are not much use to these realistic minds. They see through at once these hollow abstractions. They are taught the essential causes of this war – the rapacious aggression of the combined capitalistic-military class of Japan, seeking new territory for expansion and glory. They are taught to hate this class – not to hate the blind fellow-workmen of Japan forced into the army to fight and die for the benefit of another class than his own and the 'Glory of the Emperor.' The world has come a long way since 1914. Then the working men entered the army completely ignorant that the war was one between rival national capitalistic classes. That working man emerged from the war – if he survived – no better off than when he entered. Millions fought and died uselessly and stupidly to maintain – or on the side of Germany, to expand – the imperial rapaciousness of their respective national capitalistic classes. The Chinese soldier in the 8th Army is teaching his fellow workmen in the partisan detachments that this war must be fought and won by the working class of China; that the war will be fought in vain if the working class who comprise the army do not benefit by that victory. There are no Wilsonian idealistic slogans heard here. The peasant will not fight to make China safe for the capitalists. But being a realist, he will fight to the death to save this country for the millions of workmen who inhabit it and whose labour make it rich. This sort of common sense is called Communism. It is also the sort of common sense that the Chinese practical mind grasps at once.

Cooperation with the Guomindang in this Region or, for that matter, in any other part of China, does not mean that the Communist Party is dispersed and absorbed into the large Guomindang. It means that the immediate aims of both now being identical, a common course of action is the best policy. The Communist Party is content to take a subordinate place, but maintains its political integrity as a distinctive party. The principles of communism are not for one moment abandoned. This is not opportunism, but realism at the present stage of the revolution. Cooperation without loss of identity, for the winning of the Anti-Japanese War and the establishment of a new democratic republic of China, is the policy of the Party. The formation, in China, of a classless Socialistic Soviet Republic, cannot be achieved quickly or at one jump. The economic and political low levels in China today forbid it. The final goal is a distant one. Revolution is a process. In this region is seen that process; that coming-into-being; that political awareness and consciousness of the masses growing into life, without which all the 'technics' of revolution are bound to fail. The Guomindang did not realize, in 1927, the revolutionary elements of the three principles. The Communist Party has taken these principles and interpreted to the people the revolutionary elements they contain. Since the Guomindang has never 'officially' abandoned these principles, although work among the people and mass organizations has ceased since 1927, and since that party has returned to those principles in its program for the war, so the Communist Party is cooperating with the Central Government. It was not drawn into cooperation, it was the first to beg and plead and insist on that cooperation.

This cooperation has produced the effect of isolating its opponents. For all they may protest to the contrary they have become pro-Japanese-Puppet-People.

This war contains, in the highest degree, revolutionary tendencies. It is the function of the Communists to lead and develop these revolutionary tendencies among the people, so that the progress from the social democratic to the proletarian revolution – its highest stage – is quickened and shortened. It is by cooperation that this will be achieved. The United Front is being enlarged and extended here daily. The Communists are the real leaders of this front. They have become the models of the masses and hold their leadership with a steadfast, proud humility.

It would be as easy to exaggerate as to underestimate the influence of the Party in this Region. Is everything in the United Front garden lovely? By no means. It is, as yet, an imperfect thing; a process, a growing development. It could not be a living, dynamic, human-relationship development and be otherwise. Are many of the bourgeoisie still afraid of the growing influence of the Communists among the people? Undoubtedly. Then why do these same bourgeoisie still support the United Front? Through self-interest. Because they see that it is only by such a government, that they will be able to retain the security and protection they, like all men, desire. The alternative is a worse one to them. So they watch, with anxious eyes and powerless hands the bonds of feudalism slipping off the arms of the workers. They must feel very unhappy.

Sung Shao Wen, Chairman of the Boundary Region, in an interview, said, 'A firm United Front Government exists here. Perfect unity holds between the Communist Party, the local provincial officials, the army and the Guomindang. All are united on the essential program of anti-Japanese imperialism and a social program of improvement in the lives of the workers. The future developments in this region must be thought of in relationship to the war situation in the rest of China. At present, the Japanese are not employing large numbers of troops in North China, but are concentrating on Central China and the capture of Wuhan. This gives us time to further mobilize the people and strengthen the partisans. It also permits us to extend this Region. Recently a large partisan detachment has gone past Beijing into east Hopei. We are enlarging. But even though the Japanese turn from the South and concentrate large masses of troops here and make a determined effort to capture this entire territory, we believe we will by then be able, at least, to maintain our position. I see the development of the Region, in a positive way.

'It is truly unbelievable that behind the Japanese lines we have been able to establish a firm, solid government. I can not think of a similar example in the history of China, nor for that matter, in the world. Even we, the Chinese, would not have believed it possible before the war.

'In Spain and in Abyssinia, the example we have given would have led to victory. We know now that Victory comes from the resistance of all the people not just the army. That is the lesson of partisan warfare.'

Questioned about education, he said, 'Our educational program is still weak. We have maintained all primary and mid-schools. Some subjects have been altered and others added according to war needs. We have edited a new series of textbooks. Outside the schools, our popular educational classes are well attended. Among the People's Guards, for example, the "short time training course" has passed 480 men and boys. We are planning to establish a National Revolutionary Middle School, to take young men and women from 16 to 24. The subjects which will be taught will include the United Front, how to train for political work, political economy and the social sciences, etc.

'I sincerely hope that other provinces will follow our example.'

The Chin-Ch'a-Chi Region is isolated from the rest of China. Yet here a great flame of determination to resist Japanese imperialism is burning in the breasts of its people and with that, is emerging, the vision of a New Democratic Republic. This region is the hope and the presage of the future China, free at long-last from the grasp of foreign imperialism. All men of good will wish it so.

Bethune did not rest in his efforts to keep Canadian and American supporters aware of the Chinese struggle. In June 1938 he wrote the following letter to a Canadian close to the Communist Party who had suggested working in China.

Northwestern Partisan Relief Committee
Hankou, China
June 29

Dear Lilian:

Your letter of May 12th came just now. In the meantime, Dr. Robert Lim came to the city from the new training centre in Changsha. We sent you a cable, signed by Dr. Lim as director of the Chinese Red Cross Medical Corps and a member of the committee that sponsors the work of the China Aid Council. He works very closely with us. He badly, badly needs a foreign secretary. And he wanted you to come and work with him. He said you could help me, because I do much work for them, but we are now in two different cities and he needs help the most. You can do the exact kind of work he requires. So he is willing to give you a maintenance allowance twice that given Chinese. That is $150 (Chinese). In Changsha free room, and board with the Red Cross Medical Corps [is] $12 a month. That would leave nearly all your wages for other expenses. If you wrote an article a week and got from the *Clarion* say $5 each time, it would give you a very good reserve.

This work, you must understand, is not with the 8th Route. But Dr. Lim gives us 4 Red Cross Medical units of 20 doctors, nurses and dressers each, he keeps us supplied with all the medicine he can, and he is aiding in supplies to our new 4th Army. Also, our comrades here believe that we must help all the Chinese armies with medical and other supplies, for the conditions in most of the armies in so far as the wounded are concerned, are simply horrible. I myself am now giving much of my time to this, aiding Dr. Lim [to] build up his work. And our comrades hope to give some aid, wherever possible, in securing a complete reorganization of the Army Medical Corps. You have the technical qualities to help, because they need someone with your technical office knowledge, your knowledge of foreign friends, you can compile reports and circulate them, correspond for them and, I am certain, be able to give the Corps good advice in many organizational matters.

If Tim Buck allows you to come, it means your own words are backed up by a responsible man, and I think there will be no danger in your case of repeating the experience with Dr. Parsons. I take it that you are not a 'soak,' and your qualifications sound to be excellent for this country and this kind of work.

There is one thing you must remember: the Japanese are coming, and the Red Cross Medical Corps will change its centre – and you must go with them. If you are determined as you seem to be, I believe you would take what the Chinese take, sharing their vicissitude, retreating with them if necessary, or going forward when possible. The Red Cross Medical Corps will take care of you in so far as it is humanly possible for them to do so.

If you come, I shall send down to you various things to do, for I have too much work on my shoulders and am often exhausted and unable to care for all the things on my shoulders. The Manchester *Guardian* of England has now asked me to supply them with a minimum of two articles a month, and more as the situation seems to warrant. This gives me a living – which has been a worry for me up to this time. Yet one month went by, after I was asked to do this, before I could find time to write one article. Last night I got off my first. I am enclosing a copy of it for you to read. You can not use it in the *Clarion* in that exact form, but you could take out of it what material you find of value for your paper. This article was read first by the comrade in the CC [central committee] of the Party who deals with me and with medical matters (Boku), and approved. So you need not fear the statements in it. I have no permission from the Manchester *Guardian* to allow its publication anywhere else. Hereafter I shall be sending pictures and various kinds of material to the *Clarion*. I'll send it to Buck's address – also this letter – in case you have started here.

I laid your letters of May 12 and 27th before Boku, rep. of the Party and the 8th Route here. We talked about them last night. He approved Dr. Lim's action, but we do not know why you have not replied to the cable. When you come, I'll bring you up to Hankou to meet all the 8th Route and Party representatives in this city. We have the strongest delegation in the Party apart from Mao Zedong, and two men commanding at the front. This is the most important place, so they keep the strongest delegation here. With your help, we could keep Canada and the USA better supplied with material.

I'll be sending Buck a copy of an important document soon – the plan of the CCP to the Chinese government and the mass organizations, for the defence of Wuhan and of all China. The Guomindang says it will itself carry out this plan – without the Communists! They have done nothing – and will do nothing. They *cannot* carry it out. We fear Hankou will be taken within a month or two.

Sincerely,
[signature missing]

One of his main contacts in Yan'an was an American, George Hatem, known by the Chinese as Dr Ma Haide. By 1938 he was a veteran with the Eighth Route Army, having come to China in the early 1930s. In this letter, Bethune also referred to Captain Evans Carlson, a U.S. military attaché, who was investigating the Eighth Route Army and its guerrilla warfare methods in the anti-Japanese campaign in north China.

General Nieh's Headquarters,
Wutaishan, July 3, 1938

Dear Ma –
Well, here we are at last. Medically things are not so bad as Smedley made out. This place is much better equipped with everything than that pest-hole, Ho Chia Chuang, Shensi. That's a hospital that should be shut down – lousy position, lousy poverty-stricken area, no food for patients, lousy equipment and a lousy, lazy staff.

This place is much better. There is organization here with all its faults.

Where is Ewen? Thank God she didn't turn up. Put her to work in the training school.

I sent you, through Dr. Chiang, a bunch of films. Did you have the undeveloped ones developed? And have they all gone off to Canada by air mail? I am sending you with this letter another bunch. Get them developed and rush off to Canada by air mail. I asked Mao Zedong to give you money for these purposes.

Carlson is gone into Hopei. I follow in 10 days. Brown goes south to Zhu De.

Best regards to Litch. How are tricks? Why not write?

This is a swell country and some swell comrades inhabit it.

With comradely greetings,
Norman

Please send the enclosed letters (one I left open for you to read), seal and send off promptly by air mail. Aye.

N.B.

By mid-July, with his leave from mission work almost ended, Brown was forced to leave. Although he expected to come back to Bethune's aid, he was not able to. Bethune's isolation grew. He was the only trained physician in the entire region of thirteen million people.

General Nieh's Headquarters,
(near) Wutaishan, July 13, 1938

Dear Ma,
An A.P. [Associated Press] Correspondent, Hanson, has just come through from Beijing and gone south to Zhu De with Brown who is on his way out to Hankou. He is a good little fellow but politically innocent. I have done my best with him.

I am enclosing some letters. Please send them on air mail. Get the money from Mao Zedong. They are important. One is a long article to the *New Masses* on this Region. It should get there quickly.

All is well. I did 8 operations today and two blood transfusions. I am tired, but enormously content.

Did you succeed in keeping Ewen? I don't need her. I have trained a first class staff and have a good interpreter.

Please send on all mail. Any news? I wish you were here.

Best regards to Li Teh,

Aye,
Norman

You can open and read it if you like. It's addressed [to] Eric Adams.

P.S. Please send me my x-ray outfit with all accessories. General Nieh has promised me a dynamo and small gas engine to run it. It will be valuable here. Can you get this off at once, Ma? Also Chinese dictionary and papers and magazines. I intend to stay here. I am the only qualified doctor in this region of 13,000,000 people. The hospital has 350 beds – 56 new admissions all wounded – this month so far. I am doing 10–15 operations a day. Come up and see me some time!

My mail is coming here in pieces – ½ the letters split or opened. Please *enclose* all letters in *new* envelopes (strong).

N.

Near General Nieh's headquarters
Wutaishan, July 19, 1938

Dear Dr. Lim:

Dr. Brown has gone out to Hankou with my report on the medical situation here. He will give it to you personally. I am taking the opportunity of a newspaper man who is also going out to follow him with a letter to you.

The Base Hospital here is at present 350 beds and filled. It should be enlarged to 500 immediately. Brown and I have done 110 operations in 25 days. These people need everything. I am enclosing a list of their drugs in stock. Pitiful, isn't it? Can you send us morphine, codeine, surgical instruments, salvarsan, carbasone (there is quite a lot of amoebic dysentery here)? No need of gauze or cotton as there is a factory at Wutaishan.

Can you help us? I am the only qualified doctor in this entire region to look after 150,000 partisans. These partisans are doing grand work and should be helped. I am staying here and Brown is returned.

With kindest personal regards,
Norman Bethune, M.D.
Surgeon, Canadian-American Mobile Medical Unit

P.S. Next week I am leaving for an extended trip of inspection of the entire region with a visit to its 7 hospitals along the railways. I hope to get into mid-Hopei and north Hopei near Beijing. I will return here.

N.B.

The lack of support from the China Aid Council caused Bethune to try to enlist the aid of a friend in New York, Elsie Siff.

Near General Nieh's Headquarters
Wutaishan, Shansi
July 19, 38

My dear Elsie –
It seems so long since we met and parted, seven months, yet they have gone quickly enough. You have been many times in my thoughts, and always pleasant and grateful ones.

As you probably know, we, that is the nurse and I, arrived in Sian and later in Yan'an, safely. Dr. Parsons fulfilled all of my forebodings, as he turned out a drunken bum. We were glad to get rid of him. Later, another Canadian, Dr. Richard Brown, a medical missionary, joined us. He and I came to Wutaishan – a month's trip, on foot and horseback, a month ago. He has gone out to raise more money and left me, once more alone. Our nurse stayed in Lan Hsing – a town about 50 miles east of the Yellow River in Shansi.

This is the centre of the Partisans. It is an organized United Front Government and has the name of Chin-Ch'a-Chi (Shansi-Chahar-Hopei Provinces) as it takes in parts of all 3 provinces. We are completely surrounded by the Japs, north, east, west and south. They hold all the towns on the railways but we still retain the enclosed country.

In this great area of 13,000,000 people and with 150,000 armed troops I am the only qualified doctor! The Chinese doctors have all beat it. I am at present 'cleaning-up' the base hospital of 350 wounded and have done 110 operations in 25 days.

I have written and cabled that damned Committee of Dodd's at 268 Fourth Avenue, a dozen times to send me over Louis Fraad but they never answer. I have wished for him at least a hundred times. All the 'doctors' in the army are former nurses. I could use Fraad. I still can use him. If the Committee won't send him, will he come by himself? Ask him. We – that is the 3 of us – Brown, Fraad and myself, can have a wonderful time here. I am intending to stay, and Brown is coming back in 3 months. There are 7 other hospitals scattered around, some no more than 50 miles from Beijing. In a week's time I am going off on an inspection trip of the whole territory, staying long enough to operate at each hospital, then moving on to the next. This will take all summer. I will return here for the winter.

Here everything is needed – all drugs, surgical instruments, etc. The patients lie on straw or reed mats, no pillows, no sheets – in their old dirty uniforms. The nurses are boys of 12 to 17. In the drug room is a dozen half-filled bottles of medicines for 350 men. Send more Carbasone – it's fine. There is no malaria here but a lot of syphilis and tuberculosis. I have started blood transfusions – 4 already, but I have only one syringe – my own – and am afraid of it getting broken. Send a lot of Spinocaine. But we need money. The hospital needs enlarging to 500. We need 400 coverlets and hundreds of other things which can be bought if we had the money. This is a 8th Route Army Hospital and is very poor. We can buy drugs in Beijing and Pao Ting! These cities are held by the Japs but our troops and partisans go in disguised as peasants and smuggle stuff out. If we had $1000 dollars (gold) we could fix this place up fine. Can you do something, Elsie, with that bloody Committee?

Remember me to all my friends and particularly to Irma, your sister and Procter, and Wiel, Elroy and Edith and Irma's sister.

With love, your comrade,
Beth

A letter to Dr Ma of 19 July includes a brief but significant note on an issue central to Bethune's international reputation – blood. Bethune reported that three of the medical staff had volunteered to give blood, 'although I must say it was only after I demonstrated that the giving of 300 cc. of blood was a painless and harmless procedure.' Chinese culture, he had found, differed from Spanish culture with regard to giving blood. Madrilenos, inspired by the needs of the soldiers defending their city from Franco's attack, had responded en masse to the blood institute's call for donations. Bethune encountered much greater reluctance among the Chinese. They came forward only after he demonstrated not just that donating blood was safe but that he, a doctor and a Westerner, was willing to give his own blood to the Chinese wounded. It was an important event in bonding Bethune and the Chinese, and it contributed to his towering reputation there. It also signalled a critical step in Bethune's own development. He had long exhibited sympathy for people – the poor in Detroit, the tubercular, the victims of fascist terror. Now he was demonstrating something deeper still – solidarity. That is, he was uniting with the Chinese people in a very tangible way, not just by lending his efforts and talent to their struggle, but by literally giving his own blood. Little wonder that on 21 August he would report in a letter back to North America that 'I am content.' He was no longer the outsider, acting upon the world; he was now an integral part of it.[17]

Sung-yen K'ou
Wutaishan
July 19, 1938

My dear Ma –
I am enclosing a bunch of letters that I would like you to send off at once, air mail. Also a letter and a telegram to the China Aid Council in New York.

Things are going well. A combination of shouts, tears and smiles has worked wonders here. Things are organized – daily lectures to the doctors and nurses, 'clean-up' squads, fly control, metal identification discs for all patients, patients' files, recreation park built with chairs for the walking wounded, specified, posted duties for all members of the staff, daily rounds. I am gradually getting the doctors to supervise the work of the nurses. There is less 'passing the buck.' Actually three volunteered for blood transfusions (although I must say it was only after I demonstrated that the giving of 300 cc. of blood was a painless and harmless procedure).

Well, let me hear from you. And for Marx' sake wrap these letters and papers in strong cloth. They are arriving in shreds.
    Regards to Li

Aye,
Beth

*Bethune was disappointed again and again in his requests for assistance from
the China Aid Council. Interception of letters, cables, and money undoubtedly
accounted for some of this lack of contact. Yet many of Bethune's letters and
reports seemed to have reached friends and comrades in North America, so that
it is clear some mail found its way through. And in any case, if the CAC was
not receiving reports from its own representative in China, duty would have
required it to discover the reason why. Clearly, negligence in New York is the
primary reason for the failure to support Bethune. Once having sent the team to
China, senior CAC members appear to have ignored it. Bethune would never
know, for example, that Dr Fraad was denied a passport by the American government and could not join him in China.[18] One letter did arrive from New
York, to which Bethune immediately replied.*

Near General Nieh's headquarters
Wutaishan, July 19, 1938

Oliver Haskell, Director
China Aid Council
268 Fourth Avenue
New York, U.S.A.

Dear Sir:
l received your letter – the first from the Committee in 7 months'
absence – April 18, 1938, on July 14, 1938.

You give me but little particulars about matters which concern the
unit and have answered only one of the many questions and demands I
have made to your Committee since leaving New York. I have sent you
over a dozen letters and cables giving you the most detailed and exact
information of medical conditions here. I have had from you no
acknowledgement of these.

I thank you for sending to Mrs. [Frances] Coleman of Montreal the
sum of $200. She is not the sort of person to ask for money. I request you
to forward to her, unsolicited, $100 a month regularly and also any sum
now in arrears since the first of the year.

I am enclosing a number of letters which may be of interest to your
Committee. I wrote you (rather sent you a copy) a letter of July 10 to
Mao Zedong, re conditions here. This was sent to Earl Browder as I had
never heard from your Committee and did not know whether it was
functioning.

I have not seen an American paper or magazine for three months.

Please send all papers and magazines and all letters. These must be strongly wrapped and addressed to Dr. Ma Haide, Yan'an, Shensi, China.

I am alone as Dr. Brown has gone out to Hankou for 3 months. Nurse Jean Ewen is working in the 120th Division Hospital of the 8th Route Army at Lan Hsing, west Shansi. Dr. Brown is returning to work as my assistant. I ask you again to send over Dr. Louis Fraad. I am alone and need help.

Sincerely yours,
Norman Bethune, M.D.C F.R.C.S.
Surgeon, Canadian-American Mobile Medical Unit

On 20 July 1938, from Sung-yen K'ou, he sent Mao Zedong a report of his work since leaving Yan'an on 2 May. During those eleven weeks he had examined 773 patients and performed 146 operations (with Brown's assistance until 13 July). He then described the improvements that had been enacted and those he proposed to make.

Comments on the Base Hospitals at Hopei Tsun, Ho Hsi Tsun and Sung-yen K'ou
1. Since my last report (July 1st), I am glad to be able to report that a great improvement has taken place in organization, cleanliness, and in construction of needed works. Some of the improvements are –

1) An operating room has been constructed and enlarged.
2) All patients operated upon have post-operative charts kept of temperature, taken twice daily.
3) Segregation of post-operative patients in one compound, and under one doctor.
4) 'Clean-up' squads to enforce disposal of refuse, food and soiled dressings; to supervise *hsiao kweis* in keeping wards clean.
5) Fly control. A very difficult problem. Mosquito netting has been put on all windows and all food boxes in wards are protected by the same. More active measures are the burning of manure piles, covering over of latrines and burning of refuse in incinerator.
6) A sterilizer for instruments and dressings has been built.
7) One hundred leg and arm splints have been made.
8) Regular weekly staff conferences. These are held every Sunday

afternoon, of the combined doctors and nurses. Here the problems of the week are discussed, criticisms made and suggestions for improvement come from the members of the staff themselves. In this, we have been very pleased with the response. There is a fine spirit of eagerness to improve and learn. At these staff conferences, all take and keep notes.

9) Duties of nurses have been outlined and printed and posted on the walls. Each nurse knows his expected duty.

10) Lectures to the staff. Two of these have already been given and more will be. They are illustrated by blackboard drawings. The subjects already taken are anatomy and the treatment of wounds. Physiology, *materia medica*, etc., will be discussed in future lectures. These lectures are held every other day from 5 to 6 p.m.

11) Regular weekly ward rounds, seeing every patient in the hospital, are made on Sunday morning.

12) Identification discs for all patients have been made. These metal (tin) discs have printed on them the patient's name and his hospital number. All patients wear these discs. The number corresponds to that on the hospital file. This makes the location of patients easier. This system, combined with a large map and file hanging on the wall of the Chief Surgeon's office, enables him to locate scattered patients with ease.

13) Complete inventories of all materials belonging to the hospital have been made. This includes drugs, surgical supplies, gauze, cotton, bandages, towels, basins, pails, etc.

14) Dressing trays have been constructed and standardized.

The projected improvements now in hand are –

1) Patients' Recreation Park. A start has been made on this, a plot of ground selected, levelled and seats (with backs) are now being built. In the ground is a cook-house which will be turned into a hall for games, writing letters, and lectures as well as a reading room.

2) An incinerator for burning soiled cotton, food, etc. is being built.

3) A de-lousing sterilizer is planned.

4) Sample hospital uniforms, pillows, coverlets, have been made and criticized, 50 of each will shortly be ready. Before being distributed, all wards will be cleaned, white washed and sterilized. One ward at a time will be taken. 50 protective oiled cotton protective sheets have been ordered to keep the new coverlets clean.

5) One dozen covered tin pails are being made for placing food and soiled dressings in away from flies. One will be placed in each ward.
6) Four stretcher racks are being built to rest stretchers on so that patients do not touch the ground. These will be placed in the Operating Room compound for patients waiting operation.
7) An illustrated booklet for doctors and nurses is in process. It will have chapters on first aid, application of splints, emergencies, drugs, anatomy, elementary physiology, treatment of wounds, etc. It will be translated by Comrade Tung into Chinese for distribution throughout the Region to all doctors and nurses. The Regional Government will be asked to print it. A further series of booklets on public health, preventative medicine, will be planned if the first one is successful.

Much still remains to be done before the 'Five Weeks' Plan' of the staff to make this the finest hospital in the 8th Route Army will be accomplished. I am firmly of the opinion that it can and will be done. All are cooperating now with that in mind. Immediate needs – A thousand % increase of drugs. One thousand dollars for new bedding, etc.

Future needs – Construction of a new operating and post-operative ward. This will cost about a thousand dollars. It will contain the laundry, sterilizing room, stockroom and doctors' offices.

Enlargement of the hospital to 500 beds capacity. Centralization of arm cases, leg cases, etc. Construction of bath house.

About $5,000 dollars will be needed in all for the winter. An appeal has been made by telegraph to America for this money. I have every confidence it will be forthcoming.

With comradely greetings,
Norman Bethune, M.D.,
Surgeon, Canadian-American Mobile Medical Unit.

Bethune's confidence in getting funds from America was misplaced. It became clear that aid from abroad would not even be sufficient to provide for his personal needs. When the Military Council in Yan'an ordered General Nieh, commander-in-chief of the Border Region, to pay Bethune and Ewen $100 (Chinese) monthly, Bethune promptly replied by telegram, refusing the salary. In fact, his accounts to the China Aid Committee showed that he had budgeted for a wage of just $1.00 a month to each member of the Canadian-American Medical Unit.

Military Council, 8th Route Army, Yan'an
August 11, 1938

To General Nieh –
1. Please give Dr. Bethune and Miss Ewen, $100.00 every month and it will be returned to you.
2. Dr. Bethune's letter to us states that the hospital needs some money for re-construction. Please instruct the hospital to act according to this program. You had better not go on in a big scale construction, that costs too much. Give us an estimate by wire and let us look it over.
3. What Dr. Bethune bought and paid for himself for cotton and gauze, etc. should be reported on the statements of the hospital.

Telegram to the Military Council, 8th Route Army, Yan'an
August 12, 1938

Replying to your telegram of August 11.38
(1) I refuse to accept offered $100 a month. Ewen may do as she pleases. Have no need of money personally, as all food, clothing, etc. is supplied me. If this money has been sent to me personally from America or Canada, make a Special Tobacco Fund out of it for tobacco and cigarettes for the wounded. I will draw from time to time, what little money I need, from Headquarters here.
(2) The above – the ordinary expenses authorized by me last month in the Base Hospitals here were approximately $1500. This was spent on materials and labour for the reconstruction of the hospital as a Model Demonstration Hospital for the Chin-Ch'a-Chi District. A medical, surgical and nursing Training School will be opened here next week. Approximately $1000 a month will be needed in the future. This is close to my estimate in my letters of May 17 and 23, from Ho Chia Chuang. It should not exceed $1500 normally. Over 100 wooden splints, and many tin and metal trays, boxes, instruments, urinals, bed pans, ward furniture, have been constructed.
Fifty complete bedding, blankets and protective sheets have been made. The object is to make this hospital a model for this district. One pamphlet, illustrated, on the treatment of wounds, has been written, and will be published in a few days. Another larger book, illustrated with over 200 drawings on military medicine, surgery and nursing for the doctors and nurses of the 8th Army, is half completed and will be sent to you for publication, within three weeks.

(3) Immediate needs are $5000 worth of medicines. These may be pur-
chased in Beijing, where contacts have been established. I am writing
full particulars of this in a letter.

(4) Please inform me of the sums of money coming in from Canada
and America so that I may know the financial position.

(5) All the above does not include larger projects for the construction
of a permanent hospital, which would cost approximately $50,000.
These plans for a permanent base hospital will be submitted to you, by
letter. What we are doing now is reconstruction with the existing materials at hand, but they are far from ideal.

(6) The need here is very great. I beg that the Military Council appeal
to Canada and America for additional financial assistance.

With comradely greetings,
Norman Bethune, M.D.,
Surgeon, Canadian-American Mobile Medical Unit.

*Bethune described in detail his plans for a model demonstration hospital and
training centre in a letter to General Nieh.*

Surgical Base Hospital Sung-yen K'ou
August 13.38

General Nieh, Commanding Officer
Chin-Ch'a-Chi Military District

Dear comrade –
You may recall that I spoke to you on August 7th, about the establishment of the model hospital here and its use as a training school for the
doctors and nurses of the military hospitals of the entire district. The
day before yesterday, Dr. Yeh introduced the subject again and told me
that you had spoken to him about this matter and had instructed him to
ask me to accept the principalship of the Training School and to abandon my plans for a tour of all the front hospitals of the District. This
letter concerns this very important matter. There are two facts now
apparent:

1. There is not a very high standard of technical skill among the doctors
   and nurses of the Sanitary Service.

2. There is a need for re-organization of the Service as well as improvement in technical training.

There are 3 ways possible.

1. The sending away of selected candidates (doctors) to Russia or to Universities in China, to be trained as fully qualified doctors. This would take 4 to 5 years. The advantages would be that the 8th Route Army would then possess its own politically reliable, fully trained medical personnel. They in turn would gradually raise the standard throughout the Sanitary Service. The disadvantages are equally obvious – the time taken and the urgent demands for even the partially trained technicians you already possess, for the needs of the moment. The changing political situation will also be the deciding factor here.

2. The sending out of the District to either modern Chinese Hospitals or to Mission Hospitals (such as the Union Mission Hospital, Hankou; or the Baptist Mission Hospital, Sian) of a certain number of doctors and nurses for a 3 to 6 months' course in surgery, surgical nursing, dispensing, etc. Arrangements for the maintenance of these doctors and nurses might, I believe, be made. These partially trained doctors and nurses, would, on their return, act as instructors to others.

3. The utilization of foreign medical units such as the Canadian-American Unit, as instructors in medical and surgical technique. This should be done by all means. The Chinese Red Cross Units (if any come here) should also be utilized in this way.

I have not mentioned the 4th way, which is already in operation, namely the 8th Route Army Medical Training School, near Yan'an. Since, however, there are no more than 5 or 6 fully qualified doctors in the entire 8th Army, it is difficult to understand how the essential training of the instructors makes them proficient enough to instruct others in anything else than the rudiments of medicine, surgery and nursing. This observation must not be taken in any way to depreciate the splendid work of that training school – work which I consider beyond praise – but merely as an objective fact. I have in this hospital recent graduates of that Training School. They are conscientious and hard-working but they lack clinical training and experience. They also lack the ability to direct the work of nurses, which is an essential duty of doctors.

To take up the immediate question of the establishment of a Training School here. The first point to be made is that it should be done. The second point is the plan of such a school.

It must be kept in mind that a medical training school is no different than a Military academy or a Party School. What is needed are –

1. A competent staff of instructors.
2. A definite planned course of instruction.
3. Textbooks.
4. A demonstration Hospital or ward to illustrate practical problems.

Have we here in Sung-yen K'ou these basic requirements? Can they be established?

1. The staff of the Training School. I do not consider the present staff of doctors under Dr. Yeh sufficiently trained or competent to act as instructors to others. I have had 2 months' close association with them and am only now beginning to see the results of my instruction to them. This instruction is most frequently not passed on to the nurses. There are a number of reasons for this serious defect. One is the language difficulty – I need an interpreter and so am unable to give systematic ward instruction myself. I see no effort of the doctors, especially the chiefs (Dr. Liao, Lin and Dr. Yeh) to systematically instruct the nurses. Although I have given a number of lectures to combined groups of doctors and nurses with the assistance of my excellent interpreter, Comrade Tung, such lectures are not enough, but must be followed up with ward instruction and constant supervision to be sure they are being put to practical use by the nurses. This is the duty of the doctors. I miss in them the ability to supervise and the activity to see that work is being carried out efficiently.

2. There are no textbooks to give the students who would come to the school. One pamphlet has been written and illustrated and translated. It will be printed at the Government's printing press shortly. Another larger textbook of about 200 or more pages is now in preparation and is being translated by Comrade Tung. It is essential that a textbook be put in the hands of the students. I am not aware of the textbook used in the Medical Training School at Yan'an. If there is one it should be brought here at once. If not, it will be necessary to wait until the textbook I am writing is finished and published. This will take 2 months.

3. A planned course of instruction. I would be glad to draw up such a course. I would suggest it be divided into 3 parts – medical, surgical, nursing and organization. The course might be 3 weeks.

4. A Demonstration Hospital. We will have this soon – in about 2 weeks. It will be a 'model' ward of 30 beds. It will be ideal for practical

demonstrations. It is costing about $2,000.00. A great deal of equipment is still necessary.

To return to the major problem of the staff of the Training School. I would be glad to accept the position of Principal if it did not involve my being restricted in my movements to this hospital alone. I wish to be free to move about the District on the different fronts and to see for myself that the Sanitary Service is working smoothly and efficiently as possible. In short I do not wish to be 'tied down' to this base hospital.

In regard to the other members of the staff of instructors, I frankly am perplexed. Perhaps the Yan'an training school will lend us one or two of their instructors. No one man can do this job – it must be done by a coordinated and efficient staff, active, eager, with imagination and ideas and the ability to instruct and supervise the work of their assistants. This present staff does not possess these characteristics.

I append a confidential report on the members of the staff of this hospital from the point of technical efficiency, etc.

The general conclusion I have come to after giving this matter a great deal of thought, is, while a Training School is necessary, it should be postponed for two months until the textbook I am writing and Comrade Tung is translating is completed. During this period I will endeavour to give the doctors and nurses more technical instruction. After the completion of the book and during the period of waiting for its appearance in print, I desire to keep to our original plan that I should take a tour of the fronts in the District. That there is a great need for this is only too evident to me – example, there has not arrived from any front hospital, many wounded comrades, who have had a fracture of the arm or leg and who have had a splint on the fracture. This shows a lack of care on the part of some of the doctors at the front. This must be corrected. The best way to correct it is to go to these doctors and instruct them in the field under actual conditions.

In conclusion, I would suggest the early calling of a conference when all criticisms will be made openly and frankly in a proper Bolshevist manner. In this way, our difficulties can be solved.

With comradely greetings
Norman Bethune, M.D.,
Surgeon, Canadian-American Mobile Medical Unit

A concluding note on the progress of re-organization.

It must not be thought that no progress has been made. On the contrary, I consider that we have come a great distance in the past 2 months.

Not being content with the rather loose organization of the doctors and nurses a conference was called at Dr. Yeh's office at Hopei Tsun on July 29th. All the doctors and political commissars of the 3 hospitals attended. I put forward the suggestion that to tighten up the organization, we divide all the doctors, nurses and orderlies into 'teams.' This would give us 5 teams composed of a doctor, 5 nurses and 9 orderlies each. To each team would be allotted a definite number of patients for which each team would be responsible. Since there are approximately 300 wounded, this would give each team 60 patients. Socialistic competitions between teams would be encouraged for neatness and cleanliness of wards, etc.

Another proposal was to keep the hospital at Sung-yen K'ou for the seriously sick (about 85) and the hospital at Ho Hsi Tsun for the slightly wounded (about 125), and use Hopei Tsun as a convalescent camp for recovery.

Another was the fitting out of the Buddhist Temple at Sung-yen K'ou as a model ward.

All three suggestions were unreservedly accepted by the conference. The senior doctor (Dr. Lin) was given the title of Team No. 1 in charge of the seriously wounded and operated cases. The other doctors were given teams according to experience. Each doctor would be responsible for the supervision and training of the nurses and orderlies under him. Nightly reports were to be made to me by the 2 senior doctors in charge of the seriously wounded. Wounded would be seen by me at any time of the day or night on arrival. In the past it was sometimes days before I was notified!

Since the introduction of the 'teams' the organization has tightened up considerably. Doctors and nurses and orderlies now know their patients and feel more responsible for them.

By the daily reports, I am able to know what is going on in the hospitals and what patients are worse or better. In the past, I not infrequently was merely informed, when I inquired about a particular patient – 'Oh, he died last week!' Since I am busy with my interpreter all day long on the book we are writing, I can not have time to get around the wards, except to see the very sick and to operate on such cases as need operation.

The model ward is nearly ready. We are held up for want of cloth for sheets. We hope to open next week. We have a centralized sterilizing plant for dressings complete with drying oven, a laundry, an incinerator, a new operating room, a new drug and gauze room, a new doctor's office, new temperature charts, records, etc., etc. At the end of the month I will send you a complete report on this model hospital.

Despite Nieh's opposition to the construction of a permanent centre in a district of guerrilla war, the Model Hospital at Sung-yen K'ou was built. Although he supervised the construction, Bethune continued to travel to inspect other medical facilities. He wrote the following letter to an unnamed Canadian friend during one of these tours. In it he foresaw the type of wound that would eventually kill him.

August 15, 1938
You won't find this little village on your map, it's so small – only a few hundred peasants living in their mud huts beside a clear-running green mountain stream, down at the bottom of a deep-cut valley, with steep mountains rising to the north and south. Looking up the valley to the west, I can see the range set between Shansi and Hopei, ten miles away, with the Great Wall running along its crest. We crossed this again to meet another mountain range, the tops of which are covered with clouds. If you look at your map you will find Wutaishan. In Hopei, the city of Fu Ping. This little village is on the road between the two.

When I say a 'road,' I mean a mule path, ten feet wide and as rough as the ingenuity of nature can construct. We rode 90 li (30 miles) yesterday and it took us from 8 in the morning to 5 at night – eight hours in the saddle. The hospital is in a Buddhist Temple, among the willow and pine trees, on a little rocky elevation above the road. (Has it ever struck you how fascinated the religious mind is by nothing less than the most beautiful, the most desirable locations?) The priests are still here – regular priests, universal types, fat, obsequious, unctuous and loathsome. (Do you remember the priests of Anatole France in *Penguin Island* – 'pious and obese'?) Three times a day I hear their chant (remarkably like high church Anglicans), their gongs and bells. The smell, pungent and sweet, of the burning joss sticks, mixes with the scent of flowers of the open court. A few minutes later the air is filled with the revolutionary songs of the soldiers. One song, like a shout, goes like this –

| Mayo Chang | We have no rifles |
| Mayo Paw | We have no guns |

| Dee ling gay | The enemy gives us |
| Women zaw, etc. | All we have, etc. |

and these sound grand after the doleful drone of 'O Buddha, I have put my trust in thee.' Well, all the gods that man has ever trusted, have failed him. Now he must think to save himself.

The court is filled with flowers in bloom. Huge pink water lilies, like fat slightly breathless dowagers after a good lunch, hang their heavy heads, as big as footballs, over the edges of black earthenware tubs. Geraniums, roses, bluebells, and phlox, provide the colours for the ornately painted doorways. Small gauze squares, washed and now hung out to dry, are spread out on the low orange trees like huge crumpled magnolia blossoms. A few pigs and dogs are asleep. The slightly wounded sit or lie on the temple steps, their bandaged arms and legs in attitudes of awkward repose. Nurses scuttle about in their white aprons. The sun comes down out of a blue sky, warm and beneficent. Across the mountain tops pass slow, majestic parades of clouds. The golden air is filled with the cooing of doves, the wind in the trees and the murmur of the distant stream. On the four sides of the court are the wards, formerly the priests' quarters and guest rooms. Here the wounded lie, on the hard-packed mud k'angs with a bit of straw underneath. They are still in their old uniforms, faded from blue to grey by a thousand suns, winds and rains. There are 75 of them. Lots are boys of 18, some are as old as 36. Most have been wounded this month. They have been carried here over steep, tortuous mountain paths, from the hills of the north and the plains of the east. Some have been carried 60 miles, with broken legs and arms, gaping wounds, infected and gangrenous. The wards are long and dark, lit only by the white-paper covered windows. The k'angs take up one side. Here the wounded lie, side by side, sometimes 15 in one row. These k'angs are really ovens, heated in the winter times, and are raised about 2 feet above the mud floors. Of course, there are no mattresses, no sheets, no pillows, just a little straw and old cotton padded coverlets. They lie, crouched up like unhappy monkeys in the zoo, regarding the world with dark, melancholy eyes or with their heads covered with towels to protect themselves from the clouds of flies. Some moan gently and persistently to themselves; there is no morphine for their pain. Others are quiet and stoical. Some are mere children – 16, 17 and 18 years of age – their grave, smooth faces showing no indication that they have seen violence and death, known fear, felt the strong inward life of courage, been acquainted with despair. And when I hurt them as sometimes I must, they weep the hopeless, overwhelming tears of little children. I was trying to persuade a little boy of 18 to let me amputate his leg. It was hopelessly smashed by a bullet. No, he would not have it off. Why not? Because if he did he would never be able to fight the Japanese again. He finally consented when I assured him I would make him an artificial leg and get him a job with the General, and in this way he would be able to still fight against the enemy. He smiled as if I had given him a present for his birthday.

8 p.m.—August 21, 1938
I have operated all day and am tired. Ten cases, 5 of them very serious. The first was a fracture of the skull with the brain exposed. It was necessary to remove 4 loose pieces of bone and part of the frontal lobe. I hope he lives as he is a regimental commander. Tonight he looks very well, is conscious and without paralysis.

It is true I am tired but I don't think I have been so happy for a long time. I am content. I am doing what I want to do. Why shouldn't I be happy – see what my riches consist of. First I have important work that fully occupies every minute of my time from 5:30 in the morning to 9 at night. I am needed. More than that – to satisfy my bourgeois vanity – the need for me is expressed. I have a cook, a personal servant, my own house, a fine Japanese horse and saddle. I have no money nor the need of it – everything is given me. No wish, no desire is left unfulfilled. I am treated like a kingly comrade, with every kindness, every courtesy imaginable. I have the inestimable fortune to be among, and to work among, comrades to whom communism is a way of life, not merely a way of talking or a way of conscious thinking. Their communism is simple and profound, reflex as a knee jerk, unconscious as the movements of their lungs, automatic as the beating of their hearts. Here are found those comrades whom one recognizes as belonging to the hierarchy of Communism – the Bolshevists. Quiet, steady, wise, patient; with an unshakeable optimism; gentle and cruel; sweet and bitter; unselfish, determined; implacable in their hate; world-embracing in their love.

August 22, 1938
A quiet day. Only three operations – two amputations and an enucleation of an eye. One of the amputation cases had a blood transfusion. The Chinese are amazed at this. I had, at first, great difficulties to get donors from among the doctors and nurses. It was only by showing

them that it was without ill effect on myself that I was able to persuade them. Now there is no more trouble.

August 23, 1938

The little boy with his leg off and colonel are both doing well, so I am happy. I have an infected finger – it's impossible to avoid them, operating without gloves in these dirty wounds. This is the 3rd in 2 months.

The partisans are great people. Not regular soldiers, but 'workers in uniform.' The average age of a soldier in the 8th Route Army is 22, while among the partisans many are 30 and over – up to 39 and 40. They are often big fellows – 6 feet sometimes with strong, burnt-black faces; quiet purposeful movements and an air of determination and courage. It's a pleasure to work on them. After I dress their wounds they rise and bow profoundly, with an inclination of the body from the waist. The father of the little boy knelt on the ground with his head at my feet to thank me.

In a speech at the opening of the Model Hospital, 15 September 1938, Bethune demonstrated the internationalist vision which nourished his actions in China. A 'peaceful and prosperous Republic of workers' could be born, he said. 'But whether it will be born or not, depends on our actions today and tomorrow. It is not inevitable; it is not self-generating. It must be created by the blood and the work of all of us who believe in the future; who believe in man and his glorious man-made destiny.'

Comrades:

I thank you for the eight beautiful banners you have given to me and for the kind things you have said about me. I feel, as I know you must feel, that today is an important day in our lives and marks a milestone (I should rather say, a li stone), on the path that our hearts and wills are set upon.

The eyes of millions of freedom-loving Canadians, Americans and Englishmen are turned to the East and are fixed with admiration on China in her glorious struggle against Japanese Imperialism. This hospital has been equipped by your foreign comrades. I have the honour to have been sent as their representative. Do not consider it strange that people like yourself, thirty thousand li away, half-way around the globe, are helping you. You and we are internationalists; we recognize no race, no colour, no language, no national boundaries to separate and divide us. Japan and the war-mongers threaten the peace of the world.

They must be defeated. They are obstructing the great historical, progressive movement for a socially organized human society. Because the workers and sympathetic liberals of Canada, England and America know this they are helping China in the defence of this beautiful and beloved country.

It is not many months since I arrived in the Chin Ch'a Chi Military District to work with you in this hospital. I used to think of it as 'your' hospital, now I think of it as 'our' hospital. For between us we have created it. We have changed each other, have we not? We have reacted each to the other in a dialectical way, I might say: modified each other; and the product of our changed relationship is this fine new hospital, the opening of which we are celebrating today. From you I have learnt many valuable lessons. You have shown me a spirit of selflessness, of working co-operatively, of overcoming great difficulties, and I thank you for those lessons. In return I may have been able to instruct you a little in the mastery of technique.

The road to victory is the mastery of technique and the development of leaders. It was the adoption of Western technique that was responsible, in part, for the transformation of Japan from a tenth-rate backward nation into a great world power in less than fifty years. Technique, in the hands of the Dictators of Finance-Capital, has made Japan the enemy of the world. Technique in the hands of the workers of China will make her a great power for world peace. Must China then copy Japan? Yes, in many ways. We must learn from our enemies; we must imitate them in their mastery of technique and surpass them in that mastery. We must use that technique for the happiness and prosperity of the millions and not for the enrichment of the few.

Now the mastery of technique in the Sanitary Service is the learning and the using of the technique of healing our wounded comrades who have fought for us and for whom we, in return, must fight. And the enemies we fight are death, disease, and deformity. Technique will conquer not all, but most of these enemies.

Technique is the term used, in general, to describe the mastery of materials and processes. It is the most improved, the most efficient way of doing things. It means that instead of being controlled by nature, we control her. So we may talk of the technique of sweeping a floor and the technique of the organization of a hospital; the technique of doing a dressing and of an operation, the technique of washing a patient, of lifting him and of making him comfortable. For each of these and a thousand other procedures, there is a right way and a wrong way. The correct way is called 'good technique' and the wrong way 'bad technique.' We must learn the good technique.

Why must we learn the good technique? Because good technique in medicine and surgery means more quickly-cured patients, less pain, less discomfort, less death, less disease and less deformity. And all these things are our job. We have only one reason to offer, one excuse when our fighting comrades at the front ask us: 'What are you doing in the anti-Japanese war?' Our answer is, 'We are curing the wounds and healing the sick.' They may say, 'Are you doing it well?' And we say, 'As well as we know how.' But that last question we must ponder in our minds – 'Are we doing it as well as we might?'

What is the duty of a doctor, of a nurse, of an orderly? There is only one duty. What is that duty? It is the duty to make our patients happy, to help them in their fight back to health and strength. You must consider each one as your own brother or father, for he is, in truth, more than either, he is your comrade. He must come first, in all things. If you do not consider him above yourself, there is no place for you in the Sanitary Service. In fact, there is no place for you in the 8th Route Army at all.

There is an old saying in the English hospitals – 'A doctor must have the heart of a lion and the hand of a lady.' That means he must be bold and courageous, strong, quick and decisive, yet gentle, kind and considerate. That applies to everyone who is engaged in treating the sick and wounded – doctors, nurses, orderlies. So be constantly thinking of your patients, constantly asking yourself – 'Can I do more to help them?' Look for ways of improving your work and mastering your technique.

At first you will need instruction and you will need supervision. So you will need leaders. But you must not get into the habit of being supervised constantly. This is only temporary while you are learning. You must finally be able to supervise your own work. So you orderlies – go to your leaders, the Chief orderly, the doctors, and the nurses, and say to them, 'What will I do next? Tell me what to do. Am I doing this correctly?' When you have finished the work you have been given to do, go to him again and say, 'Give me more work.' After a while, he will get very tired of your insistence, and to get rid of you, he'll make you a nurse. And, when you're a nurse, go to the doctor of your team, to your leader, and say, 'Show me how to do this. Am I doing this dressing correctly? Is there a better way to do it? What is the reason for this way? Give me more work to do.' Then, he in his turn will get very tired of you and your insistence, indeed, and to get rid of you, he'll make you a doctor like himself. And, when you're a doctor, go on in the same way making a great nuisance of yourself, creating a big disturbance with your activities, go around eagerly looking for work. Do the work of two or three other doctors, be constantly studying how to improve your technique, be constantly thinking of the comfort and well-being of your patients. If other doctors go and see their patients once a day, or once every other day, you go two or three times a day to see them. Then, after a while, General Nieh will hear about you and he'll make you the Chief doctor of one of the military sub-districts. And there you behave as before, constantly discontented with yourself and your work, constantly thinking and planning to improve the conditions of your patients and constantly imparting instruction to others. Then Comrade Mao Zedong will hear about you and will want to make you the chief of the Sanitary System of the whole 8th Route Army. Then there will be a friendly fight between Comrade Nieh and Comrade Mao Zedong as to who will have you, for Comrade Nieh won't want to let you leave his division!

Now, comrades, we need technique and we need leaders to apply that technique. The ideal is the trained, conscientious technical leader. What are the qualities such a leader must possess? (1) the ability to organize, (2) the ability to instruct, (3) the ability to supervise. Organization means planning – planning as a whole and planning in detail. Instruction means the communication of that plan to others, the teaching of correct technique; supervision means the constant inspection of the progress of the plan, the correction of faults, the modification of theory by practice. And above all – work, work, work.

The Army is hungry for leaders. Every department is looking for leaders. It needs leaders more than it needs rifles and food.

One of the tasks of this hospital is to develop leaders. And when I say leaders, you must not consider I am thinking only of generals, colonels, and chairmen of districts. No, I am thinking of the whole army and the whole district from the big leaders at the so-called top, to the little leaders at the so-called bottom. But there is, in truth, no top and no bottom. That is a false conception. Our organization is not like a house – settled, static and still. It is like a globe – round, fluid, moving and dynamic. It is held together like a drop of water, by the cohesion and co-operation of its individual parts. So, when I think of leadership, I think, principally, of the 'little' leader of small units, and not so much of the big leaders of great units. This development of the 'little' leaders is the absolute necessity for the revolutionary reorganization of human society into autonomously acting, socially conscious individuals. When that has been accomplished, leaders (like the State itself) will gradually disappear. So, even though you need leaders now, and will for a long time to come, you must begin to learn not to depend upon (I mean not to get into the habit of leaning heavily on) your leaders. Be a leader yourself, though you only lead yourself, for every leader starts by first leading himself.

Those of us who are your leaders now because of our experience, are trying hard to be displaced. We are eager for you to take over our jobs and our responsibilities. Then we will be able to sit back and admire you (yes, with friendly envy) for the way you have excelled us.

We need leaders and especially small leaders, to act as germinating centres to penetrate the whole masses of the people and arouse them to realities and show them the way out of poverty, ignorance and misery. It is the lack of small leaders who make dictators possible, and substitute instead so-called 'great men,' 'great heroes,' whom we are asked to admire and worship and to be led by them like sheep.

But to return to our particular work. Doctors – instruct and supervise your junior-doctors, nurses and orderlies. Lead them; show them an example of energy; of self-disregard; of consideration. Nurses – instruct your orderlies; lead and supervise them; be diligent and quick; don't talk so much and do more work; do not be so apt to give each other advice when you know no better yourselves. Learn to act independently without the help of a half-dozen others. Don't ask others to do things you can do yourself.

In regard to conferences, they are necessary and good, but only good if followed by action. Talk is no substitute for action. Words were invented by man to describe action. Use them for their original purpose.

Today we have accomplished what we set out to do – the fulfilment of our Five-Weeks' Plan of making this hospital the best in the 8th Route Army. I think it is the best in the 8th Army and I have seen most of the others. But we must not stop here. We must plan and work to make this hospital the best in the entire Chinese National Army of which we are a part. That is the goal we must set ourselves. It will take more than five weeks, I assure you. Can it be done? Yes, I am sure it can. How? By the hard work of every comrade. It must be done co-operatively, by energy, by enthusiasm. You have that energy and that enthusiasm – apply them to that great task. No work is small, no work is unimportant.

If one fails in his duty, all suffer in consequence – if one excels in his work, all gain as a result. Yet, one last word of warning, let us be on our guard, in spite of our success, against wishful thinking; against self-deception; against the confusion between our desires and our actual accomplishments. Let us be ruthless in our criticism, be cruel to personal vanities, be indifferent to age, rank or experience, if these stand in our way. Let all theories be subjected to the bright clear light of practice. Only in this way will our concepts mirror reality.

Let me conclude. I want to thank all who have made this splendid hospital, of which we are so proud. I thank the carpenters who have worked so hard making the buildings, the alterations, the ward furniture; the iron smith for the Thomas splints. I want to praise the doctors, nurses and orderlies for their splendid work. Especially is it just to praise the volunteer civilian nurses, many of them old in years, whose loving care for the wounded has been, and is, a daily lesson to all of us, in faithfulness and devotion to duty. The civilians of the village, both men and women have been co-operative and cheerful in accommodating such large numbers of wounded staff in their houses, often to the great inconvenience of themselves. I want to thank the Management Department and Superintendent's Branch. If I would mention names, I might mention a dozen worthy of praise, but I will mention only two. One is Comrade Liu, our political director, for his tireless activity; and Comrade Tung, my other self, assistant and interpreter, without whose patience, good humour and intelligence, I would be lost.

I cannot close without expressing my admiration for the courage and uncomplaining spirit of our wounded, both of the 8th Route Army and the Partisan Detachments. For these there is nothing we can do, less than to give them the utmost consideration, care and skill, in return for what they have endured and suffered for us. For they have fought, not only for the China of today, but that emerging, great, free, classless, democratic Chinese Republic of tomorrow, which they, and we, may never live to see. Whether they and we will ever live to see that peaceful and prosperous Republic of workers doesn't matter. The important thing is that both they and we, by our actions now, are making that new Republic possible, are assisting in its birth. But whether it will be born or not, depends on our actions today and tomorrow. It is not inevitable; it is not self-generating. It must be created by the blood and the work of all of us who believe in the future; who believe in man and his glorious man-made destiny. Only in this way is it inevitable. Let us raise our voices so that those who are lying in the wards and cannot move yet, hear us. 'Comrades, we salute you! We shall repay your suffering with our loving care.' Before the graves of those who have fallen, whom we have been unable to save, let us say: 'we shall remember the sacrifices of the dead.' Our goal is the free China for which they died. In their memory, in devotion to our great cause, let the living and the dying seal our comradeship. In struggle and sacrifice we shall have one purpose, one thought. Then we will be invincible. Then we will know that even if we do not live to see it, some day those who come after us will gather here, as we do today, to celebrate, not merely the building of a model hospital, but of a great and democratic republic for the liberated people of China.

Bethune's energy and talents seemed boundless and took him far beyond medicine. Even in remote districts, he found ways to project word about the anti-Japanese struggle to the outside world.

Sung-yen K'ou
Shansi
Chin-Ch'a-Chi Military District
Sept. 30, 38

Dr. Ma Haide,
Yan'an, Shensi

Dear comrade –
Your undated letter (why in hell don't you date your letters!) received Sept. 15, 38. As it was accompanied by another from Dr. Sung, of August 10, 38, I take it that yours was written about the same time. Your letter contained much information about which I am very much interested.

I am glad you have had the films developed and sent to Canada. In future however we intend to develop the films here as we have received some photographic material from Tientsin and we have an excellent photographer. We will send you, for the use of the People's Foreign Relationship Association, prints of our stuff. While I am on this subject, I might as well go on and tell you about our Publicity Bureau. If you have access to my report to General Nieh, of August 23, 38 (a copy of which was sent to Comrade Mao Zedong) you will see that I advocated the establishment of a Department to collect and rewrite articles for the domestic and foreign press and not to rely on the reports of such observers as Hanson, Brown Lindsay or others coming to our District, however sympathetic they may or may not be. The matter was taken under consideration, and the arrival of your letter of Sept. 15, telling of the Yan'an Association, was sufficient to spur us on to action. A Publicity Bureau has now been formed; the first meeting was held on Sept. 26 to consider plans of organization. At that meeting, attended by the 4 members of the Bureau, namely – Comrade Tung (my interpreter) was elected Chief of the Bureau with special charge of the literary and educational field and to act as liaison officer between the Chinese section of the Bureau and the English section; Comrade Teng, of the Political Bureau attached to General Headquarters, was appointed in charge of the political and mass organizations section; Comrade Sha, formerly editor of the County Press, and now photographer attached to General Headquarters, was appointed in charge of the military section and photographer of the Bureau; I was appointed as in charge of the English section, with special attention to hospitals, public health, etc.

The name of the Bureau was chosen as 'The Chin-Ch'a-Chi Branch of the People's Foreign Relations Association of Yan'an.' It should be noted that we consider ourselves as a branch and not as an independently acting Bureau. Only by centralization of the collection and placement of information, will overlapping and non-utilization of the domestic and foreign fields be prevented. Yan'an is the logical place for such centralization. We intend to supply Yan'an with the material we collect. At the same time, we will offer suggestions as to its placement to the Central Association, if we consider such called for. We suggest that a very careful analysis of the fields be made by the Yan'an Association, both in China and abroad, with special attention to the liberal bourgeois press, magazines and periodicals. Of course, our own press should be supplied also.

It was decided to call a conference of the press, the Government and the mass organizations, to discuss the appointment of our representatives in all departments in the District, including the Army. This conference has been called for in one week. Tentative plans for an office staff, were made.

In particular, each member of the Bureau pledged himself to personally write at least one article a month, in addition to the collection of more material. We want to know what is going on in the entire District and to 'tell the world' about it. If the Yan'an Association wants, at any time, 'special' articles on different phases of our activities, we will try and supply such demands.

It was suggested that our plan be adapted for a dozen other districts in China where the activities of the Party and Army are permitted to be known. We have made plans to buy a movie camera to take films of the Army and Partisans. Also a collection of photographs to form a travelling exhibition. We badly need an enlarger and large sized printing paper. Could you get this in Sian for us? Has anything been done about my suggestion for a travelling projector of movie films to come from Canada to tour the District? I ask this because I have received no mail from Canada for several months – no letters or papers and am cut off from the world!

Please send me some books in English. I have read all I possess a dozen times.

Later –
Owing to the critical military situation (we are being attacked by large concentrations from the south, west and east) the conference has been postponed. Our lovely new Model Hospital on which we spent so much care and work, has been evacuated to the east, and is now a Divisional Hospital. The Japanese are within 55 li of us. I am standing-by to proceed to the front as a Mobile Operating Unit. Expect to move up (that is to near Wutai) tomorrow. A determined attack is apparently being made on Wutai city.

I have just time to enclose my speech on the opening of the Sun Yat Sen Model Hospital (Sept. 15) and a copy of a letter I wrote to a friend of mine last month. I am sending the copy of my address to Toronto and New York (the Canadian and American CP), in case you might think of using it. It accompanies my monthly report and was written not with publication in view, unless they thought fit. Your association might use it if considered suitable – also the letter, which is nothing out of the way, but I enclose it as a sample, if your association would like more of the same type. Comrade Tung will send you an article on the Model Hospital. Frankly I have been so busy getting this hospital on its feet; writing 2 books on surgery and medicine; a weekly medical bulletin to the front line medical service and doing 115 operations this month, that I have but little time left for writing letters and articles.

Having a grand time! Only wish I had an assistant. What in hell is that damned American Committee doing? Why don't they send me help?

With comradely greetings to all. Remember me to Li Teh.

Salud
Norman

Bethune continued to refuse the monthly salary offered by the Military Council of Yan'an.

Sung-yen K'ou
Sept. 30, 38

General Nieh,
Military Headquarters

Dear Comrade –
Dr. Lin has brought to me tonight, the sum of $301.00 for my acceptance. This sum seems to be made up of $100.00 for myself personally; $102.20 I am supposed to have spent for drugs; and $98.80 I have spent for gauze and cotton. In respect to the first item of $100.00 I repeat my telegram of August 12, 38 to the Military Council of Yan'an, in which I refused to accept this money and suggested it be turned into a special tobacco fund for the wounded. I can only repeat this suggestion. In regard to the other items, I have no knowledge of the sum of $102.00 supposed to have been spent by me on drugs. In regard to the $98.00 spent on gauze and cotton, of this sum I only contributed $70.00, the remainder having been given by Dr. Brown. As this money was given me by Dr. Chiang at Lan Hsien on June 6th before leaving for Wutai, it was not my money I spent but that belonging to the medical service of the 8th Route Army. The receipt for this has been sent to the chief of staff, Yan'an.

It is inconceivable that I should be supposed capable of accepting $100.00 a month personally when other doctors receive $1.00 a month and General Nieh himself, the magnificent sum of $5.00 a month.

In addition, I have no need for money as everything I need is freely supplied me.

With comradely greetings,
Norman Bethune. M.D.

Bethune's mind seldom rested. He had suggestions on many issues, even nonmedical matters such as boosting recruitment and raising the level of consciousness of the non-combatant Chinese population.

Nan Ping, 4th Sub-District
Oct. 22, 38

General Nieh, Commanding Officer
Chin-Ch'a-Chi Military District

Dear Comrade:

As a result of a visit to Headquarters of the 4th Sub-District, it has occurred to me that some methods to encourage recruiting and to permit the soldiers to take a permissible pride in their army record and experiences and to deal (in part) with the problem of soldiers absent without leave or even deserters, would be useful at the present time. The following suggestions have been made to Commander Hsung. They were found extremely useful in the 1914–1918 war.

1. Service stripes. These are narrow strips of ribbon or braid about one inch long and a quarter of an inch wide, of red or any other colour, worn on the uniform just above the lower end of the sleeve. Each strip represents any given time of service, say 6 months. A soldier with 2 years service would be entitled to wear 4 such stripes. They are sewn, horizontally, one above the other at a distance of ½ inch.

2. Wound stripes. The idea is the same as the service stripes, with a braid of a different colour and worn on the opposite sleeve to the service stripes. They are sewn on the sleeve in a vertical manner, instead of horizontally. Every time a man is wounded on service he becomes entitled to wear one such stripe.

3. Army Enlistment Plaques. Of stone, on which the names of the men who have joined the army are cut. These plaques to be set up in each village in a prominent place, preferably at the village gate, for all to read and see. Sufficient space should be left on each to add additional names.

4. Soldiers' Families Stars. Made of paper, about one foot wide and printed in red, blue and white. To be distributed to the families who have sent men into the army. To be hung inside or outside the house. One star might be given for each man sent.

5. Medals for Mothers and Wives of soldiers killed or dying on service. Should be good quality, on enamel, with the soldier's name engraved on it.

6. Military funerals. Not sufficient attention or respect is paid to the dead in our hospitals. A cemetery should be set apart in each village. A meeting should be held in the dead soldier's village attended by political workers and representatives of the man's comrades from his regiment, to hold a short memorial service. His courage should be praised and the ideals for which he fought brought back to the attention of the villagers, and an appeal to replace him in the ranks made. Music-bands, bugles – are essential for the best effect of such a service.

7. To the relatives of every man killed in action or dying of wounds, letters should be written by the soldier's commander or by the doctor in

the hospital, without delay. This letter should describe the manner of his death to his relatives. If the man dies in hospital, the doctor should notify the man's company commander. Then too, the Government should write or send to the relatives, an official letter of regret, printed or engraved in a suitable manner on good paper so that it may be hung or framed. This document should be countersigned by the Commanding Officer of the District.

8. All villages containing deserters or men absent without leave, should have sent to them representative soldiers of proved political worth and military experience to describe the truth to the villagers of life in the army and to counteract the injurious effects of deserters' stories – by means of which lies they defend their absence from the front. As frequently as circumstances will permit, men should be given leave to return to their own villages to describe the things they have seen of Japanese brutality and ruthlessness, to awaken the villagers to the situation.

With comradely greetings,
Norman Bethune, M.D.

Although it would be destroyed by the Japanese only a few weeks after it opened, demonstrating the error of constructing permanent facilities in an area dominated by shifting war fronts, the Model Hospital at Sung-yen K'ou, while it survived, did improve the state of medical training and care in the Chin-Ch'a-Chi military district. (I have excised sections of Bethune's monthly report which conveyed relatively insignificant details about his activities.)

Chang Yu, 4th Sub-District
Nov. 1, 38

General Nieh,
Commanding Officer,
Chin-Ch'a-Chi Military District

Dear comrade,
I enclose my monthly report ending Oct. 31.38.

I am happy to report that the patients are in better condition than at any time since June; that the organization of the Sanitary Service is greatly improved; that more and increased attention is being paid to the comfort of the patients. This reflects great credit on the chiefs of the service.

At a conference held today, many new plans were discussed. I have not the slightest doubt but that they will be put into force.

I enclose a memorandum presented to the conference for discussion. The greater number of the points it contained were accepted.

Comrade Tung, two doctors taking my course in Operative Surgery, an operating-room nurse and myself, are leaving for the north to the 1st and 3rd. Sub-District Divisional Hospitals at the end of a week. We will be away, in all probability, about two months.

Copies of an article Comrade Tung and I have written on a staff conference held at Hung Tsi Tien on Oct. 19, 38 are being sent to Dr. Ma Haide, Tim Buck and Earl Browder. I am enclosing one copy for yourself for censorship. Perhaps some of the discussion should not be published. On the other hand I feel strongly that, if printed exactly as it is, it will give a truer and more authentic picture of the work of our District. I am suggesting to Comrade Ma that the story might be sent to International Press Correspondence or some such periodical. The story will be published in our Canadian and American party periodicals. If you have any objections to some points in the story being told, will you please 'blue-pencil' them, not only in your copy but in the copies being sent to Yan'an, Canada and America – the letters of which I am leaving open? If on the contrary you approve of the story as it stands, will you send the batch of letters to Mao Zedong, who will send them on.

With kindest regards to yourself and to Mrs. Nieh, and all comradely greetings,

I am, yours faithfully,
Norman Bethune M.D.

Monthly report of the Canadian-American Mobile Medical Unit –
Sept. 28–Oct. 31, 38

This month we have been practically on the move for the entire month as a Mobile Unit.

...

Total number of patients personally examined for the first time – 303.
Total number of operations performed – 132 (75% of these were debridements).
Distance travelled – 525 li (175 miles) on foot and by horse.

...

Comments – 1. As a result of our experiences of not only this month but from the previous three, we have come to some very definite conclusions in regard to the raising of the technical standards of the Sanitary Service. One is that the Team idea is excellent and should be more universally employed. An extension of this same idea would be to subdivide the teams up still more into nurses' units within the doctors' team. The house becomes the unit of the team. Put a nurse in charge of one or even more houses and make him responsible for that house or houses. Committees of doctors, nurses and orderlies should meet regularly once a week. Once a month a general Hospital Conference should be held of delegates from these various committees.

2. In the 4th Sub-District hospital (Dr. Liao) the technical abilities of the staff are below the average. Organization is poor. The comfort of the patients is being neglected. We found the best way to tackle this problem was to take over for a week or so, half a dozen wards and to demonstrate to the hospital staff the correct methods. We have done so at Hsiao, Chia Ho and at Nan Ping. There is a great place for these Travelling Educational Units employed in this way.

3. The construction of a 50 bed hospital at Chang Yu is nearly completed. It will be occupied by typical, assorted cases of wounded for ward training of the student nurses. A wide variety of wounded is being selected.

4. We feel very pleased indeed with the results obtained at the Model Hospital at Sung-yen K'ou, which are now beginning to show themselves. A very great improvement in technique has been obtained, and as a result the condition of the wards and patients very much improved. The staff are very anxious to learn new methods and the finest co-operation has been obtained from all. Special attention should be drawn to the work of Dr. Yeh and Dr. Lin, not to mention Political commissar Liu.

5. The shortage of surgical instruments is still acute, especially for knives, artery forceps, surgical scissors, catgut and silk ligatures. Efforts should be made immediately to buy these in Beijing or Tientsin, especially in view of the conditions in the south. Bandages, cotton, gauze supplies are adequate at present. The stock of antiseptics is very low, also anaesthetics.

6. I must acknowledge my sincere thanks and appreciation for the thousand and one kindnesses I have received at the hands of all our comrades. It would have been impossible to have been treated in a more considerate and co-operative manner than has been demonstrated by all, from General Nieh to the youngest orderly.

7. We are all looking forward to increased efficiency in the next

months to come. The results have shown that it is not necessary to have any ideal 'Model Hospital,' that every hospital can be made a model one, if sufficient organization, energy are applied to the task. Our educational work in the future will be directed towards transforming the ordinary, dirty house of the peasant into a clean, comfortable hospital ward for the wounded. This is far simpler than sounds possible. But it needs a lot of educational work to open the eyes of some members of the Sanitary Service to these possibilities!

With comradely greetings,
Norman Bethune. M.D.
Medical Advisor to the Chin-Ch'a-Chi Military District

This lengthy report – parts of which I have excluded – describes the reality of guerrilla warfare and practical government in the battlefront areas Bethune served.

Chang Yu, Hopei
Nov. 1, 1938

A *Hsien* Government at Work in the Fighting Area in North China
'Tungtzemen,' the chairman said, in a quiet voice and paused. I glanced down the long line of polished lacquer tables, placed end on end, around which the 20 delegates were sitting on rough stools and benches. The air of the warehouse – cool and dank, with the faint odour of burning wood still hanging about its stained walls and high ceiling – became still. All eyes were fixed on that short figure standing opposite me, dressed in faded blue jacket and trousers; her face, broad and pale; serious and serene. An emergency staff conference of the Ping Shan Ksien Government was about to open.

It was the morning of October 19, 1938. Outside, the sun was coming over the mountain tops and falling in long slanting rays on the white cement roofs of the houses still standing and into the blackened, brick-strewn compounds. We were 17 li (52 miles) from the enemy. Their cavalry could reach us in an hour. That morning, early, we heard their machine guns and the faint crash of their artillery to the east. They were firing on our partisans, gathered on the hills and hidden in the deep mountain valleys.

The town of Hung Tsi Tien was nearly deserted except for soldiers, government officials and a half dozen merchants selling oil, cigarettes, meat and vegetables on the sidewalks of the long, winding ruined main street. A barber had set up his chair in the street and was already at work. An old man was raking among the ruins of his burnt house, for his remembered precious belongings. Laughing little boys, perfectly naked in spite of the cool morning air, played among the piles of scattered bricks. Outside the government offices stood a sentry in his patched, yellowish-green cotton uniform, wearing on his sleeve the badge of the Chin-Ch'a-Chi Military District and in his cap, the round metal disc of the National Chinese Army. The sling of his old rifle was made with a piece of bandage, but the yellow handles of the 4 hand grenades stuck in his belt were new and shiny. On his bare feet he wore Sechuan sandals with woven cloth rag soles and bright red and green wool tops. Over the great toe of each was a green and red wool tassel like what milliners used to call 'pom-poms.' Across the low tops of houses, I could see standing on a hill, a Buddhist Temple, its open doors disclosing within, blackened walls and roofless rooms. A flock of pigeons wheeled and swung in its aerial ballet. The town was very quiet, very still; desolated; exhausted like one after a fever; yet with an air of waiting; of expectancy.

Two weeks ago, a force of 1150 Japanese had left Ping Shan city, 60 li away to the east and raided this town. Warning had been given in time and the enemy entered a deserted town – not a single inhabitant remained, not a pig not a sheep was left behind, not a sack of grain or even a pail to carry water, was left for the use of the enemy. Then, fearing for the safety of their line of communication, they retired, first setting fire to 60 houses with kerosene and incendiary bombs. Their losses were 100 men, ours 50.

This town is in the *hsien* (or county) of Ping Shan, west Hopei province, lying in the angle between the Tai Yuan-Cheng Ting railway (the Cheng-Tai lu) running east and west, and the line from Cheng Ting north to Beijing (the Pei-Han lu). It is roughly triangular, measuring about 75 miles from east to west and 50 from north to south. The base of the triangle lies to the west and is bounded by the great Shih Pa Pan range of mountains between Hopei and Shansi provinces. The eastern apex is part of the Hopei Plain, the north and west are mountainous. Running through it from west to east is the large Hu To River. Feeding this are half a dozen smaller streams from the north which flow down the steep valleys between the parallel ranges running north and south. The villages – from 50 to 300 families each – are strung along these streams like buds on a willow branch. There is a motor road from Shih Chia Chuang (the junction point of the Cheng-Tai Lu) to Ping Shan. The Japanese control this road. From Ping Shan to Hung Tsi Tien, the road is fair and can be used by bicycles. From this point westward, there is only a mule track, running along the river bank. The roads running north and south through the mountain valleys, are narrow, rocky, winding trails, impassable except by horse, mule or on foot. The Japanese are in possession of one-fifteenth of the *hsien*'s territory – its eastern angle. This proportion, incidentally, is the proportion the Japanese hold of the entire North China!

The inhabitants of the *hsien* number 250,000, living in 300 villages. There are no habitations outside of the villages and towns. The principal industry is farming – 95% of the population are farmers or members of farmers' families. Of these farmers, only three are large land owners, possessing from 500 to 1000 mu each. (A mu is one third of an acre.) The remaining farmers are divided into 4 classes. First, those owning outright the land they till. There are 10,000 of these. The average holding of a family of 5 is 5 mu ('One mu, one mouth'). Second, those farmers who own a little land and rent some more to make up, again, an average of 5 mu. There are 20,000 of these. Third, those who own no land at all and rent – still again an average of 5 mu. Of these there are 16,000. The fourth class are the agriculture wage labourers numbering 10,000. These work where they can find work to do and take their wages in grain or cloth. They may handle as much as $5.00 or $10.00 a year in addition.

A farmer tilling either his own or rented land possesses his own implements. These consist of a hoe and a mattock for digging the soil. If more prosperous, he may own a wooden plough with an iron plough share, an iron spade and a wooden harrow. Ploughing is done by men and mules – very occasionally by oxen. The grain is cut with a small hand scythe. The rakes are of cane or made of the 3 prongs of a tree branch. Baskets are woven cane or fibre. Grain is stored in woven bins or earthenware pots.

The only metal worked is iron, with the exception of a little spinning of pewter for wine cups, in the towns. Apart from iron, the most precious metal is tin in the form of Standard Oil or Shell company kerosene and gasoline cans. These are put to innumerable uses.

Depending on his prosperity, a farmer may own a donkey, a mule, a pig and half a dozen hens. He may own a sheep or goat. These are herded communally, in charge of a goat herd and a small boy. They are pastured on the steep mountain slopes all day and return to the village at night. There are wolves in the northern mountains.

Two crops a year are grown. Wheat (of the quality corresponding to our Canadian Number 2, hard) corn, millet, oats, gaolian, peas, beans, cabbages, onions, garlic, carrots, turnips, red peppers, bread-fruit, apples (in the north), potatoes, dates (which grow on small thorny trees and are not very sweet), hemp and tobacco, are the principal agricultural products.

The staple food of the people is millet and boiled flour dough strips, rather like large flat macaroni. Soya bean curd, vegetables and steamed wheat flour, unleavened bread, and occasionally a little pork, is the remainder of the people's food. Meat is a luxury. So also is tea. Rice is not grown and in consequence not eaten. Nothing is eaten or drunk without being cooked or boiled. There is no milk. The goats are not milked. Children are fed at the breast up to the age of 3 or 4. Children begin to work in the fields at 5 years of age. There is a high percentage of illiteracy, especially in the distant mountain villages.

The little farms (gardens we would call them) lie alongside the streams or on terraces built up on the sides of the deeply-gouged, treeless mountains. These terraces are the product of centuries of labour. There are literally thousands of these narrow ledges. They range from the size of a blanket up to half an acre, each retaining on its rock-buttressed shelf, its cup full of the precious earth. They rise one above the other, with mathematical neatness, like the giant steps of here, a colossal capitol; there a towering pyramid; and here again as of some vast veranda.

The general physique of the people is excellent. Men of six feet in height are not uncommon. Their complexion is a ruddy brown. The women are shorter, but sturdy and not unhandsome. They wear through the dark coil of their hair a single, thick silver pin, silver bracelets on their wrists and silver rings on their fingers. The health of the survivors of childhood – infant mortality is high – is on the whole good. Chronic nasal and respiratory diseases are common. Every other person has a cough. Trachoma is prevalent.

Such is the country – wild and mountainous, and its people – poor, good-natured, hardy and strong.

The government of the *hsien* is supported by taxes. Of these there are three – the land tax, an import and an export tax. Only land owners pay the land tax – 40¢ on the mu per year. The farmer who tills rented land is not taxed directly – he pays his tax in the increased rent he is forced to pay the actual owner of the land. All land is not taxed equally – much poor land, and river land subject to floods are not taxed. The land of soldiers has a reduction of 20%. Much of the work of the tax department of the government has been in tracing down the hundreds of tax evaders, which, up to last year, under the old provincial government, had enjoyed a comparative freedom from taxation by means of the well-known official 'squeeze' system of bribery to government officials. This has, needless to say, been completely abolished. The income from the land tax amounts to $60,000 a year. Half of this goes to the district government. The import tax is collected on luxuries only. Necessities of life are not taxed. Cigarettes pay 100%, cotton products 20%, toilet articles 5%. The collection from this tax is $24,000 a year. It goes to the district government. An export tax is placed on all products in which the enemy are in need of. Cattle and cotton are both prohibited to be exported; eggs pay 20%, skins and leather 10%, pigs' bristles 10%, etc. This tax produced $12,000 a year.

The total income of the *hsien* is in the neighbourhood of $42,000 a year. This supports 40 officials. These are – the magistrate, the head of the government and his secretarial staff; the staff of the departments of administration, finance, education, law, and that of agriculture and industry. The highest salary paid is that to the magistrate – $18.00 a month. He has voluntarily reduced this to $10.00

The government of the *hsien* is in the hands of the people acting through the Village Conference. This is an unique institution. It meets every two weeks and is attended by two delegates or deputies from eight different organizations. The mayor of the village represents the village council, while the Peasants' Union, the Workers' Union, the Women's Union, the Young Men's Union, The People's Guards and the School Teachers each sends two delegates. Included in the conference are two representatives from the gentry (rich peasants, wealthy merchants and members of the professional classes if there are any). To this conference come representatives from the *hsien* government to explain the program and policy of the government and, in turn, from this conference, deputies are chosen to attend the monthly staff conference of the government. It is this monthly staff conference that decides the government's policy. It is such a conference that is being held this morning.

'Tungtzemen,' the chairman repeated, 'this emergency staff conference has been called to put before you the work of the past two weeks for criticism and analysis and to make plans to deal with the new situation that confronts us. The purpose of the conference is also to find a way to stress the work of the mass organizations and to find a way so that we may be able more effectively to help our troops in the defence of our district. I will call on Comrade Lui to speak.' As she finished, a tall, lean figure rose. He seemed about 35 years of age. He was dressed in a long, rough, blue cotton robe. His hair was shaved short. His face was dark-brown and lined; the lips thin, the nose large, and straight, the eyes serious and intelligent. His hands, resting on the table in front of me, were broad and thick – the hands of a farmer, of a worker. I whispered to my interpreter, 'Who is he?' 'The chief of the Peasants' Union. He represents 30,000 small farmers,' was the reply. Lui commenced by outlining the good points of the government's work. He praised the bravery of the staff of the Women's Union who had not retired to the rear on the Japanese advance but, instead, had, by a round-about way, made their entrance into the enemy's territory to carry on their secret work. He reported the mobilization of 20,000 people's guards in the period from September 24 to October 5. In one district (the 5th), 2,000 had been mobilized in 6 hours alone. These had acted as transport for the army, carrying food and ammunition, as stretcher-bearers for the wounded and for destroying the roads. He then went on to describe the 'Chian Pi Ching Y'eh' – the policy of evacuation of villages before the arrival of the enemy. At Hung Tsi Tien, for example, all food had been removed, all precious things had been hidden or carried away. Nothing was left but empty houses. The Partisan squads of the People's Guards – small bands of local civilians, young boys of 12 and old men of 50, armed with ancient rifles, swords and spears – had been very brave. Forty of these had attacked a force of 100 puppet enemy (the Traitor Army, composed of Chinese attached to the Japanese troops). Eight boys with only 3 rifles between them had killed 6 of the enemy. In regard to anti-traitor work, he was able to report that there was no traitor activity to the west of Hung Tsi Tien. To the east, 5 traitors had been caught and killed. The propaganda work was improving. The people were awakening to the situation and saw for themselves that our propaganda was true when their houses were burnt and their relatives shot by the Japanese. One small boy of 12 had been shot by the enemy for singing an 8th Army soldiers' song. The Peasants' Union had given the army 600 catties of cakes, 105 sheep, 76 pigs, 20,000 catties of bread, 1500 pairs of shoes, and 1000 persimmons.

Learning from the experience of 10 months ago, the leaders of the union had not collected together in one place, but had spread themselves out into the small villages to assist the work of the junior leaders. 'The members of the Peasants' Union are fearless,' he said. 'Their spirits are high. Last time some of us retreated when the enemy were 100 li away. This time, we stayed when the Japanese were only 7 li distant.' The people are beginning to realize that this is a protracted war; that a decisive victory is impossible at the present time, so they are not discouraged.

These were the good points. Then he went on to discuss the weak ones. 'Let us criticize ourselves severely, comrades,' he said. 'We will have to acknowledge that independence of spirit is, as yet, not fully developed among the lower leaders. Instructions are not transmitted quickly enough through the ranks. Our communication network is not fast enough. For example, the food stocks of the village of Ko Su were not removed in time, owing to delay in messages. Some of the People's Guards watch only for a frontal attack and fail to guard the rear. Some villages did not resist. Only in a few villages was a determined effort at resistance made. Of course, there is much excuse to be made for these comrades, armed as they were with only old flint-lock rifles and rusty swords. They felt themselves powerless against the machine guns and cannon of the Japanese. But we must fight with the weapons we have as we are not likely to get others, unless we capture them from the enemy.'

Traitors still act as guides to the Japanese troops and continue to cut the telegraph wires. We must re-double our efforts to catch these traitors. Then, too, our propaganda work needs strengthening. The lower leaders are not active enough in explaining the war to the people. Our slogans, when they fall or are torn from the walls are not always repaired. The Young Men's Union at Huei Sheh had retired on the approach of the enemy saying to the troops, 'our work is during peace, your work is to fight.' Needless to say, this is very wrong. In time of war, there is no difference between us; we all must fight.

He sat down and the Chairman rose again. She was a woman of about 25, a member of the Central Committee of the Women's Union and a representative of the District Government. She proceeded to give an account of the military situation. The Japanese had transferred 3 or 4 divisions from the Yangtze River front to make the attack on this district, because we had become the centre of Japanese resistance in North China and were becoming a serious menace to the enemy's military and political position. It was an acknowledgement by the Japanese both of the failure in North China and a tribute to the resistance of the people of the Chin-Ch'a-Chi military district. That is the reason for the recent attack on our district. He has set himself the work of capturing all our important cities and towns in the North. Then by connecting up these basic centres by motor roads, he will attempt to control our district. To this end he has taken already the cities of Lai Yuan, Lin Chu, Kuang Lin, Wu Tai, Tai Hsien, Ting Hsiang, Tang Hsien, Wan Hsien and Fu Ping. Thus he hopes to separate our troops and drive them into the remote mountain regions. He has commenced already to build a motor road and railroad at Wu Tai and Chu Yang.

'Let us examine the strong points and the weak points of the Japanese position in our district. One of his weak points is that he does not have enough troops to distribute among all these cities and to hold them all. He must depend on building up a great Traitor Army to do so. Even in his attacking forces, there are many Chinese Puppet soldiers. He mixes these Chinese traitors with his own troops as he is aware that they are unreliable. The recent mass surrender of 800 puppet troops, after killing their Japanese officers, is a demonstration of this. Then, too, he has suffered many casualties – 400 at Po lan and 500 at Wan Kuai. On the other hand our losses have been small – 350 at the outside.'

I leaned over and said to my friend – 'I can confirm that. Our hospital has treated only 200 wounded in the past two weeks and we received the majority of them as we were closest to the fighting on the southern route up to Wutai.' The chairman went on – 'the other weak point of the enemy is the extreme difficulty he experiences in transporting food and military supplies through hostile territory. In the attack on Wu Tai, he was forced to employ air planes to drop ammunition to his troops. He was forced to burn the bodies of his dead – and, the civilians declare, of his seriously wounded also – in a great pyre at Liang Chia Ch'ai, in Shansi, since he was unwilling or unable to transport them either back to Yu Hsien or forward to Wutai. The hatred of the people is his greatest obstacle. That is the reason he sees he must construct motor and railroads through our territory for his armoured cars and tanks. Mule transport such as we employ is, for him, too risky. In addition, owing to the highly mechanized nature of his army in small valley fighting, such weapons as artillery, tanks and even air planes are unsuitable for our particular type of terrain. He can use them either not at all, or, at the most, with a great loss of their efficiency.

'Now let us consider some of his good points. He is excellently equipped. His weapons are first class. His officers are well trained. The Japanese soldier does not shrink from hand to hand fighting. He is quite brave. He lacks initiative, however, and fights in a routine way. It is interesting to note that so many of the Japanese soldiers are men of 30 to 35 years of age. In the diaries of the dead we have found, very frequently, anti-war leaflets. One of the strong points in the enemy's tactics is his method (as in the capture of Wutai) of moving forward in divided divisions and concentrating their attack on a given point. His scouts, contrary to his practice of a few months ago, now are placed well in advance of his vanguard and main force. He places his puppet troops in the vanguard. The propaganda of the enemy in the territory he has taken, is extensive, although at times rather crude and appealing to the worse instincts of the civilians. As example some of his slogans used are – "We are not fighting the Shansi and Hopei troops, we are only fighting the Red Army." Another of his slogans is – "The Red Army is the enemy of the civilians. Follow us and what we capture will belong to you." This, of course, is a direct incitement to plunder.

'Now let us look at some of our strong points. In weapons and in numbers, our troops are increased. They have gained much valuable experience in fighting in the past two weeks, and as a result our casualties are less. Our fresh soldiers are inclined to take too many risks and endanger their lives carelessly. They are learning how to fight. Our chief weapon is the hand grenade. That means close fighting. Our soldiers are brave to the point of recklessness.

'The government has led the people; has led the fighting and not retired. As a result, the people's faith in the government is strong. This faith is shown by the people not retiring on the advance of the enemy until the government orders them to do so. The work of the mass organizations in helping the troops has been excellent.

'Still,' she continued, 'we have our weak points. Our people are poorly armed and as a result are sometimes reluctant to attempt armed resistance against the well equipped enemy. The people of Pi Lan Hsien fled when the enemy were 20 li away leaving food and other material to fall into the enemy's hands. Terrified by the sound of artillery, their only thought was to escape from the sound of the guns; happy when they could hear them no more. Conceptions of "Peace at any Price," still exist among some of the backward villages. They do not realize that this is exactly the attitude that the Japanese desire to cultivate.

'What are our duties? They are to stress pure propaganda among the people; to tell them the truth about the war. Our staffs must go to the lower leaders to encourage them and to assist them in mobilizing the people more extensively to join in the fight. Also we must enlarge our partisans; we must lead our people to greater efforts with armed resistance.'
...
The colonel of the 7th regiment then spoke. He was a boyish-looking young man of 25. He looked about 19. I learnt later that he had 8 years'

experience in actual fighting and had been wounded 4 times. He told of the conditions in the army; of their high spirits and morale, and described, to everybody's great amusement, a story of two regiments. It seems that certain old provincial prejudices still exist slightly among the troops. For example, the 7th Regiment has been called the 'Shan Tao San' – 'the Potato Eaters' – because they are all natives of Shansi Province. Some soldiers of other regiments – natives of Hopei province – did not like at first to fight beside them. This was, of course, a relic of the old inter-provincial rivalries and antagonisms. But now all is well, for they said – 'we must take the policy of the United Front. If the Communist Party can co-operate with the National Party, then we should co-operate with the Shansi troops.' A year ago such a declaration would have been impossible.

This ended the general discussion. The chairman then re-capitulated the points raised and threw these problems open for detailed discussion. They were –

1. The enlargement of the army; how this was to be done.
2. Chian Pi Ching Y'eh; how to supervise it and make it more prevalent.
3. Economic and financial problems.
4. Co-operation and unity in work; how to achieve.
...

The Chairman then reviewed the practical points raised and then placed the next item on the agenda on the table, namely the policy of Chian Pi Ching Y'eh, or the method of evacuation of villages on the route of march of the enemy. A number of delegates joined in this discussion, including 2 young girls from the Women's Union. They spoke quietly and diffidently at first, then, as they became more assured, with stronger voices and conviction. They were dressed like the Chairman, in the standard faded blue jacket and trousers. Their faces were broad and sunburnt; their expressions modest and courageous. They were about 22 years of age. Their thick black hair was cut short and bobbed. They wore no ornaments of any kind. In their reports, they said that the evacuation work near the government's offices had been done excellently, where it was supervised, but not so well at places farther removed. This kind of work needed close supervision ...

A representative of the Peasants' Union pointed out some difficulties and mistakes. ...

Again the chairman re-capitulated the points raised and said – 'The Mass Organizations should make use of their organizational facilities to supervise the evacuation of villages and to take charge of the civilians who have been evacuated. The C.P.C.Y. is not a policy of running away, but a policy of obstructive resistance' ...

At this point, an adjournment was made for lunch. It was a merry, gay and noisy meal. Great steaming pots of hot cabbage soup were brought out into the open court and consumed amid shouts of laughter, especially when some greedy delegate spent too much time in search for the rather rare pieces of pork. The noise was terrific. The Chinese are great aspirators of food – this on account of the inefficiency of chop sticks to transfer fluid or semi-solid food from bowl to mouth. Following the soup we had hot steamed bread rolls, made from unleavened wheat flour. Then back to work again.

The Magistrate outlined some of the financial problems of the *hsien* ...

There followed a discussion on the problems of leadership. It was the consensus of opinion that central, collective leadership was necessary for the co-ordination of work, both in their own and in enemy territory.

By this time, it was 6 o'clock and the conference had a recess. Candles had already been lit and placed on the table, throwing into high relief earnest, brown faces, and casting on the wall behind great wavering shadows of bent heads and shoulders. Outside through the open door, I could see the first pale stars. It was quite cold. The town was silent.

There arose a demand for a song from the chairman. After a little demur, she consented and in a clear, good voice sang this soldier's song –

> 'We are an oppressed nation,
> We must resist our oppressors.
> Only by resistance can we win our liberation,
> Only by fighting, can we continue to exist.
>
> 'Answer the enemy's furious attack,
> People of China! arm yourselves; push forward.
> Drive the Japanese out of our territory,
> Only with our blood shall we consent to peace.'

It was a fine, brave song.

Then it was the turn of the foreigner, but not the stranger, to sing. So I sang a song that the Thaelmann Battalion of the International Brigade used to sing in Spain. And as I sang I remembered with pride those strong comrades fighting with the same high courage as their Chinese brothers, in the same great cause. I remembered the millions of comrades all over the world fighting for the liberation of mankind from poverty, ignorance, ignominy, so that they and their children could live with dignity; enlightened, prosperous, peaceful and happy. 'Yes,' I thought, 'this is a cause worth fighting for. This is the answer to every man's question to himself – "What shall I do with my life?"'

Then the conference got down to business again. Comrade Wang of the Mass Movement Department, spoke. He was young, vigorous and decisive. 'We are in danger. The enemy has made plans to crush us completely. We must realize the seriousness of our situation and be prepared to die, if necessary, for the liberation of the Chinese nation. ...

'I propose the formation of a "Fighting Area Mass Mobilization Committee," to include members of every organization of the army, and of the government, to tackle the problems we have heard discussed today.'
...

After a great deal of discussion, it was the decision of the Conference to establish a 'Fighting Area Mass Mobilization Committee' for the central leadership and co-ordination of all anti-Japanese activities in the *hsien*; that this committee should prepare a collective plan to assist, instruct and supervise the work of all organizations; that this committee should not act in an executive manner, but be a machine to connect up the various organizations' work. Five [*sic*] members were elected to prepare such plans – the magistrate, the chief of the Peasants' Union, a delegate from the Mass Organizations Department, and a captain of the People's Guard.

The conference closed at 9:30 that evening.

As we separated, the stars were shining through a thousand perforations in the dark curtain of the sky. It was cold and clear, with the amazing, dead silence of the Chinese night. On the wall of a burnt-out house, the flashlights in our hands lit up a slogan written in great black characters – 'Except by fighting, there is no other Road to Life.' It was a complete description of the day.

Norman Bethune
and
Tung Yueh Chian

Waging an effective propaganda war continued to be one of Bethune's preoccupations. He envisioned a plan to use captured Japanese soldiers in this propaganda campaign.

Letter to Chin-Ch'a-Chi Military District
Chang Yu
November 2, 1938

We have, as you know, two wounded Japanese prisoners at Hua Mu Base Hospital. One is an officer of senior rank, on whom we have operated twice on his badly wounded leg. He is now able to walk with the aid of crutches. He is perfectly aware that it is entirely due to the good medical attention he has received that he did not either lose his leg or his life. The other has a moderately severe bayonet wound of the head which is nearly healed. Although neither of these prisoners can understand nor read Chinese, yet they manage to convey their gratitude to the staff of the hospital for their humane treatment.

When I was last at Hua Mu, on October 27th, I took photographs of these two prisoners in a group with Dr. Lin, dressed in his operating room gown marked with the red cross and wearing the arm band of the 8th Army. I myself was taken in a similar group.

Now I suggest we send these men a Japanese interpreter and have them write letters to their relatives in Japan and enclose the photos. In addition, we should have a statement of their letters printed with their photographs and use these as propaganda leaflets in enemy territory and abroad.

Greetings
Norman Bethune, M.D.

After the Japanese destroyed the model hospital at Sung-yen K'ou in October, Bethune turned his attention to developing a mobile medical team that would serve the front. The first test of his unit was at the battle of Hei Ssu in late November. In this report to General Nieh (sections of which I have omitted), Bethune described the conditions which made such mobile operating units imperative. He also explained the philosophy behind the mobile units, which would become identified with Bethune: 'The time is past and gone in which doctors will wait for patients to come to them. Doctors must go to the wounded and the earlier the better.'

Yang Chia Chuang, at Sub-District North Eastern Shansi
Dec. 7, 1938

General Nieh, Commanding Officer,
Chin-Ch'a-Chi Military District

Dear Comrade:
I have the honour to present the following report for the month of November of the Canadian-American Mobile Medical Unit.

Following our conference with you on October 29th, in which we received permission to go to the 1st Sub-District, we left Chang Yu on November 6th. Our unit consisted of Dr. Wang, Dr. Yu, Comrade Tung and myself. Drs. Wang and Yu were attached to our Unit for instruction in surgery. We travelled via Fu Ping to give Comrade Tung the opportunity to see his successors in the office of magistrate of that *hsien*. We arrived at Chia Kuan on the 19th, being met by Dr. Ku, chief of the Sanitary Service of the 359th Brigade and Political Commissar Yuan of the same brigade. The Commander of the Brigade sent his regrets at not being there to meet us but was away on a tour of inspection of the front. The following day, we travelled to Ho Chien Tsun and Chu Hui Tze, two villages containing the wounded of the 359th Brigade to the number of 225. We operated on 7 cases here, then travelled to Hsia Shih Fan, the office of the Sanitary Service of the Brigade and examined 20 cases. Travelled to Chuan Lin Kiou and examined 27 more cases of wounded of the Brigade. On November 22nd, 35 wounded arrived from north of Lia Yuan, having been 3 days on the road without attention. We operated all night and the following day. As a result of my strongly expressed feelings of indignation that such lack of attention should have been shown the wounded by the Sanitary Service of the Brigade, the Commander, who stayed up all night and the following day while we were operating, agreed that a radical change should be made and promised that on the next occasion of a planned action, that our Mobile Unit should be placed immediately behind the regiments in action, to render operative First Aid. He also agreed that Rest Stations should be placed on the road from the front to the rear. This was impressed on him by seeing two cases of gangrene of the arm occur as a result of tourniquets being left on for several days without attention.

On the 26th, we left for the Base Hospital at Yang Chia Chuang and inspected 60 cases. Decided to operate on 40, but owing to the receipt of a letter from the Commander on the evening of the 27th, that an action was planned for the morning of the 29th, north of Lin Chu, we left on the 28th and travelled 120 li northwest to Tsai Chia Yu. Here we were told to proceed to Hei Ssu, 55 li northwest. We arrived at 3 p.m. and found excellent arrangements had been made by the commander for our First Aid Station. We were 25 li behind the 8th Regiment attacking the Kuan Lin-Lin Chu motor road, and about 35 li from the 7th Regiment and 45 li from the 9th Regiment, all in action on this road. A very fine organization of stretcher bearers had been formed. We received our first patient at 5:15 p.m. – seven hours and 15 minutes after he had been wounded. For the next 40 hours we worked without rest, and operated on 71 cases. We were joined on the 30th day by Dr. Lu of the Yan'an Medical Unit and by another doctor of the Sanitary Service of the 359th Brigade, who relieved us for the evening of that day, permitting Drs. Yu and Wang and myself to take some rest. We finished operating at 10 a.m. on the first of December. By that time all the patients except two had been evacuated to the rear. These two were one perforation of the lung with haemorrhage that was unadvisable to transport for ten days and the other was a skull wound who refused to go to the rear. Only one patient died – a case of multiple perforations of the intestines in whom a resection of the bowel had been done. He died from shock, in spite of a blood transfusion. Dr. Wang gave 500 ccs. of his own blood at 3 a.m. in the morning of the 30th and went on working for twelve hours. Very great praise should be given this doctor for this action. I desire to bring this to your official attention for commendation. I also wish to mention the work of Comrade Tung, who in spite of a severe tonsillitis and running a high fever, gave over 50 anaesthetics. The work of Drs. Yu and Chia was also very fine.

We left at 11:30 a.m. December 1st for the 8th Regiment, accompanied by Brigade Commander Wang and his staff. Here we had a conference with the medical officers of the Regiment and critically reviewed the work of the past two days.

On December 3rd, we travelled to the Brigade Hospital at Chu Hui Tsu to inspect the cases we had operated on at the front ... One-third of all cases operated on escaped without infection. We regard this as a great advance. The incidence would have undoubtedly been higher except for the unavoidable delay between the time the wound was received and the time on which it was operated. This, at the best, was 7 hours and 15 minutes and at the latest was 40 hours. The average was 24 hours for all wounded. I regard this as satisfactory as can be expected under the circumstances, as the country is very mountainous and transportation as a result slow.

Another important factor must not be forgotten, that these cases received no attention whatever between November 30th and December

3rd with their arrival at the Brigade Hospital – a distance of 110 li. There were two rest stations between but no arrangements made for dressings, at these stations. In spite of this, one-third arrived three days later without infection! Now if these two factors of time between wound received and operation and the factor of intervening dressings between the Mobile Unit and the Base Hospital could be controlled, I feel that we could expect no more than 33% infections instead of 66% that occurred. The saving in time spent in hospital would be enormous, to mention only one result that would follow non-infected wounds.

No tourniquets were applied and no amputations done. All wounds were debrided. All fractures were operated on at once and splints applied. There were 4 fractures of the skull, with 3 herniation of the brain. None have died, to date.

Our equipment was found to be adequate. It consisted of a collapsible operating table, full set of surgical instruments, anaesthetics, antiseptics, 25 wooden leg and arm splints with ten iron Thomas leg and arm splints, sterile gauze, etc. All was placed on 3 mules. The three doctors and anaesthetist (Tung) were mounted. The remainder of the personnel of the Unit, namely operating room nurse, cook, 2 orderlies and 2 grooms, were on foot. The unmounted personnel and mules with equipment were never more than 2 hours in arriving at a destination later than the mounted personnel. This was due to the very difficult country traversed which made walking practically as fast as riding.

...

Conclusion:

We have demonstrated to our own satisfaction and I hope to the satisfaction of the Army commanders the value of this type of treatment of wounds. It is expected that it will revolutionize our present concepts of the duties of the Sanitary Service. The time is past and gone in which doctors will wait for patients to come to them. Doctors must go to the wounded and the earlier the better. Every Brigade should have at its disposal a Mobile Operating Unit such as ours. It is the connecting link between the Regimental Aid posts and the Base Hospital. In this interval between the Regiment and the Rear, in the past, the wounded have been neglected. This neglect must cease ...

I am perfectly aware of the difficulties of correct placement of such an Operating Unit in guerrilla warfare. But, if the communication by wireless of the separated military units be tightened up so that in the case of unanticipated action or spontaneous action, in which no time could be given to send word to the Operating Unit to get into position, the Operating Unit could immediately be dispatched to meet the wounded on their way back to the rear, a lot would be gained. The Operating Unit, in ordinary times should work at the base hospital and only go into action when the number of casualties are greater than the regimental doctors can take care of efficiently.

That brings up a very important point of the improvement of the First Aid at the Regiments. I would suggest that these regimental doctors be given an intensive 2 week course of instruction at the Base Hospitals and that in addition they should have attached to them for their instruction a trained member of the Operating Unit, since the types of operations performed at the front and at the base are entirely different.

We have now returned to the Base Hospital at Yang Chia Chuang where there are 147 sick and wounded. 130 are wounded, 40 are serious. All will require operation. We found Dr. Chang in charge. He has 16 nurses. The organization of the hospital is fair. The staff is inadequate. Owing to the inefficiency of the Sanitary Service of the 359th Brigade, it is imperative that all serious and moderately seriously wounded be removed from the Brigade Hospital to our Base Hospital immediately and our Base Hospital reserved only for the seriously wounded of the 359th Brigade and the 1st Sub-District Regiments. To this end, I have discharged today 20 cases and have sent letters to the Chiefs of the 359th Brigade and 1st Sub-District Sanitary Services, that they should send us at once all their fractures, all head, chest and abdominal wounds. Frankly, I cannot trust these types of cases in the hands of the doctors and nurses of these Sanitary Services. Too frequently it is seen that owing to neglect, patients develop bed-sores that are more serious than their original wounds!

I would advise that this Base Hospital be strengthened by the permanent addition of both Dr. Wang and Dr. Yu, who I am now training in surgery and both of whom are making excellent progress. I have also attached, temporarily to our Unit, Dr. Lui of the Yan'an Unit, for instruction. He will work in the 8th Regiment later. Owing to the poor quality of the medical work in this sub-District, I suggest that the Yan'an Unit be broken up and its members dispersed among the hospitals here. This sub-District is a very active one from the military point of view, has nearly 1000 wounded. The 359th Brigade is very energetic and as a result has a high proportion of casualties. These amount to at present in the neighbourhood of 325 wounded (approximately 10% of strength).

With comradely greetings,
Norman Bethune

Surrounded as he was by people needing his attention, Bethune was nonetheless isolated by language and culture. He spoke only a few words of Chinese, so that he was able to communicate only with and through his interpreter. For Bethune, a great raconteur and talker, this was trying, and he showed this frustration in a letter to Dr Ma.

Base Hospital
Yang Chia Chuang 1st Sub-District

Commander Wang 359 Brigade
December 8th, 1938

My dear Ma –
I'm getting used to not hearing from you! By God, I've got to! Another two months and no reply. The Yan'an Medical Unit arrived on the 25th of November, but brought no letter from you. I had been looking forward to this Unit to bring me some books, magazines and papers and a letter from you telling me the news of the outside world. But, they brought me instead an x-ray without a dynamo and without the upright (iron) so that the business won't work. They also brought me an opened tin of Canadian cigarettes, a bar of chocolate, a tin of cocoa, a tube of shaving soap. These were all very welcome, but I would have exchanged them all for a single newspaper or magazine or book. Incidentally, everything I have ever received from Yan'an has been opened. This includes all my letters. Some parts of letters are missing. Please, double wrap all articles and letters in protective and seal. Chinese curiosity is very strong.

I have not seen an English language newspaper for over 6 months with the exception of the *Japan Advertiser* of April 18, left behind by the Japanese in a Shansi village. I have no radio. My isolation is complete. If I did not have enough work to fill 18 hours a day, I certainly would feel discontented.

Will you do this for me? Just one thing! Send me 3 books a month, some newspapers and magazines, I won't ask you to write letters. I would like to know a few facts – Is Roosevelt still president of the United States? Who is the prime minister of England? Is the Communist Party in power in France? Some other facts would be welcome also – What is the China Aid Council doing for China, for the 8th Route Army? How much money have they sent? Are they sending more doctors or technicians? Am I to have assistance? Am I to have the medical supplies

I have been asking for for 5 months? I have exactly 27 tubes of catgut left and 2 lb. of carbolic acid. I have one knife and 6 artery forceps – all the rest I have distributed. There remains 2½ lbs of chloroform. After that is finished we will operate without anaesthetics.

Now, for Marx' sake, get busy!

I am sending you a short story, 'The Dud.' It is based on an actual occurrence. Also an article called 'Wounds.' Duplicates are sent to Tim, in Toronto. I have been too busy to do more. Travelled 855 li last month, 113 operations. Set out first frontline Operating Unit on Nov. 29, 30 and operated on 71 cases in 40 hours. We were placed 25 li behind the 8th Regiment of the 359th Brigade in action. 33% of our operated cases escaped without infection, when seen 4 days later. Usual monthly report sent to Mao Zedong.

What is Ewen doing? What is Brown doing?

What does America say? What does Canada say?

All the above would seem that I was complaining bitterly of my lot. On the contrary. I'm having a swell time!

Best regards to Li The,

With comradely greetings,
Norman

In the midst of all this work, on 20 December 1938 Bethune completed a seven-thousand-word constitution of the 'Special Surgical Hospital,' detailing the rights, duties, and responsibilities of all the personnel in the hospital, including patients and committees involved in it. This was approved by the provisional central committee of the hospital on 28 December 1938. (It is not included in this volume.) Astonishingly, he also found time to write fiction, and one of his most enduring works, the passionate essay 'Wounds.' 'The Dud' and 'Wounds,' both completed about December 1938, were published in Canadian and American left-wing publications in 1939.

The Dud

'Ai Yah,' the old man murmured to himself and rested on his hoe, straightening his old bent back.

His face was burnt deep brown; wrinkles encircled his eyes, running down in deep grooves past the compressed corners of his mouth. The upper part of his body, from the waist, was bare. Below, he wore a many-patched pair of faded blue cotton trousers. His feet were bare. Around his head was wrapped a towel, from below the edges of which the white hair sprung, still strong and vigorous.

His body was bathed in sweat. It was very hot. Overhead, the sun was a great shimmering, brazen ball in a cobalt blue sky. Beneath, the brown, brittle earth threw back the sun's rays, like a reflector, into his bent face.

It was a morning in May, on the Hopei plain, outside the city of Pao Ting. Slender willow trees edged the little fields covered with the plush-like growth of the young green corn. The fields stretched away to the city's wall, rising in the near distance.

He could just make out with his old eyes the Japanese sentry standing, rifle in hand at the city's gate. Blue Jays flashed their white striped wings in the sun, making, with their harsh cries, the heat even more intense.

'Ai Yah,' the old man breathed. Life was very difficult. He had to eat much bitterness. First there was his cough. It never seemed to improve. Then his only son had left to fight and joined the Partisans, leaving no one at home to till the farm except him and his lame son-in-law.

Then the Japanese were hard people. They took half his crop and paid him nothing. They constantly bothered him with questions – where was his son, did he write, what did he say? They even threatened to shoot him. But the old man pretended to be stupid and would tell them nothing.

Then there were the weeds. Weeds everywhere. How could one keep up with their growth? Cut them down and they seemed to spring back to life again overnight. His life seemed to him to be just one great never-ending struggle with his enemy – weeds. There must be a weed devil in the earth, with a hundred thousand heads, a million lives; persistent, deathless, mocking.

For over seventy years the old man had fought his enemy and yet here they were as strong, as impudent, as unconquerable as ever. It was very discouraging. Every trouble in the old man's life became for him a weed of some kind or another. His cough – that was a weed; his having to work in the fields again – that was a weed; the absence of his son – that was a weed; the Japanese – they were weeds, the biggest weeds of all.

And with the thought of weeds, there rose in the old man's mind the picture of a great green field. It was China. The whole of his country was for him just one vast farm – one big fertile acre of earth. And he saw this great field overrun with the weeds of the enemy, choking out the life of the young green corn; bold and arrogant. When he struck viciously at a particularly big, insolent weed with his hoe, he would murmur to himself, 'Yeh Pen Kuei Tzu, Japanese devils, there, take that,' as he dug it up, flung it aside and crushed out its life with the heel of his hoe.

The sun rose higher. The old man worked on. Coming to the end of a row, he stopped short in amazement. There, at the edge of the field, was a curious hole in the ground and sticking up in the centre of it, something that looked like a big black turnip with its top cut off.

For a moment he could not think what it could be. Then he remembered. Yes, there could be no doubt about it! It was a shell! He had seen hundreds of shells in the city, stacked up in rows like wood. The Japanese brought them from Pei Ping by train. Once he had been forced to unload a whole carload. He had seen the enemy put them into guns as long as his carrying pole and as big around as the black earthenware pot he had at home. These guns went off with a tremendous crash. They fired at men they couldn't even see, hundreds of li away.

He and his neighbours had often talked about these guns; what terrible weapons they were; how many the enemy had; and what a pity that our troops had none.

But to be sure, we did have one, just one. It had been captured in a raid the month before. He remembered his son, who had stolen home for a visit, telling him about this one gun of theirs; how proud the Partisans were of it; how much it must have cost; how few shells they had and how careful they had to be of them so that none were wasted.

Was it one of theirs or was it one of the enemies? It lay pointing towards the city. It must have been fired at the city and fallen short. Then there was no doubt of it. It belonged to the Partisans.

'Well, well,' muttered the old man, 'isn't that just like those young fellows. Here they go simply throwing away one of their few precious shells. Why, it's scandalous! Young men are always wasteful.'

He stared at it with increasing indignation. A plan grew slowly in his old mind. Raising his head, he called, in a voice shaking with excitement and anger, to his son-in-law working in the next field. 'Kuai Lai, Kuai Lai, come here quickly.' The young man hobbled over. 'Look,' said the old one, pointing at the shell, 'just look at that. That's the way those young fellows of ours expect to win this war. Why, they have so many shells they can waste as many as they please, it makes no difference,' he exclaimed sarcastically. 'That's the work of my son Chu. Undoubtedly, he is responsible. He was always extravagant. Don't you remember the time he spent a dollar, a whole dollar, for a book? Yes, it's that same careless one. If I had him here I would tell him what I think.' His voice rose in indignation as he regarded the buried shell.

But the young man was paying him but little attention. With a cry of wonder and delight, he was down on his knees, scooping away the earth from the shell. In a moment he had it free. 'Look, father, it's iron. This pointed end is brass. We will now be able to have a new ploughs-hare. Why, it's worth $10 at least. What a find. What luck.'

He lifted it carefully, cradling it in his arms like a baby, regarding it with pleasure and pride, stroking its shining brass nose and smooth black sides with a living, rough brown hand, seeing already the new ploughshare and the brass lamp to be made from it. 'Why, we're rich!' he exclaimed in excitement.

But the old man would have none of it. 'No,' he said firmly. 'We must give it back to them. It mustn't be wasted. They must use it again.' And in spite of the young man's protests, he made him fetch the donkey, made him place the shell in one of the wicker baskets, balancing the one on the other side with earth. Then with the shell covered with leaves to conceal it, he drove the donkey out of the field and turning its head away from the city, started down the long, dusty road in search of his son.

The great green chequered plain stretched ahead to the distant pale horizon. Bluebells and pink phlox flowers sprang up in the grass along the road. The brown water in the criss-cross irrigation ditches barely stirred. Poplar and willow trees stood tall and shining, each lifting its umbrella of green, motionless, into the still, blue sky.

The old donkey plodded on, the old man following in the cloud of dust stirred up by the feet of both. They were soon covered with a pale brown layer which clung to their skins and filled ears, nostrils and eyes, with its fine particles. Perspiration ran off the old man's face, making lit-tle rivulets down his cheeks. He wiped it off impatiently with his towel.

It was very hot. The whole air visibly vibrated. The dust particles danced in the waves of heat. The sun seemed like a heavy copper cap on his head. The distant line of the horizon moved up and down with a fine unsteady motion before his eyes. It was noon. Other farmers were stretched out beneath the trees for their noonday sleep, but still the old man plodded on, driven by determination and anger.

He collected burning words for his son like a man selecting jewels. Only the sharpest, the most bitter, would do. 'I'll tell that young man what I think of him.' He had a mission to perform, he had a work to do. He felt strong, proud and arrogant.

Li after li he urged the donkey on. Neither one of them had ever been so far away from home in their lives. 'Why, I must have come fifty li,' the old man muttered. They passed through village after village, which to him had been only names before, which he had never seen in all his seventy years. To all questions from whence he came, he replied, 'I come from the east,' and to those inquiries where he was going, the noncommittal 'I go to the west' was his answer.

Now, he didn't know exactly where he would find his son. Chu would never tell him where the Partisans were. 'You see, father,' he would say, 'we Partisans never stay in the same place for long. One day we are here, the next, a hundred li away. We are like birds in the sky or like fish in a deep pool. Like a hawk, we swoop, and strike and fly as fast away. Like a fish we dart to the surface from beneath the shadow of a rock and as quickly swim away.'

So the old man's task to find his son was likely to be a difficult one. And so it proved to be. To his questions where the Partisans were to be found, none knew, or if they did, would not tell. It was only by chance that late in the afternoon he happened to recognize a young neighbour of his standing in a village street. He knew that this neighbour and his son were in the same detachment, so his son could not be far away.

They greeted each other with the warmth of old friends. The young man expressed his surprise at the old man being so far away from home. 'Why, Lao Pai, white-haired one, what are you doing here? Have you come to join the Partisans?' he asked jokingly. But the old man was serious. This was no time for jokes.

'Where's that son of mine?' he asked. 'I've got something to tell that careless one. I've got something to give him, too,' he added mysteriously. 'He's not far away,' said the neighbour. 'Come, let us go and find him.'

Close at hand they found the Partisans. They gathered around the old man and his donkey, in a great circle in the village street. Nearly a hundred of them. He knew most of them by sight and many by name, and they knew him. They were farmers like himself.

They greeted him with shouts of welcome. Yet for all that they were old neighbours of his, somehow they seemed strange to him. They seemed to have changed. Perhaps it was the faded green uniform of the Chin-Ch'a-Chi military district they wore, instead of the blue trousers and jacket of the farmer. Their faces seemed to have changed too. Burnt by a thousand suns, winds and rains to the colour of the earth itself, they expressed determination and purpose. They carried themselves more erect. They seemed at the one and the same time to be more serious and yet more gay. They moved more quickly; spoke with more decision. It was very puzzling.

Perhaps it was the new Japanese rifles that each man carried; perhaps the yellow hand grenades on their belts, but the old man suddenly felt he knew them only as strangers. Even his own son seemed to have changed. Some of the anger and most of his assurance oozed out of his finger tips. He felt that superiority. They had become, instead of just old friends, that rather mysterious, separate, rather awe-inspiring Collective Thing – the Army. And he was just a *lao pai hsing*, a civilian, an individual.

So the old man suddenly forgot most of the bitter scornful words he had carefully been collecting all day long. He looked at their strong courageous faces and the arrogance melted out of him. When he spoke, the very sound of his voice surprised him, so gentle it was. Only his parental authority which they all would recognize as his right, supported him. He addressed his boy.

'My son, I have brought you something.'

'Fine,' they all shouted. 'What is it? Cigarettes? We need those.'

They crowded around the old man, and lifted up the leaves in the basket. 'No, it's something that belongs to you.' Bending over, he raised the shell in his arms. 'Here, that's yours, isn't it? Now, comrades,' he spoke gently and almost apologetically, 'I found this in my field. It didn't go off, so you must have fired it wrong. I've brought it back to you, so you can use it again.'

For a moment there was silence in the crowd. Then gales of laughter burst from their open mouths. The street rocked with their shouts. The old man looked at them in speechless amazement; waves of non-understanding passed across his face as clouds across the sky. He turned his head this way, then that. It was inexplicable. His brow wrinkled in perplexity. He shook his old white head. He could make nothing of it. It was beyond him. They were mad. He suddenly felt just a very tired old man.

Automatically, he placed the shell back in the donkey's basket. There was nothing to do but go home. His day had been wasted. He looked at the soldiers, at his own son, with sorrowful reproach. But none could speak; all were overcome with laughter. They thumped each other on the back, or collapsed into each other's arms, overcome by mirth. The old man picked up the donkey's reins and started to lead him out of the encircling laughing crowd.

His son was the first to recover and to understand. He laid his hand on the old man's sleeve. 'No, father, you mustn't go.'

'Comrades,' he said, turning to the others, and indicating to them with his back to his father, that they must support him, 'comrades, we are all greatly obliged to my father. He has done us a great service,' scowling as he spoke, at one or two who threatened to burst into laughter again, at this remark.

'Yes, yes,' they shouted, understanding at last the old man's mistake and eager that he should be deceived. 'Yes, you have been a true soldier. We are grateful to you.' Now they crowded about the old man and praised him. 'We will use it again,' they lied gracefully.

Gradually his old lined face broke into smiles. Gradually he began to feel important again. He felt he was one of them. He felt strong and authoritative. His assurance returned like a tide. They had made a mistake, but now they knew he was right. 'My boy, you must never do that again.'

'No, no,' they all shouted earnestly. 'We apologize. It was certainly wrong of us. In the future we will be more careful. We won't let that happen again, we tell you.'

So the old man was happy again. He had rooted up a big weed that day. He had done something to clear the field of China.

Wounds

The kerosene lamp overhead makes a steady buzzing sound like an incandescent hive of bees. Mud walls. Mud floor. Mud bed. White paper windows. Smell of blood and chloroform. Cold. Three o'clock in the morning, Dec. 1, North China, near Lin Chu, with the 8th Route Army.

Men with wounds.

Wounds like little dried pools, caked with black-brown earth; wounds with torn edges frilled with black gangrene; neat wounds, concealing beneath the abscess in their depths, burrowing into and around the great firm muscles like a dammed-back river, running around and between the muscles like a hot stream; wounds, expanding outward, decaying orchids or crushed carnations, terrible flowers of flesh; wounds from which the dark blood is spewed out in clots, mixed with the ominous gas bubbles, floating on the fresh flood of the still-continuing secondary haemorrhage.

Old filthy bandages stuck to the skin with blood-glue. Careful. Better moisten first. Through the thigh. Pick the leg up. Why it's like a bag, a long, loose, red stocking. What kind of stocking? A Christmas stocking. Where's that fine, strong rod of bone now? In a dozen pieces. Pick them out with your fingers; white as dog's teeth, sharp and jagged. Now feel. Any more left? Yes, here. All? Yes, no, here's another piece. Is this muscle dead? Pinch it. Yes, it's dead. Cut it out. How can that heal? How can those muscles, once so strong, now so torn, so devastated, so ruined, resume their proud tension? Pull, relax. Pull, relax. What fun it was! Now that is finished. Now that's done. Now we are destroyed. Now what will we do with ourselves?

Next. What an infant! Seventeen. Shot through the belly. Chloroform. Ready? Gas rushes out of the open peritoneal cavity. Odour of faeces. Pink coils of distended intestine. Four perforations. Close them. Purse strong suture. Sponge out the pelvis. Tube. Three tubes. Hard to close. Keep him warm. How? Dip those bricks into hot water.

Gangrene is a cunning, creeping fellow. Is this one alive? Yes, he lives. Technically speaking, he is alive. Give him saline intravenously. Perhaps the innumerable tiny cells of his body will remember. They may remember the hot, salty sea, their ancestral home, their first food. With the memory of a million years, they may remember other tides, other oceans and life being born of the sea and sun. It may make them raise their tired little heads, drink deep and struggle back into life again. It may do that.

And this one. Will he run along the road beside his mule at another harvest, with cries of pleasure and happiness? No, that one will never run again. How can you run with one leg? What will he do? Why, he'll sit and watch other boys run. What will he think? He'll think what you and I would think. What's the good of pity? Don't pity him! Pity would diminish his sacrifice. He did this for the defence of China. Help him. Lift him off the table. Carry him in your arms. Why, he's as light as a child! Yes, your child, my child.

How beautiful the body is; how perfect its parts; with what precision it moves; how obedient; proud and strong. How terrible when torn. The little flame of life sinks lower and lower, and, with a flicker, goes out. It goes out like a candle goes out. Quietly and gently. It makes its protest at extinction, then submits. It has its say, then is silent.

Any more? Four Japanese prisoners. Bring them in. In this community of pain, there are no enemies. Cut away that blood-stained uniform. Stop that haemorrhage. Lay them beside the others. Why, they're alike as brothers! Are these soldiers professional man-killers? No, these are amateurs-in-arms. Workman's hands. These are workers-in-uniform.

No more. Six o'clock in the morning. God, it's cold in this room. Open the door. Over the distant, dark-blue mountains, a pale, faint line of light appears in the East. In an hour the sun will be up. To bed and sleep.

But sleep will not come. What is the cause of this cruelty, this stupidity? A million workmen come from Japan to kill or mutilate a million Chinese workmen. Why should the Japanese worker attack his brother worker, who is forced merely to defend himself? Will the Japanese worker benefit by the death of the Chinese? No, how can he gain? Then, in God's name, who will gain? Who is responsible for sending these Japanese workmen on this murderous mission? Who will profit from it? How was it possible to persuade the Japanese workman to attack the Chinese workman – his brother in poverty; his companion in misery?

Is it possible that a few rich men, a small class of men, have persuaded a million poor men to attack, and attempt to destroy, another million men as poor as they? So that the rich may be richer still? Terrible thought! How did they persuade these poor men to come to China? By telling them the truth? No, they would never have come if they had known the truth. Did they dare to tell these workmen that the rich only wanted cheaper raw materials, more markets and more profit? No, they told them that this brutal war was 'The Destiny of the Race,' it was for the 'Glory of the Emperor,' it was for the 'Honour of the State,' it was for their 'King and Country.'

False. False as Hell!

The agents of a criminal war of aggression, such as this, must be looked for like the agents of other crimes, such as murder, among those who are likely to benefit from those crimes. Will the 80,000,000 workers of Japan, the poor farmers, the unemployed industrial workers – will they gain? In the entire history of Wars of Aggression, from the Conquest of Mexico by Spain, the capture of India by England, the rape of Ethiopia by Italy, have the workers of those 'victorious' countries ever been known to benefit? No, these never benefit by such wars.

Does the Japanese workman benefit by the natural resources of even his own country, by the gold, the silver, the iron, the coal, the oil? Long ago he ceased to possess that natural wealth. It belongs to the rich, the ruling class. The millions who work those mines live in poverty. So how is he likely to benefit by the armed robbery of the gold, silver, iron, coal and oil of China? Will not the rich owners of the one retain, for their own profit, the wealth of the other? Have they not always done so?

It would seem inescapable that the militarists and the capitalists of Japan are the only class likely to gain by this mass murder, this authorized madness. That sanctified butcher; that ruling class, the true State stands accused.

Are wars of aggression, wars for the conquest of colonies, then just Big Business? Yes, it would seem so, however much the perpetrators of such national crimes seek to hide their true purpose under the banners of high-sounding abstractions and ideals. They make war to capture markets by murder; raw materials by rape. They find it cheaper to steal than to exchange; easier to butcher than to buy. This is the secret of this war. It is the secret of all wars. Profit. Business. Profit. Blood money.

Behind all stands that terrible, implacable God of Business and Blood, whose name is Profit. Money, like an insatiable Moloch, demands its interest, its return, and will stop at nothing, not even the murder of millions, to satisfy its greed. Behind the army stand the militarists. Behind the militarists stand finance capital and the capitalist. Brothers in blood: companions in crime.

What do these enemies of the human race look like? Do they wear on their foreheads a sign so that they may be told, shunned and condemned as criminals? No. On the contrary, they are the respectable ones. They are honoured. They call themselves, and are called, gentlemen. What a travesty on the name! Gentlemen! They are the pillars of the State, of the church, of society. They support private and public charity out of the excess of their wealth. They endow institutions. In their private lives they are kind and considerate. They obey the law, their law, the law of property. But there is one sign by which these gentle gunmen can be told. Threaten a reduction on the profit of their money and the beast in them awakes with a snarl. They become as ruthless as savages, brutal as madmen, remorseless as executioners. Such men as these must perish if the human race is to continue. There can be no permanent peace in the world while they live. Such an organization of human society as permits them to exist must be abolished.

These men make the wounds.

8

Martyr:
China, 1939

Nineteen thirty-nine was the last year of Bethune's life. On 4 March he turned forty-nine, marking the date by writing a three-thousand-word letter to comrades in Canada after operating through the entire night. Despite his age, he maintained his hectic pace, leading his mobile operating unit through the rough Chin-Ch'a-Chi border region to dozens of battles and skirmishes with the Japanese. In one Japanese offensive in April, his unit operated for sixty-nine consecutive hours on 115 wounded men, a feat of endurance and dedication which further enhanced his stellar reputation in the Eighth Route Army.[1] This work often took him right to the shifting battle front. Yet he made light of the extreme danger constantly at hand. In one report, he noted in passing that his unit was nearly captured, leaving one end of a village just as four hundred enemy troops entered the other.

Still, after a year of superhuman exertion, Bethune showed signs of wearing down physically. One of the most obvious symptoms was that his prodigious written output of 1938 slackened greatly. In 1939 his writing was confined mostly to letters and relatively brief reports on medical conditions at the many rudimentary hospitals he visited. These reports also took on a new tone which is important to explore.

In China, Bethune embarked on an experiment – as often in the past, with himself as subject. The central problem of the experiment was this: Is it possible to create a new man? By 1939 he had drawn close to answering the question. The Bethune who entered China in January 1938 was not the same Bethune who died there in November 1939. Two years, extraordinary conditions, and inspiring people produced an immense change in him. By various accounts, he arrived in China as he had been for years: troubled, angry, aggressive, self-abusive, and charismatic. Reports during the early months of 1938 from people like Jean Ewen and Dr Robert Brown give us a portrait of an irascible Bethune who was abusing alcohol. But those who knew him near the time of his death present him as almost a saint, still rough-edged to be sure, but marked mostly by a spirit of selflessness. Whom do we believe? Our tendency, of course, is to trust the former. Our rational Western mind prefers the evidence we glean from lengthy experience. We dismiss miraculous conversions. And although we might not like to acknowledge it, the source of the evidence is also a factor in our decision. The observers who insist on an unreconstructed Bethune are Westerners; those who portray a saintly Bethune are Asians. And the Asians, we fear, are biased by their communism.

But is it possible that Bethune did in fact change? We know from credible witnesses that both egoism and altruism always coexisted – sometimes not peacefully – within Bethune. Under duress – for example, in his last weeks in Spain – the troubled, egotistical side of Bethune gained the upper hand. Could it also be that different conditions engendered a compassionate, selfless, and content Bethune?

His own writing points to an answer. Comparing his use of the words 'happy' and 'content' in correspondence from Spain to that from China yields an intriguing contrast. Bethune's words from Spain have an institutional, formulaic tone. 'All are well and happy,' he wrote on 8 February 1937. A cable of 5 May 1937 repeated – far from convincingly – the stock phrase: 'All representatives [at the blood transfusion unit] content.' In the same vein, he wrote from China on 22 May 1938, 'We are happy and content in our work.' But by 13 July his words had taken on a new, more genuine tone: 'I am tired, but enormously content.' His letter of 21 August 1938 probably best elaborated on his new sense of personal satisfaction, explaining: 'It is true I am tired but I don't think I have been so happy for a long time. I am content. I am doing what I want to do.' And on his last birthday, 4 March 1939, he wrote in the same tenor: 'I am very happy and content.'

What was the cause of his sense of fulfilment? Clearly it was the people with whom he worked, especially the communists and partisan fighters. On 23 August 1938 he wrote: 'The partisans are great people ... [with] quiet purposeful movements and an air of determination and courage. It's a pleasure to work on them.' And describing untrained medical staff on 4 March 1939, Bethune observed that 'although I am often irritable at their ineptitude and ignorance ... their simplicity and eagerness to learn combined with their true spirit of comradeship and unselfishness, disarms me in the end.' Under such influences, a new Bethune was emerging. The Bethune of old – 'arrogant in the service of humanity,' as Donald Jack has characterized him[2] – was being trans-formed. This is confirmed by Dr Ma Haide, an American who knew Bethune in China, who has said that Bethune began 'to lose his impa-tience ... There was a certain calmness of spirit that gradually descended upon him.'[3] By 1939 Bethune appears also to have been able to slay another of his personal dragons – alcohol. Ted Allan asserts that Bethune was drinking excessively during his first months in China. He has written that Dr Robert McClure, then a missionary but later the moderator of the United Church of Canada, 'had to personally treat Bethune in China for this affliction. But Bethune, inspired by the hero-ism and sacrifice of the Chinese, overcame his illness.'[4]

Although he was far more emotionally composed, Bethune's letters to North America did still reveal a man yearning for a release from his lin-guistic and cultural isolation. In January 1939 he reported that he had not read an English-language newspaper in eight months. Even mail arrived only every two and one-half months. His spirits remained high, but notes of nostalgia for his past life crept in: 'I dream of coffee, of rare roast beef, of apple pie and ice cream. Mirages of heavenly food! Books – are books still being written? Is music still being played? Do you dance, drink beer, look at pictures? What do clean white sheets in a soft bed feel like? Do women still love to be loved?'

This need for reconnection to North American culture, complemented by the unsolved problem of how to coax aid from there, led him to resolve to return home on a fund-raising tour. In October, preparing conditions to leave, he set out to inspect the twenty base hospitals in northwest Hopei Province. The tour was interrupted by a Japanese offensive, which forced him to return to the front lines. Operating on a wounded soldier, Bethune cut his finger, and infection set in. He fought valiantly, but in his weakened condition he was unable to defeat it, and he died of blood poisoning on 12 November 1939.

Bethune's death launched a scramble to memorialize him and capital-ize on his martyrdom. Some of this was mendacious, some of it sublime. In the former category, we can place the eulogy by Earl Browder, the general secretary of the Communist Party of the U.S.A. His effort to por-tray himself as responsible for sending Bethune to China, for instance, bordered on deceit. Speaking to a party meeting in June 1940, Browder said:

We sent our ambassador to China, one we need to mention very often, as a symbol of what America should do for China – Dr. Norman Bethune ... He was not known as a Communist ... But when Dr. Bethune, at my proposal, immediately and unhesitatingly agreed to go to China to serve the Eighth Route Army with the miserable equipment of $5000 worth of drugs and tools, he knew that the chances of his coming back were very small, and he said: 'I accept on one condition, that if I don't come back, you will let the world know that Norman Bethune died a Communist Party member.'[5]

Serious distortions of fact in Browder's statement demand to be corrected. Bethune probably decided to assist the communist forces in China in July 1937. We know from secret RCMP reports that when he spoke in Vancouver on 1 August the fact that Bethune was bound for China was well enough known in the Communist Party for local RCMP officers to report it to headquarters.[6] The American party became involved only after Canadian communists decided that they were already fully extended in meeting the demands of the struggle in Spain. Roderick Stewart has written that in September, near the end of the tour, Bethune approached Communist Party of Canada leader Tim Buck to ask him to support the scheme. 'Buck telephoned Earl Browder, the Chairman of the American Communist Party, to determine what arrangements could be made with the Chinese.'[7] In other words, Bethune decided on his own to go to China, then sought aid from the communist apparatus. And while he went to China as a Communist Party member, it was the Communist Party of Canada, not of the U.S.A., in which he was enrolled. Jean Ewen, who was at a meeting between Bethune and Mao in late March 1938, recalled Bethune presenting his Communist Party card to Mao, a card signed by Tim Buck. Mao said, 'We shall transfer you to the Communist Party of China so that you will be an inalienable part of this country now.'[8] Finally, it is true that the CPUSA did send Bethune off to China with $5,000 in medical supplies, the Canadian party being unable to contribute because of its existing commitments to Spain.[9] But that was the last assistance he received from communists in North America. In truth, Bethune's comrades in North America let him down.

More fitting tributes to Bethune can be found in Lincoln Fisher's obituary in the *American Review of Tuberculosis* and Mao Zedong's widely known essay on him, 'In Memory of Norman Bethune.' Fisher's comment concluded eloquently: 'With no thought of sacrifice, he laid down his life for strange peoples upon alien soil.'[10] In a brief essay published 21 December 1939, Mao also focused on Bethune's selflessness: 'With this spirit everyone can be very useful to the people. A man's ability may be great or small, but if he has this spirit, he is already noble-minded and pure, a man of moral integrity and above vulgar interests, a man who is of value to the people.'[11] It was not surprising that Mao chose to dwell on this one of Bethune's many strengths. It confirmed Mao's own voluntarist perspective, which over the course of fifty years guided his efforts to reshape China. From the beginning of his political activism, Mao argued that objective conditions – China's dire poverty, its lack of trained experts and political leaders, its apparent impotence in the face of powerful enemies like Japan, the Soviet Union, and the United States of America – were secondary to the initiative and will of the Chinese people and their leadership. In Bethune, Mao was graced with a martyr who shared his own faith in the power of human audacity. Indeed, if Norman Bethune had not existed, Mao might have had to create him. As it was, Mao had little need even to tailor Bethune. In his life up to his arrival in China, Bethune showed again and again the passion which Mao believed could animate millions. Bethune's fierce desire to live and willingness to innovate medically had allowed him to conquer his own tuberculosis. His contempt for stifling conservatism had driven him away from medical, social, and political orthodoxy. His deep personal hatred of fascism had put him on a course for Spain while the communist movement was still deciding how to raise a volunteer force. And that same anti-imperialist passion had hurled him into a guerrilla war in the remote Chinese interior at a time when only a few maverick leftists in North America grasped the importance of the Chinese struggle. In Bethune, Mao found a kindred spirit, animated by an unswerving determination to create a just world.

Isolated in north China, Bethune did not learn before he died that a generalized war had broken out in Europe in September 1939. It would become an anti-fascist alliance in June 1941, when Germany attacked the Soviet Union. Then, in December 1941, the United States was thrust into the war, and a Pacific stage was added to the European theatre. With that, the anti-Japanese struggle which had been waged single-handedly by the Chinese from 1931 was linked to a massive international coalition to defeat fascist and militarist aggression. Had he lived, Bethune would doubtless have rejoiced to see millions embrace his vision and set to the task of eradicating fascism from the world. It was a cause for which he had fought passionately from the moment he embraced communism in 1935 until he lay down his scalpel in China in 1939.

In a letter to Canadian friends and comrades, Bethune described the difficult conditions in the areas surrounded by Japanese forces. So desperate was he for medical supplies that he mentioned a plan to go in disguise into Beijing to buy them, a plan the Eighth Route Army command decisively rejected.

Yang Chia Chuang
North-East Shansi
Chin-Ch'a-Chi Military District
China
January 10, 1939

My dear comrades,
I received your last letter of July 17th on November 22, 1938 and was most certainly delighted to hear from you. As you know, I have no radio (Dodd forgot to give us the one he promised) and receive no newspapers, so am very ignorant of the affairs in the outside world. I have not seen an English newspaper for 8 months now. I receive mail about every 2 and half months apart. So you can well imagine my delight to receive your letters, especially as they give me important news of changes at home. In fact, if it were not for your letters, I should be in the dark as no one else writes me on these matters. I am sorry that the books you sent me have not arrived. I am very short of books as I have read and re-read all I have a dozen times.

My life is pretty rough and sometimes tough as well. It reminds me of my early days up in the Northern bush. The village is like all other Chinese villages, made of mud and stone one-storey houses, in groups (families) of compounds. Three or four houses are enclosed in a compound facing each other. In the compound are the pigs, dogs, donkeys, etc. Everything is filthy – the people, their houses, etc. I have one house to myself. It has a brick oven running along the single room. In this I have my cot and table. I have made myself a tin stove in which is burnt coal and wood. The windows (one) are papered with white paper. The floor is packed mud, so are the walls.

The country is mountainous and bare of trees except in the little valleys. Streams run in the valleys. They are now completely frozen over. There was an inch or so of snow in December, but that has gone in the

January thaw. The weather is now mild – about 20 or 30 degrees above freezing in the day, but falling to 10 degrees above at night. The worst feature of the climate is the biting high winds that come down from the Gobi Desert to the northwest. They blow up great whirling clouds of dust and snow.

We are about 65 li (22 miles) south of Lin Chu, which is occupied by the Japs. The Japs are all around us – west on the Ta Tung-Tai Yuan railway, north on the Ta Tung-Kalgan line and the motor road which runs parallel to this, east and west about 50 miles south of it, to the east, the Japanese hold the big cities and towns between us and the Beijing-Hankou Line, while to the south, they hold the Tai Yuan-Shih Chia Chuang Line, also. Here they are putting in a wide gauge track to replace the old narrow gauge lines.

We are in close contact with the Manchurian troops in Suei Yuan province (inner Mongolia). These are our allies.

The Japanese plans are to drive west along the south and north. The south attack will be made along the Lung Hai Line to Sian and then west to Lan Chow in Kan Su province. The northern drive will be west through Suei Yuan province and inner Mongolia, also to Lan Chow or the line from Lan Chow which goes northwest into Turkestan. This is very important as all our Russian aid comes down this line.

About the contradictions in the Chinese Government! I know nothing. There undoubtedly exists a set which are willing to make peace with Japan. This is, of course, exactly what the Japanese want to do now – a quick war and a quick peace. We want a long war and no peace until the Japanese are driven from China. I put this at a minimum of 4 years.

If we can prevent them cutting off our Russian supplies, we can go on for a long time. The country is independent for food. Its man power has just been touched and not exhausted. We believe the man power of Japan is nearly exhausted. Their troops are much older now. Conscription is digging deep into their available supply. There is no conscription as yet in China. At the beginning of the war it was said that in fighting efficiency 5 Chinese were equal to 1 Japanese. This has been reduced to 3 and 1. This year it will be lowered to 2 to 1. Then the tide will turn. Till then guerrilla war and the avoidance of a stand face-to-face with the more technically efficient Japanese Army is the military policy.

We are about 100 miles west of Beijing. Later on in the year, I will make an attempt to get into Beijing to buy medical supplies. I think it can be done. We have had foreign sympathizers come to us from the city and return.

Next week we leave this place and go east into Hopei (East Hopei). The following month we plan to cross the Pei-Han line into Mid-Hopei, which lies west of Tientsin. This large area is held by us.

Last month I sent to Canada one short story – 'The Dud' – and an article called 'Wounds.' This last is one of the best things I have written, I think. What happened to my articles on the 'Cave University at Yan'an,' and the one about this District? Were they ever published? I wrote another called 'Staff Conference.' All of these were about 5000 words in length, each. I hope they have not been lost.

Well, I will leave you now. Let me confess that on the 1st of the New Year I had an attack of homesickness! Memories of New York, Montreal and Toronto! If I were not so busy I could find reasons enough for a holiday.

With the kindest remembrances of you all,

Norman Bethune,
Medical Advisor to the Chin-Ch'a-Chi Military District

On his birthday on 4 March, Bethune again wrote to Canadian comrades with an explanation of the nature and strategy of the anti-Japanese guerrilla war.

At the front, near Ho Chien, with the 120th Division
March 4th/39

My dear Tim and comrades in Canada –
I am trying to establish a mail route to you through the kindness of the A.P. [Associated Press] in Beijing by using the U.S. diplomatic bag. This is necessary as the Japs are censoring both incoming and outgoing mail, books and periodicals. I don't know whether this will be successful or not but if it reaches you, please send a cable to Professor M. Lindsay, Yen ching University, Beijing, saying – 'Letter OK.' (unsigned). You can try and send me a letter addressed to him for 'Rev. H.N. Bethlehem.' It must be very carefully and cryptically worded of course. If we can establish this route it will be most valuable.

I have sent you regularly every month since coming to China, reports on my work – over 20 to date – but whether or not you have ever received them, I know not as I have not received any letters or communications from you. I have however received 3 letters from Lilian, 1 from Philip and 2 from Eric and several from Montreal comrades. I have had

3 letters from the China Aid Council – all from Haskell none from any other member of the Committee. I have had also 1 letter from A.M. in Vancouver. That is all. The letters from the C.A.C. were dispatched on Aug. 23 and Sept. 20/38. They arrived here on Jan. 14/39. The part of my mail that reaches me (about 1 in 10) comes through Yan'an. This is a long trip, from Hong Kong and a longer one from Yan'an to G.H.Q. in west Hopei. Then it has to come here – another month or so. We are about 150 miles south of Beijing and 50 miles west of Tientsin. If we can establish a route through Beijing, our letters should reach each other in about 2 months. They will be carried down from Beijing by missionary sympathizers, who are constantly going to and fro from their missions in the Japanese-held cities.

First, I will tell you about our work, but I expect you have received some at least of my monthly reports which have been pretty detailed. Since the new year, we have been very busy on organizational and educational work. This has taken us into all the 6 sub-districts of our Military Area, each one of which has one or more hospitals. A good deal of re-organization was necessary. Last month alone we travelled 1198 li (400 miles) in the mountains of west Hopei and onto the plains of Mid-Hopei. After a year in the mountains, it was a great pleasure to be on flat ground again. The mountains are very fine but the travelling is arduous – constantly on rough donkey paths along the beds of the swift mountain rivers, then up and over a mountain pass of several thousand feet into another valley and so on. We walk most of the way, although we have horses. Walking is faster. It is very hard on our feet as we wear nothing but cotton slippers. They only last a few days – often less than a week. We average 75 li (25 miles) a day. I have been given a fine brown captured Japanese mare, in addition to much other Japanese captured stuff – overcoat, cap, etc. After a week of travel we are dirty, lousy and flea-bitten. We sleep in the villagers' houses on their k'angs, which are heated mud-brick ovens. Our hospitals are simply the very dirty civilian houses made of mud-brick and stone, one story high. They are very cold and draughty. The windows are of paper – mostly torn. The floor is mud.

The villages are scattered along the streams in the valleys, wherever there is any land to scrape off the mountains. (Did you ever receive an article entitled 'Staff Conference,' I wrote last year in Sept.?) Here I described the country and the life of the villages. Each village contains from 20 to 200 families. They are desperately poor. The wounded (over 2000 now) are scattered in the villages – from 50 to 200 in a village. They are housed with the civilians so the overcrowding is pretty bad. We travel to one of these 'hospitals,' inspect the wounded, re-organize the staff (the hospital staff consists of 'doctors' of 19 to 22, not one of whom has had a college education or been in a modern hospital or medical school; the nurses who are boys of 14 to 18, just peasants). Imagine the average standard! Imagine their knowledge of hygiene, anatomy, physiology, medicine and surgery! Yet this is the only material we possess and we must make the best of it. They are very eager to learn and to improve themselves and are constantly asking for criticisms of their work. So that although I am often irritable at their ineptitude and ignorance, their lack of order, their carelessness, yet their simplicity and eagerness to learn combined with their true spirit of comradeship and unselfishness, disarms me in the end.

Well, after the C.P. convention of the north China area in west Hopei, in Feb. 39, we came here, crossing the Pei Han R.R. just north of Ting Hsien. We passed within 1 mile of the Japanese garrisons on the R.R. All the barking dogs had been removed from the villages near the R.R. by the civilians so that we can move at night without giving the alarm. After crossing the R.R. we travelled another 3 days (or rather nights) to this place. Here we are completely surrounded by the Japanese – no farther in any direction than 15 miles. All the roads are dug up to impede the progress of their motor cars, armoured cars and tanks. They are constantly shelling the villages where they think there are troops. Their biggest gun is 105 mm. It can fire a distance of about 10 li. They have many other smaller field guns, also air planes. We have none of course. Our division of approximately 15,000 men is scattered among the villages. There are over 10,000 villages in mid-Hopei. The Japanese hold the big towns and cities, we hold and control the countryside and small villages.

This is great cotton country. To the west near Tientsin, 75% of the crop was cotton. By our government regulations, no more than 5% of the crop is allowed to be cotton. The rest must be food grains. It is the opinion of competent foreign observers in Beijing that the Japanese are getting little out of the exploitation of the land in north China but only out of the mines. The enemy wants peace badly. We want a long and protracted war. I do not think the Chungking Government would dare – even though one or two may desire peace – to ask for peace. The feeling of the people – the masses – is against peace until the Japanese are driven off the land. Their anger and determination is growing daily.

The Japanese military mind is very stupid. They burn the civilians' poor houses and kill them, then expect the civilians to co-operate (sic!) in building up a new China! With peace and good will between the two nations! (Like little Red Riding Hood said to the wolf, 'What big teeth you've got, grandmamma!')

If the Chungking Government bourgeoisie ever tried to bring about peace – I don't think that at all likely – the class war (now suppressed) would flare into a flame. This United Front is one of the 'temporary blocs' that Marx and Lenin were so insistent about. As I see it here, the United Front is holding together remarkably well in spite of some efforts of former provincial officials (now returned) to break it down. This is entirely due to the astuteness and flexibility of the C.P. policy. I must say that the Chinese C.P. is the 'best' national C.P. I have ever seen. Of course there is a historical reason for this. They have had the enormous advantage of 20 years' actual experience. The party contains a very large number of very clever and experienced comrades. Their theoretical knowledge standard is high. In addition they have the advice and assistance of the Russian comrades. Leftism is very much frowned down upon. It is, of course, in most cases, simply due to inexperience. Far more emphasis is put on teaching the masses local self government and mass organization. Graft and 'squeeze' in local governments has entirely disappeared. Whenever the 8th Route Army and its political staff arrive in an area, order and honesty come into governments, who are taught how to govern themselves democratically. The political people in the 8th R.A. simply act as advisors and supervisors. Of course to do this effectively, our people must hold and do hold the chief positions in the mass organizations – Peasants' and Workers' Unions, Union of Women, etc.

The longer the war goes on the stronger our party becomes. It grows by leaps and bounds. No wonder it is feared by the bourgeoisie! The Guomindang is caught in a contradiction. If they abandon a district (as they abandoned Mid-Hopei in 1937) the 8th Route Army and C.P. move in to the danger spot. They establish a United Front Local Government – not a Soviet – with any of the remaining government officials. This the Guomindang of course dislikes. Yet at the same time they want to win the war so these efforts of the 8th R.A. must be tolerated. They discover that the 8th R.A. can arouse and has aroused a fiercer spirit of resistance among the masses than they were able to do. Some times the old officials (such as Lu Chung Lin, former governor of Hopei) come back and try and regain their old holds. But the masses have had a taste of honest self government and won't go back to the old ways. Governor Lu

Chung Lin was appointed by the Guomindang. He abandoned this area in 1937 by going south on the Japanese advance. Now he wants to return and actually did attempt a come-back. He has petitioned to have the Mid-Hopei area added to his region – that is southern Hopei. But northern Mid-Hopei is now a part of the new United Front Chin-Ch'a-Chi Military District. The Guomindang is perfectly aware that Lu Lin could never hold this region against the Japanese and that the 8th R.A. can. So the Guomindang has refused him. I bet it didn't like it! Don't think that the Guomindang has abandoned its hate and fear of the C.P.! It is simply caught in a contradiction of antagonistic desires. At the present time, the hate and fear of the Japanese predominate.

The tasks of the C.P. in different parts of China vary. They vary even within a short distance – in west Hopei and east Shansi from Mid-Hopei. In Shansi, the governor, Yen Shi Shan, had held complete political power for 20 years. He gave them a stabilized form of feudal government. That province, being situated farther inland, had not come under, to any extent, the imperialistic influences of Hopei. This province was semi-colonialised. Although in Shansi democratic government was non-existent, and the officials all appointed by the Governor, on the whole it was comparatively honest and reasonably efficient. The people were docile and inexperienced in the management of their own affairs. In addition, the governor and the Shansi troops never wholly abandoned the province – only retiring from the north to the south. Many minor officials held their ground, such as in Wutaishan. These were later to form the United Front Government with the C.P. and the 8th R.A. But the historical conditioning of the people under the semi-feudalism of Yen Shi Shan made the work of the C.P. more difficult among the masses since they were indifferent to local self government, being satisfied with the comparatively mild semi-despotism of the old government. But west- and Mid-Hopei had a different history. For years, it had been a battle ground for contending war-lords and politicians, each one of whom in turn practised extortion and despotism on the masses. Its people were accustomed to changes of government – the succession only varying in its degree of dishonesty and misuse of power. So the masses were ready for an honest government. They leaped at the chance of local self government. Their consciousness of the need for reform was higher. In addition they were near the sea (Tientsin) and so had early become colonized in part by imperialistic nations. Along with this commercial imperialism had come Christianity with the missionaries and its vague democratic spirit. Last of all, to make the task of the 8th R.A. and the C.P. easier, the former Governor and the majority of his officials had fled, leaving the country bare of the machinery of state. The people thus more easily took power (with the advice and assistance of the 8th R.A. and the Chinese C.P.) into its own hands and set up its own local government. The Chin-Ch'a-Chi Military Region Government welded these together. Thus the incoming political workers of the 8th R.A. immediately began to utilize all these factors – 1. The absence of the former state machinery. 2. the higher cultural level of the masses. 3. the higher political consciousness of the masses. 4. the general dissatisfaction with former experiences in despotic governments.

It is extremely interesting to watch the growth of anti-Japanese feeling. This has been largely increased by the Japanese occupying the large cities and towns in this region. Before, when the Japs held only the really big cities such as Beijing and Tientsin and a few others, the peasants and petty bourgeois were largely unawakened to their danger. The enemy was too far away. 'Out of sight, out of mind.' But when the enemy actually did come into their lives by burning *their* houses and killing *their* relatives and stealing *their* goods, it was a different thing. Now the whole countryside is aroused against them. Recruiting is increased, mass organization work is easier.

Wherever the 8th R.A. goes it leaves an indelible mark among the people. It is a true 'People's Army.' It is never separated from the masses. It is composed almost entirely of peasants and workers. It is their army. The political workers who accompany and talk the language of the army are mostly peasants and workers too with the addition of students. They talk the language that the workers understand. They have lived their life. They show the peasants and workers a new vision of life. Soon a spirit of determination to resist Japan to the death appears. The peasants attend all the meetings of the soldiers; they learn their slogans and sing their songs. They copy the hygiene of the army. Villages become tidier, the people cleaner. They learn rudimentary army discipline. They drill in awkward military formation, their Self-Defence Corps equipped with old flintlock rifles and rusty big swords. They give presents of grain, fruit and shoes to the troops, wash their clothes, carry their wounded, transport their supplies. I have never heard a word of complaint from a civilian when asked to leave his village and his farm, often for days, to transport wounded or supplies. Soldiers occupy half his house, crowding him and his family (often as many as 6 or 8) into one room where they all sleep on the same *k'ang*. The civilians act as spies and intelligence officers, guides and scouts. To see a civilian in a tattered old blue long gown, in an old straw hat but with an old flintlock rifle across his shoulder, leading a regiment along a steep narrow mountain path, is at the one and the same time both a splendid and laughable sight.

This war will not be won by the great military leaders or the professional soldiers – it will be won by the peasants, in and out of uniform.

The women are playing an increasingly important role. In the village I am writing from – 45 li from the enemy – is a dramatic company of players composed of 10 young men and 4 girls. They put on shows and performances for the troops at the front. Then the women in the Women's Unions are working for the army – making shoes, repairing and washing uniforms. They play an important but hidden role in the influence they exert on their own men folk. Women are being aroused from centuries of patriarchal feudalism to take part in local governments. They actually are beginning to eat with men! They are found not only in local governments but even in the *hsien* and central government. Many of the best women workers are students from the cities. How I wish our own Canadian students would take a lesson from these girl students here, and put their 'book learning' and their 'culture' at the disposal of the workers in their fight for a new and better life. Then and only then, will students be able to justify their lives, ennoble such culture, use such education. It must be used for others. Not only must they do so for the sake of others, but for their own sake too – for the deepening of their own personalities and the enrichment of their own lives through service.

Today is my 49th birthday. I have the proud distinction of being the oldest soldier at the front. I spent the day in bed. I went to bed at 6 a.m., having operated all night from 7 p.m. the day before. We did 19 operations last night on 40 seriously wounded who had arrived from a battle near Ho Chien. After dressing all the wounded we started to operate on those needing operation. Three fractures of the skull were trephined, 2 amputations of the thigh, 2 suture of perforations of the small intestines, half a dozen bad fractures of arms and legs, and the rest smaller operations. We defeated the enemy. He left 50 dead – a most unusual thing for him to do. We captured 40 rifles. We lost 40 men – a rifle for a life. That is the way we get our guns.

Now I will close, comrades. I am very happy and content except I would like to hear from you. You keep on your fight, we will do the same here. It is all the same battle. We are bound to win.

With warmest comradely greetings,
Norman

In a report to support committees, Bethune summarized the unit's performance during four months of constant trekking and front-line medical practice. In it he referred to the chronic problem of lack of trained personnel and supplies.

Shin Pei, West Hopei
July 1/39

Report to Committees in New York, Hong Kong and London
This report will be a survey of the work of the Canadian-American Mobile Medical Unit for the period from February 1, 1939 to July 1, 1939 – a little over 4 months spent working in Central Hopei, south of Beijing and west of Tientsin, under very active conditions of guerrilla warfare. I have already submitted reports for February and March which included 3 memoranda on the sanitary service and suggestions for improvement.

1. During the 4 months' period, our Unit was in 4 battles – at Liu Han (at the crossing of the Hu To Ho) on March 14 to 19; at Ta Tuan Ting on April 15; at Chi Huei on April 26 to 28th; and at Sung Chia Chuang on May 18th. In none of these engagements was the Unit ever farther than 8 li from the firing line and at times even closer.

2. The total number of operations performed in the field were 315, not including 1st Aid dressings.

3. The total distances travelled in Mid Hopei were 1504 li (500 miles).

4. The number of operating rooms and dressing stations set up was 13.

5. The number of new Mobile Operating units organized was 2 (one for the troops of General Lui and the other for the troops of General Ho Lung).

6. Number of training courses given to doctors and nurses – 2.
Comments:

1. The month of April was our busiest month at the battle of Chi Huei where out of a total of 400 Japanese engaged, 340 were either killed or wounded. Our casualties were 280. Our Unit was situated 7 li from the firing line and operated on 115 cases in 69 hours' continuous work.

2. The Unit was very nearly captured in the village of Szu Kung Tsun about 40 li northeast of Ho Chien. With ten minutes warning at 5 a.m. we left one end of the village as 400 of the enemy entered. All the staff and equipment were saved owing to the smart work of our capable manager (W. Long) and to the fact that the entire staff were mounted and carried all equipment in saddle bags. If we had been carrying our equipment in the ordinary way it would have had to be abandoned with

the mules. The patients were either hidden in straw or carried on the backs of the civilians. No patients were captured.

3. Two Japanese prisoners (wounded) were operated upon (one with an amputation of the thigh) and ten days later both returned to the enemy at Ho Chien.

4. Fifteen operations were performed without anaesthetic as we ran out of chloroform. We also ran short of antiseptics and gauze but a small quantity was obtained from Pao Ting.

5. At Chi Huei and at Sung Chia Chuang the temples in which our operating rooms were located were under artillery fire, but we had no casualties.

6. The transport of over 1000 wounded from Central Hopei to West Hopei was successfully accomplished without the loss of a single case. As this trip is a dangerous one, passing close to many enemy-held cities and takes over one week, it reflects the highest praise on the staff work of Headquarters and the intelligence department. All wounded were transported disguised as civilians.

7. There are now no hospitals in Mid-Hopei. All the former hospitals of the six sub-districts have been sent to the west, and the sanitary work is being done by the regiments and brigades and partisan detachments Sanitary Services. It is hoped that the examples we were able to set up of Mobile Operating Units (really Divisional Field Hospitals but with only temporary bed accommodations) will be widely copied. This year it is hoped to set up 7 such Operating Units (one for each Division or each sub-district of partisan brigades).

8. The supply of drugs and medicines is pretty poor in most places in Central Hopei. Difficulty is being found in getting supplies from Tientsin. The missionaries are being closely watched. One lot of drugs were examined on the way by the Japanese and when told that they were going to a mission hospital, they made a note of all bottles and packages and later checked up on the Mission. The Mission reported that the drugs had been 'stolen' by the partisans – to account for their non-arrival.

9. We were able to construct a new form of transport for Field Hospital equipments to carry all necessary for an operating room, a dressing room and a drug room. All this equipment, sufficient for 100 operations, 500 dressings, and making up 500 prescriptions can be carried on two mules. A description of this transport will be found in the book which I am writing called 'A manual of organization and technique for divisional field hospitals in guerrilla war.'

10. I enclose expense accounts up to date ...

11. Personal expenditures (food, etc.) as I cook my own meals: April – $30.30; May – $21.68; June – $18.62

These accounts are certified by the manager of the Unit (W. Long) and enclosed.

12. I believe that everyone was satisfied that operations can be successfully performed in the field by mobile operating units only one or two miles from the front. Not only can they be performed there, but it is essential that they should be. As an example of this, I will mention the two cases of perforation of the intestine by rifle bullets operated on. The first case was operated on 18 hours after wounded and the second 8 hours after being wounded. Both cases had almost identical wounds – the bullet entering the abdomen at the level of the umbilicus. Both had ten perforations and tears of the small and large intestine with escape of intestinal contents into the abdominal cavity (including round worms!). Also there was in both cases a big haemorrhage from tear of the mesenteric artery with the abdomen full of blood. Both were operated on at night in a dirty Buddhist temple by the light of candles and flashlights. The first case died the following day but the second made an uneventful recovery, in spite of being transported 60 li every night for the following week on a rough stretcher. The differences between life and death was the difference between 8 hours and 18 hours.

Two blood transfusions were given at the front in very difficult conditions. I would bring to your notice that Tung (my interpreter) saved another life by giving a second (in 4 months) blood donation; and to Dr. Chang who went on working for 12 hours after giving 300 cc. of blood.

The successful application of Thomas Iron leg splints for fractured femurs was demonstrated. This should be routine practice especially for Mid-Hopei, where long transport from east to west must be done. Unfortunately, I have exhausted the supply of skin adherent I brought from America and we had no adhesive to use or elastic bandages.

Of course, the great obstacles to such treatment are two:

1. Untrained doctors.
2. No surgical instruments to give surgeons to do the work even if they were capable.

I have come back with my mind thoroughly made up that the education of the doctors and nurses of this region is the main task of any foreign unit.

But, why, oh why, are we not receiving more help from both China and abroad? Think of it! 200,000 troops, 2,500 wounded always in hospital, over 1000 battles fought in the past year, and only 5 Chinese graduate doctors, 50 Chinese untrained 'doctors' and one foreigner to do all this work.

13. In conclusion, the Unit left Mid-Hopei at the end of June as the rainy season was approaching and there was little expectation of fighting in the near future. I must thank all commanders (especially General Ho Lung and General Lui) and all ranks for the wonderful reception they gave us and the most splendid co-operation at all times.

Norman Bethune, M.D.
Medical Advisor to the Chin-Ch'a-Chi Military District

Carelessness among untrained medical workers continued to infuriate Bethune, as he indicated in the following letter of rebuke. He also acknowledged the assistance of 'Miss H.,' Kathleen Hall, a nurse from New Zealand who was director of the Anglican mission at Sung Chia Chuang, 250 kilometres southwest of Beijing, in the area where Bethune's unit was active.

Ho Chia Chuang
July 31, 1939

Dr. Yeh,
Chief of the Sanitary Service, Chin-Ch'a-Chi Military Region

Dear Comrade:
I have sent you yesterday and again today a large amount of medical supplies brought from Beijing recently by Miss H. On being received I found them very carelessly packed and I have repacked them as best I could without making a permanent job of it. They will all require repacking in new boxes.

I have in front of me as I write, the lists of drugs as taken up to Beijing for the purchasing agents there. I will comment on these lists.

1. There are 8 lists of drugs, made out by as many people but who made them out is impossible to say as none are signed, none dated. Why did you permit this carelessness? Did you not insist that *all* requisitions for drugs should be made through your central office? Apparently not, for as a result there is a great deal of duplication. Miss H. tells me that

the purchasing agents in Beijing were very confused. In future, I would strongly advise that all requisitions should come only through your office and that all lists should be personally checked by you.

2. Not only were there too many lists, but they were all made out, without exception (your own included) in a very careless and slipshod manner. Over 50% of the drugs were spelled incorrectly, there were no numbered items. You must impress on your office staff the necessity of neatness and correctness. You must check these things yourself.

3. The ordering of special drugs (especially ampules) must stop. Such items as 'Vita-Sperm' are both useless and expensive. A tonic of strychnine and iron is a better medicine at one-tenth the cost.

4. There has been ordered enormous amounts of digitalis, digitalin, digitalis folia. You must bear in mind and impress on your medical officers that digitalis is not a general heart tonic. Its only use is in auricular fibrillation. In my one and a half years' experience in the 8th Route Army I have seen only one case in which I would have ordered digitalis. The ordinary rapid heart of the young soldier is not improved by digitalis. It is merely a reflex symptom of nervous origin. Sedatives are indicated. You have ordered enough digitalis to supply an army of 10,000,000 men! In your weekly letter to medical officers (which, as you perhaps remember, I started last year and personally wrote 4 letters, and which I hope you have continued) I would suggest that you bring this matter of digitalis to their attention.

5. You must reduce and discourage the use of hypodermic injections. This practice is the refuge of the quack. It is, of course, encouraged by the large commercial drug houses. There are only a half dozen drugs that are best given by hypo – such as arsenic and bismuth for syphilis, insulin for diabetes, morphine for pain, various vaccines and serums. Iron is not one of them – there is no need for the Ferrous Cadacoylate ampules you ordered or for the pneumococcal serums also.

6. I notice that none of your lists contain Liquid Paraffin. How are you going to make up Bipp? Bipp is the best substitute for first aid treatment wounds which cannot, for one reason or another be debrided. For ordinary diarrhea (not bacterial or entamoebic) chalk or kaolin is cheap and inexpensive – less than bismuth, but I see you have ordered none. You have no tragacanth, no flavours, such as licorice. You ordered Vaseline without specifying whether white or yellow – the former is best for ointments, the latter for wound dressings. Antipyrine and Pyramidon have been cut off your lists by the medical advisors in Beijing. I agree with this. There is a widespread impression among your doctors that it is

more important to reduce fever by any means than to find out its exact cause and treat the cause. The most effective and cheapest way to reduce fever is by cool water sponge. Improve your nursing standards and you will use fewer drugs.

7. Pancreatin, pepsin and diastase were ordered in 20 lb. lots. These are needless.

8. Last summer I gave you 1 lb. of Tannic Acid. Its use is in a 4% solution for burns. You have ordered 10 lbs. This is very bulky. I think it more than you will need.

9. There is no need for cocaine when you have the synthetic substitutes, such as novocaine. Its only use is on mucous membranes in eye and nose operations.

10. You have ordered 6 abdominal retractors with a lot of other surgical instruments and although you state the catalogue number, you fail to state what catalogue. There are hundreds of surgical catalogues.

11. Probably the most serious point was your failure to order any skin adherent (such as B-D Adherent), Sinclair's glue, flannel cloth and elastic bandages for skin traction in fractures, especially of the femur. I demonstrated on a number of cases to you last winter the proper methods to put up fractures of the thigh by means of the Thomas splint and by Russell traction. Yet when I asked Dr. Wang (who I especially trained in this work) how many cases he had put up since I left he told me none. What are you doing about this most important matter? How many cases of fractured femurs have you in all the hospitals and how are you treating them? I suggest that you make a personal investigation of this at once. It is more important that you treat fractures properly than you teach doctors how to do abdominal operations.

Two weeks ago I was asked to see a company commander at Shin Pei. He had been wounded at Wan Hsien the day before. He had a compound fracture of the thigh. The medical officer of the Cavalry Regiment had sent him to Shin Pei without a splint of any kind – a distance of 60 li. And this in spite of my efforts to teach the doctors of this region the first aid treatment of fractures and having written a book on the subject! Do you not agree that this doctor should be severely criticized? But it means also that you also are to be criticized for this condition. What are your inspectors doing? Do they not send in reports as to the number of splints in every battalion and regiment? Do you require of them that they should do so?

12. In regard to the packing and transport of supplies. The habit of the 8th R.A. in packing drugs in paper must stop. It is wasteful. Order at

least 500 tin containers with lids for all drugs. When it is considered how far these drugs must be transported, how expensive they are, at what risk to life they have been brought here, it is necessary to impress on all ranks the importance of care and prevention of waste. You must order at least 25 new boxes. A lot of drugs and boxes have been spoilt and broken by poor packing and rain.

13. Standard form for requisitions of drugs must be written and mimeographed.

14. Have you appointed a Formulary Committee as I suggested? Are they at work? I should like them to meet here with me in preparing a list of standard solutions, stock mixtures and prescriptions.

15. There are 2 or 3 graduate nurses come down from the P.U.M.C. Have they been attached to the Medical school staff? One, I know has been here 3 weeks and has been given no work.

Please let me have a reply to this letter.

With comradely greetings,
Norman Bethune, Medical Advisor

Bethune was pleased by the performance of his mobile medical unit, and hoped to form similar ones in each of the subdivisions of the Border Region. This would require skilled medical personnel. Lacking such personnel, he resolved to train them himself and revived the idea of a central school along the lines of the model hospital which the Japanese had destroyed the previous year. On 15 July he completed a detailed memorandum on the make-up, curriculum, and special needs of such a medical training school. But the Eighth Route Army simply did not have the funds to create it. In the absence of money from the China Aid Council, Bethune resolved to return to North America to raise it himself, as he explained in the following report, from which some sections were cut by its recipient.

Ho Chia Chuang, West Hopei
August 1st/39

Monthly report of Canadian-American Mobile Operating Unit
Since returning to West Hopei from Mid Hopei, I have been engaged in the past 4 weeks to organizational work. I have seen the director of the Medical School and his staff and talked over their problems with them. I have presented to them a memorandum on the organization of a Medi-

cal School with detailed curriculum and schedules of courses – both for doctors, surgeons, refresher courses for old doctors, nurses (specialist nurses) such as anaesthetists, masseurs, pharmacists, ward and operating room supervisors. I enclose a copy of this memorandum. I would like to put down some of my thoughts on this subject:

1. The importance of an efficient Medical School can not be exaggerated. This Region needs a Medical School badly. The present standard of both doctors and nurses is very low. It must be raised. But how?

2. There must be brought into the Sanitary Service a much higher grade of personnel than is entering it at present. The present policy of using young boys of 16 to 18 as nurses must cease. It is not only bad for the patients (such boys are young and careless) but their presence stops more intelligent and better educated men from entering, when they see young boys dressing wounds they are apt to think that such work is easily learnt and requires no special education or training. As a result, such superior men would rather go into other departments rather than the Sanitary Service. This is quite easily understood.

3. Not sufficient encouragement is given to women to enter the S.S. They are especially adapted to such work as pharmacists, anaesthetists, masseurs. There are a number of young women now entering other departments (such as the Political Department and Mass organizational work) which should be taken into the S.S.

4. A special appeal should be made to Kan Ta students to enter the S.S. after graduation. The same applies to the Party School.

5. Too few of the regimental, brigade and divisional commanders realize their responsibility in supervision of the S.S. They may deplore, as often they do, the low state of this department, but I have found practically none who actually inspect and supervise their S.S. medical officers.

6. I feel too that the political workers among the S.S. are far too young in most cases.

7. Now that a number of graduate doctors have come from the Mid-Hopei S.S. to the West Hopei and have been taken to form the nucleus of the Medical school staff the standard of training should be raised considerably. But there is lacking still not only a number of trained staff doctors to act as instructors, but there are practically no books, no models for teaching anatomy, no histological or pathological sections, no bacteriological equipment. The school can only be set up by the expenditure of about $2000. It will then need a minimum of $3000 a month to keep it going – counting 200 pupils and a staff of 100 at $10 a month

each for maintenance. Another $1000 is not too much to spend on setting up a small Model Hospital of 100 beds to be run as an adjunct to the School for teaching purposes. I am aware of the pressing need for money in the Region and feel that an increased effort must be made to bring more money in, both from China and abroad. I am completely in the dark as to where the money from America (supposed to be over $1000 (gold) a month) is going to. I am not told where or how it is being used. I have written the Trustee committee in Yan'an so often in the past 12 months without reply, that I am tired of writing them again. I have come to the conclusion that I must leave the Region temporarily and go to Yan'an and return to America to raise the guaranteed sum of $1000 (gold) a month that the Medical School needs. How else can that money be raised except by wide-spread appeal of one such as myself who knows the needs of this region thoroughly after spending more than 15 months here?

8. I have come to some very definite conclusions as how best foreign comrades and friendly sympathizer technicians can help the Chinese in their great fight. One way (and not the best) is to come and work as independent units and try to do as much work as themselves are capable of. This is the way missionaries work. It is not a good way. It is true that an energetic unit can do a considerable amount of useful work in a year – as an example, any Red Cross Unit or even our own Canadian-American Unit which performed over 750 operations last year. But when such a unit moves on, the essential conditions still remain. They have left no permanent record of their work outside of their cured patients. The Chinese themselves must be educated to carry on after such a foreign unit moves away. That to my mind is the test of its real worth. How many Chinese technicians has such a unit trained? Has the general standard of technical work been raised? Are the Chinese now capable of carrying on by themselves? The answer to such questions is the indication of the worth of foreign units.

9. Such educational work is admittedly very difficult. First there is the great obstacle of the language, then the low standard of education of the workers to be trained, then the lessened amount of actual work that the unit can do while training uneducated workers, its lessened efficiency during this period. The lack of standards of efficiency such as the western nations are trained in is very discouraging to western workers – the slackness, inability to master detail, carelessness in supervision by seniors and the whole general manner of haphazard working of the Chinese 8th Route Army Sanitary Service. Yet slow as this work is, it must

be done. This is the heritage of the past and we have no other. We must work with the imperfect human material we have.

10. We must get more money, more and better men, more materials for work. I have been sending reports to the Chinese National Red Cross for over a year asking for help for this Region but have never had a reply in return. If the money from America and Canada is being sent to the Chinese Red Cross and only a portion allotted to the 8th Route Army and from that only a still smaller part sent to this Region for my work, then I must return to America and Canada and tell the people about the needs of this Region to get money especially for the medical work here.

11. I have finished the book on the Organization and Technique for Divisional Mobile Operating Units. It will be about 150 pages with 50 illustrations. It is very detailed. It is based on my practical experiences for the past 6 months at the front. The translation is now under way by Comrade W. Long and should be finished in 3 weeks. I would like it printed here.

12. The medical supplies obtained in the past 3 months have chiefly been the result of the energy of Miss K. Hall of the Anglican Church Mission at Sung Chia Chuang. About $15,000 has been spent. This amount of supplies should see the S.S. through the winter. As a result of her activities, her Mission has been burnt by the Japanese. I have always felt and expressed some months ago that too much should not have been asked of these sympathetic missionaries, but more organization of an underground transport service would have prevented this attack. Again, the local press were unwise enough to print an article praising Miss Hall for her assistance. This paper is undoubtedly read by the Japanese. Of course, there are other factors such as spies and the current manufactured so-called 'Anti-British Sentiment' in China which does not exist except in the minds of the Japanese. There are still large amounts of supplies that have been bought in Beijing, Tientsin and Pao Ting that have not been brought out for the lack of a Chinese organized transport. This work must be organized at once. Miss Hall can not be used again. Her life is already in danger owing to her help to the Region. The same applies to other missions such as the American Board Mission in Pao Ting. There have been many arrests of the Chinese there and the American missionaries are nervous and dare do no more to help. In fact, when I asked one of them to send me 10 lbs. of chloroform and 10 lbs. of carbolic acid when I was in Mid-Hopei in June, I received a reply that it would be done this time but I must not ask them to do it again.

So it comes down to this – either the Region organizes its own underground purchasing and transport service or else all materials must be brought from the south.

13. I am trying to persuade Miss Hall to join the Canadian-American Unit and give up her own missionary work. Around her I propose to gather a nucleus of trained graduate nurses from the P.U.M.C. (we have 2 now already) and with such a staff, set up a small model hospital to be used in connection with the teaching of the Medical School. She is considering the matter. It would mean her leaving (resigning) from her mission. She is also thinking of going to New Zealand to raise more money for this Region. Between the two of us, I feel that we can raise enough for the medical educational work of the Region, but it would mean that both of us would have to leave here temporarily for 6 months to 8 months.

14. One of the big problems that I am confronted with is what to do with the old former badly trained medical officers, many of whom have been in the Red Army. They have got into a lot of very bad habits and are tending to be very cliche [sic] and somewhat bureaucratic. They are technically inefficient but of course politically fine.

...

16. I would suggest the calling of a Conference of the Chiefs of the S.S. and discussing the points brought out in this letter.

With warm comradely greetings,
Norman Bethune, M.D.,
Medical Advisor to the Chin-Ch'a-Chi Military District

PS   Dear Tim [Buck]

No letter or word from you 1 or 1½ years. I sent Lilian a cable in spring this year from Beijing. She could come through there. No reply. I am returning this winter.

I sent cable to [name deleted] asking for $1000 for hospitals last winter. No reply.

N.

In August, Bethune began to set out his travel plans to comrades and friends in North America. The letters – to Tim Buck and his friend John Barnwell, copies of which also went to other friends – described Bethune's extreme poverty and the hardship imposed by his remote work, distant from all English-speaking company.

G.H.Q. West Hopei
August 15/39

Dear Tim and Canadian Comrades –
I last wrote you a letter on March 4th from Mid-Hopei. I am afraid it was lost. I am sending you a copy. These letters are going out with an English visitor (Professor M. Lindsay of Yin ching University, Beijing) who has just arrived from Beijing and is on his way to Hong Kong. He should reach there in 2 months.

This is to let you know that I am coming home for a short time. The General [Nieh] did not, at first, want me to go, but we must have more money. I don't know where the money from America is going, the only thing is I am not getting it here for my work. I have started a Medical Training School and need $5000 a month (about $1000 gold). We have no books, no instruments (mine are all distributed) and very little drugs. The Chin-Ch'a-Chi Government is poorer on account of more soldiers in the army and we have had very serious floods this summer so that thousands of square miles are flooded and crops ruined. We have 2300 wounded in hospital. Every day there is one or more battles. We need more doctors – more of everything! And we are not getting it, from America. Why not? If the China Aid Council won't help, we must set up special committees for this Region.

I have suggested to the Government a Government Public Health Service for the civilians. We need money for that too. The poverty of this area is very bad. The health of the women and children is poor. We must help them. I want to set up co-operative workshops to make our own surgical gauze, cotton, splints and artificial legs.

There are a thousand problems. The people of Canada and America must be told about these things from one, such as myself, who has lived and worked among these splendid and heroic Chinese.

I have been alone for over a year – no letters, no books, no periodicals, no radio. I must have help to go on.

I plan to leave here in November – somewhere about the 1st or 2nd week – go across Shansi and down to Yan'an on foot. This is about 500 miles. It will take 6 weeks. From there I will go the Chungking and then to Yunnan in the south, arriving at Hong Kong (through French Indochina) sometime in January. I will take a freighter from there to Hawaii to avoid Japan. I should be in San Francisco about the end of February/40. I want to stay in Canada for about 3 or 4 months to collect more money and supplies – and men if I can – and then come back here next summer.

Well, comrades that is the present plan. I hope you agree. It seems the best thing to do.

I am fairly well. My right ear has gone completely deaf for 3 months. My teeth need a lot of attention and my glasses are giving me trouble. Outside of these minor things and being rather thin, I'm OK.

I have no clothes. My civilian clothes were lost from Hong Kong on the R.R. to Hankou in March last year. Will you please have the China Aid Council send enough money to get me clothes, pay passage to America, pay dentists and doctors in Hong Kong? Perhaps they should send about $1000 to the China Defence Committee in Hong Kong.

I am bringing back all the negatives I have. I only wished I had had a movie. I cabled several times from Beijing to New York but could get no reply.

With the warmest comradely greetings, both to yourself and all comrades,

I remain, as ever,
Norman

On the border of north western Hopei, China
Chin-Ch'a-Chi Military District
August 15/39

Dear Comrade,
It seems such a long time since we last met and so much must have happened to you. It has certainly happened to me. These last (nearly two years) now, have been very full, so full that I hardly know where to start to describe them to you. So this account will be a disconnected one at best. But I am anxious that you should receive one letter at least of those I have written you, for I have written before, but I am supposing that you never received them as I have had no reply. That is what I have come to accept, more or less resignedly, as part of this life. The mails are very irregular. It takes at least 5 months for any letters to reach me after they have arrived in China. I calculate that I get only 1 in 25. Books and periodicals are even worse. I have received none in one and half years. My reading consists of years old San Francisco papers used as wrappers for sugar, tea and cakes by merchants. I am thoroughly conversant with the doings of the 'smart set' and the vagaries of Hollywood, but of anything of importance, I know less than an Arctic explorer. He, at least, has a radio, I have none. It was three months before I knew that Madrid had fallen!

The work that I am trying to do is to take peasant boys and young workers and make doctors out of them. They can read and write and most have a knowledge of arithmetic. None of my doctors have ever been to college or university and none have ever been in a modern hospital (most of them have never been in any hospital) much less a medical school. With this material, I must make doctors and nurses out of them, in 6 months for nurses and 1 year for doctors. We have 2300 wounded in hospital all the time. These hospitals are merely the dirty one-story mud and stone houses of out-of-the-way villages set in deep valleys overhung by mountains, some of which are 10,000 feet high. We have over 20 of these hospitals in our region which stretches from Beijing in the north to Tientsin in the east, south to Shih Chia Chuang, west to Tai Yuan. We are the most active partisan area in China and engaged in very severe guerrilla warfare all the time.

The Japanese claim they 'control' this region. The claim is absurd. What they control are the large towns and cities of the region which is an entirely different thing. There are 22 cities. They hold these. There are 100 large towns. They hold 75. There are 20,000 villages. They hold none. 'Holding' a city means something like 'holding' a tiger. You feel rather proud of 'controlling' such a big fine beast but rather afraid also of what he may do if you relax your vigilance.

The Puppet Governments set up by the Japs seem to work in a sort of fashion in the cities. In the countryside they are complete flops. Our own local governments are the only ones recognized by the people. To them they pay their taxes. Japanese taxes are pure and simple robbery and extortion, capricious, uncertain and based on the simple gunman principle – 'How much have you got?' Our taxation is a fixed tax on the land such as the peasants are accustomed to paying for centuries. This year, 1939, the taxes for 1940 have been paid as usual a year in advance. 90% of the customary amount ($1,200,000.00) has been already paid.

My own opinion is that the Japanese can never conquer China. I think it a physical impossibility. They haven't the troops to do it. The country is too big, the people too numerous, the feeling against the aggressor, among the masses too intense. Even at present, the Japanese army is nothing but a police force. They seem held up in their advance. And in the meantime, China is building an enormous army of 20,000,000 men. Next year this army will take the offensive.

The war will be a long one. We want it to be protracted. We are planning on a war lasting at least ten years.

The Anti-British sentiment in China is a purely Japanese manufactured article. The real Chinese feel very friendly to England and America.

We must help these splendid people more than we are doing. We must send them more money and men. Technicians of all kinds are badly needed, doctors, public health workers, engineers, mechanics – everybody that knows some technical specialty well. Last year I travelled 3165 miles, of which 400 miles were marched on foot across Shansi, Shensi and Hopei Provinces. 762 operations were performed and 1200 wounded examined. The Sanitary Service of the army was re-organized, 3 textbooks written and translated into Chinese, a Medical Training School established.

It's a fast life. I miss tremendously a comrade to whom I can talk. You know how fond I am of talking! I don't mind the conventional hardships – heat and bitter cold, dirt, lice, unvaried unfamiliar food, walking in the mountains, no stoves, beds or baths. I find I can get along and operate as well in a dirty Buddhist temple with a 20–foot high statue of the impassive-faced god staring over my shoulder, as in a modern operating room with running water, nice green glazed walls, electric lamps and a thousand other accessories. To dress the wounded we have to climb up on the mud ovens – the *k'angs*. They have no mattresses, no sheets. They lie in their old stained uniforms, with their knapsacks as pillows and one padded cotton blanket over them. They are grand. They certainly can take it.

We have had tremendous floods this summer. It's been hellish hot and muggy. Rain for 2 months coming down like a steady shower-bath turned on full. I am planning to return to Canada early next year. I must leave here sometime in November and go 500 miles on foot over to Yan'an. From there by bus – I hope down through French Indochina. Then boat to Hong Kong, another boat (a freighter to Honolulu to avoid Japan) then another boat to San Francisco.

I want to raise a guaranteed $1000 (gold) a month for my work here. I'm not getting it. They need me here. This is 'my' Region. I must come back.

I dream of coffee, of rare roast beef, of apple pie and ice cream. Mirages of heavenly food! Books – are books still being written? Is music still being played? Do you dance, drink beer, look at pictures? What do clean white sheets in a soft bed feel like? Do women still love to be loved?

How sad that, even to me once more, all these things may become accepted easily without wonder and amazement at my good fortune.

The China Aid Council seems to its China representative in the field to be rather neglectful. I have received three letters from them in 20 months. The last was received on Jan. 14th, 1939 – over 7 months ago. That letter was mailed from New York in Sept. 20, 1938. As a result I am completely in the dark as to the American developments, money, supplies, etc. It is really on account of this ignorance that I am forced to come back. Why have they kept me so uninformed? Perhaps it was too much to expect that some of the individual members of the Council should write me but why has not the secretary done so officially? That, I think, is not unreasonable.

Goodbye for the present, dear friend and comrade,
Beth

In a brief letter to the Trustee Committee in Yan'an he announced his intended visit to Canada.

G.H.Q. Chin-Ch'a-Chi Military Region
August 16, 1939

Dear Comrades:
I am leaving this region to return to America about the first week of November if I can clean up my work before. My new book on 'Organization and Technique for Division Field Hospitals in Guerrilla Warfare' has been written and is more than half translated. It will go to the press in about three weeks. Then I must make a fast inspection trip of all hospitals (20 now) before leaving. The medical school with 150 students is on its feet. We need 1000 medical books.

I plan to be away in America for 3 or 4 months, returning next summer. I must have a guaranteed $1000 gold monthly for this region alone. I'm not getting it. I don't know where the money from America is going to. I can get no information from the Trustee Committee or America, so I'm going to find out for myself!

My teeth and eyes are bad. Completely deaf in one ear for three months, a little thing with the 8th Route Army chronic cough, otherwise OK.

Goodbye for the present. Inform Dr. Ma Haide I received his letter written March 10, 1939 on June 2, 1939. I thank him for the information it contained.

With comradely greetings,
Norman Bethune
Medical Advisor to the Chin-Ch'a-Chi Military District

While on the hospital inspection tour, Bethune was asked to assist an army bri-
gade under attack. While operating on a soldier with a leg fracture, he cut his
finger, and the cut became infected. Weak and fatigued, he struggled to survive.
He wrote his last letter to his interpreter, Lang Lin, just the day before his
death. (My source for this letter is Roderick Stewart, Bethune, *pp. 159–60.)*

On the north bank of Tang Ho near Hua Ta, West Hopei
November 11, 1939

I came back from the front yesterday. There was no good in my being
there. I couldn't get out of bed or operate. I left Shih Chia Chuang (I
think) Hospital of Central Hopei troops on 7th. Pan and I went north. I
then had infected finger ... Reached Tu Ping Ti late at night ... We go
over west and joined at 3rd Regiment sanitary service on 8th about 10 li
east of Yin Fang. Had uncontrolled chills and fever all day. Temp.
around 39.6 C., bad. Gave instructions I was to be informed of any
abdominal cases of fractured femur or skull cases ... Next day (9th),
more vomiting all day, high fever. Next day (10th) regiment commander
(3rd Regiment) instructed I be sent back, useless for work. Vomiting on
stretcher all the day. High fever, over 40 C. I think I have either septicae-
mia from the gangrenous fever or typhus fever. Can't get to sleep, mentally very bright. Phenacitin and aspirin, woven's powder, antipyrine,
caffeine, all useless.
    Dr. Ch'en arrived here today. If my stomach settles down will return
to Hua Pai Hospital tomorrow. Very rough road over mountain pass.
    I feel freely today. Pain over heart – water 120–130°. Will see you
tomorrow, I expect.

Norman Bethune

In The Scalpel, The Sword, *Ted Allan and Sydney Gordon stated that*
Bethune wrote 'his last will and testament to Staff Headquarters' in the last
days of his life.[12] *Like much of their book, the source of the 'will' was Zhou*
Erfu's novel, Dr. Norman Bethune.[13] *The document they presented raises*
several issues of historical authenticity. Certainly it is entirely plausible that
Bethune would attempt to sum up his experience in China when it became clear
that he was dying. However, several aspects of the 'last will and testament' are
not credible. For example, it quoted Bethune as writing, 'All my photographs,
diaries, narratives and all the motion pictures of our army are to be turned over

to T.B. [Tim Buck]. Inform him that a motion picture will be completed soon.'[14] But as recently as 15 August, Bethune had written to comrades in Canada, 'I only wished I had had a movie.' Despite several cables to New York seeking movie equipment and funds, Bethune received nothing. The statement also warned General Nieh to 'never buy medicine in such cities as Pao Ting, Tientsin and Peiping again. The prices there are twice as much as in Shanghai and Hong Kong.' This flies in the face of both logic – Pao Ting was some 200 kilometres away, whereas Hong Kong was more than ten times that distance and could be reached only by land routes over rough country – and Bethune's concerted efforts of the previous year to establish a secure supply line to Beijing, Pao Ting, and Tientsin.

Nonetheless, some elements of the 'last will and testament' ring true. erhaps the most important is Bethune's conclusion that 'the last two years have been the most significant, the most meaningful years of life. Sometimes it has been lonely, but I have found my highest fulfilment here among my beloved comrades.' Bethune's letters confirm that in China he had found a movement, a community, and comrades with whom he was at home, politically, emotionally, and physically. When Bethune died early in the morning of 12 November 1939, he was not alone. Indeed he might have been less alone than he had been for years. He was among caring comrades with whom he had shared a powerful common experience. They had fought together to eradicate imperialism from China and to crush the scourge of fascism. If he did not in fact write it in so many words in his final testament, Bethune must certainly have felt that 'my only regret is that I shall now be unable to do more.'

Appendix 1:
Report on the Actions of the
Canadian Delegation in Spain

*The confusing, dubious situation surrounding Bethune's recall from Spain is
illustrated in the following report from Spanish authorities. The exact charges
against Bethune were frustratingly vague – reflecting the ambiguous, highly
charged atmosphere in the Republican ranks in the spring of 1937. The Spanish
authorities clearly believed he was consorting with unsavoury people and suspected that members of the transfusion team, Bethune included, were engaged
in spying. Little is known about Kajsa von Rothman, the person singled out for
the most critical attention, although she was almost certainly Bethune's lover.
(In a conversation with me, Ted Allan indicated that in Madrid he chanced upon
Bethune in bed with a naked young Swedish woman, a liaison confirmed in
interviews of Henning Sorensen by Roderick Stewart.)[1] This report declares
that Ted Allan and Henning Sorensen's letter of complaint to the Communist
Party of Canada led to Bethune being recalled to Canada, although the party
had previously been made aware of difficulties in Spain. It also indicates that
the Spanish were dubious about Bethune's technical capacity to establish a
blood transfusion service, since his previous experience had been in surgery and
tuberculosis. (Rosa Stewart, Bryan Nethery and Marc Hunter each helped me
to translate this report from Spanish. To give the reader a sense of the original, I
have reproduced the shifts in verb tense and other grammatical peculiarities.)
Source: National Archives of Canada, Mackenzie-Papineau Collection (Moscow
Archives), Fonds 545, file list 6, file 542, 1937–1940, report of 3 April 1937.*

Background:
Approximately in the month of October [1936], Henning Sorensen
(Danish) arrived in Madrid, and said he arrived from Canada where he
lived, and was sent here with the mission of determining in what way
Canada could contribute economically to the republican cause. Accord-

ing to information from this Henning, a Committee for the Assistance of the Spanish People had been formed in Canada, whose purpose was collecting funds and sending them to republican Spain.

After a series of measures, there are plans to set up a blood transfusion service, for which the Canadian doctor Norman Bethune arrived in Madrid. He had full authority to set up such a service and administer the donations from Canada. At this time Sorensen lends his services as a secretary to Mr Bethune.

In collaboration with the S.R.I. [Socorro Rojo Internacional, a relief agency for the families of political prisoners], which gives him a place to stay and other facilities to set up his equipment, Dr Bethune organizes the blood transfusion service on Principe de Vergara, #36.

Due to Mr Bethune's technical deficiencies, collaboration was requested from a Spanish team that already was working in San Carlos, and who currently do all the work, leaving Dr Bethune as the Director of the service and administrator of the funds.

From this moment forward, a series of foreigners begin to arrive, some in the capacity of reporters, others as chauffeurs, who lived with the team.

In the first days that the Spanish team was active, Bethune moves to Valencia and Barcelona to see about extending the service to all fronts, in collaboration with Military Health.

The doctor negotiates with the Headquarters of Health Services of E.M. [probably should read S.M. – Sanidad Militar, or Military Health] a contract which, as a project, is presented for the approval of the Ministry of War. Since it seems that the contract presented will not be accepted [sic], the Canadians and Military Health are beginning to work with each other. But when Mr Bethune failed to send to Valencia the promised quantities for the installation of the laboratory there, the first differences of opinion arise. The mentioned doctor, being summoned repeatedly to Valencia by the Headquarters of Health Services of E.M., refuses to leave Madrid, where he resides, and orders his secretary, Henning Sorensen, to break with Military Health. He yields finally when faced with a final threatening call and explains that Canada has passed a law which does not permit its citizens to participate in the Spanish war, which is the reason he cannot hold to that which was agreed in the mentioned project contract. He also complains that it is the Spanish State that has not fulfilled its part of the contract (payment of wages to the personnel). He immediately returns to Madrid.

Before the collaboration with the Spanish team, the Canadians working independently, there occurs the following incident:

In the place where the team was located, Principe de Vergara, #36, a series of foreigners would gather, which raised the suspicions of Henning Sorensen, who let this be known to the one in charge of the Socorro [Rojo Internacional], and he, in turn, informed the police. As a result of this, all the foreigners were detained, and among them Bethune, Henning, and Seise [Hazen Sise], whom the Socorro took responsibility for and were released; not so the rest. Among those detained were a commander, Harturg, of Austrian nationality, and one Kajsa. This last one, after checking many things out, was set free. The commander disappeared and they say he was executed.

Kajsa's background:

(Swedish, it seems that she lived before the movement in Barcelona, where she lived comfortably. After the movement, she enrolled as a nurse in the Pillar of Iron, becoming affiliated with the C.N.T. [Confederación Nacional de Trabajo, the anarcho-syndicalist labour federation]. Before or after this she belonged to the Scottish Field Hospital, from which her commander, Miss Jacobsen, kicked her out, along with other foreigners. On this occasion she was detained as well, but she was soon set free. The aforementioned Miss Jacobsen, who was asked by the Chief of Health Services about the reasons for the expulsion, refused to give any, but it appeared that it was due to immoralities. She acts as speaker on the Swedish broadcasts of radio U.G.T. [Spanish government radio]. On a certain occasion she was at the point of being detained again for asking suspicious questions of the guard at the Arganda Bridge, on the occasion of one of her strange trips. This was avoided by the documents carried by the transfusion team's chauffeur.)

Upon Bethune leaving, this Kajsa remains in Madrid as his secretary, and in the first days of this absence, more foreigners are added to the team. (Miss [Jean] Watts is a good friend of Kajsa, and claims to be a reporter, a militant from the Communist Party, and reporter for the party's newspaper in Canada.) Kajsa makes frequent trips to the fronts, morning, afternoon, and sometimes even at night. She cannot be found at the team's housing, her whereabouts are not known. The medical personnel do not know what she does, because she doesn't tell anyone what she does, limiting herself to mentioning that she is gathering information with regard to the needs for transfusions at the fronts.

Currently, and due to Kajsa's initiative, it is said, there exists with the team a series of detailed maps, similar to military maps.

A month ago, Allen May, a delegate of the Committee in Canada, arrived in Spain. He has remained with the team in Madrid as secretary.

A little before, Ted [Allan] also arrived, a communist of long-standing and reporter for various newspapers.

On one of the last of Bethune's trips, which he frequently takes to France to collect the money from America, he brought with him from Paris a movie camera, with its camera man (a Hungarian). Among the equipment there are several small photographic machines.

Of a series of pictures that were taken of hospitals, none have been seen, and the negatives disappeared when Kajsa was left alone.

Many times it has occurred that during a determined trip, one of these foreigners may have remained in one of the towns near the front in order to do something. Later, the need for a new trip was contrived – even at late hours of the night – for nonexistent transfusions, evidently with the sole objective of picking up the foreigner. This foreigner is one Tom [Walmsley], Canadian or American [British], who is not part of the team.

There is a truck assigned to the transportation of blood that carries out no health services. On the contrary, it does nothing but take trips between Madrid, Valencia, Barcelona, and Perpignan, driven by Sise, Canadian.

A grave fact, of very special nature, that speaks of the morality of these elements or of some of them, and it is not known if it has had some source [been confirmed] is the following:

A room on the floor that is used by the team on Principe de Vergara, 36, was sealed by the Chilean Embassy. When the team occupied it, it was broken into by Bethune and another or others. It's known that two trunks in it were also opened by said individuals; in them it seems there were jewellery and documents whose whereabouts are now unknown.

A suspicious fact which should also be considered is that Mr Bethune openly takes detailed notes of the locations of bridges, crossroads, distances between determined points, journey times, etc., writing it all down carefully.

Of all the foreigners mentioned, there are two who deserve from the informers a certain guarantee: Henning Sorensen, Dane, and Ted, Canadian, who have sent a letter of complaint to the Communist Party of Canada, via the Provincial of Madrid, denouncing the unclear conduct of Dr Bethune, and requesting his dismissal and the naming of another director.

3 April 1937

Appendix 2:
Chronology of the Life of
Dr Norman Bethune

4 March 1890	Born in Gravenhurst, Ontario, in the Presbyterian manse; spent his youth in Beaverton, Toronto, Aylmer, Blind River, and Sault Sainte Marie, and his summers around the Muskoka lakes
1909–11	Student at the University of Toronto, preparing for medical studies
1911–12	Labourer-teacher in lumber camp near Whitefish, Ontario, under auspices of Frontier College; reporter for *Winnipeg Telegram* from April to August 1912
1912–14	Medical student at University of Toronto
8 Sept. 1914	Enlisted with No. 2 Field Ambulance Army Medical Corps, serving as a stretcher-bearer
29 April 1915	Wounded at Ypres; spent six months in hospitals, mostly in England
1915–16	Returned to medical studies at University of Toronto in accelerated program
Dec. 1916	Graduated Bachelor of Medicine, University of Toronto
25 April 1917	Joined the navy as surgeon lieutenant and served aboard the aircraft carrier HMS *Pegasus* for fourteen months
1919	Internship at the Great Ormond Street Hospital for Sick Children, London. Medical practice at Ingersoll and Stratford, Ontario
1920	Worked in surgery at the West London Hospital and studied at the Royal Infirmary in Edinburgh
3 Feb. 1922	Elected Fellow of the Royal College of Surgeons, Edinburgh

1922–3	Resident Surgical Fellow of West London Hospital
13 Aug. 1923	Married Frances Campbell Penney
spring 1924	Travelled in Europe for honeymoon and study – Italy, Switzerland, Austria, Germany
fall 1924	Set up practice in Detroit, Michigan, serving mostly working-class, immigrant patients
fall 1926	Overworked and growing weak, diagnosed as having tuberculosis
1 Oct. 1926	Left Detroit for Calydor Sanatorium, Gravenhurst
16 Dec. 1926	Admitted to Trudeau Sanatorium, Saranac Lake, N.Y. Persuaded Frances to separate; after six months in Trudeau, returned to Detroit
early 1927	Again at Trudeau Sanatorium, created a mural, with short poems, called *The T.B.'s Progress*. Read about new achievements in pulmonary surgery and insisted on being operated on
24 Oct. 1927	Divorced from Frances
27 Oct. 1927	Given artificial pneumothorax treatment, after which began to improve
10 Dec. 1927	Complete recovery; discharged from Trudeau
April 1928	Moved to Montreal to become first assistant to Dr Edward Archibald at the Royal Victoria Hospital, Medico-Surgical Pulmonary Clinic
1928–32	Specialized in thoracic surgery; at the same time taught at McGill, lectured and demonstrated at Trudeau
11 Nov. 1929	After persuading her to rejoin him in Montreal, remarried Frances
1931	Became associated with Pilling and Son, Philadelphia, which manufactured his medical instruments
March 1932	Acting head, thoracic surgery, at Herman Kiefer Hospital, Detroit, for six months; later at Maybury Sanatorium, Northville, Michigan, and American Legion Hospital, Battle Creek, Michigan. After Detroit, demonstrated and lectured in the United States; then returned to Montreal
26 Nov. 1932	Appointed to Sacré Coeur Hospital, Cartierville, Quebec, as chief of pulmonary surgery
30 March 1933	Second divorce from Frances
June 1935	Elected as council member of the American Association of Thoracic Surgery

July 1935	Sailed to Britain en route to the International Physiological Congress in the USSR; spent several days in London with Marian Scott and her son, Peter
Aug. 1935	Attended congress in Leningrad and Moscow
24 Aug. 1935	Sailed from Southampton to Montreal; arrived 31 August
fall 1935	Organized the Montreal Group for the Security of the People's Health, which began to study and report on the desperate medical situation of Quebec's people
Nov. 1935	Joined the Communist Party of Canada
Dec. 1935	Helped to organize and finance the Montreal Children's Art Centre
20 Dec. 1935	Reported on the Russian trip to Montreal Medico-Chirurgical Society
July 1936	Montreal Group for the Security of the People's Health issued manifesto to candidates in the August 1936 Quebec election
Sept. 1936	Volunteered for medical work in Spain
24 Oct. 1936	Left Canada for Spain
3 Nov. 1936	Arrived in Madrid. Decided that blood transfusion at the front should be the focus of the Canadian effort in Spain
Nov.–Dec. 1936	Travelled to London to study the problems of blood transfusion and to purchase necessary equipment and truck
12 Dec. 1936	Arrived back in Madrid with Henning Sorensen and Hazen Sise to organize donor system and the work of the Canadian Blood Transfusion Service
Dec. 1936	Blood transfusion service established and functioning, serving Madrid and other fronts
Dec. '36–Jan. '37	Several radio broadcasts from Spain to stimulate help for the loyalist cause
7 Feb. 1937	Evacuation of Malaga; blood transfusion team helped to transport some of the 150,000 refugees to Almeria. Soon after, wrote the pamphlet *The Crime on the Road: Malaga-Almeria*
19 April 1937	Submitted his official resignation as head of the transfusion unit, which was taken over by the Spanish Ministry of War

18 May 1937	Left Spain for fund-raising trip in Canada and the United States
8 June 1937	Arrived in New York
June 1937	Edited film *Heart of Spain* in New York
14 June 1937	Triumphant homecoming meeting in Toronto, followed by similar event in Montreal to begin tour
June–Sept. 1937	Speaking tour in Canada and the United States
Oct. 1937	Left Canada for New York to prepare to lead medical unit to guerrilla troops in China
8 Jan. 1938	Sailed from Vancouver for Hong Kong with Canadian-American Medical Unit to China; arrived in Hong Kong on 27 January
22 Feb.–22 Mar. 1938	Long trek to Sian from Hankou
31 March 1938	Met Mao Zedong in Yan'an; proposed creating mobile operating unit working close to battle lines
24 April 1938	Travelled north from Yan'an to put medical unit into action near front lines
June 1938	Arrived in Chin-Ch'a-Chi Region and here became medical advisor to Eighth Route Army. Besides operating on and treating the troops, organized model hospitals and courses for doctors and nurses, wrote textbooks, and helped to set up public health systems
4 March 1939	Forty-ninth birthday – 'the oldest soldier at the front'
Aug. 1939	Continued to work in west Hopei; proposed to return to North America to raise money for hospitals and medical school
Oct. 1939	Began inspection tour of hospitals before leaving for North America
28 Oct. 1939	Called to the front because of heavy fighting; sliced his finger and contracted infection while operating on a soldier
12 Nov. 1939	Died in village of Huang-shih K'ou, Hopei Province, China

A Note on Sources

The material in this book comes from a variety of places. A considerable amount – including short stories, poems, articles by Bethune and others quoting him, open letters, and medical articles – was published during Bethune's lifetime. I've located them by going to the original publications. I have obtained the majority of Bethune's work that was not published – letters, reports, cables, and the like – through Ted Allan.

How Allan obtained Bethune's records, how he controlled them, and how he came to give me access to them should be explained. Most of this material was provided to Allan by the Communist Party of Canada (CPC) sometime around 1942, when Allan first took on the task of writing Bethune's biography. Whether or not what was made available included everything the party had on Bethune is unclear, although it seems unlikely. (Allan, for instance, claimed to have himself written reports from Spain depicting Bethune as drinking excessively and near a nervous breakdown, and I have not found them in any archive, including his own papers.)[1] After ten years of unsuccessfully trying to complete the biography, Allan, with the assistance of the Communist Party, recruited fellow communist Sydney Gordon to the project, and the documents became their joint archive.

Allan obtained Bethune's personal letters to his former wife, Frances Coleman, in another way. In 1942 he interviewed Frances and collected her letters from Bethune, paying her $200 as an advance on royalties for the biography. Arrangements were to be made with the American publisher Little, Brown to pay her 'a definite [but unspecified] percentage of royalties on the book.' Allan later contended that Frances had given him exclusive permission to use her information and Bethune's correspondence.[2]

Although Allan and his co-author kept these documents, they began to become public through mischance and disorganization. Allan provided the National Film Board of Canada with copies of Bethune's letters to Frances for its 1964 film on him, then forgot he'd done so. In 1971, when he and Gordon attempted to sue the NFB for violating the copyright of *The Scalpel, The Sword*, the NFB produced a letter from Allan allowing it to quote from the letters. 'The East and my face are both red,' a chastened Allan confessed to his lawyer. 'I forgot ever sending that letter.' He also admitted that his claim to own Bethune's letters to Frances was baseless: 'In reply to the NFB's query: Did I ever get the letters copyrighted? No.'[3] Nonetheless, Allan acted swiftly in 1970 when Roderick Stewart informed him that he'd found copies of the correspondence in another place, the Metropolitan Toronto Library. He threatened Stewart with legal action to prevent him from using the letters in his new biography of Bethune,[4] and he issued a decree making that repository, as well as the papers he'd deposited in the Osler Library at McGill University in Montreal, closed except with his permission. This prohibition remains in place as of this writing. Everyone who wishes to consult the material must first obtain the permission of Allan's daughter or son.

In the half-century from Bethune's death to his own, Allan consistently attempted to monopolize Bethune and his memory. He turned Bethune into a lucrative commodity and attempted to corner the market on him by asserting constantly that he had a 'copyright' over Bethune's writings. The claim is legally dubious and morally baseless. Copyright of unpublished material remains forever with the author or his heirs, unless otherwise assigned. If Bethune assigned anyone his rights – and clearly the thought of anyone making a profit from him would have infuriated him – it was the Communist Party of Canada. Allan and Gordon themselves wrote in *The Scalpel, The Sword* that just before his death Bethune gave 'his last will and testament to Staff Headquarters.'[5] (A search of Allan's papers has yielded no evidence of this document.) According to this 'will,' Bethune declared that 'all my photographs, diaries, narratives and all the motion pictures of our army are to be turned over to T.B.' – Tim Buck, leader of the Communist Party of Canada. These were the records the CPC provided to Allan and Gordon in the 1940s. The party also paid Gordon a salary 'for some weeks' while he rewrote Allan's rough draft.[6] Given its central involvement in the project, the Communist Party's claim to ownership is probably the strongest. Indeed, Allan's lawyer acknowledged as much in 1971 when he wrote that 'at least half of that material [Bethune's writing] was (*and remains*) the property of the Communist Party of Canada.'[7] By 1977 the Communist Party had grown weary of Allan's avarice. Asked to mediate between Allan and Gordon, who had fallen out over who should profit more from possible film deals then in the works, CPC leader William Kashtan came down firmly against Allan's attempt to claim Bethune unilaterally. 'It is indefensible to argue that ... you have the right to appropriate all the film benefits and financial gain for yourself,' he wrote to Allan. 'We [the Communist Party] do not feel that we can grant you the right to use, without our consent, any of the extensive materials we made available to you through the late Tim Buck and others.'[8]

This rebuke did not force Allan to relinquish his hold on Bethune. Through the 1980s he parlayed his association with Bethune into film-script-writing deals that brought him hundreds of thousands of dollars. The contract to write the script for the film *Bethune: The Making of a Hero*, for instance, called for Allan to be paid $400,000.[9] In the early summer of 1995, Allan could not turn his back on one more scheme to wring more revenue from a communist who himself died in complete poverty. He signed a deal with me in which he agreed to allow me to reprint the portion of Bethune's writings which he claimed to control, in exchange for half the net proceeds of this book. The proceeds, which will go to Allan's son and daughter, will not quite equal those from the film deal: they'll get half the advance on royalties from the publisher, which was a four-figure sum, and half of any royalties that might accrue after the advance is paid. Allan died mere weeks after signing the contract, asserting to the end his 'copyright' over Bethune's writings.

In recent years, the National Archives of Canada has acquired Allan's papers, which include material from Bethune. Although researchers required his permission to view them until 1995, at his death that barrier was removed. In short, material written by Bethune exists in the Metropolitan Toronto Library, the Osler Library, the National Film Board, and the National Archives of Canada. Allan was a prodigious photocopier, with the consequence that most of what exists in the first three places can also be found in the National Archives. The National Archives of Canada also has a small collection on Bethune himself and the papers of Marian Scott, which include letters and poems Bethune wrote to her. Interested researchers are encouraged to try that location first.

Doing justice to Norman Bethune's memory demands a radically different handling of this invaluable resource. All the documents which originated from Norman Bethune or his wife, Frances Penney, and which are in the closed Allan collections in the above libraries should be made available without restriction. The 'copyright' on Bethune's own words exercised by the Allan family should be passed over to the Canadian public. It is time to recognize that Norman Bethune belongs to all of us.

Notes

1 Introduction

1 Ted Allan, 'With Norman Bethune in Spain,' in *Norman Bethune: His Times and Legacy*, ed. David A.E. Shephard and Andrée Lévesque (Ottawa: Canadian Public Health Association, 1982), p. 157

2 In an explanatory note in 1978, Zhou wrote that except for Bethune and the Communist Party and Eighth Route Army leadership, the people portrayed in his novel were 'all fictitious composite characters ... The events in the story are also all the result of accumulation and combination.' Even though it was fictional, Allan and Gordon made considerable use of it, acknowledging in 1952 that they were 'immeasurably helped' by Zhou's work. Indeed, Allan admitted privately in 1971 that Zhou 'deserves more credit for our Chinese section than we gave to him.' Gordon, however, was less willing to concede Zhou's contribution, dismissing the work as 'a Chinese fictional story, written in a puerile style, making Bethune look like a half-idiot.' Taken as a whole, the 1971 controversy does cast into doubt the veracity of *The Scalpel, The Sword* and explains some of the book's serious shortcomings. See Zhou Erfu, *Doctor Norman Bethune*, trans. Alison Bailey (Beijing: Foreign Languages Press, 1982), p. 5; Ted Allan and Sydney Gordon, *The Scalpel, The Sword: The Story of Dr Norman Bethune* (Toronto: McClelland and Stewart, 1989; first published 1952), p. viii; National Archives of Canada (NAC), MG30 D388, vol. 1, file 1–28, Allan to Ma Haide, 18 Oct. 1971, and file 1–15, Gordon to Edward Lewis, 10 Oct. 1971.

3 NAC, MG30 D388, vol. 1, file 1–23, Allan to Gordon, 23 April 1971

4 Roderick Stewart, *Bethune* (Toronto: New Press, 1973)

5 I owe these observations to Bill Livant, who has raised the points in discussion with me and in his unpublished paper 'Bethune and Blood: A Compari-

son of Two Biographies,' University of Regina, 1979.
6 Roderick Stewart, *The Mind of Norman Bethune* (Toronto: Fitzhenry and Whiteside, 1977)
7 A related issue has been raised by an anonymous reader of the pre-publication manuscript of this book, who suggested that Bethune 'fabricate[d] the truth for the sake of the [Communist] Party.' The charge is utterly spurious. Bethune's writing demonstrates again and again his uncompromising nature. His detailed reports from China, for example, are valuable precisely because of their frankness. If a medical comrade deserved praise, Bethune issued it forthrightly. But if a comrade or a hospital was condemnable, he spared nothing in saying so. He described the hospital at Ho Chia Chuang, Shensi, for instance, as a 'pest-hole [which] should be shut down – lousy position, lousy poverty-stricken area, no food for patients, lousy equipment and a lousy, lazy staff.' His communist affiliation, if anything, seemed to make him more candid. Even in Spain, where political delicacy was considered vital because of the conflicts among the various left-wing factions, he bluntly called for the Canadian blood transfusion personnel to be withdrawn because of what he saw as interference by the Spanish government. After he returned to Canada in 1937, he was instructed by the Committee to Aid Spanish Democracy to conceal his political affiliation. Against his will, Bethune temporarily denied being a communist. But deceit was contrary to his nature, and he was soon openly and proudly announcing he was a red, to the committee's chagrin (see chapter 6). In short, suggestions that Bethune fabricated the truth in the interests of the Communist Party are the inventions of people whose own political bias is so extreme they stoop to pathetic innuendo.
8 Link published the murals in a pamphlet, *The T.B.'s Progress: Norman Bethune as Artist* (Plattsburg, N.Y.: Center for the Study of Canada, SUNY, 1991), which unfortunately received very limited circulation.
9 Hazen Sise, 'The Vivid Air Signed with His Honour: In Memory of Norman Bethune,' in Shephard and Lévesque, eds, *Norman Bethune*, p. 162
10 Metropolitan Toronto Library, Baldwin Room, Ted Allan Papers, Bethune folder C, Fisher to Ted Allan, 4 June 1942
11 Lee Briscoe Thompson, 'Norman Bethune and His Brethren: Poetry in Depression Montreal,' in Shephard and Lévesque, eds, *Norman Bethune*, p. 111
12 Norman Bethune, 'A Plea for Early Compression in Pulmonary Tuberculosis' (see chapter 3)
13 *Globe and Mail*, 7 March 1996, p. A1
14 Letter to Marian Scott, 5 May 1937

15 Wendell MacLeod, Libbie Park, and Stanley Ryerson, *Bethune, the Montreal Years: An Informal Portrait* (Toronto: James Lorimer, 1978), p. 98

16 Bethune to Canadian comrades, 10 January 1939. See chapter 8 for entire letter.

17 See chapter 7 for entire text.

2 Adventurer: Youth to December 1927

1 Roderick Stewart, *Bethune* (Toronto: New Press, 1973), pp. 2, 169; Department of Foreign Affairs and International Trade Access Request A-3149, passport application for Henry Norman Bethune, M.D.

2 Much of this biographical detail is based upon Stewart, *Bethune*, pp. 1–18.

3 Ted Allan, 'With Norman Bethune in Spain,' in *Norman Bethune: His Times and Legacy*, ed. David A.E. Shephard and Andrée Lévesque (Ottawa: Canadian Public Health Association, 1982), p. 158; Jean Ewen, *China Nurse: 1932–1939* (Toronto: McClelland and Stewart, 1981), p. 77

4 Stewart, *Bethune*, p. 12

5 Ibid., pp. 18, 28

6 Bethune to John Barnwell, 5 Sept. 1934 (see chapter 3); 'The T.B.'s Progress,' *The Fluoroscope* 1, no. 7 (15 Aug. 1932)

7 Eugene P. Link, *The T.B.'s Progress: Norman Bethune as Artist* (Plattsburg, N.Y.: Center for the Study of Canada, SUNY, 1991), p. 2

3 Crusader: Montreal, 1928–1934

1 G.J. Wherrett, 'Norman Bethune and Tuberculosis,' in *Norman Bethune: His Times and Legacy*, ed. David A.E. Shephard and Andrée Lévesque (Ottawa: Canadian Public Health Association, 1982), p. 68

2 Ibid., p. 67

3 Donald Jack, *Rogues, Rebels, and Geniuses: The Story of Canadian Medicine* (Toronto: Doubleday, 1981), p. 473

4 Roderick Stewart, *Bethune* (Toronto: New Press, 1973), p. 69

5 Metropolitan Toronto Library, Baldwin Room, Ted Allan Papers, Bethune folder C, Pilling to Allan, 1 May 1942

6 David A.E. Shephard, 'Creativity in Norman Bethune: His Medical Writings and Innovations,' in Shephard and Lévesque, eds, *Norman Bethune*, pp. 94–8

7 Stewart, *Bethune*, p. 34

8 Ibid., p. 60

9 Wendell MacLeod and Hilary Russell, 'Norman Bethune: A Biographical Outline,' in Shephard and Lévesque, eds, *Norman Bethune*, p. 3

10 Stewart, *Bethune*, pp. 45–6
11 Ted Allan, 'With Norman Bethune in Spain,' in Shephard and Lévesque, eds, *Norman Bethune*, p. 157
12 Metropolitan Toronto Library, Baldwin Room, Ted Allan Papers, Bethune folder C, Barnwell to Bethune, 28 Aug. 1934
13 Ibid., Barnwell to Bethune, 4 Dec. 1934

4 Convert: 1935–1936

1 Roderick Stewart, *Bethune* (Toronto: New Press, 1973), p. 69
2 On 25 October 1935, three days *before* Bethune formally wrote to refuse the offer to become president of the association, the RCMP in Montreal reported the fact to headquarters in Ottawa: '[H]e is not ready to take the step yet. He wishes to study more about Communism first' (CSIS Access 117–91–22, report of 25 Oct. 1935). The force was slower in documenting his membership in the Communist Party, not recording that until 6 November 1936 (ibid., report of 6 Nov. 1936).
3 Stewart, *Bethune*, pp. 74–9; Libbie Park, 'Norman Bethune as I Knew Him,' in Wendell MacLeod, Libbie Park, and Stanley Ryerson, *Bethune, the Montreal Years* (Toronto: James Lorimer, 1978), pp. 120–9; Libbie Park, 'The Bethune Health Group,' in *Norman Bethune: His Times and Legacy*, ed. David A.E. Shephard and Andrée Lévesque (Ottawa: Canadian Public Health Association, 1982), pp. 138–43
4 Metropolitan Toronto Library, Baldwin Room, Ted Allan Papers, Bethune folder C 62–88, Scott to Allan, 29 April 1942
5 Park, 'Norman Bethune as I Knew Him,' pp. 114–15
6 National Archives of Canada, MG30 D399, vols 14–15, Marian Scott lecture notes, 1979, file 1
7 Ibid.
8 Metropolitan Toronto Library, Baldwin Room, Ted Allan Papers, Bethune folder C 62–88, Scott to Allan, 29 April 1942
9 Interview with Peter Dale Scott, 2 October 1995
10 It is not certain whether Bethune's portrait was placed in the Scott home at that time. Peter Dale Scott is 'pretty sure I remember it [the portrait] at 451 Clarke Ave., where we moved in 1941' (communication to author, 30 Sept. 1996). By 1941, of course, Bethune was a dead hero, whose portrait would have been much safer to hang.
11 Department of Foreign Affairs, Access Request A-3149
12 Park, 'Norman Bethune as I Knew Him,' p. 107
13 Ibid., p. 126

Notes to pages 118–25 377

5 Anti-fascist: Spain, November 1936 to May 1937

1 Hugh Thomas, *The Spanish Civil War* (London: Eyre & Spottiswoode, 1961), p. 306; Martin Lobigs, 'Canadian Responses to the Mackenzie-Papineau Battalion, 1936 to 1939' (M.A. thesis, University of New Brunswick, 1992), p. 10
2 National Archives of Canada (NAC), MG30 D187, vol. 35, file 4, transcript of CBC interview, 1939, pp. 3–8
3 *Norman Bethune: His Times and Legacy*, ed. David A.E. Shephard and Andrée Lévesque (Ottawa: Canadian Public Health Association, 1982), p. 104
4 Canada, House of Commons, *Debates*, 19 March 1937, pp. 1939–62
5 Rose Potvin, ed., *Passion and Conviction: The Letters of Graham Spry* (Regina: Canadian Plains Research Centre, 1992), pp. 104–5
6 Ibid.
7 Thomas, *The Spanish Civil War*, p. 304; RCMP documents show that the Communist Party of Canada began active recruitment of volunteers in December 1936. See Michael Lonardo, 'Under a Watchful Eye: A Case Study of Police Surveillance during the 1930s,' *Labour / Le Travail* 35 (Spring 1995): 35–6.
8 NAC, MG30 D187, vol. 9, file 14, 2 December 1936
9 Ibid., vol. 43, file 18, outline, n.d.
10 NAC, Mackenzie-Papineau Collection (Moscow Archives), Fonds 545, file list 6, file 542, 1937–1940, report of 3 April 1937 on the Canadian delegation in Spain (see Appendix 1 for translation)
11 Sise's recounting of the unit's problems can be found in his papers at the National Archives of Canada, MG30 D187. In particular, see vol. 6, file 8, correspondence 1937–9, letters of 4 May, 29 June, and 30 July 1937; vol. 10, file 9, manuscripts, pp. 16, 29, 63, 64, 82; and vol. 35, file 4, CBC interview. For Bethune's liberal use of CASD money, see T.C. Worsley, *Behind the Battle* (London: Robert Hale, 1939), p. 247 and *passim*.
12 Roderick Stewart to author, 14 January 1996
13 Stewart, *Bethune*, p. 106
14 NAC, Mackenzie-Papineau Collection (Moscow Archives), Fonds 545, file list 6, file 542, 1937–1940, report of 3 April 1937 on the Canadian delegation in Spain
15 Thomas, *The Spanish Civil War*, pp. 309, 317
16 *Daily Clarion*, 1 March 1937, p. 1; 13 March 1937, p. 1; and 17 April 1937, p. 2
17 *Daily Clarion*, 3 March 1937, p. 1
18 See cable of 12 April 1937, below.
19 Stewart, *Bethune*, p. 106; Ted Allan, 'With Norman Bethune in Spain' in *Norman Bethune: His Times and Legacy*, ed. David A.E. Shephard and Andrée Lévesque (Ottawa: Canadian Public Health Association, 1982), p. 158; NAC,

MG30 D388, vol. 1, file 1–34, Allan to *China Daily*, 2 June 1987, and accompanying notes

20 R.S. Saxton, 'A Study of the Madrid Transfusion Service,' McGill University, Osler Library, ACC 637/1/33

21 Allan, 'With Norman Bethune in Spain,' p. 158

22 Ted Allan, interview, 8 June 1995

23 Allan, 'With Norman Bethune in Spain,' p. 160; NAC, MG30 D187, vol. 43, file 18, outline, n.d. and untitled chronology, n.d.

24 Worsley, *Behind the Battle*, p. 247

25 Ted Allan, interview, 8 June 1995; Roderick Stewart, interview, 5 January 1996; NAC, MG30 D187, vol. 43, file 18, outline, n.d.

26 Kate Mangan, 'Memoirs,' February–March 1937, in the possession of her daughter, Charlotte Kurzke, of Downham Market, Norfolk, England. I am indebted to Ms Kurzke for this reference.

27 NAC, MG30 D187, vol. 43, file 18, chronology. Subsequently, Bethune rationalized his return from Spain this way: 'I did not return to Canada at my own request, but at the request of the other Canadians in Spain, who in a conference of us all in Madrid in April 1937 decided that the film should be accompanied by me.' See *Daily Clarion*, 7 September 1937, p. 4.

28 Like so many women, Kajsa von Rothman's Spanish Civil War experience has remained secondary to that of the male volunteers. Kajsa's involvement in the transfusion unit was ironic because Bethune had earlier dismissed the idea of a woman serving with it. When Bethune met Hazen Sise on 29 November in London as he collected equipment to go to Spain, Sise's friend Moran Scott asked to return with them. Sise reported that 'Bethune put his foot down. He thought the situation was too dangerous. He didn't want to have the responsibility of a woman with him on the Unit and because we [were] literally racing to get to Madrid before the trap closed ... [A]fter I'd been in Spain even for a week or two I could see that there were a great many girls who had come out ... doing all sorts of jobs to help' (NAC, MG30 D187, vol. 10, file 9, manuscript, 'The Canadian Blood Transfusion Unit,' p. 12).

29 Thomas, *The Spanish Civil War*, p. 616

30 Ted Allan and Sydney Gordon, *The Scalpel, The Sword* (Toronto: McClelland and Stewart, 1989), pp. 135–6, 208–12

31 Paul Weil, 'Norman Bethune and the Development of Blood Transfusion Services,' in Shephard and Lévesque, eds, *Norman Bethune*, p. 178

32 Lobigs, 'Canadian Responses to the Mackenzie-Papineau Battalion,' p. 10

33 Worsley, *Behind the Battle*, pp. 280–1

34 NAC, MG30 D388, vol. 16, file 'Bethune Series 14,' Spence memo, 12 August 1937, containing cable of 31 May from Allen, May

6 Propagandist: North America, June 1937 to January 1938

1 *Daily Clarion*, 6 September 1937, p. 12
2 National Archives of Canada, MG30 D187, vol. 35, file 'Bethune – George Mooney Manuscript, 1948'
3 Roderick Stewart, *Bethune* (Toronto: New Press, 1973), pp. 112–13
4 *Daily Clarion*, 6 September 1937, p. 12.
5 *Winnipeg Free Press*, 21 July 1937, p. 5
6 *Daily Clarion*, 23 June 1937, p. 4
7 Ibid., 7 September 1937, p. 4
8 *Winnipeg Free Press*, 21 July 1937, p. 5; *Vancouver Daily Province*, 2 August 1937, p. 5. The desperation of the Depression, however, was evident from the collection at other cities. In Sudbury on 11 July, seven hundred people gave just $22.40. See Stewart, *Bethune*, p. 109.
9 Martin Lobigs, 'Canadian Responses to the Mackenzie-Papineau Battalion, 1936 to 1939' (M.A. thesis, University of New Brunswick, 1992), pp. 153, 282
10 CSIS Access 117–91–22, report of 9 August 1937. For personal testimony, see, for instance, Mark Zuelhke, *The Gallant Cause: Canadians in the Spanish Civil War, 1936–1939* (Vancouver: Whitecap, 1996), p. 130.
11 Roderick Stewart, *The Mind of Norman Bethune* (Toronto: Fitzhenry and Whiteside, 1977), p. 74
12 Stewart, *Bethune*, p. 110. The RCMP reported that a communist in Vancouver was severely reprimanded by party leaders for publicly asking Bethune on 1 August whether he was a communist, to which question Bethune replied affirmatively (CSIS Access 117–91–22, Cadiz to the Commissioner, RCMP, 4 August 1937).
13 *Saskatoon Star-Phoenix*, 24 July 1937, p. 3
14 *Regina Leader-Post*, 23 August 1937, p. 3
15 *Toronto Globe and Mail*, 16 June 1937, p. 4
16 *Toronto Daily Star*, 16 June 1937, p. 2; Stewart, *Bethune*, pp. 110, 113
17 Jean Hamelin and Nicole Gagnon, *Histoire du catholicisme québécois* (Montréal: Boreal, 1984), p. 383
18 *Daily Clarion*, 2 October 1937, p. 1, and 8 October 1937, p. 3
19 Lobigs, 'Canadian Responses to the Mackenzie-Papineau Battalion,' p. 118, citing RCMP Records, file, 'Committee to Aid Spain (28 January 1937 – 20 December 1939),' RCMP report of 18 August 1937
20 *Toronto Daily Star*, 15 June 1937, p. 11
21 Stewart, *Bethune*, p. 114; CSIS Access 117–91–22, Cadiz to Commissioner, August 1937; *Daily Clarion*, 29 October 1937, p. 3

22 *Daily Clarion*, 7 June 1937, p. 1; 14 and 15 July, p. 1; 16 November, p. 7;
    6 December, p. 3; and *passim*
23 Edgar Snow's *Red Star over China* (New York: Random House, 1938) was
    not officially published until 1938, but on 2 January of that year Bethune
    wrote a letter to Marian Scott urging her to read it; see chapter 7 for text of
    letter.

7 Anti-imperialist: China, 1938

1 'Henning Sorensen to Graham Spry: A Letter,' in *Norman Bethune: His Times
   and Legacy*, ed. David A.E. Shephard and Andrée Lévesque (Ottawa: Canadian Public Health Association, 1982), p. 156
2 Ma Haide, 'Norman Bethune in China,' in Shephard and Lévesque, eds, *Norman Bethune*, pp. 182–4
3 Jean Ewen, *China Nurse: 1932–1939* (Toronto: McClelland and Stewart, 1981),
   p. 69
4 Ted Allan and Sydney Gordon, *The Scalpel, The Sword* (Toronto: McClelland
   and Stewart, 1989), p. 191; cf. Zhou Erfu, *Doctor Norman Bethune* (Beijing: Foreign Languages Press, 1982), p. 24
5 Gordon wrote to Allan: 'There is no evidence for what is put into Bethune's
   mouth as a diary note about Mao. There is no such diary note, I have established ... The big issue is the Bethune interview with Mao. Since I wrote it, I
   should know what I am talking about ... I constructed a dialogue out of
   Bethune's theses in general ... and ideas of Mao's. I thought in 1950 that was
   permissible. Since then both Bethune and Mao have become world personalities about whom one cannot write in this manner any more.' Allan actually
   accepted Gordon's demand to cut the statement from the new McClelland
   and Stewart edition, although for unknown reasons this was not done in the
   1971 or 1989 reprintings. National Archives of Canada (NAC), MG30 D388,
   vol. 1, file 1–15, Gordon to Allan, 25 May 1971, and file 1–27, Allan to William
   Kashtan, 13 Sept. 1971 and 16 Sept. 1971, to Jack McClelland, 16 Sept. 1971
   and to Ma Haide, 30 Dec. 1971.
6 Mao Zedong, 'On Protracted War,' in *Selected Military Writings of Mao Tse-
   tung* (Beijing: Foreign Languages Press, 1972), p. 191. I'm indebted to Bill
   Livant for this observation and for drawing my attention to this essay.
7 See letter of 10 January 1939.
8 Roderick Stewart, *Bethune* (Toronto: New Press, 1973), p. 156
9 NAC, MG30 D388, Acc 93/100, vol. 1, no file name, Haskell to Bethune,
   18 April 1938
10 Ewen, *China Nurse*, pp. 50–2

11 Alvyn J. Austin, *Saving China: Canadian Missionaries in the Middle Kingdom, 1888–1959* (Toronto: University of Toronto Press, 1986), p. 252. I wish to thank Karen McIvor for pointing out this source to me.

12 Ewen, *China Nurse*, p. 67

13 Min-sun Chun, 'China's Unsung Canadian Hero: Dr. Richard F. Brown in North China, 1938–39,' in *East Asia Inquiry*, ed. L.N. Shyu et al. (Montreal: Canadian Asian Studies Association, 1991), pp. 116–19; and Karen McIvor, '"Those of Strange Tongues": The Anglican Mission in Honan, China, 1910–1948,' unpublished paper, University of Victoria, 1992, pp. 21–4

14 This report contained a very detailed breakdown of medical services in Sian, much of which has been omitted here. For the original, see NAC, MG30 D388, vol. 14, file 16–5, item 41, medical notes, 23 March 1938

15 Ewen, *China Nurse*, pp. 95–6

16 Ibid., p. 99

17 Bill Livant, 'Bethune and Blood: A Comparison of Two Biographies,' unpublished paper, University of Regina, 1979, pp. 7–8, 11

18 Stewart, *Bethune*, pp. 156–7; Roderick Stewart, *The Mind of Norman Bethune* (Toronto: Fitzhenry and Whiteside, 1977), p. 102

8 Martyr: China, 1939

1 Roderick Stewart, *Bethune* (Toronto: New Press, 1973), pp. 153–4

2 Donald Jack, *Rogues, Rebels, and Geniuses: The Story of Canadian Medicine* (Toronto: Doubleday, 1981), p. 466

3 Cited in Stewart, *Bethune*, p. 163

4 National Archives of Canada, MG30 D388, vol. 2, file 2–2, Allan to Kroonenburg and Clermont, 26 Sept. 1988

5 *Daily Worker*, 6 June 1940, p. 6

6 CSIS Access 117–91–22, Cadiz to the commissioner, RCMP, August 1937 [exact date deleted]

7 Stewart, *Bethune*, p. 114

8 Jean Ewen, *China Nurse: 1932–1939* (Toronto: McClelland and Stewart, 1981), p. 88

9 Stewart, *Bethune*, p. 114; and Stewart, interview, 2 March 1996

10 Lincoln Fisher, 'Obituary – Norman Bethune, 1890–1939,' *American Review of Tuberculosis* 41 (Jan.–June 1940): 820

11 Mao Zedong, 'In Memory of Norman Bethune,' in Stewart, *Bethune*, p. 197

12 Ted Allan and Sydney Gordon, *The Scalpel, The Sword* (Toronto: McClelland and Stewart, 1989), pp. 311–12

13 Aside from variations introduced by translation, *The Scalpel, The Sword*, pp.

311–12, reads virtually identically to Zhou Erfu, *Dr. Norman Bethune* (Beijing: Foreign Languages Press, 1982), pp. 224–6.

14 Significantly, if this is indeed Bethune's last will, Ted Allan's claim to own copyright to Bethune's letters from China is shredded. In the statement, Bethune granted the copyright to Tim Buck, not to Allan. See 'A Note on Sources.'

Appendix 1: Report on the Actions of the Canadian Delegation in Spain

1 Ted Allan, interview, 8 June 1995; Roderick Stewart, interview, 5 January 1996

A Note on Sources

1 National Archives of Canada (NAC), MG30 D388, vol. 1, file 1–34, Allan to *China Daily*, 2 June 1987, and accompanying notes
2 Ibid., vol. 16, file, 'Bethune Research, Correspondence, 1942–1951,' Allan to Coleman, 23 February 1943; vol. 1, file 1–21, Allan to Stewart, 8 October 1970
3 Ibid., vol. 1, file 1–24, Allan to Deutsch, 1 June 1971
4 Ibid., vol. 1, file 1–21, Allan to Stewart, 8 October 1970. Unknown to Allan and Gordon, the letters had been placed in the Toronto library by Rita Patterson, Gordon's former wife.
5 Ted Allan and Sydney Gordon, *The Scalpel, The Sword* (Toronto: McClelland and Stewart, 1989), pp. 311–12
6 NAC, MG30 D388, vol. 1, file 1–19, Gordon to Allen, 5 May 1971
7 Ibid., file 1–15, Deutsch to Gordon, 4 Oct. 1971; my emphasis
8 Ibid., file 1–34, William Kashtan to Allan, 14 Dec. 1977
9 Ibid., file 1–39, Michael Prupas to Mike Zimring, 9 Nov. 1984

Bibliography of Bethune's Works

Published Works

Articles, Pamphlets, Poems, and Stories

'Compressionist's Creed.' *Journal of Thoracic Surgery* 5 (Feb. 1936)

The Crime on the Road: Malaga-Almeria. Madrid: Publicaciones Iberia, 1937

'The Dud.' *Toronto Clarion,* 8 July 1939

From Hankow to Sian. Toronto: Canadian League for Peace and Democracy, 1938

'Letter From Dr. Bethune to the Committee in Aid of Spanish Democracy.' *New Frontier: A Monthly Magazine of Literature and Social Criticism* 1, no. 10 (April 1937)

'A Letter to Canada from Doctor Bethune.' *Daily Clarion,* 4 April 1938

'Red Moon.' *Canadian Forum* 17 (July 1937)

'Reflections on Return from "Through the Looking Glass."' *Bulletin of the Montreal Medico-Chirurgical Society,* March-April 1936

'Take Private Profit Out of Medicine.' *Canadian Doctor* 3, no. 1 (Jan. 1937)

'The T.B.'s Progress.' *The Fluoroscope* 1, no. 7 (15 Aug. 1932)

'University in Caves Is Training Ground of China's Victory.' *Daily Clarion,* 2 Aug. 1938

'With the Canadian Blood Transfusion Unit at Guadalajara.' *Daily Clarion,* 17 July 1937

'Wounds.' *In Away with All Pests: An English Surgeon in People's China: 1954–1969.* By J.S. Horn. New York and London: Monthly Review, 1969

'Youth Will Be Freed.' *Daily Clarion,* 22 Nov. 1937

Medical articles

Items marked by an asterisk have not been reproduced in this volume.

'A Case of Chronic Thoracic Empyema Treated with Maggots.' *Canadian Medical Association Journal (CMAJ)* 32 (March 1935): 301–2

'Cotton-Seed Oil in Progressively Obliterative Artificial Pneumothorax.' *American Review of Tuberculosis* 26 (Dec. 1932): 763–70*

'Maggot and Allantoin Therapy in Tuberculosis and Non-tuberculous Suppurative Lesions of Lung and Pleura: Report of Eight Cases.' *Journal of Thoracic Surgery (JTS)* 5 (Feb. 1936): 322–9*

'New Combined Aspirator and Artificial Pneumothorax Apparatus.' *CMAJ* 20 (June 1929): 663*

'Note on Bacteriological Diagnosis of Spirochaetosis of Lungs.' *CMAJ* 20 (April 1929): 265–8*

'A Phrenicectomy Necklace.' *American Review of Tuberculosis* 26 (Sept. 1932): 319–21

'A Plea for Early Compression in Pulmonary Tuberculosis.' *CMAJ* 27 (July 1932): 36–42

'Pleural Poudrage: New Technique for Deliberate Production of Pleural Adhesions as Preliminary to Lobectomy.' *JTS* 4 (Feb. 1935): 251–61*

'Silver Clip Method of Preventing Haemorrhage While Severing Interpleural Adhesions, with Note on Transillumination.' *JTS* 2 (Feb. 1933): 302–6*

'Some New Instruments for Injection of Lipiodol: Oil-guns and Combined Cannula and Mirror.' *CMAJ* 20 (March 1929): 286–8*

'Some New Thoracic Surgical Instruments.' *CMAJ* 35 (Dec. 1936): 656–62*

'Technique of Bronchography for General Practitioner.' *CMAJ* 21 (Dec. 1929): 662–7*

(with) D.T. Smith and J.L. Wilson. 'Etiology of Spontaneous Pulmonary Disease in the Albino Rat.' *Journal of Bacteriology* 20 (Nov. 1930): 361–70*

(with) W. Moffatt. 'Experimental Pulmonary Aspergillosis with Aspergillus Niger: Superimposition of this Fungus on Primary Pulmonary Tuberculosis.' *JTS* 3 (Oct. 1933): 86–98*

Unpublished Works

'Encounter.' Unpublished short story in the papers of Marian Scott, National Archives of Canada, MG30 D399, vol. 14, file, 'Correspondence to Marian Scott, Jan. 36 to June 36'

'The Patient's Dilemma, or, Modern Methods of Treating Tuberculosis.' Unpublished radio play, Ted Allan papers, Osler Library, McGill University

Illustration Credits

National Archives of Canada: portrait of Frances Penney, PA 116911; 'Compressionist's Creed' and Christmas card (filling-station), MG30 D388, accession 93/100, vol. 1; pneumothorax pump, PA160619; rib shears, PA1600723; 'Lost' poster, MG30, D399, vol. 13, file 'Bethune Correspondence to Marian Scott, July 1935 to Oct. 1935'; self-portrait, 1934 (black and white version), PA119069; self-portrait, 1935, PA114793; Bethune in bed with jaundice, C41380; 'Viva Espana,' Charles Comfort, C139723; photo of Bethune, Ho, and Brown, PA114783

National Film Board of Canada: self-portrait, 1934 (black and white version in NAC, PA119069)

Osler Library of the History of Medicine, McGill University: *The T.B.'s Progress* (Trudeau Sanatorium murals), presented to the library by Dr Eugene Link; nurse's medal, Ted Allan Collection

Parks Canada, Bethune Memorial House, Gravenhurst, Ontario: photo of Mao Zedong

Royal Victoria Hospital, Montreal: *Night Operating Theatre*

Index